The Ancient Mediterranean

The Ancient Mediterranean

Michael Grant

Charles Scribner's Sons
New York

Library of Congress Catalog Card Number 69-17047

Printed in Great Britain

To Giuseppina and Paolo Rossi

Contents

List of Illustrations

Between pages 140–141

Acknowledgements

The author and publishers would like to thank the following for supplying photographs for this book: Eduardo Ortega, plate 1; University of Reading, plates 5, 6, 7, 8, 9; Rolf Ammon, plates 10, 36; Director of Antiquities, Cyprus, plate 11; Moroccan Tourist Office, plate 12; Mansell Collection, plates 13, 17, 23, 29, 31, 38, 46, 50, 54, 56, 66, 68; Musées Nationaux, plates 14, 22, 24; British Museum, plate 15; Glasgow Art Gallery and Museum, plate 16; Victoria and Albert Museum, plate 18; National Council of Tourism in Lebanon, plate 19; Varoujan, plate 20; Museum of Damascus, plate 21; Ashmolean Museum, plates 28, 33; Staatliche Museen, Berlin, plate 30; Museum of the Antiquities of Tel-Aviv-Jaffa, plate 34; Paul Popper, plate 37; Moderno Bini, plate 39; German Archaeological Institute, Athens, plate 42; Enit, Rome, plate 47; Tunis National Tourist Office, plate 49; National Museum of Archaeology, Sofia, plate 52; Leningrad, Hermitage Museum, plate 53; Spanish National Tourist Office, plates 55, 59; Oscar Savio, plate 61; Royal Air Force, plate 62; Giraudon, plate 70; John Freeman, plate 71. The photograph on the jacket is by J. Allan Cash.

The publishers acknowledge the following sources of the quotations used in the text: Penguin Books for *The Letters of the Younger Pliny*, translated by B. Radice; Thucydides *The Peloponnesian War* translated by R. Warner; Sophocles *Theban Plays* translated by E. F. Watling; and *The Hittites* by O. R. Gurney. Mentor Books for *Three Great Plays of Euripides* translated by R. Warner; and Petronius *Satyricon* translated by W. Arrowsmith. Jonathan Cape for Virgil's *Georgics* translated by C. Day Lewis. Loeb Classical Library for Pliny's *Natural History* translated by H. Rackham; and Aristophanes' *Plays* translated by B. B. Rogers. University of Chicago Press for *Euripides*, and *Greek Tragedies* edited by Grene and Lattimore; and *Greek Lyrics* edited by Lattimore. Eyre and Spottiswoode for *Poems* by A. Tate. Centaur Press for *The Poems of Sertus Propertius* translated by A. E. Watts. Hamish Hamilton for *Poets in a Landscape* by G. Highet. Doubleday and Co. for Homer *The Odyssey* translated by R. Fitzgerald. University of Michigan Press for *Hesiod*, translated by R. Lattimore. Washington Square Press for *Polybius* translated by R. Chambers. Routledge and Kegan Paul for *Aeschylus* translated by

Lewis Campbell. Thames and Hudson for *Six Poems of Modern Greece* edited by E. Keeley and P. Sherrard. Phoenix House for *Voices from the Past* by J. M. Todd. Heinemann for *The Odes of Horace* translated by Lord Dunsany. Macmillan and Co. for *The Tower* by W. B. Yeats.

The grand object of all travel is to see the shores of the Mediterranean

SAMUEL JOHNSON

Preface

This book has been written in the belief that we cannot understand our past, and cannot therefore understand ourselves, unless we know something of the Mediterranean sea and coasts that made us what we are.

An eighteenth-century view attributed to those shores *almost all that sets us above savages.*[1] Most of that statement is still valid today. Not all of it, perhaps. For example, television and washing machines are among the things that set us above savages, and it would be rather far-fetched to trace them back, however indirectly, to the mechanical devices which were discovered in ancient Alexandria. But before they were invented a huge proportion of our civilised heritage already existed, and that, almost in its entirety, came to us from the ancient Mediterranean – from Greece and from Rome and from Israel.

This fact is given too little prominence today because so many other ancient cultures, some of them from much further afield, have now been discovered. Yet it still remains true that the Mediterranean was the region from which civilisation came our way. What the new discoveries have made it impossible to believe any longer is that civilisation was 'invented' in that area. For the Mediterranean peoples did not originate but transformed, and it is their transformation of ancient, more easterly cultures that has impinged upon the world and upon ourselves.

Why were these eastern borrowings so thoroughly and invigoratingly changed in the Mediterranean area? This book will try to determine, at each stage, the particular contribution exercised by the sea and coastlands themselves. By this means I hope it will prove possible to throw some light on the eternally absorbing problems of why it was in Greek lands, and nowhere else, that the Greek achievement took place; and why Rome grew to a monstrous size while other Italian foundations, possessing apparently equal advantages, are silent villages or meadows today.

This operation of simultaneously assessing both outside influences and the Mediterranean environment which transfigured them has to call on the varied findings of historians, classicists, geographers, archaeologists and historians of art. The effort to combine their results requires apology, since a single author cannot be a master of anything like so many disciplines, if indeed he is master of any. And yet surely the attempt at a synthesis, however inadequate, is justified and indeed necessary, because each of these groups of scholars has shown an inevitable inclination to describe recent developments in the technical terms which are peculiar to its own trade. But, with due respect to the distinguished labellers, does it really convey any general message, for example, to describe three successive forms of Levant culture as proto-Neolithic, Aceramic Neolithic A, and Aceramic Neolithic B? In endeavouring to combine the conclusions from different fields, each with their different forms of expression, into a single story, I have felt it ought to be practicable to avoid using technicalities as esoteric as all that.*

Archaeology, with its new techniques under ground and under water and in the air, has continued to provide discoveries that are especially remarkable. They have made it impossible to write a story such as mine without trying to start at the beginning. Gone is 1846 when Grote could decide to start the 'real history' of Greece with the first recorded Olympic Games (776 BC). Nowadays any account of Mediterranean life must begin not in the eight century BC but, however sketchily, in the eighth millennium BC: if not indeed in the fortieth. The drama is already a long one, and the period of written history is only its final scene – or perhaps not even that, if our own age of writing is to be followed, as some believe, by a post-literate epoch.

I have carried my account on to the fourth century AD, when the ancient world may be regarded as giving place to the Middle Ages. There was, it is true, no particular need for the story to stop at the end of antiquity. According to one view the Mediter-

* Some are, however, recorded in the notes at the end of the book.

ranean age, although that was when its decline began, did not finally vanish until another four hundred years had passed: by which time the European age was about to start, and was destined to continue until it was superseded by our present Atlantic epoch.[2] Or perhaps (admitting that all these designations are rather vague and inadequate) we should instead speak of Mediterranean and Atlantic ages only, and miss out their European intermediary – like Theodore Roosevelt who regarded the Mediterranean era as having died in the fifteenth century AD when America was discovered. And there are other reasons, too, why we might choose to regard that century as terminating the Mediterranean era. For, until then, the most civilised power of the western world had continued to reside in this region – namely the Byzantine empire, which, contrary to the nationally minded textbooks of our northern countries, remained of outstanding significance throughout most of the medieval epoch, although finally in diminished form.

And yet, in a sense, Byzantium brought a certain anticlimax to the Mediterranean. That sea, in its previous, Roman, centuries, had been unified from end to end. It was the first time in its history that this had happened, and it was also the last: for when the Byzantines lost the west, the unification split apart and has never been reassembled. For that reason I felt that the period of Roman rule ought to be treated as the climax of this book, and that a suitable terminal was the event which heralded the renewed Mediterranean division, namely Constantine's refoundation of Byzantium as his new capital Constantinople, the future Istanbul.

The waters which that city adjoins cannot be described as Mediterranean without slightly stretching the meaning of the word. For the site chosen by Constantine stands, instead, upon a strait beside an adjunct or extension of the Mediterranean, the Sea of Marmara; and beyond the eastern and northern extremity of the strait lies the Black Sea. And yet, although these two stretches of water are not parts of the Mediterranean in the same sense as the Aegean and Adriatic and Ionian and Tyrrhenian seas, its history cannot be written without saying something about them.

The existence of such loose ends and overlaps is sometimes felt to make it useless to suppose that there are any definable or self-contained 'regions' of the world at all. This is the same sort of argument as the assertion that a historian has no right to detach one special *period of time* from another. But for practical purposes, if any history is to be attempted at all, such a conclusion is unhelpful; and the same applies to regions. Certainly, none are self-contained. But that does not mean that units with a distinguishable and definable homogeneity cannot be identified. One recent suggestion would deny such a character to the Mediterranean on the grounds that it ought instead to be grouped together in a single bilobal system with the whole of the near and middle east including Iran.[3] Such a view evidently deserves a measure of sympathy in the light of the oriental influences which have played so decisively upon the Mediterranean. Nevertheless, a glance at the map is enough to show that the Mediterranean remains a valid unit in itself, because of the simple geographical, physical fact that its shores encircle this single, interconnected stretch of water. Borrowings have come from the hinterlands, but if any sort of regional history can be written at all then the Mediterranean is a region.

A history of so large an area must seek to pinpoint, at each epoch, the most significant developments that were taking place. The term 'significant' is obviously ambiguous, and so are words such as progress or advance, which may often be progress on a material plane but retrogression in terms of human behaviour and happiness. Besides, far the greater proportion of the ancient populations remained predominantly, unchangingly, uneventfully agricultural throughout the whole of antiquity – worshipping the Mother Goddess in some form or other, and remaining hostile to any progress or advance, or unaware that it was taking place. Nevertheless, the historian is obliged to concentrate largely upon change – upon the innovations in ideas and techniques that influenced the future and provided such a huge proportion of the ingredients of our own civilisation. The mobile elements are what stand out, for history cannot help being a success story: a record of what people did, not of what they failed to do.[4]

With that in mind, I shall devote more space to the eastern than to the western Mediterranean. This is because ancient Syria and Asia Minor and Egypt are even more important factors in the making of the Mediterranean world than, for example, ancient France and Spain. The latter countries contained the seeds of modern France and Spain and of other developments beyond them. But from and through Syria and Asia Minor came the seeds which, together with those more familiar ones from Egypt, fertilised the entire Mediterranean world. These well-attested facts are obscured in our general culture because such eastern shores are far less well known to us than the coasts of France and Spain, and are still for the most part a good deal more inaccessible, because of distance and human obstacles. But yet another reason for our comparative neglect of that part of the Mediterranean is parochial unwillingness, conscious or unconscious, to see ourselves as the offshoots of orientals: the sort of unwillingness which made Greeks and Romans view history as a millennial Trojan or Persian war between east and west, and which induced the designers of nineteenth-century stained glass windows to make Jesus into a Nordic blond. Now that the Levant is again an explosive, major insecurity zone in the 1960s AD as it was in the 1960s BC, perhaps the time has come to remind ourselves again of its eternal role as a cauldron of fluctuating, pullulating influences – a role, as will be seen, which owes a lot to the country's natural configuration.

But I have tried to strike a balance between such factors and the significances of other and more westerly Mediterranean lands. That would, in any case, be my inclination on personal grounds, since having spent five years of my life in a country which borders the eastern Mediterranean I now live only a few miles from its more westerly shores. Yet the secrets of this sea and coastland are so subtle and various that few people, and certainly not myself, can regard themselves as anything but beginners in its understanding.

I want to acknowledge the valuable help I have received from Dr I.E.S. Edwards, Professor Estyn Evans, Mr W. Fuge, Mr Denys Haynes, Professor E.M. Jope, Professor Seton Lloyd, Mr J. Mellaart and Professor Stuart Piggott. I am very grateful to Mr Julian Shuckburgh and Mrs Patricia Vanags of Messrs Weidenfeld and Nicolson for their unfailing assistance, to Miss Suzanne Harsanyi for collecting the illustrations and to Mr James Best for his advice. Acknowledgements are also due to

Mankind (Los Angeles) and *History Today* (London) in which certain material from Parts I and II has appeared. In conclusion I thank my wife for everything she has done to bring the book into existence.

GATTAIOLA 1969 MICHAEL GRANT

PART ONE
The Mediterranean in Early Times

I

The Mediterranean and its Beginnings

The Mediterranean and its lands

The deep gash of this sea, two thousand three hundred miles long and never more than five hundred wide, was created by a vast geological upheaval which piled up mountainous folds around the sunken trough.

In Europe and Asia Minor the convulsions and collapses produced a row of peninsulas, and the impact of storm-sped waves on the outcrops of softer rock between hard buttresses has warped and scarped and notched their shores. These intricate coasts strongly encourage intercommunication. But never far behind them, forming part of a complex belt of high relief that extends all the way from Spain to Indonesia and Japan, are the sharp-cut, endlessly varied heights. In some areas, such as Dalmatia which is the Mediterranean Chile, these mountains cut the coast off from its hinterland almost completely; though usually the process is less drastic, and the faults and subsidences provide a generous supply of passages. And yet the tendency still is for the mountains to negative the coasts, throwing off in opposite directions the human activities which the sea has tended to join. These dramatic and paradoxical conditions have inspired much wonder and curiosity, prompting men to make their first climatological and oceanographical observations, to recognise the geographical significance of the folded relief, and to note for the first time the whole intricate relationship of history and geography with which this book is concerned.

Behind the mountains that fringe the northern shore lay countries which were destined, much later, to take the lead from Mediterranean powers. The Asian and African hinterlands contain much larger expanses of territory which ring their Mediterranean coasts not only with mountains but also with desert, which in Africa extends right down to the seaboard. 'The geologists, those historians of silent revolutions, show us that the Mediterranean has arisen in reaction to the deserts like a liquid response to endless drought, or a majestic signpost pointing in the opposite direction. The Mediterranean is the anti-desert.'[1]

Surface evaporation from the sea is extremely high. Little more than one-fifth as much is made up again by rain, and less than one-twentieth by rivers; one-thirtieth flows in from the east through the Bosphorus, and the whole of the remaining seventy per cent enters from the west, through the Strait of Gibraltar.

Since the surface of the Mediterranean lies between four and twelve inches lower than the Atlantic ocean outside, this water is driven in at a speed of nearly five miles an hour, forming a current which extends two hundred and fifty feet downwards. So huge and pressing an intake would be far too large for the existing basin if there were not also a compensating outflow. This outgoing water, like a similar much smaller expulsion through the Bosphorus, moves out far *underneath* the surface since its more salty content makes it heavier than the incoming current.

A second factor which helps to prevent the intake from swamping all before it is an underwater shelf at the strait which is twelve hundred feet high and acts as a gigantic lock. One effect of this barrier is to reduce the tides of the Mediterranean to a mere fraction of those of the Atlantic, scarcely exceeding a maximum of twenty inches. Another result is to keep out the cold deep Atlantic currents so that only the warmer surface water is admitted. Consequently the high temperature which the inland sea derives from its sunny climate is not eliminated by the Atlantic influx. The Mediterranean retains, on an average, a temperature eighteen degrees higher than the Atlantic, and is, indeed, the hottest of all seas in the temperate zone.

Its civilisations, in their finest forms, did not extend for more than a few miles inland – only a little beyond the sites of

Cnossos and Athens and Rome. Within these limited dimensions there are slopes overlooking the sea, and small intensively irrigated plains with mountain foothills at the back.

The mountains look on Marathon,
And Marathon looks on the sea.[2]

The variety within these diminutive areas has multiplied contacts between varied experiences, activities and outlooks. It has also provided a balanced diet. Meat and milk from the slopes combine well with the cereals, olives, vegetables, grapes and other fruits from the terraces and plains.

These lands are mostly made of limestone, and there is an exhilarating lucidity in the spare relief of their cleanly chiselled shapes. Hard-faced and resistant to surface disintegration, this limestone can stand up to the annual ravages of frost and heat. But since, unlike most rocks, it is readily soluble in ground water containing carbon dioxide, deep cracks and fissures from erosion are often to be seen. This makes the calcium carbonate in the limestone dissolve, leaving underground tunnels, swallow holes and caves, and above them a scene which is uneven and sparse. Here grow those aromatic and yet tragic scrubs of the often treeless Mediterranean coastlands.* 'The impenetrable bush is intertwined like locks of hair laced together, and then is thrown on the back of the mountain like an inextricable fleece.'[3] But often even the scrubland is gone, when the heavy, retentive loam associated with the limestone base has been eroded away completely, leaving utter bareness in its place.

Dead mountain mouth of carious teeth
That cannot spit.[4]

Such erosion is the work of men and goats (p. 14). Their deforestations have released decomposed organic matter into the violent, erratic Mediterranean rivers. History has been made by the few relatively stable (though still dangerous) exceptions, the Nile, Tiber, Po, Ebro and Rhône. But most of the other streams flowing into this sea are alternately bone-dry and destructively torrential: setting a grave problem of how to stave off floods and yet also conserve their waters. A proportion

* The maquis (macchia) and more earthbound garrigue.

of the water from such torrents is absorbed through cracks from which it later wells up again in springs and streams. But the greater part roars down to the sea, drastically encroaching on its outlines throughout the centuries by the construction, behind offshore spits and bars, of marshy deltas which have assumed ever changing and growing contours.

Although Mediterranean people are surprised by the frequency with which an Anglo-Saxon makes conversation about the weather, this is not because it is unimportant to their lives and histories. But they take its supreme importance for granted. The primary functions of Zeus were connected with the rain and the return of fine weather, and the Romans, like the Italians today, used the same word for weather as they used for time. However, this climate is singularly different from the assurances of tourist publicity. For one thing it does not lend itself to any simple, sweeping explanation, but is as complex and elusive as any other upon earth. In particular, the climate of the Mediterranean, like its culture, defies analysis *in isolation*, since it is profoundly receptive to outside meteorological influences, which its own disturbed local conditions then transform. Yet in spite of these local disturbances, there is no fundamental difference in the weather all the way between Gibraltar and Beirut; the eastern city is hotter, but the principles are the same. They rest upon an alternation between hot, rainless summers and warm, humid winters. The most adverse feature is the summer drought, which in some parts of the area lasts as long as five months. All over the Mediterranean the regime of the Sahara desert takes over for a long period, so that Atlantic cyclones scarcely enter, the sun can blaze for ten hours a day, and the whole region seems to have lost any contact with the north and west. With mean temperatures in or near the eighties (or nineties along the African coast) all vegetation withers. The light off Asia Minor 'seems to melt, as if it were eating the islands; it lies heavy like the sheaves of a yellow harvest made of air, flattened into wide smooth circles by the sun.'[5] In winter, on the other hand, the moist Atlantic westerlies and cyclones break through. Except for sharp periods – when the weather-talk becomes more indignant even than in England – the climate is some ten degrees warmer than London because of the high surface temperatures of the sea.

The same sort of Mediterranean climate exists in certain distant countries of similar latitude north and south of the equator, such as southern California, central Chile, the Cape Province of South Africa, and southern Australia. In such countries spring comes dramatically, making it easy to understand why the Earth Mother was worshipped. 'There is nothing there of the ordered progress of the English spring – the flowers come all of a rush. One week there is nothing but spikes and buds, then the temperature rises or the wind drops, and whole tracts turn lilac or scarlet.'[6] Autumn brings an equally spectacular change, when the drought-bound countryside is transfigured by rainfalls which last for fewer days than in the north but provide a drenching abundance. In many parts of the Mediterranean these two seasons, spring and autumn, give a double rain-maximum, especially heavy where steep mountain faces force the air-currents upward into a more chilly atmospheric stratum. The major emphasis is on autumn, when the closed sea has been heating up for months.

These startling spring and autumn transformations mean that the Mediterranean, situated halfway between the tropical and temperate zones, possesses not one climate but two. Vigorous vegetation is encouraged, because summer sunshine brings crops to ripeness and open winters do not totally suspend the growth of plants or cultivation of the soil. But this sort of seasonal behaviour also sets the cultivator extraordinary problems, for the two indispensable gifts of wetness and warmth do not appear simultaneously. When the sap is flowing strongest and its need for drink is greatest, the moisture is turned off. Such dissociation between the maxima of rainfall and heat provides a safeguard against excessive evaporation, but it also restricts natural flora to types which can tap far-off, deep water supplies and survive. The rest all depends on human effort and ingenuity: and how great they have been will be shown in this book.

The earliest Mediterranean peoples

Perhaps man originated in southern Africa; but current research is now leading to the possibility that there was an even earlier form of ancestral humanity on the northern confines of the Indian peninsula. At all events, human beings of the same genus though not the same species as ourselves were living in the cracks of Chinese rocks in about 400,000 BC, and eating one another. Yet they understood, too, how to protect and warm themselves by the use of fire, which was also employed by other peoples of comparable date to harden the pointed ends of wooden spears. Crude implements were employed as tools, and their shapes very slowly became better and more practical. Flint, easily and evenly fracturable, became a favourite material, and its flakes were thinned down, edged, and grasped in the hand as 'hand-axes' for cutting meat, scratching up roots, and shaping wood. Africa has been recognised as the cradle of these industries, which produced such tools without much specialisation over huge areas and enormous passages of time. Africa seems to have learnt of fire from Asia in approximately 55,000 BC. Some five or maybe fifteen thousand years later, men started to construct shelters for themselves. Marks in the ground denote the tents set up by mammoth-hunters at Molodova on the right bank of the Dniester, three hundred and fifty miles from the Black Sea; and similar sites have been identified close to the sea itself, in the Crimea.

Near the shores of the eastern Mediterranean, people were still living in caves. Yet they were already burying their dead carefully in deliberate postures which suggest that they held some sort of religious beliefs. A cemetery containing ten of these skeletons, with their legs bent and drawn up, has been discovered upon a terrace in front of a cave on Mount Carmel. This ridge divides the maritime strip of the Levant (between Asia Minor and Egypt) into two parts, the larger – including a little of Israel, the whole of Lebanon, the Syrian shore, and the Hatay province of Turkey – to the north, and the smaller – containing the greater part of Israel's coastline – to the south. Carmel narrows from landward into the only headland for hundreds of miles, a steep promontory running out into the sea on either side of the plains of Sharon and Jezreel (Esdraelon). Waves of innumerable armies have surged through the defiles of the mountain and past its seaward base, and the caves on the slopes have often afforded refuge.[7] The earliest inhabitants needed protection not only from their fellow-men but also against the monstrous hippopotamuses, elephants, rhinoceroses and cave-oxen which infested the area. These lavish jungles were not yet the parkland or garden orchard which is the meaning of the name 'Carmel'. Yet they were far enough south to escape the ice ages which periodically covered more northern territories and directed their evolution. Glaciation farther north meant, at most, increased rainfall here (p. 19).

The first inhabitants of the Carmel caves belonged to a branch of the species *Homo sapiens* known as Neanderthal man, whose remains, found also at the gates of Rome and in many other Mediterranean regions, have testified to his beetling brows, retreating chin and stooping gait. But then a further stage of habitation on the same mountain and in a cave near Nazareth, across the Jezreel plain, has yielded skeletons of mixed structure which set the pattern for the racial blendings that have continued ever since. These skeletons represent several stages of transition and probably cross-breeding between Neanderthal man and our own branch of the species (*Homo sapiens sapiens*), which had originated somewhere in south-western Asia and subsequently moved westwards and northwards into Europe, absorbing as well as destroying Neanderthal man at some date before 30,000 BC.

Homo sapiens sapiens, 'modern man, as handsome and as wise as us',[8] gradually revolutionised human life by establishing far better methods of hunting, based on novel and effective weapons. These were produced by distinctive techniques of stone-working, in which regular blades superseded crude flakes and chisel-like graving-tools were used. The successive cultures which augmented or superseded old implements by these new ones are mostly described by French names, but the peoples in question were by no means limited to France. There are very early sites in Cyrenaica on the north coast of Africa, and remains of the ensuing periods have also recently been found on Italy's heel and in Greece and Afghanistan. Indeed the earliest major phase of these developments seems to have been centred upon western Asia, where its thickest deposits occur.

Subsequent migratory groups squatted on open sites in semi-subterranean houses, walled with branches and perhaps brushwood, and roofed with turf. A complex of post-holes recently found in a cave mouth at Kastritsa near Janina (north-west Greece) represents the oldest man-made habitation so far known in Mediterranean lands (*c.* 15,000 BC). The nomadic hunters of this period followed reindeer and mammoth over great distances, decked themselves with personal ornaments, and moulded stone or ivory or clay into small figures of women, generally with exaggerated sexual characteristics. The production of these figures had started in the south Russian plain and middle Europe (*c.* 25,000 BC), and spread west to France and Italy, which was perhaps reached across the head of the Adriatic, still dry land at that time. Whatever their exact religious significance, such statuettes bear witness to the concern with fertility which continued throughout the ancient Mediterranean world. No idea was more persistent than the conception of an inexhaustibly fertile female power of the earth, regarded with envy and hope because of the full bellies that she could offer these men living near the edge of human subsistence. And through images of this kind an endeavour was presumably made to exercise ritual encouragement of the generation of children, which such feminine fecundity likewise guaranteed.

These little figures, sometimes weirdly effective in appearance, are the first three-dimensional works of art. But art truly came into its own among the series of cultures which followed next, starting in about 15,000 or 12,000 BC and maintaining its distinctive features until the ninth millennium. These peoples made lance-heads and harpoon-heads out of the antlers and bones of their prey the reindeer, which proliferated in the severe, cold, dry climate of many south European regions. The last major ice advance at its maximum development covered the British Isles and much of Germany, but ice-free territories fringing the glaciation were a mixture of tundra, steppe and Alpine flora which provided perfect conditions for grazing. In these circumstances, hunters developed close associations with the individual herds that were their living larders and walking wardrobes and raw materials, and such, in all probability, was the earliest origin of animal domestication (p. 14). The culture in which these favourable conditions were at their ebullient height is fittingly called Magdalenian after a French locality, for although its manifestations extended all the way from Mediterranean Spain as far as Poland and then south-west Germany, the nucleus was in France.

Some of the sites are open-air camps. But many are caves; and certain of them were decorated with paintings and engravings. This art was highly concentrated in three mainly inland regions of France, but it also flourished in the coastal areas of Spain and in central and southernmost Italy and Sicily, including Levanzo which then formed part of Sicily but is now a short way out from its coast. Paintings of mammoths have also recently come to light on the River Byelaya in the southern Urals, and engravings occur in two caves very close to the Mediterranean coast of Asia Minor. Previous ideas that this was purely or even mainly a Franco-Spanish art must be abandoned. The pictures, coloured with ochre, manganese and charcoal, comprise many subjects, including a large number of different animals and the earliest known human portrait (*c.* 12,000 BC). Did man revere these animals, or was it rather that he considered himself as one of them? Arguments about the meaning and purpose of the representations, drawing or rejecting analogies with present-day Australian aborigines, have been continuous. But clearly these immensely varied products of a complex and very long-lived civilisation, in so far as we can understand their meaning at all, need not one single explanation but many.

> Within any one cave it is possible to imagine . . . that some representations were the work of children (perhaps some of the floor engravings), that some were used in acts of sympathetic magic (perhaps some of the representations pierced with holes), that some were placed in particular situations in order to please (perhaps some of the open-air low reliefs), and that some were illustrations of myths and traditions (perhaps those with contain imaginary creatures, anthropomorphs and unexpected combinations of animal species).[9]

There is also a French theory that the paintings, which include many symbolic representations of women's organs, are primarily intended to convey a sexual significance symbolising the antithesis between the male and female principles.[10]

Since the activity of these artists can be so variously interpreted, it is useless to speculate how they balanced and reconciled the abstract and naturalistic elements in this earliest Mediterranean art. But if men, or even women or children (or cripples?), could be allowed time off from food-gathering to undertake this work, then economic development and surplus planning must already have reached fairly advanced levels. Although reindeer-hunting was their principal occupation, the peoples who made the paintings also collected sea-fish such as wrasses which could be caught off the rocks, spearing them or using line or net or trap. Moreover, Mediterranean sea-shells and fish-bones have been found in caves far inland in the Dordogne; so that there were already interchanges of goods over a fairly wide area. But the fish-bones include no sea-fish of any but inshore-living species, and do not therefore necessarily presuppose the existence of boats at this date. Sicily, it is true, had been inhabited since *c.* 25,000 BC, but here again the lower sea-levels during the last Ice Age make it hard to be sure that the two-mile passage across the Straits of Messina had necessitated the use of any sort of vessel.

The change came in about 8000 BC when water-crossing devices were increasingly used in Europe. For the Mediterranean there is no direct early evidence, but its first boats may have been logs, dug-out tree trunks, or rafts made of light wood-frames covered by skin or bark. These fragile craft evidently made it possible to add to the precarious resources of the period by camping on offshore islands. For in most of Europe a gradual retreat and disappearance of the glaciation had caused the semi-arctic stretches of land on its fringe to become dense forests of pine and birch, so that areas available for grazing animals were drastically reduced. The scattered communities of human beings, who still had to hunt and gather food since they had not learnt to produce any themselves, coped with these severe environmental changes by adapting their traditional techniques. In all parts climatically influenced by the end of the glaciation, conditions became much harder than they had been in the previous epoch. Game was smaller, and so therefore were tools. During the eighth millennium BC, upon the shores of seas and lakes in southern France and many other parts of western Europe, at least two main races of cultural descendants from the Magdalenians, living in caves or sandy open ground, were using flint scrapers, awls and chisels of bone, and red-deer antler harpoons. This could, in the long run, be a more promising environment because it was less frozen. Yet life was more arduous than before, and the centres of material progress moved far to the south, where they remained for many millennia.

Westwards to Israel and the Jordan Valley

The discontinuity caused in Europe by conditions following the last Ice Age was far less marked in other continents, because the freeze-up had been too far away for its termination to exercise a profound effect. But recent examinations of animal bones, marine food shells and other deposits in Cyrenaica confirm that the climate in this area had hitherto been wetter and cooler than it now became, and that the change brought results which in many African regions were disastrous. A similar modification occurred in nearer Asia, but here, on higher ground at least, with favourable effects. For, while Europe temporarily regressed, there were striking advances in the well-watered foothills area which includes north Mesopotamia and extends beyond it on either side from the Taurus mountains to the Kurdish borderlands of Iraq and Persia and their continuation along the Zagros range. These developments occurred because the area possesses the extraordinary advantage of being a natural habitat of four of the principal essentials of civilisation, in their wild form: emmer wheat (which after cultivation and crossing with another weedy grass provided the most commonly grown modern variety), barley which was evolved into the two-row and then the six-row cultivated form (p. 22), and goats and sheep.

The 'noble grasses', wild grains of wheat and barley that are ancestral to our own cultivated crops, are found from the Adriatic to the Caspian, but their original native place has been variously assigned to Abyssinia and Afghanistan. If, as seems probable, Afghanistan was their original home, then they spread westwards very early onto the Kurdish hillsides, and it was there, in all probability, that the first deliberate cultivators were to be found. The two or three thousand foot altitudes of watered foothills and plateaux which these grains favour were provided by the gently sloping basin floors fed by Kurdish mountain streams. But for direct evidence of cultivation, it is necessary to wait until another date and place (p. 21).

As regards cattle, however, there is early evidence from this area. At a date estimated by radio-carbon tests at *c.* 10,000 BC a shelter in north-eastern Iraq was occupied by hunters who specialised in wild goats in the same way as earlier European communities had closely associated themselves with particular herds of reindeer or other animals (p. 10). About a thousand years later, changes in the ratios of age-groups and sexes, which can be deduced from bones found on such sites, imply a process of selective herding of goats and sheep for their food and skins. This is half-way towards full domestication. As in the Sudan to-day, the animals had no doubt gathered near human beings, in time of drought, for food and drink and survival. They grew accustomed to eating what man fed on; and they stayed and were then encouraged to stay, because their products were what man wanted for himself. Milk has helped civilisation more than meat, and woollen clothes have given men the possibility of moving from one climate to another. Modern sheep are derived from the urials whose native habitat extended westwards from Persia to the Mediterranean.

On the sites in northern Iraq the proportion of sheep to goats gradually and greatly increased. But goats, too, were valuable for milk, meat, skin and hair; and they could eat anything, and find their own way.

> Their pasture is an Arcadian forest or height,
> where they feed
> On prickly brambles and on thorn-bushes that
> love a hillside.
> Unherded they remember to come home.[11]

The goat contributed beneficially to the clearance of the forests, but he is also one of the principal causes of the erosion which has destroyed the woodland floors of Mediterranean and near eastern lands, preventing new growth and exposing the topsoil to storms. 'While Corydon sported with Amaryllis in the shade their goats devoured the saplings that might have renewed the forests.'[12]

Stock-rearing has rarely been dominant in western Asiatic or Mediterranean life, because of the fierce droughts and need for long annual journeys. But sheep and goats can walk far for their food and be none the worse for it, and these rising uplands of northern Mesopotamia must have been acquainted from a very early date with the institution of transhumance, the type of pastoralism in which the sheep are driven up to lofty hillsides in spring to return to the plains in autumn. This practice long antedates domestication. In northern Greece, people and the herds to which they attached themselves were moving upwards from winter to summer pastures more than twenty thousand years ago. Many were the ancient territories that owed their original settlement to this custom, 'elongated pastures along which ebbed and flowed the pastoral resources of the nation'. In this vestigial form of nomadism, which still survives today (p. 28), the peoples of the hills and plains enrich one another's experience, but they also develop age-long hostility to one another. Moreover, driving the animals uphill lost the plains one of their few sources of manure, and driving them down again hinders cultivation (except of fodder) and takes away labourers. Yet transhumance was a principal formative element during the crucial transitional periods between hunting and domestication.

These people in northern Mesopotamia buried their dead in graves with stone walls and settings, and ritual red ochre decorations, that suggest mortuary cult. The handmills (querns), mortars and pounders that they used suggest that foodstuffs were already being ground. They may have been nuts or acorns or berries or vegetables, but they could also have included cereal grains. For tools occasional use was made of obsidian, which must have been brought all the way from the north or west of Lake Van. This invaluable material – of which there is a whole cliff in Wyoming's Yellowstone National Park – is a volcanic rock, equivalent in chemical composition to granite, formed by the cooling of viscous lavas containing a high concentration of silica. The sharp edges of its smooth, curved surfaces, often black in colour, are not crystalline but glossy owing to rapid cooling, and are easily split and chipped into sharp points and blades. Although it is unlikely to have been the very earliest object of widespread trade, it is the first traded substance of which there are material remains.

In spite of their approaches to food-producing, these peoples were still food-gatherers and hunters; and there were further groups of a somewhat similar kind, but not yet enjoying all the same natural advantages, in Crimea and Transcaucasia. Others again are to be found in the Mediterranean coastal areas and hinterlands of Israel – six hundred miles from the Kurdish foothills, so that if there was a process of transmission (as seems probable) then unknown intermediaries must have played a part. The culture is known as Natufian, after a cave above the Wadi el Natuf north-west of Jerusalem. At a date which radiocarbon tests place before 9500 BC, people came to the area from the north and settled upon its hillsides. Some of these new arrivals lived in caves, for example on the slopes of Mount Carmel, where they chose hollows facing the marshes of the Mediterranean coastlands. Other dwellings, oval or circular, were on open terraces in front of the caves, such as the three successive villages at Eynan (Ain Melaha) in the upper Jordan valley. Although these were only concentrations of a few hundred people, they pointed the way to every sort of future co-operative activity. Indeed, the existence of such humble groups already presupposed a certain degree of coordinated and purposeful thinking. This had come about because of the need to be near supplies of water. Eynan, for example, overlooked the pools of Lake Huleh (which has now been drained).

Nevertheless this was still only a transitional stage. Even if the open-air settlements were permanent, they may not have been intended for residence all the year round: perhaps they and the caves were occupied at different seasons of the year. For in spite of the concentration on water areas, the Natufians were still for the most part food-gatherers on the old pattern. They hunted the abundant woodland fallow deer and gazelle, in circumstances suggesting the same sort of special relation with their herds as other communities had formed with reindeer and now goats (p. 14), and they speared and hooked fresh-water fish from Lake Huleh and local streams. And yet, unlike any previous people at present known to us, they also made use of flint headed and bone hafted implements which have been identified as reaping knives or sickles. A peculiar lustre on the edges of these tools reveals that they were used to cut some crop. This is likely to have been a cereal; for handmills, grinders, mortars and pestles made of locally quarried basalt have also been found. Accordingly the Natufians had some knowledge of the techniques of harvesting. And so they also understood the passage of the seasons – one of the gifts which Prometheus claimed to have given mankind.

> No token sure had they of winter's cold,
> No heralds of the flowering spring, or season
> Of ripening fruits, but laboured without wit
> In all their works, till I revealed the obscure
> Risings and settings of the stars of heaven.[13]

And as the millennia moved on, this knowledge of the changing year gave renewed intensity to the immeasurably ancient cult of the Earth Mother, and made men reflect about their own condition.

> The changing year's successive plan
> Proclaims mortality to man.

Wild wheat, barley and rye had spread westward to the fertile parts of Israel, and this greatly contributed to its early cultural advance. But the identification of hoes at so early a date is not yet certain, and although these people reaped, we cannot yet tell if what was reaped had previously been sown or modified by breeding.

As for the Natufians themselves, their skeletons show them to have been small-boned people about five foot tall, with long skulls and delicate features. Perhaps they were among the ancestors, still undifferentiated, of later Semites and Hamites. Or typical Mediterraneans? But this entire area has always been 'a melting pot for the peoples and civilisations which have seeped into it from its continental hinterlands'[14] – starting with the very earliest inter-breedings of *homo sapiens* – so that the Natufians were probably thoroughly hybrid already. So were elements in their culture, for they practised at least three different forms of burial. Their art, consisting of reliefs and sculptures which ranged from naturalism to stylisation and included abstract representations of human heads, points forward to the future but also looks back to cave-designs of many millennia earlier. These sculptors studied wild life, such as the deer they hunted, but there is no definite proof that the Natufians domesticated animals. Elsewhere in the Mediterranean, the domestication of sheep and goats can be traced on sites of southern and western France, at a period which further research may conceivably show to be not very much later. There is also new evidence from many strata in the La Adam cave of the Dobrogea (Rumania), where remains show how wild animals were gradually tamed and bred.

Early in the eighth millennium BC, at least one Jordan valley settlement had become a substantial place surrounded by fortifications. This was Jericho, five miles north of the Dead Sea and just over forty from the Mediterranean. Jericho had already existed in the previous phase, and by about 7000 it had become a ten-acre community of round or oval mud-brick hog-backed houses on stone foundations, with walls and floors coated with layers of mud plaster. The area of habitation was surrounded by a massive stone wall, twelve feet high and six and a half feet thick, with a circular stone tower adjoined by a deep, wide ditch. Our knowledge is so fragmentary that this cannot be claimed as the first of such defensive systems ever to be devised. But it is a very early and spectacular example.

Nevertheless, Jericho's population was probably not more than about two thousand. Though walled and architectural, this was still a village rather than a city. The place occupies a sort of mid-way position in the emergence of civilised man.[15] It is also transitional in another respect, because for more than a thousand years after these fortifications were built the people of Jericho still made no pots; their dishes and bowls were of fine limestone instead. Nor had pottery yet appeared during the initial years of the seventh millennium, although artists already produced large-scale statues, and added careful modelling to human skulls for some ritual purpose in connection with the worship of their ancestors.

Jericho commanded the Dead Sea and its resources of salt, bitumen and sulphur. Obsidian and other stones were imported from Asia Minor, turquoise matrix from Sinai, and cowries from the Red Sea. But the place also possessed a vital resource of its own. Although situated a thousand feet below sea-level in the waterless desert of the Jordan valley, where there are only five inches of rainfall annually as against thirty-five at Beirut, drinking-water in abundance comes from a powerful spring throughout the year. This well-watered land probably developed the cultivation of wheat and barley which Natufians had foreshadowed or begun. At Beidha, two hundred miles south of Jericho, barley was already being cultivated soon after 7000, though it had not yet acquired all the characteristics of the cultivated form; the nature of the emmer wheat also found there suggests a stage of genetic transition. Moreover, the same techniques had now reached the Mediterranean shore, where a community contemporary with Jericho was built on top of an earlier habitation upon Mount Carmel.

Other cultures going back to the same period as the Natufians are detectable in Asia Minor, near the caves beside the Bay of Antalya (Adalia) which earlier inhabitants had adorned with engravings (p. 11). Squatters of the ninth millennium BC, who may have been their descendants, occupied rock-shelters formed by rain-floods which corresponded to the last Ice Age of more northerly territories (p. 9). Although these people lived near the sea, there is at present no evidence that they ventured upon its waters, but finds include fragments of harpoons which may have been used for spearing fresh-water fish. There are also fanged arrow-heads of individual shape, and sickle blades which suggest that cereals may already have been reaped. Red ochre was used for painting floors, and there are still some exiguous survivals and continuations of earlier cave art.

One of these shelters, nearly a thousand feet above sea-level, stands at the head of a shallow valley which is traversed by a narrow pass and may have given these people access to the lofty interior plateau of Asia Minor. For there, in a narrow but fertile valley a little over two hundred miles away, a site going back at least to the mid-eighth millennium BC has now revealed over six thousand two hundred pieces of obsidian. This is the largest discovery of the material so far to have been made anywhere in Asia Minor. The stone could have been quarried not very far from where the collection was found, and from this and other centres there developed an industry which was destined to become the object of widespread trading in bulk. Whether these cultures of Asia Minor derived any cultural influences from the Kurdish regions seven hundred miles to their east cannot yet be said. But it is likely that they did.

South-eastern Asia Minor and the Lower Orontes

However, for direct information about early agriculture, it is necessary to move back to Asia Minor and to the site now known as Çatalhüyük, which is the Turkish for forked hill. This double eminence stands about sixty-five miles north of the Mediterranean, at the nearer end of the line of early civilisations which stretches from these Taurus foothills through Turkish Mesopotamia into Iraq and Iran (p. 13). Çatalhüyük is in the plain of Konya (Iconium), which is now largely steppe or saline wilderness but then contained grasslands and open woods. With its three basins, each commanding a land-route of its own, this is the largest single alluvial plain on the plateau of Asia Minor.

Here, at a place three thousand feet above sea-level, a dozen successive levels of ancient Çatalhüyük rise, one above the other. The settlement attributed to the mid-seventh millennium BC presents what may be the earliest known example of houses that are formally planned and grouped. Rectangular in shape unlike the round or oval dwellings of Israel, these buildings for the first time have the appearance of a town. Urbanisation is coming into existence. Çatalhüyük conforms with suggestions that the development of towns requires elevated ground away from swamps, and that the borders of desert regions were particularly suitable for ancient human concentrations. Such an urban concentration 'defies the land, contradicts nature in the lines of its silhouette, denies all nature.'[16] But it also leads to interchanges of ideas, techniques, forms of organisation and artistic styles. A town can only come into existence if there are material conditions which provide a surplus of food – and if the means are available to bring it together at that particular spot.

The people of Çatalhüyük employed stamp seals and made skilful use of many polished stones. Several varieties of obsidian, perhaps derived from earlier industries of this part of Asia Minor (p. 19) by direct continuity, were utilised in abundance to make chipped tools and polished mirrors which were the finest of their time. Obsidian was also exported southward on a large scale, impinging directly on the economy of the Mediterranean coastlands, from which sea-shells came back to be used as beads. Probably Çatalhüyük held a monopoly of the obsidian trade both with Syria, from which it obtained fine flint in exchange, and with Cyprus. Obsidian found in Cyprus with a radio-carbon date of *c.* 5690 BC has now been identified as originating from Çiftlik in southern Asia Minor.

Another important activity was the hewing and carving of wood, mainly oak or juniper, probably floated down the neighbouring River Çarsamba to the town. Unique fragments of woven and twined materials, including probably flax, have been preserved in carbonised form, and so has the earliest known warp-weighted loom.

Some of the products of what must have been an outstanding textile industry are imitated by local painters. Certain of the artists of Çatalhüyük show the goddess of fertility in various forms, as a young girl, a mother giving birth, or an old woman. Others favoured animal symbolism, engraving red or black bulls on the walls of shrines, or painting them on fine white plaster in colours mixed with fat. These are the earliest murals so far discovered on any man-made wall. Throughout the seventh millennium there are still perceptible echoes of the old animal art of cavemen five thousand years earlier. Yet the severe abstractions that were to rule the aesthetics of the next few thousand years – art for art's sake – are also detectable. The older, more naturalistic style can be linked with the gathering of food, and the more novel abstractions may be due to the greater distance from wild beasts which characterised the new sort of settled agricultural life.

For at Çatalhüyük this settled life has started. The age of food-gathering is nearly over and this is an age of food-production. Sheep and goats are now domesticated, and stock breeding is under way; the auroch (an extinct species of wild ox or bison) was still hunted, but this was also perhaps the moment of its domestication. Moreover, people are not only harvesting grain, but they are deliberately cultivating it with an elaborateness that had not, as far as we know, been seen before. This creation of agriculture was no sudden discovery, but a long evolutionary process (p. 13) which had now reached its culmination. The reproduction of grain plants from seeds was an easily observable phenomenon, and at Çatalhüyük observation led to action.

The grains found on the site include remains of cultivated wheat and barley. Destined to become the pillars of Mediterranean life, these were probably the first crops to be sown and harvested for human food, in conditions when men were not secure or knowledgeable enough to plant olives or vines. The carbohydrate content of grain supplemented the protein of the hunters and herdsmen and provided a balanced diet. Man-and-crop became a new symbiotic unit, wholly interdependent. The pursuit of agriculture enhanced men's love of home and feeling for the earth and sense of property; and what Aristotle said, that 'most of mankind get their living from the land and from cultivated plants',[17] remained true throughout the entire duration of the ancient world.

Less protected by its natural covering than barley, wheat is nevertheless the most valuable among cereals. It has been found at Çatalhüyük in both emmer and einkorn (one grain) forms, derived from two species which grew and still grow wild in the near east (p. 13). Hybrids too, have come to light, bearing witness to a long previous history of partly accidental, partly intentional selection, acclimatisation, and improvement. Excavations at Çatalhüyük have also provided examples of six-row barley, a more evolved version of the simpler two-row rype which was closer to the natural form. Barley is far less exacting then wheat, since it starts to grow early, does not need rich or humid soil, requires less moisture in its ripening stage, and resists alkaline and saline influences alike. It is therefore well adapted to the drier parts of the Mediterranean area where it remained the chief cereal until after the Middle Ages. Barley-cake and porridge or broth were cheap staple foods, and it appears that beer, too, was already known at Çatalhüyük.

Not long after the beginnings of the town, a primitive pottery was being made there. This was not apparently a new craft, because it may already have existed for millennia in the hills of eastern Iraq and Iran. The original idea perhaps came from plastering baskets with clay, as is done in Syria today. Pottery is not all-important to students of the past, since it can no longer be employed as the chief index and criterion of prehistoric development. Quite powerful and advanced communities prospered without it, including, for all practical purposes, Çatalhüyük in its early years, since it was not until *c.* 5900 that the town's ceramic industry became extensive and efficient. Nor, even when such an industry had come into existence somewhere, was it always in close touch with other artistic or political and social developments. Nevertheless, wide ranges of fabric, shape, finish and decoration make pottery a sensitive indicator. For since pots could be so easily broken, they were only used for a short time, and therefore reflected current fashions. At the same time, however, they were not easily destroyed even by fire, and in most soil conditions display an extraordinary capacity for survival. Ancient Mediterranean peoples were rarely rich enough to use vessels of precious metal, and pottery was used in ancient times for many more purposes than today. Though its makers are veiled in the anonymity which is so inevitable in pre-literate communities, their work tells us something aesthetic, industrial and social about themselves as well as their clients: 'every potsherd in any waste heap is the response of somebody's hand and brain to somebody's need.'[18]

The clay of which pottery is made is waterproof and cohesive when dry, and plastic when wet. But the most highly plastic clays have a tendency to crack, which ancient potters learnt to counteract by admixtures of sand, ground rock or ash. Since clay is the product both of crystalline and volcanic rocks, it provided a choice of colours ranging from white and cream to the tan and coral-red which came from the iron oxides of limestone soils. To offset weaknesses due to the crudity of early kilns, potters built up vulnerable lips and edges by additional applications of clay. This procedure, which started as a functional need, eventually produced shapes justifiable on artistic grounds alone; the craftsman needed judgment as well as technical skill. It was again for artistic reasons (and with due regard to the luminous qualities of his particular clay) that he began to incise the surfaces of pots while they were still damp, to create an additional tone by firing, to apply and burnish a shiny slip, and finally to paint the surface. Although these processes did not yet achieve great sophistication at Çatalhüyük, its potters between *c.* 5900 and 5650 BC were already producing shades of red and buff, and finally streaks of red paint appeared as well.

The use of pottery kilns was soon adapted to the melting of metals, since they were the only known furnaces capable of achieving the temperatures required. At Çatalhüyük this process did not go beyond the fabrication of copper and lead beads and pendants. Yet metallurgy had now begun. Its invention comprised a number of successive discoveries – the malleability of copper, its fusibility, and the reduction of copper from ores.

Alloys were still to come, but man had discovered he could transmute one natural substance into another.

A series of long-drawn-out processes had profoundly modified human life. This was not the single Neolithic revolution which was once believed in, since the processes were varied, gradual and spread over large areas and long periods of time. Tools had been drastically altered, food-producing had replaced food-gathering, animals were domesticated, villages and then towns had come into existence, weaving and spinning and pottery and metallurgy were introduced. In the regions where these decisive developments slowly took place, the changes had vast social consequences. Population increased to figures at least ten times higher than three thousand years before. Yet such increases were not large enough to absorb and cancel out the economic surpluses provided by these new activities. The surpluses were, it is true, still too small to require any full-time specialisation. Yet they sufficed for the establishment of rudimentary governmental systems – and for the provision of a certain amount of leisure. 'Culture begins when you stop wondering where your next meal is coming from':[19] and there was certainly culture at Çatalhüyük.

This place and its surrounding plain possessed three outlets to the world outside. A western route went on into inland Asia Minor; a southern track reached the narrow plain of the River Calycadnus (Göksu) where it entered the Mediterranean opposite Cyprus; and a road leading south-east from Çatalhüyük likewise reached the sea, but at a more profitable point, for it passed through the Taurus mountains into one of the richest and most influential of Mediterranean lowlands, the plain of Cilicia. That plain, bounded by the horseshoe of mountains and sea, lies in the lowest and farthest corner of the peninsula of Asia Minor, at its right angle with the Syrian coast. In contrast to inhospitable shores farther west, this is mostly a garden-land of rich stoneless loam, watered by two large rivers that run into the Mediterranean some forty miles apart, the Cydnus and Pyramus, or Seyhan and Ceyhan. At the western extremity of the plain, from a very early date, there was a town and port at Mersin. Beside a stream (now two miles from the coastline) rises an eighty foot mound in which a descent through no less than forty levels brings the spade to a town of the seventh millennium BC. Its harbour faced across the Mediterranean towards Egypt, and this may have been the region from which Egyptians learnt to cultivate the vine (p. 50).

But Cilicia, while passing on its advantages elsewhere, itself received benefits by land from the interior of Asia Minor. It is true that Taurus, though attractively rich in minerals, presented a formidable obstacle. This range, rather than the actual geographical point of division between Asia Minor and Syria, was often considered as the real border between the two countries,[20] for the Cilician Gates which penetrate its heights are precipitous, and their descent was long and rough. Yet contacts were made through the barrier, and indeed this was the principal means by which the higher civilisation of Çatalhüyük reached the Mediterranean. Its pottery was known to the local craftsmen of Mersin, who then made their own wares and decorated them with impressions of sea-shells or fingernails in a manner peculiar to the region.

The road which went northwards from Mersin forked to the left into the interior of Asia Minor and to the right round the Gulf of Alexandretta into Syria. Here, pointing southwards to the reentrant angle of the sea, is an extension of the Taurus mountains, the richly wooded Amanus (Nur) range. Crossing over Amanus by the historic Syrian Gate or Belen Pass, the traveller reaches another stretch of country which has played an even more decisive part in bringing civilisation to the Mediterranean, the small plain known as Amik (Amuq), 'the depression'. The River Orontes (Asi), after flowing northwards parallel to the Syrian shore, has here turned sharply to the west some twenty miles before debouching into the sea between Amanus on its right and Mount Casius (Akra) on its left. As the river turns towards this pincer (the site of the later Antioch), its basin widens into the Amik plain, which was one of the principal centres of Mediterranean civilization from the earliest times until the sixth century AD, when an earthquake converted the whole area into a stagnant lake.*

* The Orontes and the small rivers Afrin and Karasu, flowing in from the east and north respectively, were dammed by the upheaval. The Orontes finally broke through into a new channel.

In the four hundred square miles of this plain, Syrian in geographical terms but now part of Turkey, the reedy water-meadows of the river's tortuous course fringed intensively cultivated lands in which emmer wheat and barley and domesticated goats and pigs flourished against a background of mountain slopes rich in timber, watered by streams and springs and fanned in summer by a north-westerly breeze that blows from the snowy peaks of Taurus and relieves the heat. The antiquity of human history in the region is indicated by the presence of two hundred mounds covering ancient settlements, including some dating back at least to the seventh millennium BC. One of them, Tell Atchana (Alalakh), was destined to attain special fame (p. 71). Reports of the partial excavation of three mounds have been published, and smaller operations have taken place at others.

These Amik communities were extraordinarily well placed to receive influences by land and sea. The Syrian Gates pointed towards the larger Cilician plain beyond, with its access to the cultures of Asia Minor. In the opposite direction, too, another major source of civilisation was readily accessible overland. For whereas the Amik plain adjoins the sea on one side, an ancient route in the other direction, across the Aleppo plateau, links it to the Euphrates where that river curves to within a hundred miles of the Mediterranean. So the Amik was a natural outlet from the Mesopotamian plains and valleys, and became one of the principal channels by which knowledge of their advanced cultures was diffused throughout the whole Aegean area.

Earliest Cyprus, Crete and Greece

To the west by sea, as well as to the north and east by land, there were places with which the Asian coastal towns could make contact. Boats of a kind had existed since about 10,000 BC (if not earlier), and people living in the Aegean area had long been transporting obsidian from island to island. During the seventh millennium there must have been vessels of a more ambitious kind, for they now conveyed settlers all the way from the mainland of Asia Minor or Syria, or both, as far as Cyprus and Crete and Greece.

In Cyprus, rich in timber, one such settlement, Khirokitia, is suggestive of contact with Syria, for its coastal hill-site within a curve of the River Maroniou looks out towards that country, and a stone vessel of the type the Cyprus community produced has been found in an early stratum at Ras Shamra on the Syrian coast. Moreover, the solidly constructed houses of Khirokitia, with their limestone foundations and cores, possess the circular shape that was traditional in Israel. A second Cypriot community of about the same epoch, Petra tou Limniti, lived on a small island in Morphou Bay off the north coast, and another was on the very tip of the easternmost Carpasos peninsula, in easy reach not only of the Amik but of the Göksu river mouth in Cilicia, which possessed access to Mersin (regarded as a possible invasion base of Cyprus in AD 1967) and formed the terminal of a route leading inland to ancient centres of civilisation such as Çatalhüyük.

Also of seventh millennium date is a settlement at Cnossos on the island of Crete. Indeed, it dates back, according to radiocarbon evidence, to a time which may be several hundred years before the first known Cypriot material. This is remarkable, because whereas Cyprus is little more than sixty miles from Syria and fifty from Cilicia, Crete is nine or ten times as far from either. Probably, however, Cnossos was colonised from neither of these regions but from the south-western coast of Asia Minor, which is only a hundred and twenty miles from the island. If so, that place of origin is still unidentifiable, though we know of an early enough Asian site, Hacilar, which is only eighty miles from the south-western corner of the peninsula. Hacilar probably derived much of its culture from Çatalhüyük, but the complexity of its cultural position is shown by skeletons of the sixth millennium which already belong to at least two races. Probably the racial mixture goes back much farther still; and no doubt it was even more complicated in the Aegean islands, when migrants from Asia had arrived and superseded or joined earlier populations.

A coastal point not far from Hacilar, then, may have been the base from which the first settlers, impelled by unknown pressures, arrived at Cnossos near the north coast of Crete. The newcomers who had navigated these difficult waters were familiar with agricultural life, and their debris, twenty-three feet below the impressive city of the future, includes mill-stones, almond seeds, and the bones of cattle, sheep and pigs. Tools of obsidian were supplied in abundance by the island of Melos which lies halfway between Crete and Attica, and a white marble statuette of a woman from Cnossos, made during the sixth millennium BC, shows that extremely advanced artistic levels had already been attained.

It was apparently from yet another part of Asia Minor, its north-western coast (where Troy was subsequently to be founded), that colonists first undertook the hundred and sixty mile crossing of the Aegean from east to west and landed on the European mainland. The boats which conveyed them, like others in more northern parts of the continent, must have been either covered with skins or made out of solid wood, like the modern dug-out canoes on Balkan lakes. In boats such as these, people arrived on the east coast of northern Greece and settled in Thessaly. There, twenty miles from the shore, beside the Peneus basin which has the largest fertile plain in Greece, they founded the village of Argissa. The earliest inhabitants, who arrived before the end of the seventh millennium, grew barley, wheat, flax and probably millet, and the animals which they bred were mainly sheep, which – like people in northern Greece today – they took to upland pastures in summer, leaving them in the rich Thessalian lowlands for the rest of the year.

> Cattle graze vigorous and strong
> On abundant fields in Thessaly beneath an ageless,
> watching sun.[21]

The people of Thessaly also had tame dogs, descended from wolves or wild canines of dingo or pariah type. Possibly the domestication of dogs came to Argissa from continental Europe, which provides the earliest discoverable examples of the practice. But this scavenger, hunter's assistant, and protector may also have had its aid enlisted independently by other agricultural peoples in Asia, and perhaps came to Greece from there.

Thessalian settlements developed and multiplied, subsequently producing vigorously painted pottery, developing a rudimentary overseas commerce, and evolving a rectangular type of residence, entered by a porch from a large open court. Models, made at a somewhat later date yet probably representing a traditional form, display gables recalling a snowy place of origin which has now been identified as Asia Minor. But these sloping roofs still remained useful to keep off the rains and snows of northern Greece. For the same reason, baked mud needed the supplementation of plaited twigs and poles, some of which were placed down the middle of the houses as props, thus creating the rudiments of two-roomed abodes and of later columnar architecture.

Whatever the reasons for the first momentous westward journey, Thessaly was a probable enough destination for emigrants from north-western Asia Minor, since portions of the two countries possessed similar terrain and climate. Another such region, likewise accessible from the Aegean, was the fertile plain of Macedonia which lay beyond Thessaly to the north. Parts of this area, too, were colonised, not later than the final centuries of the seventh millennium. Of this date is the settlement of Nea Nikomedeia, situated six miles from the present Verria upon a low mound, between two rivers which contained plentiful fish, the Haliacmon and slightly more distant Axius (Vardar). The Thermaic Gulf of the Mediterranean, into which these rivers lead, is now over thirty miles away, but in those days it came up almost to the village itself.

Whether the newcomers to Macedonia arrived overland from Thessaly or by sea from Asia Minor, a link with the latter country is indicated by the rectangular shape of their single-roomed, mud-plastered, gabled houses, which they built of woven reeds and disposed within a double ring of mud walls in an open formation different from the cramped warrens of the torrid middle east. Pottery and other artifacts likewise show the influence of Asia Minor, and so also perhaps do five female statuettes of clay, found in a building which was probably a shrine. Certain forms of pre-Greek place-names (p. 86), which later survived on the mainland, confirm the assumption of this trans-Aegean association, since they are also found over a wide area extending to the farthest extremities of Asia Minor.

First links with the Euphrates and Tigris

Such then were some of the European offshoots of the cultures which were transmitted across the Aegean from adjacent parts of Asia Minor, but which most noticeably flourished at the other, Cilician, end of the peninsula, and in the lower Orontes (Amik) plain.

In those regions the sixth millennium brought further development. Dark, burnished pottery was now being made in Cilicia, and products only slightly less advanced came from a place on the Syrian coast just over fifty miles south of the Amik. This was Ras Shamra (Ugarit), which had already begun its long history with a period in which no pottery had been made. The rectangular shape of its plaster-floored houses was more reminiscent of Asia Minor than of the round or oval dwellings of earlier Israel and Cyprus. A vigorous culture related to Ras Shamra spread south of the town, extending over much of what was later to be called the Phoenician coast, with ramifications in inland Syria and Israel. The pottery of these centres differs from the Anatolian plateau because of its keen interest in decoration, displayed in a variety of textured surfaces which imitate basketry vessels.

The immense history of one of the Phoenician towns had now begun. This was Byblos (Jbail). About ninety miles south of Ras Shamra, its first site stood upon a defensible group of sand dunes on the Mediterranean shore. Free-standing houses, at least several hundred in number, were scattered on either side of a deep ravine. Wheat was grown and perhaps barley, domesticated animals were probably kept, and the activities of the inhabitants included hunting, fishing, weaving and spinning.

Byblos, Ras Shamra, Mersin and the Amik plain are all less than two hundred miles from the River Euphrates, and by the early- and mid-sixth millennium there is a strong similarity between the pots found at such sites and those which turn up in Mesopotamia, even at its remotest extremities. The centre of this cultural diffusion was somewhere in the foothills of northern (now Turkish) Mesopotamia, in the middle of the creative Taurus – Zagros zone which seems to have originated the cultivation of crops and domestication of animals (p. 13). Recent discoveries, beside the Tigris, of sixth-millennium figurines with inlaid eyes form a link between the decorated skulls of Natufian Jericho and later Mesopotamian sculpture.

That was a region from which advanced modes of life

radiated not only eastwards far beyond the Tigris, but westwards to the Mediterranean as well. For during the last years of the fifth millennium BC a new and vigorous way of life which pervaded northern Mesopotamia extended over very large areas. A wide uniformity of culture hints at some sort of coordinated activity, comprising an extensive trade ranging far into Asia Minor, and from the Persian Gulf to the Mediterranean. The central designs and customs spread in only slightly modified forms through the adjacent areas of Syria and Cilicia. Consequently, the designs of this predominantly Mesopotamian civilisation are echoed in pottery produced both on the Lower Orontes coastlands and at Mersin.

From now on, with enormous results for Mediterranean culture, influences from the Mesopotamian hills and other parts of the creative east were destined to be channelled abundantly through such maritime outlets. For example this civilisation of the later sixth and earlier fifth millennium greatly developed and diffused the techniques of working copper and lead from the metalliferous hills of northern Mesopotamia and the Taurus. In each town, too, the cobbled streets tell of an organised social effort. The thick-walled, stone based underground vaults of these peoples were destined to have a long, strange history elsewhere, notably in Asia Minor and Crete; and themes such as the double axe and bull's skull were likewise to reemerge there after thousands of years had passed. The polychrome pottery of this time, still hand-made and decorated with figurative designs, is the most perfect ever to be seen in Mesopotamia, and was finely adapted in the areas roundabout. Such, then, were the novel developments breaking westwards into the Mediterranean lands of Turkey and the Levant.

Next, in *c.* 4300 BC, northern Mesopotamia started producing much more skilful metalwork, including cast axes of copper. These may not have been a great improvement on stone as far as agriculture was concerned, but they were more efficient instruments of war: lighter and stronger, less fragile, easier to shape and repair, more sharply edged. The production of such tools presupposed that their communities disposed of substantial food-supplies, since the quarrying and trading were full-time jobs, and often had to be conducted on mountainsides where no crops could be grown.

And yet north Mesopotamia, where such advances were achieved, was already by that time ceasing to be the central point of near and middle eastern civilisation. Its river, the Euphrates, navigable from the present Turco-Syrian frontier downwards, could convey the country's discoveries and treasures farther south, on air-filled goatskin floats, rafts, basket-work coracles and canoes; and its early name, the Copper River, indicated what some of those cargoes were. Not long after the middle of the fifth millennium, the whole nucleus of civilisation had shifted south in the same way, and had taken root in the flat, hot southern extremities of Mesopotamia. These lands are over five hundred miles from the civilized foothills and nearly seven hundred from the Mediterranean. And yet their influence on the Mediterranean world, through Asiatic outposts and Egypt, now became enormous.

The new way of life, which had reached maturity in this area by *c.* 4400–4300, again had a wide distribution, extending all the way from Zagros to Syria and Taurus; at Mersin this culture propagated four successive villages, which in due course developed a fortified wall with towered gateway. But since now, for the first time, its centre of diffusion lay far to the south, the civilisation has taken its modern name from a mound close to where the lower Euphrates and Tigris meet before their combined debouchment into the Persian Gulf.

The first occupants of the area maintained a uniform civilisation for nearly seven hundred years. Their greenish, black-painted pottery resembles products from the slopes of south-western Iran, and suggests that this was the country from which some of the new arrivals came. A desiccation, starting in *c.* 6000 BC, may well have made the Iranian grasslands too dry for all its inhabitants to sustain life there any longer. At first they probably moved to the border slopes between the higher country they had abandoned and the torrid lowlands below; and then they or their descendants moved down. Changing and adapting the customs they had brought from the hills, these immigrants or invaders set themselves the novel and immense task of reclaiming the scorching, untamed jungle swamps near the head of the Persian Gulf.

Scourged alternately by droughts and irregular floods, this territory was also choked with tangles of thick high weeds and filled with many dangerous animals. Yet it teemed with fish, wild fowl and pig, had access to salt deposits, and consisted of alluvial soil which would yield eighty-six times the sowing. And clearance, though tough, was not impossible, because there were few if any substantial trees to clear away. At first, irrigation only amounted to digging breaches in natural embankments, but then came more elaborate processes of draining and digging small canals. Skilled farmers as well as stock-breeders, the inhabitants grew emmer wheat, using a plough better than any to be seen elsewhere. The local products which had helped to entice the new settlers to the area included date-palms, and these were now cultivated and soon artificially pollinated, supplying a reliable, nutritive, annual crop.

This activity took place within the narrow region later known as Sumeria, rarely more than forty miles wide, at the far south-eastern end of the fertile Crescent. Anxiety-ridden myths of the region reflect the exacting challenge of overcoming menaces in these laborious conditions. Mastery was only possible by the conscious collaboration of a considerable number of people prepared to dam and dike and clear and dig. This joint action was organised by townships which grew to unprecedented sizes, developing new high levels of internal organisation and a more advanced urbanism than had ever existed elsewhere. The thirteen cities of Sumeria each became a small self-contained city-state, anticipatory of many such organisms in the near east and Greece. References in myths and epics suggest that in early days the control of these cities was divided among the heads of the families whose combined efforts were needed to wring a living from the land. But political unification between cities was hampered by their separateness, each an enclave in its own environment, separated by waste lands and seeking, like the Greeks of later times, to overcome their neighbours by war.

Since this was a country lacking in stone, towns were still built of mud and clay, taken from vast deposits along the river banks. These lumps, however, were no longer merely pressed together and heaped in piles, but shaped and prefabricated by moulds and then dried in the sun, reinforced with twisted reeds, and damp-proofed and cemented with the country's bitumen, which was known for thousands of years before its oil. But the mud was still unbaked, and consequently its use for architectural purposes demanded blocks that were solid, simple and right-angled. Such were the materials now used for constructing temples–often many successively, one on top of the other–upon low platforms of brick or stone. More impressive still were the characteristic enormous stepped towers (Ziggurats) which 'reached unto heaven' and helped to inspire the pyramids of Egypt.

Throughout the middle years of the fourth millennium all such ideas were actively advanced during the evolution of a culture which is named today after a site which lies halfway between Basra and Baghdad. These people developed city life and architecture, carved human heads very sensitively, and made use of mass-manufactured pottery employing the potter's wheel, which added rhythm and movement to ceramic form.

This was truly a golden age of Mesopotamian discoveries. For example, pictures were inscribed on seals, which were at first plain stamps but soon became incised cylinders imprinting the clay on which they were rolled. Next came tablets on which the earliest writings appeared, initially in the form of outline representations of objects. But then these were gradually formalised into groups of inverted wedges, each group representing a single sign, and each sign phonetically rendering a syllable or word or sound, with special marks for numerals. Out of the large number of signs that were employed from time to time, about three hundred came into common use. To begin with, these were traced by hand, but before long the impressions were instead made by wedge-shaped styluses. The material was damp clay, which would not have served very well for hand-made picture-signs but made an excellent and readily available receptacle for these simple, symbolical 'cuneiform' impressions.

Moreover, once baked, the clay would last imperishably in a dry climate for thousands of years. Durability was important because this writing (though not intelligible to us in its earliest stages) was evidently first used for temple accounts and inventories recording the accumulation, storage and distribution of surplus wealth. This ingenious art of painting words and of speaking to the eyes, the mother of orators and father of artists, could assert rights over tools or cattle, recall things that had to be done at particular times, and communicate with people who were far away. Imitators, too, appeared in remote lands. The writing of Mesopotamia was adopted not only in Egypt, perhaps through traders' meetings on the south Arabian or Somali coasts, but even apparently in a valley deep in the interior of Rumania, where recently discovered inscriptions show clear debts not indeed to the Mesopotamian language, but to its script, which had gradually percolated by way of Syria or Asia Minor.

A clay model of a south Mesopotamian sailing boat suggests the increased effectiveness of river and maritime communications which made such contacts possible. On land, too, a further advance of the fourth millennium was the invention of the wheel, at first solid and later spoked. The flat lands near the mouths of the Tigris and the Euphrates are an appropriate place of origin for the first wheeled vehicles, which were drawn by wild asses and took the form of four-wheeled draught waggons and two-wheeled carts for fighting. This opening up of traversable regions to movement and to access from the highlands and elsewhere caused stimulating exchanges between settled and nomad populations. But it also made for more frequent wars.

The various developments of this period were pushed further ahead still, before and after 3000 BC, by peoples possessing a more advanced culture, which is named today after a site near the later Babylon. Buildings developed recessed panels, floral tracery, and pilaster columns which possessed plant-like capitals and were overlaid with bitumen and mosaic designs copying palm-bark. There were further extensions of the same culture in north-eastern Syria, where a temple of Mesopotamian type has been found. City life of the new kind was spreading, and at Tarsus in Cilicia, for example, there existed a flourishing town from *c.* 3000–2400 BC. The large thick bell-shaped pots of the same phase, with their geometric or naturalistic designs in black or red paint, are found in more westerly regions of the same foothills as well as at Byblos. Cylinder seals of similar origin occur as far afield as Persia, the Caspian, and the remotest extremities of Asia Minor.

Although cultural advances cannot always be too readily equated with changes of population, one of these last two cultural pushes surely signalised the arrival of the Sumerians in south Mesopotamia. Whether they came up the Persian Gulf by sea or down from the hills by land, their woollen garments and cloaks seem to suggest origins in the mountains of eastern Iraq or western Iran. They called themselves 'the black-headed people', but their race, or mixture of races, remains obscure. So does their language, which is neither Semitic nor Indo-European but agglutinative, and has no known affinities. They shared the city states of Mesopotamia with Semitic-speaking peoples of unknown geographical origin (not necessarily nomadic), in a duality more intricate than plain opposition, for race and language did not always coincide; though on the whole Sumerians predominated in the south and Semitic speakers farther up the rivers.

When the Sumerians had established themselves in their new homeland, trade turned into imperialism on a scale which for the first time brought the militarism and aggression of major powers as far as the north-east corner of the Mediterranean. Shortly after 2400 BC the Sumerian monarch of the south Mesopotamian town of Umma claimed divine sanction for his rule 'from the lower to the upper sea' – perhaps the Persian Gulf and Mediterranean respectively. Even if this was less an accomplished fact than an unfulfilled hope, the boast implied a historic and sinister assertion of universal monarchy, or at least international acceptability as an arbiter. Very soon afterwards a Semitic ruler, from his capital at an unidentified centre near Babylon, crossed the land-bridge from Euphrates to the Mediterranean, and led raids into Syria, Asia Minor and Cyprus, 'across the sea of the setting sun'. His particular aims, like those of his equally aggressive grandson and many subsequent monarchs, were the Silver Mountain (Taurus) and the Cedar Mountain or Forest (Amanus or Lebanon). Mesopotamian epics, too, spoke of mythical heroes who had been to the Forest, and had killed its wild guardian.

Before the end of the third millennium another south Mesopotamian city, Ur, built up a careful legal system and an unprecedentedly efficient empire which (through its Assyrian successors) helped to mould many subsequent imperial organisations. The writ of Ur extended eastwards to Susa in Persia, and its trade went farther still, to the valley of the Indus. In the west, Phoenician Byblos was under the rulers of Ur, who imported timber and metals from Cilicia and Syria, exporting statuettes and precious materials in return.

The control of this system was facilitated by the domestication of the horse. It is uncertain whether an earlier horse found in Israel was domesticated or not, but the peoples of south Russia and perhaps Baluchistan had already tamed steppe ponies; and from there the practice had gradually spread to the equally level lands of Mesopotamia, where horses were probably ridden before 2000 BC and then harnessed to vehicles in place of wild asses or oxen (p. 35).

But by the end of the third millennium Ur had fallen. The occasion was one of those major, complex convulsions which wandering peoples inflicted at intervals upon the civilised centres of the ancient world. The same phase of disturbance destroyed more westerly cultures which had been in close touch with Mesopotamia. Devastation raged throughout Asia Minor, right from the Cilician cities to populous centres on the Black Sea coast.* The Konya plain was ravaged and so was a community which had flourished a hundred and thirty miles to its west. This was Beycesultan, situated near Lake Burdur on an ancient trade route beside a crossing of the Menderes (Maeander), before that river descends for another hundred and thirty miles – and three thousand feet – to the Aegean. One of the centres of a fourth and third millennium culture, the place seems to point forward to the times when advanced civilisation would move to those Aegean shores – unless indeed, unknown to us, it had already done so. Between Beycesultan and the sea lay rich deposits of emery, a dense granular variety of corundum or aluminium oxide which is nearest to the diamond in hardness and attracted great esteem as a resistant abrasive of hard surfaces. Found in reddish soil in the form of blocks or fragments embedded in crystallised limestone, emery was in great demand in Egypt, which probably learnt its use from centres such as Beycesultan in Asia Minor. But by the termination of the third millennium all these linked cultures, from Mesopotamia to the Mediterranean, had been violently destroyed.

* In *c.* 2300 a great wave of Indo-European-speaking peoples, using a Luvian dialect (p. 86), seems to have swept over Asia Minor from the direction of the Bosphorus.

2

Egypt

The delta of the Nile

After 10,000 BC, the moisture-laden winds shrank northwards away from Africa, and large tracts which had previously been fertile became uninhabitable. The expanses west of the Nile delta, formerly open grassy veldt, became the Great Sand Sea, and the lands to the east turned into desert as well. And so the populations of these desiccated areas entered the delta, in a series of waves continuing until the sixth millennium BC (p. 13).

The Nile is a classic, extreme example of the influence of geography upon history. More than four thousand miles long, completely dwarfing all other rivers which flow into the eastern Mediterranean, this is the only stream which rises in the tropics and then enters the climatic belt where the earliest human civilisations arose. For much of its length it passes through a well-defined trench, between two and fifteen miles in width, flanked by imposing limestone bluffs and waterless desert. But the banks themselves are rich with deposits of black mud and silt brought by the Blue Nile and Atbara from the high Ethiopian plateaux. For the heavy monsoon rain of those highlands combines, each June, with the melting of their snows to raise the level of the river between twenty-five and fifty feet, bringing a rich alluvial soil that covers thousands of square miles of cultivable land – a fine, heavy and tractable mud, divested *en route* of its coarser detritus by natural dams of granite within the river-bed. The ancient Egyptians named their country the Black Land.

Although its southern regions have always exercised their influence on national development, what directly concerns a history of the Mediterranean is lower Egypt, comprising the river delta. Here, almost a hundred miles before the Nile reaches the coast, its main channel has divided into a number of branches (seven main ones in ancient times), which empty their waters separately, enclosing between them this triangle of oasis-land built by river-borne silt at the expense of the sea.

Along the smooth desert of the coastline itself lies a strip of swamps and flats and brackish lagoons and sandy isles which the ancient Egyptians called *ta-meh*, the land under water. But the rest of the delta could be made extraordinarily productive. Every year, just when all plants were withering under the summer sun, the whole territory was inundated and for a time totally covered. The inhabitants conceived the primordial situation as watery, and had a song which said, 'the shepherd is in the water, along with the fish'. But when the flood receded, its muddy sediment remained, reviving the soil and raising the river banks so that irrigation of the flanking area was easier.

The climate, however, was forbidding, for the eastern basin of the Mediterranean lies considerably nearer than its western shores to the equator, and the region goes through very torrid periods. Rain, known to the Egyptians as 'a Nile in the sky', hardly falls at all beyond the delta's apex, and only very sparsely in the delta itself, though it is just within reach of Mediterranean breezes.

Before human habitation, this was as horrible a jungle swamp as the even hotter lands of southern Mesopotamia. But reclamation was easier because of the greater regularity of inundations and the timing of their arrival, which preceded the planting season and yet was late enough for the drenched land not to have dried out until the crops were sown and well set. The earliest inhabitants of the delta learnt gradually how to encourage these natural processes, and the water-lift or well-sweep still in use today, with its bucket carried by a long weighted beam on two stakes, goes back to remote antiquity. Drains and dams harnessed the floods and added new cultivable lands. Dykes and causeways and embankments were constructed, and finally canals, which often followed natural depressions, and yet needed to be dredged to keep their channels free. With these aids, after the river had subsided in November or early December, the rewards took the spectacular form of three annual harvests. For this is the most fertile country in the world.

And yet forethought was needed, not just for the day as in

more backward lands but a whole year ahead. Moreover, as in Mesopotamia, drainage and irrigation wanted and promoted the pooling, distribution and direction of human effort, and the investment of present energies for future advantage. Ultimately, the successful fulfilment of these challenges produced resources large enough to support the whole superstructure of literate civilisation.

Although immigrants to the delta probably closed in from both flanks, those who brought the more developed techniques of agriculture came from the east and north: namely, from the territory of the Natufians who had evolved comparatively advanced ways of life in Israel and the Jordan valley. That is to say, the earliest civilisation of lower Egypt originated from the Levant.

In due course these occupants of the delta began to cultivate emmer wheat and barley – both of which are shown in their earliest picture-script and had again, in all probability, been imported from Asia. Their growth was easy since the cultivator was presented each year with an almost ready-made seed-bed, in which all he had to do was to open up shallow channels with a hoe and tread the seeds into the soft mud. The grain was converted into cakes and porridge. Beer too was brewed from barley flour and varieties of wheat, the half cooked loaves being crumbled into a honey-sweetened liquid to which yeast had been added. Other staple crops were millet, a fruit like the cherry, and figs, which beyond the delta's southern rim gave place to dates on tall and slender palms. The principal Egyptian tree, the sycamore, produced wood which might be used as a material for furniture, but its grain lacked the smoothness to provide straight planks. In early times, however, there were other useful timber trees and brushwood on what are now arid margins. The large, fleshy, hard-shelled fruits of the gourd were hollowed out and used to make utensils of many kinds.

The meadowlands and pastures on the borders of the flood plain supported sheep and goats. These were of Asian origin, but the more numerous oxen may, like local pigs and asses, have been indigenous. As elsewhere, the bull was regarded as a symbol of fertility. Early kings are shown as pastoral chieftains, with goat-beards and animal tails. Burial-places of bulls and sheep appear in early strata of habitation, for these animals were revered for their fecund correspondence with the inscrutable ways of nature. They also possessed a close and intricate relation to human beings, who often lived with them in the same houses. In later times men were called upon to say, as life ended, 'I have not done evil to men: I have not ill-treated animals.'[1]

Cemeteries suggest that this reverence was extended to the wild beasts which the first inhabitants of the delta had found there in savage, overwhelming abundance. Accordingly there were many animal-headed gods and local totems, which seem to echo the far earlier products of cave art. Respect was extended to lions and leopards hunted by spearmen in the neighbouring pampas-like open spaces and deserts, and the lion in particular (sometimes half-humanised as a sphinx) passed into the repertoire of Mediterranean art as a symbol of kingly majesty.

The earliest story of coastal Egypt is almost entirely lost beneath the delta's accumulations of alluvial silt. This grave hiatus in Mediterranean history is only slightly mitigated by discoveries in the Fayum depression, a fertile and pleasant oasis in the Libyan desert, twenty-five miles west of the Nile and forty miles south of the delta.

During the fifth millennium BC the northern shoreline of Lake Fayum, which is linked to the river and stood 180 feet higher than it does now, was occupied by hamlets or camping sites, built mainly on reeds. The people who constructed them were fowlers and fishermen, but their agricultural qualifications are demonstrated by subterranean basketry-lined communal granaries, straight-handled and flint-toothed wooden sickles, threshing-flails, handmills (querns) and mealing-stones. Cereals, then, were already stored; and specimens found in the Fayum differ from the wild species and suggest the likelihood of cultivation. Grain-pits and graves alike were lined with mats woven of grass and rushes, and remains of a crude form of linen point to the growing and processing of the flax-like *ensete*, which requires light fertile soil and ample irrigation water. A beginning, then, already had been made with the development of Egyptian linen, which was to become the finest in the world. These dwellers in the Fayum also made coarse cups and bowls of clay, a material in which the soft, plastic, sticky banks of the Nile are peculiarly rich.

Early in the fourth millennium, we have evidence from the very fringes of the delta itself; for Merimdeh ben Salama, where this has been found, is only just outside the apex of its western arm. Here was another place which possessed its own threshing floors and granaries. These people also practised the domestication of cattle, goats, sheep and pigs – unlike, perhaps, the occupants of the Fayum village from which Merimdeh may well be derived. Its habitation, too, was of a more permanent character, comprising low, strong oval constructions built of lumps of mud. The leathery vessels which these people made represent the same stage as others found as far afield as south-eastern Spain.

Other sites of the earlier fourth millennium are identifiable in upper Egypt, where they were much more likely to be preserved. The craftsmen on these sites prepared the way for later sculptural developments by their skilful moulding and engraving of birds, hippopotamuses, fish and antelope on slate palettes, which were used to pound bright green malachite (copper carbonate) as eye-paint, whether for reasons of hygiene, religion or cosmetic decoration. These populations of upper Egypt also exploited the flat tabular flint of the Nile cliffs to become the best flint-workers in the world, and made stone vases and pottery which developed fanciful shapes with a red burnish and varied decoration. Some of this pottery is made of imported clay which presumably, being fragile and bulky, came by sea and not all the way by land. Gold and alabaster were also brought for long distances, and copper was used not only in the form of malachite but also in metallic form for small ornamental objects such as pins. Since, however, 'there is no rational correlation between importance and evidence',[2] it may well be that the delta, from which we have no contemporary information, was the first part of Egypt to develop these metallurgical techniques, in view of its greater proximity and accessibility to the Sinai peninsula where copper was abundantly available and could be exploited under Asian tuition.

But upper Egypt, too, had direct links with Asia, by way of the Red Sea, and in the next stage this was the region that developed a more advanced culture. Perhaps grain was now not only boiled for porridge but baked for bread; and these people also produced stone vases, fired a local glass-like quartz (faïence), worked skilfully in gold, carved large statues of the gods, and made pottery by novel techniques and with varied figurative decorations, including flamingoes, ibexes, human beings and plants. After about two centuries, this culture spread upwards into the delta. Now, at last, there was a measure of cultural uniformity for the whole of Egypt; and leadership may for a time have been asserted by the northern borrowers, since their totems appear on boats depicted in the south.

Egyptian funeral monuments of many periods have survived in the desert sands, but we know far less about the dwellings of the living people in their villages and towns. In oases of the western desert the wood-framed mud-brick houses were located where water was available, but in the delta, on the contrary, they stood on natural or artificial mounds to afford refuge from the floods. Sometimes these centres of population were raised very high, like Bubastis (Bast) – later famous for its festival and avenue of trees – on an eastern branch of the delta twenty-five miles from the sea. The whole delta, except for its marshy regions, teemed thickly with such conglomerations of people, like an ant-hill or one long suburbia.

The first Mediterranean nation

Attached to the towns of the delta were clan areas, which in early days remained independent of one another because the marshes made communication difficult. But in c. 3100 BC the whole of lower Egypt became a single state, and at about the same time upper Egypt, despite its strangely elongated shape, became another. The unification of these two territories, each within itself, facilitated effective irrigation. The first capital of the northern kingdom was Buto (Dep) by the Nile's Rosetta branch. The inhabitants of this town, from which only a few mounds survive, could see the Mediterranean from the heights of their temple-pylon erected to the cobra-goddesss who presided over these delta peoples and 'knew the Great Green Sea'.

In building such towns, the old lashed bundles of stalks, rush matwork, palm thatch, plastered plaited twigs and lumps of mud were now gradually superseded by sun-dried mud-brick. The mud was indigenous and available in enormous quantities, and when this product is churned into a thick paste with water, mixed with straw or reeds or flax, and sprinkled with sand to prevent cracking, it develops great plasticity and can be moulded into excellent bricks, more resistant to fire and weather than stone, and easier to produce, transport and lay. Nevertheless, under the stimulus of this locally accessible material, the techniques for its employment were borrowed from Mesopotamia. For although the bricks used in the two countries were not of the same size, and techniques also were different, the Egyptian pilasters and recessed panels, which now appeared along the desert fringe on rectangular platforms covering subterranean tombs, were based on models from southern Mesopotamia (p. 34).

Excavations have also revealed objects imported from that country, including cylinder seals which Egyptian craftsmen soon proceeded to imitate. For a time too, fantastic, symmetrically arranged Mesopotamian animals are copied – and adapted to become the griffins of Egyptian art, which also displays the Mesopotamian hero wrestling with two lions. This theme appears engraved on an ivory knife handle found near the beginning of the desert route to the Red Sea, and the reverse side of the same object displays river ships of a type belonging to the Tigris. The potter's wheel was also introduced from Mesopotamia at about this time or soon afterwards.

An even more significant development of the later fourth millennium was writing. These 'hieroglyphs' expressing sounds and ideas likewise owe their origins to Mesopotamia. But the two thousand or more signs that came into use also included many based on plant and animal forms found in Egypt. Many new complexities and subtleties were introduced. Furthermore, the occasional use of symbols indicating that only initial consonants should be pronounced meant that an approach was already being made to alphabetic methods.

Perhaps this Egyptian script originated in the delta, where in ancient times the principal writing material, a member of the sedge family known as the papyrus, existed in such particular abundance that it became the symbol of the area. The rushes of this plant, now found in its natural state no nearer than the marshes of the southern Sudan and upper Jordan valley, are shown in reliefs and paintings growing to more than human height. The papyrus supplied a host of needs. For human consumption, it was boiled or roasted or chewed raw like sugarcane today. It was used for the construction of boats, cloths, coverlets, sandals, cords and mats. But above all it was employed for writing purposes. The pith of its stems was cut into layers from six to fifteen inches in width. Two of these layers, one set horizontally and the other vertically, were fastened together and dried in the sun, and then twenty or more of these double strips were pasted end to end in rolls. The result was a light, portable object, admirably receptive of black or red ink, which continued in use over the entire Mediterranean area for thousands of years.

'Set your heart on being a scribe,' said an Egyptian, 'for a book is of greater value than a house, than the tombs in the west. It is more beautiful than a castle, or than a sculptured slab in a temple.'[3] For the Egyptians formed a different concept of writing from their Mesopotamian teachers, using inscriptions not only for purposes of accountancy and recording, not only to adorn their monumental art, but above all to produce the first Mediterranean literature.

The introduction of writing seems to have coincided with a shift in the nature of the language. The concise, concrete, realistic, observant Egyptian tongue had been a very early fusion of two ingredients. African, Hamitic strains were dominant, but there was also a Semitic element from Asia, and this now became stronger at African expense. Moreover, the skulls and skeletons of the slight, long-headed, oval-faced earlier inhabitants (more negroid towards the south) became mixed with broader-headed types. These, like the new features in the language, came from Asia, though whether by conquest or peaceful migration, by sudden incursion or long infiltration, as a dynastic élite or a mass movement, cannot yet be determined.

At all events Egypt, from about 3400 BC onwards, was being transformed very rapidly, and the influences which caused the transformation were Asian. In fact the country became in some measure an outlying branch of a common east Mediterranean culture. Yet it also impressed upon its borrowings a distinctive stamp: 'a foreign "know-how" was quickly seized upon and enthusiastically adapted to Egyptian conditions by a people ripe for a change.'[4] Egypt, that is to say, accepted very many of its institutions from Asia but then modified them radically – a classic situation in Mediterranean lands and one which was destined to reappear in Greece.

For Egypt, belying its later capacity for isolated unchanging conservation, was less cut off than has been supposed. The country is a tube which can be entered at the bottom as well as the top. As the events of AD 1967 have recalled, there are two direct land links through metal-rich Sinai from the centres of habitation in Israel, one along a coastal route and the other through the interior. Moreover the delta, like upper Egypt, has a land-corridor to the Red Sea, on the way to Arabian and Somali shores where further meetings between Egyptians and Asiatics could take place. And then there was also Egypt's northern, Mediterranean coast, which may already have witnessed embarkations, though direct evidence for such activity still belongs to the future.

In *c.* 3200 BC the two kingdoms of lower and upper Egypt, already to some extent sharers of a homogeneous culture, were politically merged and made into a single unit by sudden or gradual invasion from the south. The conquest, traditionally attributed to 'King Menes', has lately been ascribed to one or more of several monarchs bearing other names. The extensive captures of oxen and goats of which one of these rulers boasts refers to the conquest of grass-lands which still survived in what is now the Libyan desert beyond the delta's western border.

The unification of Egypt's two parts was signalised by the establishment, near their junction, of a new city which soon became the country's capital. This was Memphis or White Walls, situated at a river ford just south of the delta, with access to cliffs made of good limestone building material. The town has gone, since it was later pillaged to build Cairo. But nearby there are extensive remains of the ten-mile-long cemetery of Sakkara, which at first probably contained the graves of private individuals, belonging to the rising administrative and professional class, while the tombs of the royal dynasty still remained in the south.

From now on monarchs wore the lower Egyptian Red Crown,

flat-topped with tall projections and a feather, as well as the conical White Crown of upper Egypt. Since the latter was their native land, the political character of the unified monarchy which now emerged was not Asian, like so much of the country's culture, but southern and African. For the king, in contrast to Mesopotamian institutions, was god incarnate, like rulers who still exist in Africa today. In his own person he represented and incorporated the natural forces personified by the gods who rose up from the grave and brought fertility. In the same spirit which enabled them to blend men with animals, the Egyptians identified this man, their ruler, with the deity, and the identification justified an autocratic form of government which constitutes one-half of our political inheritance from the Mediterranean world.

Although a variety of different customs and dialects resisted the forces tending towards unification, this had been imperatively demanded by the need for coordinated, communal effort, organisation and discipline over as large a range of the river as possible, in order to bring irrigation to the highest productivity. At the outset of the unification period, artists show monarchs opening canals; every place in the kingdom was now within ten miles of some waterway or other.

This improved agricultural system supported increases of population and permitted the growth of specialised trades and of capital. Relying on a large hinterland as well as a coastline, Egypt was by far the largest state the near east or Mediterranean had ever seen. Its services taught the world a new bureaucratic complexity, for the effective exploitation of the Nile required elaborate calculations, measurements, and systems of law and taxation, all of which were facilitated by the recent development of writing and numeration. Absorbed in its own elaborate and prosperous life, so well protected by desert and sea that little money or energy had to be devoted to defence, Egypt now began to assume that formidable conservatism which became so striking a characteristic of its politics, religion and art. This immutability, accentuated perhaps by the eternally renewed spectacle of the Nile, was reflected in temperaments of smiling, complacent, serenely urbane tranquillity, very different from the vigilant anxiety which Mesopotamians derived from their more hazardous physical conditions.

The Old Kingdom

Yet Egyptian monarchs of the third millennium BC did not rest content with their own country, but exploited the access opened up by the Mediterranean to wider horizons beyond.

Greek visitors later described this coast as inhospitable, since the adjoining shallows and maritime stretches were full of silt, and behind wind-blown sand-bars and shoals, between the delta's shifting arms, lay soggy marsh. Because of this unwelcoming strand and the ever-present menace of pirates, the chief Mediterranean harbour-towns were situated some little way inland: Buto or Dep (Tell el Farain) in the west, Pernefer and Tanis beside one of the river's eastern arms, and the hitherto unidentified Great Port. In the derelict fringes between these places and the coast lived Swamp Men who ventured upon the sea so that the Egyptians, eaters of fish, could supplement river catches by marine varieties. Fragments and scales of fish have been found in early Egyptian stomachs, and Israelites later remembered with longing 'the fish which we did eat in Egypt freely'.[5]

Salt, too, the earliest major item of Mediterranean trade, is particularly abundant on this shore. Shallow lagoons at the mouth of the delta formed natural pans from which it could easily be collected. 'Men may live without gold or silver but not without salt',[6] which they need, especially in hot climates, to preserve their fish and meat. Inland peoples were deprecated as saltless.[7]

But it was not only for salt or fish that the Egyptians turned towards the sea which they described as Great and Green. For their experiences on the Nile prompted them to extend their navigation to this much wider expanse, and such ambitions may have been among the motives which impelled southern monarchs to invade the delta. The people of Mesopotamia had learnt to sail on their rivers, and the depiction by Egyptian artists of Mesopotamian-looking boats suggests an initiative from that area (p. 44). But the navigable length of the Nile made it far superior to the Euphrates or Tigris as a school for sailors. The earliest Egyptian name for a boat means 'binding', and refers to vessels made from lashed bundles of papyrus or other reeds to which were gradually added planks of sunt-acacia and other woods dovetailed together without keels or stems or stern-posts. By *c.* 3200–3100 BC these Nile craft were hoisting their first sails, perhaps evolved accidentally through observing the wind's inflation of animal-skin banners set up on board for religious ceremonies. With these sails filled by the prevailing north wind, Egyptians learnt how to struggle against the stream – and a vital method of harnessing inorganic energy to provide motive power had been mastered.

And so came the time when these craft, perhaps after initial ventures on the Red Sea, took to the Mediterranean. At first they were merely outsize river boats, but then the Phoenician port of Byblos helped to devise more maritime forms of construction (p. 62). During the third millennium BC one Egyptian monarch after another sent fleets into this sea both for commercial and warlike purposes. Westward links between Egypt and the fertile Libyan coastal strip of Cyrenaica were mainly by sea, but more important were the marine routes leading to the north and east. For since its local timber was not very serviceable for building ships, Egypt formed early, vital, contacts with Byblos to bring fir, cedar, pine, cypress and juniper from northern Syria and Lebanon. At the outset of their unified kingdom Egyptians were using flask-like pots which are also found at Byblos and were probably of Syrian origin; and Syrian slaves, too, came to be in great demand. The earliest recorded expedition to those shores took place in *c.* 2800 BC, and thenceforward captive Syrians, like negroes from beyond Egypt's southern frontiers, featured regularly among the decoration of royal footstools. In about 2600, forty vessels delivered cedarwood to King Sneferu, and he also became a ship-builder on his own account. A wooden boat buried by the next monarch Cheops beside his pyramid has a centre-board keel and a stern shaped like a papyrus bundle.

The twenty-fifth century BC witnessed a great increase in travel and trade. Immense quantities of cattle were captured from Libya, and fleets built for transporting soldiers to the Syrian coast displayed two-legged masts, tall slender square sails, and huge hawsers which were bound round their hulls and could be tightened on a pole. In *c.* 2300 a ship 102 feet long, with triple steering oars, could be built in seventeen days. There was no royal navy, but traders were given armed escorts. An

Egyptian officer left an inscription – such as no private individual could have recorded in Mesopotamia – boasting of the punishment of 'the Asiatics who dwell in the sands'.

At some period during the third millennium BC these increased contacts with the north brought from Syria or Cilicia one of their most important products, the vine. The Egyptians were less interested in the olive, since they obtained their vegetable oils from other sources. But soon after the country had become a single kingdom it began to cultivate grapes in order to make wine. The vine, like wheat and barley, was ascribed to the God Osiris and the legendary past, but it was not introduced into Egypt until long after its cereals. Vines, in their best known form, were native to north-eastern Turkey, or the southern shores of the Caspian, or, most probably of all, the region of the Caucasus which lies between those two territories. Wherever cultivation actually started, it eventually spread southwards, probably by way of Cilicia, and extended into Syria. Vines figure very prominently in the Old Testament, where they are attributed to Noah and their fruitfulness symbolises Israel. It was probably from there, not long after the initial period of unification, that they came to Egypt. The vineyards of the Fayum were particularly celebrated, and royal properties in the north-western regions of the delta in due course developed advanced specialisation, with labels defining *clos*, year, vintner and quality. Grape seeds found in early tombs closely resemble species still extensively cultivated today. At first, vines were allowed to trail along the ground or were attached to fig-trees like creepers, but later they were trained on forked vine-poles instead.

During the period known as the Old Kingdom (*c.* 2700–2160 BC) the arts of Egypt developed astonishingly. Stone-working, as always largely determined by available local materials, achieved great virtuosity. Employing excellent copper saws and chisels, and using moistened quartz sand as an abrasive, these sculptors handled stone almost as easily as clay. Yet they did not model the bodies of their gods or kings, but carved them into powerful, simplified outlines which emphasise the compact solidity of the block – and stress the gulf separating god or king from ordinary man. Southerners used their local basalt or hard granite, while northerners had finer, softer limestone at their disposal. Apart, however, from the distinctions thus imposed, stylistic variations were few, and the result was that blend of geometrical, formal southern regularity and keenly observed northern, Mediterranean naturalism which continued to prevail throughout Egypt's artistic history.

But sculpture, even when it was as spectacular as the seventy-five foot Sphinx of Chephren (*c.* 2550), remained subordinate to the supreme Egyptian art of architecture. This now included buildings of unprecedented size, made possible by the concentration of power in the hands of a single autocrat, whose pretensions necessitated a level of grandeur that had never been seen anywhere before. When he was dead, above all, the mortal impermanence of the monarch – who was also the supreme giver of life – had to be resisted by the preservation of his body, to ensure the return of his soul after long aeons of time. The observation of bodies that had been sterilised and preserved, first by the hot desert sand and then by artificial mummification, raised men's hopes of material immortality, and led to uniquely lavish magnificence in the provision of tombs and their furniture, huge human gestures to overcome this transitory life on earth.

The first royal tombs of the unified kingdom were low flat-topped mounds of sand supported by brick walls and solidified by rubble. Then came the pyramids, designed to reproduce such sandheaps in stone. From a date shortly after 2700 these great structures began to extend along a low ridge of desert beside the Nile's west bank, starting a hundred miles from the Mediterranean. The six-staged, two-hundred-foot-high step-pyramid built in a huge compound at Sakkara, the work of the legendary architect Imhotep, resembled earlier Egyptian architecture in deriving inspiration from Mesopotamia, where the terraced Sumerian Ziggurats supplied models. But whereas those had been made of mud-brick, the pyramids were of stone – the earliest sizeable stone buildings erected anywhere in the world. Masonry was still small-sized and reminiscent of mud or reed construction, but a recently discovered tomb-complex of a date before 2600 already displays large stone blocks which show no debt to those earlier materials.

The climax was rapidly reached in the next century, the time of the immense pyramids of Giza, which no longer have steps but sloping sides. The sharp lines of the Great Pyramid of Cheops (*c.* 2575), accentuated and paralleled by the even planes of the desert, rise to a height of nearly five hundred feet, not exceeded anywhere in the world until modern times. In addition to the smooth outer facings of white Tura limestone which have now disappeared, over two million local limestone blocks were used. Some of them weigh as much as 220 tons, and there are thirty-ton granite monoliths – which must have been transported downstream for five hundred miles or more. Accuracy to an almost infinitesimal degree was displayed by the quarriers and masons, with their sledges, rollers, levers, thick fibre ropes, chisels, wooden wedges, and mallets.

During the months from July to October, when the ground was flooded and could not be tilled, a vast population was available for the forced labour that was required. The pyramids symbolised the preeminence of service to the king. They also proclaimed, more impressively than any building ever before, his eternal life. The Ziggurats had enabled Mesopotamian rulers to commune with the sky, and a sacred text relating to the pyramids similarly proclaims that a 'staircase up to heaven is laid for him so that he may mount up to heaven thereby'.

Heaven meant the sun, and the very form of the pyramid, like the sacred discs surmounting obelisks, seems to represent the sun's rays shining down on earth. Solar worship was an obvious outcome of the ancient, universal awe of nature. Some African tribes, who knew the sun in its most terrible guise, saw it as a devil, but veneration of its beneficence was much more usual. In the Mediterranean world there are none of the subtle soft hesitations of northern horizons, and the sun though sometimes fierce is a glorious giver of life. At its cult-centre Heliopolis beside the delta's apex, a city second only to Thebes in holiness, legends told of a primeval hillock emerging from the chaos of the waters and giving birth to the sun-god, who was in turn destined to create the other divinities; and his daily conquest and rebirth gave people faith in victory over death.

Scrutinising the motions of the sun by day and the stars by night, the astronomical experts of Heliopolis achieved a solar calendar, the ancestor of our own which they needed to predict the movements of the river. Architects, too, who worked in this climate, were influenced and directed by the sun, because their buildings had to be designed in accordance with its sharp light and shade. At a second Giza pyramid, sunlight came in

> by oblique openings cut in the tops of the walls where they met the roof, and fell upon the polished alabaster floor, casting a diffused glow upon the twenty-three statues of the king, hewn from green diorites, alabasters and green schists.[8]

In later buildings vivid streaks of light were made to descend through huge gratings. On certain mornings,

> as the sun comes up above the eastern hill-tops, one long level beam strikes through the doorway, pierces the inner darkness like an arrow, penetrates to the sanctuary and falls like fire from heaven upon the altar at the feet of the gods.[9]

Since enough light came through the doors and apertures in the roof, there was no need for windows, which would only have admitted the heat – and unbroken massive walls provided uninterrupted surfaces for hieroglyphs and paintings.

In the sun's strong rays and shadows the high cliffs, which this land of contrasts has scored with horizontal strata and vertical weathering, dictated the rectilinear, prismatic, cubic post-and-lintel architecture which monopolised the temples of the Egyptians and was then taken over, in modified forms, by the Greeks. This is a style of horizontal beams beneath a cornice evolved from the overhangs that had once protected walls of mud; perhaps an even earlier source was the natural pressure of flat clay roofs upon a structure of reeds. The vertical columns supporting the beams were derived from the central poles that had propped up tents and huts.

In Egypt these columns had originally been bundles of plants or single stems or trunks, and even after the introduction of stone their decoration continued to be reminiscent of such origin. For architects and designers, being mostly conservative, tend to create the appearance of old materials – nowadays for example by making an electric fire look like a coal one – and the Egyptians felt disinclined to sever their unusually intimate association with nature, which again emerged strongly from fine naturalistic paintings of the twenty-seventh century BC, mirroring splendid real gardens of the same epoch.

Early Egyptian ceilings imitate the palm-logs that had been the earliest roofing material; tiles copy rush-matting or interlaced reeds and twigs. The fluting and ribbing of columns, which was later perpetuated in Greece, is another feature found very early in Egyptian stone buildings, where it reproduces the sharp edges of palm or papyrus stalks. Greek styles are again foreshadowed when columns taper upwards like sheathed stems or tree-trunks, and a contrary downward tapering, as though the tree-trunk is inverted, anticipates Crete. Moreover in the long past days when the columns had just been plants lashed together, these bunches, just above the point where they were tied, had broadened out into mop-like clusters of heads which may have been the prototypes of Egyptian and Greek capitals. The purpose of these, in stone architecture, was to broaden the columns beneath their lintel, which thus became reduced in span and strengthened, in accordance with carefully worked out proportions.

Capitals were distinctively painted, and their shapes retained echoes of plant origins. Often these designs recall the closed papyrus flower, or its bell-shaped open form. But just as the papyrus symbolised lower Egypt, so architects also made great use of the upper Egyptian emblem, the blue lotus. Its half-opened petals, which had already been depicted by Mesopotamian designers, appeared as often as the papyrus upon the capitals of Egyptian buildings. The lotus was used for other purposes also, since loaves were made from the centres of its blossoms, and their colour and scent were great favourites in bowls and wreaths. Lotus and papyrus alike were symbols of the fertility given the country by the overflowing Nile. So, in equal measure, was the date-palm, and this too is imitated by columns and capitals.

The first Mediterranean empire

In *c.* 2200 the unified Egyptian state fell apart. The disintegration was probably initiated by great hereditary landlords, and stimulated by Asian immigrants and wanderers – small traders, caravan men and displaced persons who had established virtually independent enclaves within the country, in which their stratified deposits, of Judaean origin, have now begun to be found. A literature of bewilderment and despair has come down from this time. 'Men do not sail to Byblos today: what shall we do for fine wood?'

Yet the pattern of unification repeated itself, since for two centuries the country became one again; and just as had happened twelve hundred years earlier, the unifiers were conquerors from the south. Thebes in upper Egypt, famed for its religion and ceremonial, became the richest and most powerful city in the ancient world. But then a new capital was established at El Lisht near the traditional centre of Memphis, and as befitted its position at the junction of the two main regions the royal city was called the Captor of the Two Lands. In this Second Golden Age the irrigation of the adjoining Fayum was enormously improved, and the eastern frontier, where Sinai's mines yielded abundant copper, was protected by a wall and linked to the homeland by a waterway, part natural and part artificial, extending from the Nile to the Red Sea.

Ships attained a length of one hundred and eighty feet, and there was an active, forward policy in all surrounding lands, involving widespread contacts with Syria and Crete. These journeyings were the cause of a romantic travel literature of great fantasy and charm, which was one of the principal ancestors of the later Greek novel.

But then followed a period of a century, or nearly two, when Egypt fell under Asian domination (? *c.* 1730–1570). The new rulers, whose skulls show large heads and strongly marked cheekbones, may have been descended from the Asian settlers in the delta; their nomenclature and probably their language were Semitic. These people now established control over all Egypt, as well as large areas of the Levant, from which further groups were attracted within the Egyptian borders. An element in these incursions was the group of Israelite tribes who came south by land under the leadership of Abraham's grandson Jacob (Israel), and settled in the eastern ranges of the delta, where they stayed for several centuries until Moses led them back to the Promised Land (p. 112).

The name by which these alien monarchs were known, Hyksos, means 'rulers of the desert uplands' or 'of the upland dwellers'. Semi-nomadic herdsmen in origin, they had developed into the type of feudal warriors who were now ruling in various parts of the near and middle east. Yet the Hyksos, in spite of Egyptian propaganda to the contrary, greatly increased the country's trade, improved spinning and weaving, introduced musical instruments, and encouraged the cultivation of olives and pomegranates.

But what changed most of all was the method of making war. New kinds of bronze swords and daggers were introduced, and a powerful composite bow. Above all the horse (p. 37), which had already made its way to the Nubian border by *c.* 1900 BC – the date of a skeleton that has been found there – was now effectively domesticated in Egypt itself, where there was plentiful fodder. Horses were utilised for cavalry and light war-chariots; and in the narrow south-eastern part of the delta the Hyksos guarded against foreign invasions by establishing a heavily fortified garrison town, at first with a large, foreign-looking, sloping embankment of pounded earth, and then with huge limestone walls of more Egyptian type. This fortress has been tentatively identified with their capital, which was called Avaris; or that may have been at a site nearer the delta's north-eastern extremity, close to the sea (p. 58).

Then came a reassertion of native power; and for a third time the movement originated from the south. The boastful forecast of a sixteenth century prince of Thebes, 'I will grapple with them, and cut open their belly', proved to be justified, since by intelligent borrowing of the military tactics of the Hyksos he successfully led a national revival against them and reestablished Egyptian control throughout the country. His major victories were won on the Nile, but during the vigorous drive towards expansion that now followed, would-be conquerors began to show themselves riding in the war-chariots that the Hyksos had taught them how to use. The main instruments, however, in these aggressive wars were the dreaded Egyptian archers, who likewise used the Hyksos bow.

Commerce soared, with emphasis on exports of the grain which Egypt now produced far beyond its own needs. During the fifteenth century BC the country was at the centre of the civilised world and at the height of its political and maritime power. Egyptian ships of this period show graceful curves of a racing yacht, or broad sails of unprecedented sizes, or high vertical prows or sterns with wicker sides to protect the oarsmen. Outstandingly active on sea as on land was Thothmes III, whose prolonged attempts to establish control over Syria were backed by the creation of a naval arsenal at Pernefer in the eastern delta.

Then followed the strange interlude of religious heresy under Amenhotep IV (Akhnaten) (*c.* 1370–1352 BC), who broke with the priests of the sun and yet laid exclusive emphasis on its ancient but now revolutionised worship. His strong feeling for nature accentuated the ever-present desire of Egyptian artists to represent natural scenes. Such tendencies, though generally subordinated to courtly and priestly conventions, had already on many earlier occasions produced detailed paintings of animals, fish, crabs, ducks, shrubs, poppies and lotuses. This secondary, lyrical, intimate style had recently become increasingly fashionable among a ruling class whose keen interest in luxurious pleasure gardens and landscaping, with extensive importations of rare flowers and trees from Asia, pervaded the poetic symbolism of the time.

> Come through the garden, Love, to me.
>   My love is like each flower that blows;
> Tall and straight as a young palm-tree,
>   And in each cheek a sweet blush-rose.[10]

Paintings of *c.* 1400 BC show the self-appointed limitations of this naturalistic art, which united almost photographic accuracy with a map-maker's absence of perspective – combining what the artist could see of nature at a given moment with what he knew belonged to the scene. Even before the religious revolution of Akhnaten (as excavations at Thebes have now indicated) these tendencies had reached a strange climax. As the depiction of human beings attained sophisticated emphasis which approaches caricature, the garden style reached out to a new delicacy and freedom, in which the characteristic formality of orderly rows was superseded by a natural arrangement of scattered groves. Amid sinuous frameworks and diagonal paths, animals are seen rapidly moving, or the kingfisher at the moment of its dive. In these landscapes and seascapes, which were to find many adapters in nearer Asia and Crete, flowers and plants are painted not as mere accessories but for their intrinsic beauty.

During Akhnaten's shortlived religious and political revolution, his residence was transferred from Thebes, which seemed too closely associated with priestly conservatism, to another town in upper Egypt, Tell el-Amarna, renamed Akhetaten after his god and himself. The king vowed he would never leave the place, and this meant that his influence in the Levant rapidly declined.

After him, however, the throne was occupied by a new series of warlike figures, notably Rameses II, who fought an indecisive battle with the Hittites at Kadesh on the Orontes (*c.* 1286) and later in his long reign achieved the more unusual feat of agreeing to a general treaty with them (p. 79). As befitted a state determined to be the major Mediterranean power, its centre of gravity had now moved from upper to lower Egypt, and the royal abodes, though movable, were generally near the sea. One such residence was at Tanis in the north-east corner of the delta, not far from the farthest frontier fortress and perhaps identical with the Hyksos capital Avaris. Tanis 'the front of every foreign country, the end of Egypt, where the warships come to anchorage when the tribute is brought', also grew to be an important military and commercial station for the Levant.

But a time came when these bastions were hard pressed, for the whole world entered upon a phase of flux and movement comparable to the convulsions at the end of the previous millennium. The delta was already dangerously full of foreign settlers and squatters, and now successive waves of violence washed against its borders from every side. At Piari, on its Libyan flank, King Merenptah fought a large-scale battle against invaders who were northerners from all lands 'fighting to fill their bellies daily' (*c.* 1221). Egyptian victory, in which the booty included nine thousand swords, brought relief.

> The fortresses are abandoned, the wells are reopened; the messengers loiter under the battlements, cool from the sun; the soldiers lie asleep, even the border-scouts go in the fields as they wish. The herds of the field need no herdsmen when crossing the fullness of the stream. The towns are settled again, and the husbandman eats of the harvest that he himself saved.[11]

But the respite was only temporary, for less than thirty years later Rameses III had to stave off a huge confederacy of peoples coming from across the sea (p. 79).

The countries which came from the Islands in the midst of the Sea* advanced on Egypt, relying on their strength. The net was made ready for them to ensnare them. Entering stealthily into the harbour-mouth, they fell into the net. Caught in their places, they were slain and their bodies stripped.

The king followed up his success by the ancient, sterile practice of invading the Levant. But the administrative machine of an almost exhausted Egypt now proved too cumbersome for large responsibilities, and as the second millennium BC approached its end, the splendour of traditional, brilliantly painted tombs at Thebes could not conceal the insignificance of the sons and grandsons of Rameses III, and the country's incapacity for further major efforts.

* Or 'from the shorelands'

3

The Easternmost Mediterranean

Lebanon, Syria and Israel

The city where the Egyptians first made maritime contact with Lebanon and Syria was the ancient port and religious centre of Byblos, with its rectangular houses and cobbled streets. This place and the adjacent strip of coast were colonised by peoples speaking a north Semitic dialect. They had arrived by 2500 BC, and perhaps a good deal earlier, since Lebanese and Syrian mountains and rivers mostly have names of early Semitic origin. Peoples speaking another variety of this language had long been prominent in Mesopotamia, but tradition held that these new arrivals in the Levant had come not from there but from more primitive territories in western Arabia. Copper statuettes show that they belonged to a herdsman type, familiar over large areas of the near east; short stocky people with neat beards and swept-back plaited hair, clothed in short kilts and broad belts fastened with tasselled cords. They called their new homeland Canaan, a name which later came to be used for territories extending widely towards Asia Minor in one direction and Egypt in the other.

Byblos stood at the northernmost point of Egypt's normal sphere of influence and virtually held a monopoly of its trade with the entire region. Indeed, during the third millennium the place had its own Egyptian temple, of which the considerable size – for it was more than eighty and later more than ninety feet in length – suggests the presence of a substantial commercial colony from Egypt. Byblos acted as a distribution point of Egyptian papyrus, for which, indeed, the name of the city (Bible) became the standard designation. The local people also re-exported copper and other metals brought to them by caravan from the mountains; and the forms of necklaces and pins of *c.* 2000–1800 BC found at Byblos, as well as Ugarit (Ras Shamra) farther up the coast, resemble those of peoples in central Europe, whose metallurgical products or techniques presumably travelled via the head of the Adriatic. The Syrian coasts north of Byblos and Ugarit were Mesopotamia's special preserve, but there was also traffic from Byblos to that country, either overland all the way or by sea to Mersin and then onwards by a road joining the main traffic highway from Asia Minor to the east.

What all other countries particularly wanted from Byblos was the timber from the Lebanon mountains in its immediate hinterland. Erosion has now stripped the hills, like others all over the Mediterranean, turning them into the *maquis* and *garrigue* scrub-land which is fragrant and rich in herbs but unprofitable for large scale cultivation (p. 5). Today a few isolated pines or oaks in a Moslem cemetery may be the sole survivors of a forest. Air-photography has revealed the abandoned cultivation terraces of the Lebanon, and already in ancient times heavy rains made the river Adonis, just behind Byblos, run red into the sea with dislodged soil (which was believed to be the blood of the dying fertility-god killed by wild boars). Yet the famous trees of Lebanon, including many from near Byblos itself, were transported in huge quantities to Egypt and utilised for a great number of purposes (p. 49).

Ship-building, for example, had already been preeminent since almost the earliest days of the united Egyptian kingdom. The people of these Lebanese and Syrian coasts were experts at every kind of woodwork, and it was they who, after graduating in lagoon fishing, constructed and also to a large extent manned the first Egyptian sea-going ships, thus becoming the first professional Mediterranean ship-builders and sailors. Unlike the Egyptians they had no great river to serve as a navigation school. No doubt they learnt from the experiences of the Nile, but for them it was the Mediterranean, sink or swim.

This was a perilous sea, because its dangers are larger than they look, and loom up with terrifying speed. Yet the Mediterranean is also the arch-temptress, since it is so free from tides and treacherous swirls and shoals. Coastal currents may distribute sand or silt, yet 'as long as you keep well offshore you can be certain of having hundreds of feet of water under your keel'.[1] Usually it is safe enough to keep going until rocks are seen ahead.

As in that other sailors' training ground, the Malay archipelago, a landmark was always available, and in this sea the position of land beyond a horizon is often indicated by small banks of cloud or migrating birds. Although it was a brave step to strike out into the Mediterranean, in its lucid air visibility extends for more than fifty miles, while mainland chains or island peaks show up for more than a hundred. Cyprus can be seen both from the Cilician and Syrian coasts, and Byblos was near enough to bring the island's mines and forests into Egyptian service. Coastal currents took a ship from Egypt to Byblos in four days, though winds or breezes from the north and northwest might double the length of the return journey. For these square-rigged ships, with their heavy mainsails and seams likely to split in a high side wind, preferred to hug the coast, only occasionally venturing upon short-cuts to a convenient harbour.

Except on arid stretches of coast, the limpid waters of rocky limestone coves were inviting to a mariner – though the Syrian shore is not too generous with such indentations. The earliest ports were just shelving strands where a vessel could be run aground and moored, at the foot of a cliff or in a little bay with a protected beach. Particularly favoured were natural harbours between two rocky terminals or half-encircling promontories, or on either side of an isthmus, leading to a peninsula or an islet joined to the mainland by a mole. 'Seamen,' said Joseph Conrad, 'look upon the Mediterranean as a man may look at a vast nursery in an old, old mansion, where innumerable generations of his own people have learned to walk. It has led mankind gently from headland to headland, from bay to bay, from island to island, out into the promise of world-wide oceans.' And the earliest initiatives seem to have been taken by these mariners from Byblos, who created and sailed the sea-going vessels that were to be depicted before long on the monuments of Egypt.

This shoreland of the northern and central Levant, home of some of the earliest known traces of civilisation, was destined by nature for prosperity. There was, it is true, a danger of unpredictable droughts, but the maritime strip, in the words of an

Arab poet, 'carried winter on its head, spring on its shoulders, whilst summer slumbers at its feet'.

Beneath me in the valley waves the palm,
Beneath, beyond the valley, breaks the sea;
Beneath me sleep in mist and light and calm
Cities of Lebanon, dream-shadow-dim . . .
And all around the snowy mountains swim
Like mighty swans afloat in heaven's pool.[2]

These mountains of Lebanon, extending from Carmel half way to the Orontes mouth, watered the narrow coastal belt with the moisture that was stored in their snowcaps and sucked down by woodlands from the west winds coming off the sea. In spite of the southerly latitude, there are rainfalls in late autumn and early spring.

Behind the Lebanon mountains lay the Bekaa plain, and behind that again, beyond Anti-Lebanon, was the plain of Damascus. These lowlands, together with the coastal strip, possessed the fertile soil which provided the 6,428 jars of wine captured by Thothmes III in Syria; and 'behold, the army of his Majesty were drunk'.[3] Indeed, earlier still, this may have been the very area from which, by the way of Israel, the Egyptians had learnt to make wine for themselves (p. 50).* Turned over with plough or hoe after the autumn rains and pruned in January or February, vineyards yielded a bewildering variety. 'It had more wine than water,' said an Egyptian about a place in western Syria. 'Its trees bore every fruit. Barley was there and wheat. There was no limit to the kind of cattle. Plentiful was its honey, abundant its olives.'

Olive-trees had grown wild in a number of lands since remotest antiquity. Though poor in soil, they were the ancestors of the cultivated tree, which does not breed true but needs to be grafted on to the wild variety. This cultivated olive played only a minor role in Egypt, but the rich yield of oil from its dark-green fruit (often allowed to remain on the tree until it becomes black) was first exploited systematically in Syria or Asia Minor;† and it was a leaf of the olive which Noah's dove took back to the Ark.[4] John Ruskin wrote of

* Unless their source was Cilicia (p. 25).
† For an olive-stone of the third millennium in Crete, see p. 88.

the hoary dimness of its delicate foliage, subdued and faint of hue, as if the ashes of the Gethsemane agony had been cast upon it for ever . . . The gnarled writhing of its intricate branches, and the pointed fretwork of its light and narrow leaves inlaid on the blue field of the sky, and the small rosy-white stars of its spring blossoming, and the beads of sable fruit scattered by autumn along its topmost boughs – the right, in Israel, of the stranger, the fatherless, and the widow – and, more than all, the softness of the mantle, silver grey, and tender like the down on a bird's breast, with which, far away, it veils the undulation of the mountains.[5]

Alone or in conjunction these trees have sometimes been regarded by botanists and geographers as the prime criterion of the Mediterranean zone. Their climatic demands are imperious and precise, for in the tropics they fail to bear fruit owing to insufficient winter chilling, but where there is severe cold and fog they are likewise not to be found. Dry summers are needed to ripen their fruit and develop its oil-content. But although an olive will use as much non-stagnant water as other trees, it can tolerate the barest and rockiest of slopes. For these trees possess a phenomenal endurance such as few others have achieved under Mediterranean conditions. The adaptations displayed by evergreens to withstand the summer droughts of this peculiar climate appear very strongly in the olive, which shares with the vines an unusual ability to reduce its transpiration or loss of moisture. Even during the most arid summers the olive-tree's roots, reaching down ten or twelve feet, tap reserves from winter rains in the subsoil and attract moisture from a wide surrounding area. These trees live to an age of hundreds of years, continuing to bear fruit even when the trunk is quite hollow or split into two. Once planted out they do not need a very great deal of attention, apart from pruning in spring. This concentrates the sap in the fruits, which are picked between October and December after all other harvests have been gathered.

On the other hand, olives are slow to start a productive life, which does not begin for seven years or reach maturity for twenty or thirty. Their growers, therefore, if the investment is not to be wasted, need orderly social conditions, since the destruction of an olive-tree, though hard to achieve since the wood is so tough, may take half a lifetime to repair. Its cultivators need to possess enough capital to be able to wait, though not too much for the means of the average independent, skilful small farmer to whom this crop is best adapted. However he and his helpers and family have to be numerous enough to carve out the hill-slopes into terraces, and construct presses for oil.

When the trees of Israel wanted a king, this was their first choice: 'They said unto the olive tree, reign thou over us.'[6] The Bible tells how its oil was used for lamps, hair and skin treatment, prayer and ritual anointings, and how the wood was employed for fuel and the construction of furniture. The tree stood for beauty, luxuriance, peace and tenacious vigour, and its greenness meant religious purity as well. 'I am like a green olive-tree in the house of God.'[7] But above all its fruit, the principal edible fat over the entire Mediterranean area, is one of the most nourishing foods man has ever discovered, and often more practical than butter, a more recent discovery which keeps less well in the heat. 'The whole Mediterranean seems to rise in the sour, pungent taste of these black olives between the teeth. A taste older than meat, older than wine. A taste as old as cold water.'[8]

Yet Syria and Lebanon and Israel, so greatly blessed by nature, are also visited with a special curse.

On the map, this area known comprehensively to the ancients as Syria, and to some nationalists as Greater Syria, looks clearly definable by the Mediterranean to the west, Turkey and its mountains to the north, Egypt to the south-west, and desert lands to the east. But this apparent definition of the region's boundaries is only an illusion. Greater Syria just does not exist. Far from being clearly defined, the territory did not need three modern Israeli-Arab wars to show its grievous lack of the geographical unity which enabled other Mediterranean countries such as Italy, Greece, Egypt or Spain to grow at different times into defensible national states. For this whole large territory contains a series of limestone ridges which instead of forming its boundaries run straight through the middle of the country in lines parallel to the coast. At the northern extremity there are Mounts Amanus and Casius, followed by Bargylus (Jebel Ansariyah) and then the most imposing of the coastal massifs, the Lebanon range. South of Lebanon are the Galilee hills, and next comes Mount Carmel, the beginning of the plateaux of Samaria and Judaea which stretch right down as far as Sinai.

Behind these various ranges are further parallel rows of eminences, Anti-Lebanon and the high ground of Transjordan. But none of these ranges provide any definable, defensible borders or calls to unity.

On the contrary, the lowlands beside and between these folds are long funnels open at each end to every sort of influence and invasion from external peoples covetous of this wealth and fertility. The two principal, parallel tubular areas inviting such encroachments are the coastal region and then, beyond the first ranges, a continuous depression running through the valleys of the Orontes, Litani (Leontes)* and Jordan and on through the Dead Sea, deepest of all subsidences in the earth's crust, to the Gulf of Eilat or Akaba. Nor is it only through the extremities of these funnels that the coastland is vulnerable, since the mountains are also broken by passes that have eternally served to introduce acquisitive armies. At regular intervals, the lofty backcloth to the sea is punctured by these ominous, historic reminders of vulnerability to the orient and Sinai; and behind the openings stretch back the classic routes into the sources of the migrations and aggressions which it was the destiny of the Levant to receive and absorb.

Owing to this centrifugal character and the absence of unifying factors, the country remained a conglomeration of small units. So, later, did Greece, and yet it achieved originality and greatness. But Greece, except for occasional dramatic events, was left alone for centuries to work out its destiny. The small states in Syria, Lebanon and Israel on the other hand were never left alone by the giants of Asia and Egypt, and so these territories, for all their resources, remained an explosive point of cleavage, an amorphous political and cultural quicksand which has still not solidified today.

'The Mediterranean is a pit surrounded by tiers of seats over which the nations are leaning, all crowded together. The same piece has been played for thousands of years.'[9] In Syria and Lebanon and Israel the scenery of this theatre was built of elements that were peculiarly inflammable. But the succession of wars and convulsions had a strange and influential sequel. For the fighting, fluctuating mixtures of peoples who came on to this small stage brought with them a host of varied institutions,

* Their sources are in close proximity beside the Bekaa plain (p. 63).

arts and objects which subsequently passed onwards and westwards from Syrian ports and transmitted civilisation to Crete and Troy and Greece and the whole of the Mediterranean world.

Between Egypt and Mesopotamia

Syria was too vulnerable to remain immune from the upheavals which devastated Mesopotamia and the rest of the middle east towards the end of the third millennium BC (p. 37). In *c.* 2100 the Egyptian temple at Byblos was burnt down, and the city's life and culture changed abruptly. Perhaps this event was part of the convulsions which, long after the first influx of people speaking north Semitic dialects (p. 60), again inundated Syria with a second wave of related invaders. These immigrants, the Amorites, were induced by the advanced prosperity of their new homeland to adopt some of its culture and to form highly developed though small and inevitably precarious city-states.

One of the princedoms was at Aleppo, to which a position seventy miles east of the Mediterranean, in the narrow belt between the Orontes mouth and the westward-curving Euphrates, gave command over a vital caravan-thoroughfare from Mesopotamia to the sea. North of Aleppo a second Amorite centre, which was to play an even greater part in ancient history, stood at the point where Turkey and Syria meet today. This was Carchemish, situated on an acropolis rising just above the Euphrates, at its great bend where there is one of the scarce fords of the river. A more southerly Amorite state, upon the edge of a belt of pasture-land, was Qatna (Mishrife), linked to the coast by a pass between Lebanon and Ansariyah, and linked also to the hinterland of the middle Euphrates by a major route.

At that point where the road reached the river stood Mari (Tell Hariri), in which a further Amorite dynasty ruled over Mesopotamian inhabitants. Already important for not far short of two thousand years, Mari passed on to Babylon, two hundred and fifty miles downstream, the timber, resin and stone of Lebanon and Amanus, and the wine and olive-oil of Syria. Mari not only controlled much of northern Mesopotamia, but possessed close and perhaps dominant relations with Qatna and coastal cities such as Ugarit; and the rulers of Mari even made contact with Cyprus and Crete. The twenty thousand surviving documents of their archives, written in Old Babylonian cuneiform characters (p. 34) dating from the eighteenth century BC, reveal in startling detail how complex the international position in this part of the world has already become. They mention more than thirty separate states, associated or divided – in modern style – by the interactions of warfare, commerce, cultural exchanges and diplomatic intrigue.

An early tablet at Mari refers to the *bit hilani*, the two-storeyed Syrian gate-house with pillars, approached by a flight of steps and leading into a wide but shallow hall. This characteristic local feature was no doubt incorporated into the royal residence, which contained more than two hundred and sixty rooms and corridors, spread over six acres round an extensive courtyard. Many of the buildings possessed very thick mud-brick walls mortared by clay and local bitumen. They were probably lit not by windows but by light-wells which also served as ventilation shafts. These foreshadow buildings erected during the following centuries in Mediterranean lands; and so do the store-rooms and plumbing arrangements of this palace, which seem to have been imitated at Cnossos. Another model of the Cretans was Mari's painting, which fuses the rigid, hieratic formalism of Mesopotamia with the freer, more fluid, naturalistic tendency of certain Egyptian art (p. 95).

Amorite rulers were also found beyond the Euphrates as far as the eastern bounds of Mesopotamia. For such was the origin of Shamsi-Adad I (*c.* 1814–1742), who created a powerful Assyrian state in the undulating, well-watered pasture-lands of the upper Tigris. Shamsi-Adad set up his own son at Mari and established close relations with Aleppo and Carchemish, from which he obtained his wine.

But meanwhile the Assyrians, masters of a formidable blend of first-class archery, administrative ability and cold-blooded negotiating skill, had also penetrated far into the middle lands of Asia Minor. Already before Shamsi-Adad, they had begun their first great outward push by establishing colonies of traders in the interior of that peninsula, especially at Kanesh (Kültepe) a hundred and ten miles northwards from the Cilician plains;* and a second centre was at Alişarhüyük, eighty miles farther inland again. Although not far from Alacahüyük with its rich, gold-filled tombs of a few centuries earlier (p. 81), these places were in backward upland country. But they were linked with home by donkey-caravans, which were particularly active at this time and conveyed cargoes back to Carchemish and from there to Assyria. Excavations at Kanesh have revealed a central hall with four pillars and a nine-foot central hearth not unlike the halls borrowed from Asia Minor by Greece (p. 28). Many cylinder-shaped seals have also been found, and compelling divine statues, and excellent pots; and commercial relations were facilitated by letters, cheques and notes of credit in Assyrian cuneiform writing.

The goods carried home by the caravans included a wide variety of metals quarried in the highlands of eastern Asia Minor, and particularly copper. Mixed with tin, this turned into bronze, which made Assyria's royal splendours possible. The Mesopotamians had known in *c.* 2500 BC that from ten to twelve per cent of tin mixed with copper would make bronze, but five hundred years passed before the use of the alloy first began to be general. Until Cyprus took the lead in *c.* 1100 BC, the principal copper mines of the second millennium were in Asia Minor, within easy reach of the Assyrian colonies. Where the tin used during the same period came from is a mystery. But importation from its later west and central European mines was probably sparse or non-existent at first, and sources in Asia Minor, at present unidentified, are again the most likely solution.

In any case, the acquisition of copper and tin required a large extension of commercial organisation. Moreover this bronze, once made and converted into tools and weapons, played a large part in developing both civilisation and politico-military power. The alloy was much more useful than copper, because it is harder and more durable, melts at a lower temperature, flaws less in the process of casting, and is protected by its tin component from discolouring oxidisations and corrosions which can poison food. Bronze nails served better than wood because

* Between 2000 and 1900 BC, in a period of changes, a new suburb was established at the foot of the Kanesh mound.

they were sharper and did not shrink, and tools of the same metal enabled builders to cut their masonry and timber more finely and easily. The same considerations applied to bronze weapons, which gained such marked superiority over all predecessors that they revolutionised warfare.

Asia Minor, thus penetrated by the Assyrians, was for the present out of Egypt's range. But when Shamsi-Adad formed an intimate connection with Syrian centres as far south as Qatna, and added further provocation by setting up a monument on the Lebanon coast, the two major powers were in conflict. For the monument was in an area which often lay under the suzerainty of the Egyptians, whose principal outpost was Byblos nearby. Byblos had recovered from its destruction three centuries earlier (p. 67). Its manufacturers showed the easy promiscuity of styles which came readily to these regions, including, for example, scabbards which had an Amorite look and crescent-shaped sword blades of an Egyptian appearance. During these early centuries of the second millennium, the Egyptians were using Byblos as a centre of expansion. Their exports reached Qatna and Ugarit, and they exercised some sort of control over most of the Lebanon coast and the Bekaa plain in its hinterland.

The threat to Egyptian supremacy from Assyria did not after all materialise, since soon afterwards that power was eclipsed and superseded by Babylonia, which was too remote to be active so far west. Even, so, however, Egypt did not remain unchallenged, for a new peril now came from the mountainous lands bordering on Mesopotamia. Here people known as Hurrians extended their influence and power over a huge area. Already before the end of the third millennium these broad-headed mountaineers had occupied a great half-circle of high country, extending from above Carchemish round northwards to Lake Van and down again to the headwaters of the upper Tigris tributaries. The language of the Hurrians may conceivably go back to certain tongues spoken in the Caucasus, and they perhaps played a part in introducing Mesopotamia to the domestication of the horse which came from the south Russian steppe (p. 37). At all events, the fringes of riding country between the mountains and deserts gave them an opportunity to develop the use of mounted warriors and chariots. This evolution took place under the influence of Indo-European-speaking peoples, who were now on the move over a vast area (p. 82). They also gave the Hurrians much of their religion. By *c.* 2000 Mesopotamian documents were showing names in the language of the Hurrians, and two centuries later they were in power as far as Mari, where four-fifths of the identifiable princes bear their names. So do leading people west of the Euphrates at Aleppo and Qatna and right down to the coastal area, to which the Hurrians transmitted Mesopotamian institutions. For although these people possessed little art of their own – except a fine type of pottery – they remained absorptive intermediaries of other cultures and brought them into the areas they infiltrated.

By the sixteenth century these Hurrians had established an extremely powerful kingdom in north-western Mesopotamia. This state of Mitanni probably had its capital on the river Khabur, which runs into the Euphrates, but its direct or indirect rule extended as far westwards as the Cilician and Syrian seaboard. There were also, perhaps, outposts on more southerly stretches of coast, since sixteenth-century burials at Gaza, in which men were interred with their horses, seem to show Mitannian influence; and marriage relations were established with Egypt.

Mitanni's principal regional capital near the Syrian shore was Alalakh (Tell Atchana) beside the Orontes in the Amik plain. In this terminal region of trade-routes to the Mediterranean, Alalakh, situated where the road from Aleppo crosses the river, had already been the site of fifteen cities, and its temple had been rebuilt to different gods as many times. The names of the population were mostly Semitic, but in the mid-second millennium their governing class was Hurrian.* A strongly fortified palace, made partly of the wood which was to be found abundantly on neighbouring mountainsides, contained narrow-footed vases of unprecedented grace. The walls were decorated with paintings which are similar to those of Crete, and seem (by an eastward – instead of the usual westward – movement) to have been influenced by them rather than the contrary (p. 95).

Between the Hurrian and Egyptian spheres of influence there

* The place had taken its name from the Hurrian deity Alalu.

was still an uneasy border area of small Syrian city-states which sought to play off the one great power against the other. But in the sixteenth century Egypt engulfed many of the coastal neighbours of Byblos, Phoenician cities which are now heard of for the first time. An even more formidable reckoning for the minor Levantine princelings came a century later from the armies of Thothmes III. Just over a hundred miles south of the Amik plain stood Kadesh on the bank of Lake Homs. Protected by the river, a wall and two moats, this fortress controlled the passage between the Lebanon and Anti-Lebanon mountains where it widens into the broad plains of north Syria. The ruler of the place now instigated a confederacy to resist the Egyptians, and he was joined by a more southerly city, Megiddo. That town, with its art blending Canaanite and Aegean motifs, stands upon a ridge halfway down to the Jezreel (Esdraelon) plain which separates the hills of Galilee to the north from those of Samaria and Judaea to the south. Commanding this gap as well as a hillroad across towards the coast, Megiddo was of such strategic importance that its name has earned a grim reputation as Armageddon. But the Egyptians, operating by land and sea from their fortified base at Gaza, crushed the confederate armies beneath the walls of Megiddo itself. As the king of Egypt complained, they failed to take this city whose 'capture is equal to the capture of a thousand cities', because they were so eager to pick up the plunder of the battlefield. However, Megiddo fell three weeks later, and the insatiably aggressive Thothmes III seems ultimately to have conquered almost the whole of western Syria, placing its towns under vassel nominees. At the price of local freedom, the whole region now possessed an unprecedented unity of rule and communications which it was not to experience again until Roman times.

Between Egypt and Asia Minor

In the fourteenth century BC all was changed when the Hurrian power, much weakened by the Egyptian expansion, succumbed to the Hittites on the other flank. Originating somewhere between the Carpathians and the Caucasus, these people had arrived in Asia Minor shortly before 2000 BC, during that huge wave of assaults from the north which extended from

India to western Europe and affected the destinies of the entire near and middle east (p. 37). The capital of the kingdom that they formed in Asia Minor, Hattusas (Boğazköy), was far in the interior of the peninsula, occupying a defensible position beside deep gorges where the plateau begins to break down towards the Black Sea. Not only was Boğazköy on a tributary of the Red River (Kizilirmak, Halys) nearby, but the town, which looked over a wide valley full of vines and olives, commanded two ancient trade routes, one from the Aegean to the east, and the other leading from the Black Sea coast down to the Cilician Gates.

The physical types of the Hittites are not easily deducible from artistic representations, since these fail to correspond with finds of skulls; but there must have been a great deal of racial mixture. Their custom of cremating the dead shows a number of resemblances to rites attributed to the Greeks in the *Iliad* (p. 143). The Hittite language seems to have possessed an Indo-European structure supplemented by an indigenous vocabulary acquired after arrival in Asia Minor. Probably there were Hittites in nineteenth-century Assyrian trading-stations, one of which was close to Hattusas; and two hundred years later a monarch fused various small plateau kingdoms into a single state, governed by laws which formed the most impressive part of this culture. The lions and eagles and other animals depicted by the Hittites, which are among their few durable artistic successes, later found their way through north Syrian successor states into the repertoire of Greek art.

What the Hittites thus handed on they had picked up from many near and middle eastern sources. The twenty thousand clay tablets found at Hattusas represent seven tongues, five native or acclimatised and two foreign. The script used for recording these languages was Mesopotamian cuneiform, borrowed through Syrian intermediaries. But inscriptions display a monumental, Egyptian appearance, and an even more important element in the mixture came from the Hurrians who gave Hattusas its religion and a dynasty of kings.

The Hittites were active traders, obtaining textiles from Syria and Mesopotamia in exchange for silver, copper and iron. This last metal, produced on a commercial scale in the mountains of eastern Asia Minor, contributed largely to their strength. Iron was not exploited until long after copper. Since it is rarely found as a pure metal, the properties of the ore were less recognisable and not so easily discovered by accident, and production of effective edges required harder and more complicated processes. Finally however, by *c.* 1400, smelting techniques became capable of making iron that was stronger than bronze. Good iron is much the better of the two, since its ores are far more common (representing 4.7 per cent of the earth's crust) and can be forged at lower temperatures. Moreover a good blade, once achieved, is keener and more lasting. Later, cheap iron tools were destined to reduce the dependence of small producers on the state and its big men. But at this stage the metal put more power into the big men's hands, because of the new effectiveness and durability with which it endowed their weapons.

The Hittites also had other formidable instruments of war; and one of the most valuable of them was the horse. Originally tamed in south Russia and then introduced to Mesopotamia (perhaps under Hurrian influence) (p. 37), the animal is mentioned in the eighteenth-century correspondence of Assyrian merchants in Asia Minor. But it was the Hittites who created or developed the expensive equipment, elaborate maintenance, training arrangements, and specialised personnel needed to make chariotry into a major military force. Hittite chariots, like those of the contemporary Hyksos kings who ruled in Egypt and the Levant, attacked inelastic battle-lines with devastating effects that could only be counteracted by the erection of great fortifications of beaten earth.

The Hittites were aggressive expansionists. The original unifier of the kingdom, in the seventeenth century BC, had claimed to have 'extended the frontiers to the sea'. It is not clear which sea he referred to, but during the ensuing centuries Hittite outposts and dependencies came into existence at Sinope on the Black Sea coast, where there were hostile populations to be kept down, and on the western Aegean shores of the peninsula which now begin to play an identifiable part in Mediterranean history. Hittite rulers also coveted the productive and wealthy Cilician plainland. When, therefore, the Hurrians of Mitanni established a protectorate over that country, it seemed a grave provocation, and there began a long period of hostilities between the two warlike states, with Syria, as usual, their battleground. Already before 1600, a Hittite seems to have reduced Mitannian Aleppo to the vassalage which gave the town its present Hittite name. This advance cut Mitanni off from its Cilician dependency and paved the way for the latter, just over a hundred years later, to come to an understanding with the Hittites. These reached the height of their power under Suppiluliumas I (*c.* 1380–1340), who reduced the Hurrians to vassaldom and consequently brought the various small states of north Syria into Hittite hands. Aleppo, which had been temporarily lost again, was retaken by him, and Alalakh and Ugarit also fell. The Hittites pushed eastwards to Carchemish, which they made into a regional capital, and down into Syria as far as Kadesh. Suppiluliumas claimed to have extended his frontier to the Lebanon, and it was in vain that a prince of Byblos declared his city to be as Egyptian as Memphis. His desperate appeals to Akhnaten went unheard, since that monarch was unconcerned with external affairs (p. 58).

The Hittite emperor was soon in a position to offer a comprehensive and honourable settlement to Cilicia, which under the name of Kizzuwatna now flourished in its own right as a strong second-class power. The walls of ancient Mersin were twice rebuilt under Hittite influence. But its marshy belt was a disadvantage, and another important centre was constructed on the ancient site of Tarsus some sixteen miles away. This place, which had already boasted a flourishing town life in the third millennium, possessed fertile territory, an important flax industry, and a vital position on roads into Syria and the plateau of Asia Minor, though it was liable to frequent, shattering devastations by earthquake. An adjoining lagoon of the River Cydnus, lined with arsenals and dockyards, was connected in those days with the Mediterranean thirteen miles to the south, so that Tarsus carried on a flourishing maritime business.

Another important Cilician city was Adana, on the River Seyhan (Sarus) inland from Tarsus, not far from the northern confines of the plain. Adana had been in touch with Egypt at least from *c.* 2000 BC, and the recognition of its name in Egyptian inscriptions suggests that it was the capital of this vigorous state allied with the Hittites. The link was of special value to them because Cilicia, with its ancient technical and commercial skills, fulfilled an indispensable pioneer role in the manufacturing and bulk distribution of high-quality Hittite ironware.

An even more important commercial community was Ugarit on the Syrian coast, some thirty miles south of the Orontes mouth, not far from the modern Latakia. Perched on a sixty-foot high coastal bluff now overgrown with the fennel from which its modern name of Ras Shamra is derived, the town was well supplied with its own crops, harvesting barley in April and wheat in May or early June. But the exceptional strength of Ugarit lay in its position on many trade routes to Asia Minor, Egypt, the islands of the Aegean and Mesopotamia. This was the first great port in the history of the Mediterranean and of the world; and during its climax between 1400 and 1200 BC, its people monopolised many of the most lucrative foreign markets. The place maintained a delicate political balance, in successive vassalage to Egyptians and Hittites, neither of whom felt willing to proceed to direct conquest. A locally-owned navy comprised at least a hundred and fifty ships, and archives often mention purple-dyed garments – in anticipation of a later world-famous industry (p. 122) – and wines of different sorts which were in demand from the Nile to the Tigris.

Ugarit also exported its own metalwork, which did not yet include iron on any appreciable scale but comprised gold, silver, and slashing swords finely made of bronze. These metal products, as well as ivories taken from the tusks of elephants which still roamed in Syria, are typical of the art of the region because of their easy and wide-ranging absorption and assimilation of all near eastern influences, which were then gradually passed on from these harbours into the Aegean world. The local god of craftsmanship seems Cretan, and a mother-goddess (accompanied by goats) seems to be of similar origin. For, like other cities along this coast, Ugarit had the closest links with Crete and then Mycenae. A surviving royal contract exempts a trader from customs duties on cargoes brought from Crete, and Aegeans had trading colonies of their own at Ugarit, with separate living quarters and burial places in town and harbour (p. 108).

There were also commercial groups from Ashdod far down on

the coast of Israel, and from Cyprus and Egypt; a passport has been found authorising a man and his son to use routes to Egypt and Hittite territories. The manufactures and cultures of all these countries were on the move, and the centre most actively concerned in their diffusion was Ugarit. Its royal palace of seventy rooms, five courtyards, a park and ornamental lake, also included a furnace for baking the clay which was used as a writing material. The documents thus inscribed include the government's extensive, varied archives, and at least four cycles of epic poetry, telling of the exploits and rivalries of the gods with a diversity of subject-matter which reflects the blend of Sumerian, Semitic, Hurrian and Hittite elements in the local population and culture. This mixture exercised a powerful influence on future Mediterranean literature, since the Greek epics that bore the names of Homer and especially Hesiod, for all their different atmospheres, owe a great many debts to the Ugaritic myths, direct or through later intermediaries (p. 152).

The main language of Ugarit's literature is a western Semitic dialect related to Hebrew, written in a Canaanite variety of the cuneiform script of Mesopotamia. This ancient form of writing was still also widely used to record the east Semitic (Babylonian or Akkadian) tongue, which was retained at Ugarit for juridical texts and served as a diplomatic international language like French and English in modern times. Yet these scripts which reproduced syllables in the old-fashioned way were increasingly found to be inconvenient because they needed such a large number of signs. Consequently, the syllabic signs were gradually reduced. Between 2000 and 1600 BC Byblos was using 114 symbols, which are unintelligible to us but seem to represent a hybrid between syllabic script and alphabet. Soon the peoples of this area were busy with at least half a dozen of such experiments; and certain signs ceased to denote whole syllables, and referred instead to their first sounds only – no longer beth (horse), gimel (corner, or camel), daleth (door), but B, G, and D. Before 1500, the scribes at Ugarit, polyglot in living and dead languages alike, were assigning such consonantal phonetic values to thirty letters of this type.

But the cuneiform method of denoting them could never conquer the world, since such wedge-like imprints only suited the penetrable surfaces of clay and stone, and these were too clumsy to become the writing materials of advanced societies. A better solution was to simplify pictorial scripts such as the Egyptian hieroglyphs, and adapt these simplified signs to the new sort of phonetic, alphabetic notation, in which, indeed, the Egyptians had themselves tentatively begun to experiment (p. 44). Towards the middle of the second millennium BC, embryonic forms of these more manageable linear alphabets were being painted on pottery at a number of Levantine centres which had easy access to Egypt, notably in the rapidly developing country soon to be known as Israel; and another alphabet was in use among Semitic-speaking people who were working in Egypt's turquoise mines of Sinai. Next, after *c.* 1500, the writing changed from vertical to horizontal, thus becoming closer to the practice of future times. Different places continued to employ variant scripts, but the first example of a fully developed consonantal alphabet that can so far be identified with certainty appears on an inscription at Byblos which probably dates from the eleventh or tenth century BC.

Although syllabic scripts continued to exist, it was this alphabetical form of linear writing which the Greeks and Romans and other speakers of Indo-European tongues took over. The nature of those languages required the addition of vowels (p. 150). But meanwhile the consonantal alphabet, adapting an Egyptian system to the purposes of Semitic speech in a simplified form that many more people could learn, was the greatest gift brought to the Mediteranean peoples and the world by that complex Canaanite, Semitic-speaking mixture of races in the Levant who fulfilled so notable a role as middlemen in every field of human activity.

In relation to the great powers of the day – the Hittites and Egyptians – these people of Syria, Lebanon and the future Israel were middlemen in the most literal and uncomfortable sense. The huge empires could not be played off against each other for ever, for they were bound to clash face to face, with the Canaanites struggling for survival between them, just as their ancestors had been sandwiched between the strong powers of earlier days.

And so the historic confrontation took place, in about 1286 BC, when the armies of Rameses II of Egypt and Mutawallis the

Hittite fought one another at Kadesh (p. 58). Although the allegedly triumphant outcome was celebrated with all the already vigorous resources of Egyptian propaganda, the battle did not bring them victory. Possibly, indeed, it was a major success for the Hittites, who soon afterwards added a region near Damascus to the territories under their control. After a period of further fighting, however, an astonishing and almost unparalleled event took place, as hard to achieve then as now. The two states, Egyptian and Asian, signed a treaty fixing relative spheres of influence in south and north Syria respectively, and agreeing to refrain from further hostilities against one another. They also undertook to provide mutual assistance in the event of any attack from a third party.

Such an agreement would, if durable, have brought peace to the shores of the eastern Mediterranean, though it would also have permanently deprived the small city-states of Syria of the measure of liberty they had retained as commercial intermediaries. However, it is not long before we hear of the Egyptians fighting against the Hittite kingdom again, this time at sea and with Cypriots also ranged against them. Yet the long-drawn-out rivalry between Egypt and the Hittites was now destined to become a thing of the past, owing to furious onslaughts which descended upon both empires from many backward peoples who were on the move again over a vast area. The desperate emergencies which descended upon Egypt shortly before and after 1200 were successfully fought off, and the country was not, after all, engulfed (p. 58). But the Hittites crumbled and collapsed, and all centralised authority vanished for a time in Asia Minor. As a widespread pattern of destruction clearly shows, invading hordes engulfed Cilicia and the whole of the Levant. Mersin, Tarsus, Aleppo, Carchemish, Alalakh and Ugarit all fell, and so did recently emerged towns of Judaea.

Who were the people who caused these massive devastations? There was a gigantic series of migratory waves, extending all the way from the Danube valley to the plains of China. Their causes cannot be determined, nor can a suggestion that drastic climatic changes played a part be confirmed. Egyptian sources call the invaders peoples of the sea, and relate them to 'the countries which are in the isles' (or shoreland, p. 59). The same records also refer to specific peoples or tribes – but their names can be variously interpreted. Probably they included dispossessed Anatolians and Aegeans; and swords, brooches, cremation rites, and ships probably of European type, also appear. The rocky southern coasts of Asia Minor, which have always served as nurseries and havens for pirates, are likely to have been used as bases, and the invaders may well have been coastal peoples who had learnt their techniques of warfare while serving the great powers as sailors and mercenary infantry.

At all events the massive, prolonged penetrations of these huge groups from the north, by sea and land, changed the whole face of the Mediterranean world, weakening Egypt and obliterating its Hittite rival. The Hittites, it is true, left behind them in north Syria a group of minor principalities which maintained a measure of continuity (p. 116). But destruction overcame many of these other small states of the Levant which, while precariously maintaining themselves between the major powers, had gathered together a mass of diversified cultural elements they subsequently passed on to Greece, Rome and ourselves.

4

The Straits and the Aegean

Troy

Near one of the colonies founded by the Assyrians in north-central Asia (p. 69) was Alacahüyük, on a tributary of the Red River (Kizilirmak, Halys). There excavations have revealed tombs of *c.* 2400–2200 – dates half a millennium before the Hittite unification (p. 74) – containing lavish treasures of gold jugs, goblets and ornaments, figures of animals in silver and bronze including stags suggestive of the steppes, and copper horns which strangely anticipate later products of Etruria and Rome.

Alacahüyük is not far from the plateau's gradual northerly descent towards the Black Sea. Across those waters, in what is now Soviet territory, were comparable and contemporary princely tombs. This Transcaucasian area, rich with the black earth which the River Kuban irrigates three times a year, has always attracted immigrant peoples. Beside the Sea of Azov and upon inland Caucasus slopes, as in many other parts of south Russia, there had been a long story of earlier cultures. Now, in the later third millennium BC, lavish burials were made at hill sites on several tributaries of the Kuban and along the coast south of its rush-grown delta.

The great royal cemetery of Maikop is some fifty miles inland on the River Byelaya. Under a mound circled by vertical limestone slabs was a rectangular wooden chamber containing precious objects which show conceptions of burial similar in many ways to contemporary Alacahüyük, three hundred and fifty miles away across an inhospitable sea and land. Axes found at Maikop, on the other hand, are of Mesopotamian style. Silver vases display lions, tigers, panthers and landscape scenes reminiscent of various regions in western Asia, from which either the vessels themselves or their makers must have been imported. Ornamental pins found in these burials are of types found in several parts of Asia Minor, and semi-precious stones come from the same peninsula, as well as from more distant parts of Asia, including Iran where similar funeral treasures have been discovered.

Archaeological and linguistic evidence combines to suggest that these widespread royal cemeteries are a product of the Indo-European-speaking peoples who were moving southwards in a mighty series of sweeps (p. 71).

Burials of comparable splendour, though reflecting different customs, also occurred at Troy, beyond the opposite extremity of the Black Sea. Between its stormy waters and the Trojans was the Sea of Marmara, dividing Europe and Asia at a crucial point of intercommunication. At each end this little stretch of water, a hundred and seventy miles long and less than fifty miles wide, narrows into slender funnels on which the history of the eastern Mediterranean has largely depended – the Bosphorus leading into the Black Sea, and the Dardanelles (Hellespont), on which Troy was located, into the Aegean. At first mariners found it hard to get into the Black Sea through the hazardous waters of the Bosphorus (p. 178), so that the Dardanelles assumed greater importance. Yet this too is forbidding to navigators, since its channel, forty miles long and averaging about a mile in width, is tortuous and full of rocks, and seethes with currents from the Black Sea. They run at a speed of four or five miles an hour, and are reinforced for nine months of the year by a strong north-easterly blast.

Buffeted by current and wind, early ships from the Aegean were hard put to it to round the first corner into the narrows, where the water speeds past the Asian shore without any back eddies to check its onrush. Sometimes tow-ropes were employed. Yet often travellers made no attempt to round the cape, but disembarked on the Asian coast just before the promontory began, and had their cargoes carried over the projecting peninsula to a re-embarkation point within the Dardanelles.

Consequently, the Asian shore of these narrows came in for more use than its European side, and this extreme bastion of Asia Minor assumed greater significance than the European

(Gallipoli) peninsula opposite. Although not so well sheltered as the other side, the Asian bank has welcoming inshore shallows; and particular attention came to be concentrated upon a little river-mouth bay just inside the strait, where cargo carried over the land from the Aegean could be re-embarked. The bay also allowed ships which had decided to sail right through to find shelter and take in water and supplies while they were waiting for favourable winds.

Less than four miles inland from this point stood Troy, controlling from its low ridge not only the Dardanelles but an important land-route on its Asian seaboard leading to a principal crossing-point of the strait. The isolated mountainous hinterland of the Troad, with its relatively inaccessible interior, was not very encouraging to travellers from the central parts of the peninsula; and Troy, accordingly, was only destroyed twice in two thousand years. Nor did the Trojans suffer from this comparative isolation, since they could live on their own food-supplies, and from the tolls they levied by piloting many a ship through the narrows and transporting its cargoes overland.

The first recorded settlements at Troy, dating from about 3000 BC and resembling others on islands nearby, were a succession of small fortresses with massive stone walls entered by a tower-flanked gate. Next, for three hundred years of the later third millennium, came the big walls and monumental gates of a larger town which buried its rulers in state like contemporary Alacahüyük and Maikop (p. 81). The whole of this Troy was only a hundred yards in diameter and extended over less than two acres, but its buildings included strong timber-laced fortifications, a spacious granary and a royal residence. This palace, consisting of several rectangular structures grouped round a courtyard, included a thirty-foot wide assembly hall, of a type which had originated in Asia Minor (p. 29).

The goldsmiths' work of these people shows an advance on anything done hitherto, and when bronze came into use the expert Trojan metalworkers provided one of the main channels by which weapons made of this alloy came to central Europe. They were also active in spinning and weaving, and produced wheel-made pottery which was almost unique in Asia Minor. Troy was now rich enough to import ivory from Syria or

Mesopotamia, lapis lazuli from eastern Afghanistan, and amber from the Baltic via the head of the Adriatic or a port in southern Russia. Artistic themes such as ships and dolphins indicate maritime exploration of the Mediterranean and perhaps the Black Sea as well. Moreover, rich settlements in south-eastern Spain, employing clay loom-weights exactly similar to those found in Asia Minor, were evidently in touch with this area, which perhaps played a part in their colonisation.

Many of the same conditions may have been reproduced in the contents of two tombs believed to have come from Dorak, which overlooked a lake from a small promontory a hundred and thirty miles east of Troy and twelve miles from the Sea of Marmara. The objects alleged to have been found there include an Egyptian tablet of mid-third millennium date – the earliest direct evidence that this area was in contact with Egypt – as well as turquoise from Sinai or north-east Persia, and a dagger-blade with a representation of a ship which provides an early example of a beaked prow for ramming.

The innumerable important centres ravaged over a period of years or centuries by irruptions attributed to Indo-European-speaking peoples of the north included both Troy and another place of ancient origin, Beycesultan in the south-west central area of the same peninsula (p. 37). Situated in a fertile agricultural area, this town seems to have recovered more quickly than Troy, for it is now possible to date the construction of its new palace to *c.* 1900 BC. This building had a hall of the shape traditional to Asia Minor, but its beams rested upon vertical posts that were resistant to earthquakes and looked ahead to classical styles. The courtyard too, surrounded by two-storeyed buildings with lighting-wells or ventilation shafts, may be bracketed with Mari as an influence on the palaces which were rising in Crete; and the altars which these people erected, and their use of wooden frameworks to hold together walls of rubble or mud-brick, may likewise have served as models (p. 90).

Meanwhile Troy, after its destruction, had been inhabited by squalid people living in heaps of refuse. But not long after the refoundation of Beycesultan, Troy also was rebuilt on a scale more worthy of its past (?*c.* 1800), probably by people who were related to settlers in central Greece and spoke much the same sort of primitive Greek. The widespread innovations introduced by these new arrivals included, in due course, cremation. Furthermore, although the town was still small, the new Trojans excelled contemporary Greece in the skill and elaboration of their fortifications, which comprised a limestone wall punctuated by four gates and enclosing a citadel nearly eight hundred feet long. A series of concentric terraces, occupied by large, generously spaced, free-standing houses, some evidently with at least one upper storey, rose to the summit where the royal palace must have risen. Pottery was of a new type, resembling that of the Greek mainland, although both sets of products probably go back to common models from western Asia Minor. Over eight thousand spindle-whorls have been found in this settlement, as well as many bones of goat and sheep, so that the spinning and exportation of cloth and textiles must have been a major activity. The discovery of the bones of horses, too, points to specialisation in the breeding and export of this animal, which was in such demand among the warlike peoples of the later second millennium (p. 74).

The Trojans had good agricultural soil and, in spite of the deficiencies of inland communications, were in contact with the Hittite interior of the peninsula. But they owed their wealth primarily to their central maritime position, which enabled them to control the traffic between Asia and Europe and to maintain commercial relations both with Greek cities such as Mycenae and with metal- and timber-producing regions of the Black Sea. Moreover, the contacts of Troy increasingly reached north-westwards into Thrace and Macedonia and contributed substantially to the diffusion of culture through and beyond the Balkan area (p. 101).

In *c.* 1275, however, the town was overwhelmed by an earthquake. Its successor, somewhat impoverished and isolated from other Aegean peoples, was likewise destroyed during the later years of the same century. Although the identity of the destroyers cannot be regarded as certain, this is generally believed to have been the Troy which according to the *Iliad* was taken and sacked by Greek invaders (p. 142). At all events, like towns on neighbouring Aegean islands and in countless other areas of the near and middle east (p. 80), the place was demolished by fire. And so again, later, was a humble Troy which had risen from the ruins and made crude knobbed pottery bearing a curious resemblance to other ceramical finds as far afield as Hungary.

Egypt alone just managed to hold its ground; but the Hittite empire which had dominated the hinterland of Asia Minor disintegrated altogether (p. 79). The Hittites had no doubt maintained important relations with Troy, amounting perhaps to a measure of supervision. Although the centre of their own empire was in the eastern part of the peninsula they also possessed important Mediterranean dependencies whose inhabitants spoke a language of Indo-European structure known as Luvian, which apparently bequeathed to the Greeks a considerable number of place-names, notably those in -assos.

At least one of these states, Arzawa, seems to have possessed its own Aegean seaboard, including 'Apašaš' which may well be the later Ephesus. Arzawa was subdued by the Hittites in the seventeenth century, but asserted its independence in the fourteenth and finally became detached from the Hittites – they were heavily engaged elsewhere – in *c.* 1200, perhaps a short time after the fall of Troy. Arzawa's eastern neighbour, whether ally or dependency or suzerain, was Beycesultan (p. 84), though it continued at intervals during these centuries to suffer destruction from unknown sources.

A closer neighbour to the Trojans, evidently, was another almost unknown but perhaps quite imposing state called Assuwa. The name is probably the same as 'Asia'; in Roman times this meant the whole of western Asia Minor, but early Greeks more or less restricted the designation to the area known as Lydia.[1] This region, then, which lay north of Arzawa, may be regarded as Assuwa's nucleus. When we hear of an Assuwan confederacy being broken by one of the last Hittite monarchs (*c.* 1250–1225), that was perhaps the occasion on which Troy succumbed. At all events, at a fairly early or even preliminary stage of these almost worldwide disturbances, the roving hordes, or smash-and grab raiding groups detached from their main bodies, demolished almost every one of these centres of civilisation in western Asia Minor.

Crete

As early as the seventh millennium BC the first people had come to Crete, presumably from Asia Minor – after somehow braving the perilous waters and winds in their tiny boats. Thereafter further immigrations took place at intervals, and pottery styles suggest that these, too, originated from various parts of the Asian coast. After 4000 there were influences from southern Mesopotamia, probably transmitted through ports on the Syrian-Lebanese coast such as Byblos. The latter half of the second millennium witnessed further new arrivals, long-headed, narrow-faced, short people like their predecessors. The cultural habits washed into the island during the upheavals of this age came from various parts of Levant as well as Egypt, the wealthiest Mediterranean state, with which Crete was in increasingly close contact by the direct sea route. The population also now included a broad-skulled element which probably originated from Asia Minor and brought the use of bronze.

Second to Cyprus by a narrow margin, Crete is both the largest and southernmost island of the Aegean.

> One of the great islands of the world
> In midsea, in the wine-dark sea, is Crete,
> spacious and rich and populous.[2]

Its shores lie sixty miles from Greece, a hundred and twenty from Asia and two hundred from Africa. The island was equidistant from Troy to the Nile delta, and from Mycenae to Cyrene. It was a stepping stone between all eastern Mediterranean lands. Occupying such a position, the Cretans seemed destined by nature (so Aristotle considered) to rule over the Greeks.

Within a compass of a hundred and sixty by thirty miles, Crete had room to supply enough food for its relatively small population. It has no imposing rivers and the plains between its lofty mountains are mostly small. But the layered (schist) valleys sought by the early settlers in preference to harder limestone break up easily into cultivated terraces and provide natural mule-roads on the slopes. Spring water was abundantly available for vines and olives and imported long-horned cattle; and forests of oak, fir, cypress and cedar, of which less than two per cent survive today, provided a wealth of ship timber.

Crete, then, had resources of its own. Yet its life-blood was maritime traffic. Natural harbours were scarce, but there is no lack of the little sandy bays and creeks which were all that early ships needed. Signet rings from *c.* 2000 BC show vessels with high sterns (and sometimes prows) propelled by fifteen oars or more on either side, and by square-rigged sails. Early Crete looked towards the oriental centres and transmission-points of civilisation, and many of its earliest collections of dwellings were situated in the warm eastern section of the island which stands nearest to Asia. Such, for example, was Vassiliki, where people of *c.* 2500 constructed large buildings with red-lime-plastered walls and made red and black pottery. The place looks both ways because it is on the north coast of an isthmus. And close beside that narrow neck, on the top of a hill facing towards Egypt, is the newly excavated settlement of Myrtos. This consisted of at least two complexes of rooms not yet divided into houses, with staircases leading to the upper parts of the site and dry-stone walls formerly topped by courses of mud bricks and by flat roofs of plaster-covered reeds, like roofs of much older centres in Asia Minor such as Çatalhüyük. Two large clay tubs found at Myrtos may have been used for wine-pressing, and the stone of an olive found in 1968 provides what is perhaps the earliest authenticated evidence for the use of this fruit, of which the cultivation was presumably learnt from the Levant (p. 63). The earliest known Aegean workshop has also come to light; clay discs found on its site indicate that the slow wheel, which had appeared in Mesopotamia two millennia earlier (p. 34), was already employed for making handmade vessels. Myrtos was destroyed by a fire of unknown origin in *c.* 2200 BC.

By the latter part of the third millennium the Cretans were producing vases cut in an astonishingly wide range of stones, which they blocked out with a tubular drill and finished by hard grinding. Although this art was stimulated by the outstanding expertise of Egyptian stone-cutters, the materials were local. Moreover, Egypt was not the only influence, since there was also close contact with the Greek archipelago (Cyclades), the peaks of a drowned plateau which studded the sea to the north of Crete. Rarely strong enough to maintain political independence, these numerous isles probably came at an early date under direct or indirect Cretan control. But many of them possessed their own markedly individual features which played leading and varied parts in the formation of Aegean civilisation. Metallurgy reached them by the great route which led across Asia Minor from east to west. Marble, however, was local, quarried in many of the islands, and already before 2000 BC their artists had created a long and wonderful series of block-like, smooth-surfaced, sharp angled human figures, endowed by the nature of their material with the harmonious geometric volumes and austere surface planes which attracted Brancusi and Modigliani*.

From the island of Naxos came emery, and from Melos and Yiali (near Cos) obsidian; a hundred blades of Melian obsidian are already to be found at Cretan Myrtos. Early in the second millennium, original schools of ceramics in the Cyclades painted their pots with maritime designs emphasising commercial activities. Meanwhile Cretan vases were decorated with varnished bands or coatings of black paint overlaid with patterns in white. Sometimes these designs, like the earliest seals of the island, are reminiscent of Egypt and the Levant, and then came a phase in which chalices with strap-like handles imitate Asian metalwork.

By *c.* 2000 the eastern region of Crete had been eclipsed by its middle part, which was a little farther away from Asia, but must always have possessed greater potential wealth and became increasingly significant as the Aegean world continued to unfold. The coastal plains, opposite one another in the middle of the island's two long sides, were connected by a low pass through the central mountain chain. Near its opening, four miles from the northern shore, stood Cnossos, ensconced in a valley fold between two slight rises. The first settlements here dated back to before 6000 BC (p. 27), and the great residences of the future were built over a mound of deposits over twenty feet deep, going back to ancient, two-roomed huts.

It was early in the second millennium BC that the major expansions took place. Only a small part of Cnossos' palace of that

* Stylised statuettes, 'fiddle-figures' (with face and neck resembling a pottery figure now found at Myrtos), had been produced at Saliagos (4500–3500), now a tiny island between Paros and Antiparos, then a hill-top in the bay where they joined.

date has survived, but the major phase of palace-building, which followed in *c.* 1700–1600, probably reproduces on a magnified scale the dispositions of the previous epoch. Many elements of construction go back to older Cretan models, but the arrangement of courtyards surrounded by two-storeyed residential quarters with light-wells or ventilation-shafts (in addition to windows) owes an extensive debt to mainland Asian palaces such as Beycesultan and Mari.

Design was clever and elastic, with masses broken up by the interplay of strong Mediterranean light and shade. Building technique, on the other hand, except for neat doorposts and a fairly advanced system of plumbing, remained rudimentary and poky. Good use, however, was made of local materials. Limestone, resistant to rain, served to pave courtyards, while internal floors were made of a fine-grained, marble-like gypsum, now scarred and corrugated but originally possessing a smooth, lustrous surface; and the use of the same material to face the walls of sun-baked brick may mean that the Cretans were the earliest people to make use of stone as a thin veneer. As at Beycesultan (p. 84), buildings were strengthened against earthquakes by horizontal and vertical timber, employed extravagantly since wood was so plentiful. Columns of various forms go back to Egyptian and other near eastern models; pillars tapering downwards like inverted tree trunks were particularly favoured (p. 54).

On the north coast, Cnossos had at least three harbours facing towards the Aegean. On the opposite side of the town a stepped, columnar portico, with a right angled turn to enable new arrivals to be scrutinised, was the terminus of the road leading inland through the mountains. Five miles before reaching the southern coast this road passed the island's second great royal residence. That was Phaestos, which occupied a dominant position on a two-hundred-foot high spur falling sheer on all sides to the fields and pasture lands of Crete's most fertile plain, the Mesara. The private apartments of the local prince were orientated to catch the cool breezes of summer, and the building was mortared with cement by the addition of a special earth from the volcanic island of Thera (Santorin). On the other, seaward, extremity of the same mountain spur, at a place now called Haghia Triada, stood a further palace, which subsequently superseded Phaestos but had first served as its harbour town. For while Cnossos, looking the other way, commanded most of the trade with western Asia Minor and Troy and Greece, Phaestos and Haghia Triada were the places which controlled the commerce with Egypt.

The other significant monuments of the Mesara are large communal vaulted tombs, which had already existed before the palaces but multiplied after their foundation. Some were circular and perhaps domed*, others square or rectangular. However, the largest of such tombs so far discovered on the island, a rectangular structure measuring one hundred and twenty by ninety feet, is on the north coast, near the town of Mallia twenty-five miles east of Cnossos. Mallia, on a little plateau within sight of the sea, possessed only a narrow agricultural hinterland and was primarily a port. Its houses, with their half-timbered, plaster-coated walls of easily workable sandstone and harder ironstone, were packed tight along narrow streets, and representations on faïence plaques show that they possessed two storeys lit by windows that could be closed by shutters and may have been covered with some sort of transparent pane.

Sixteen miles south-east of Mallia was a little valley with a low hill surmounted by another town, Gournia, facing out upon the sea from an isthmus where earlier settlements had stood (p. 88). Gournia sloped upwards in tiers of dwellings made of small stones set in clay, except for the principal mansion which was built of squared masonry. A further settlement, its houses all of stone and its floors paved with slate, was planted on an islet of the adjoining bay, facing a small harbour. More to the east again, at the extremity of the island, was a palace, Kato Zakro, where current excavations may greatly improve our knowledge of this part of Crete. The objects already discovered include some of the most impressive finds in the island, including a superb drinking-horn of rock crystal.

One of the many things that are still uncertain is the political relation of these centres to one another. It is very likely, however, that Cnossos exercised some sort of supremacy throughout the island, though at times this may have been shared with Phaestos. The authority of the Cretan rulers was strengthened

* For Mesopotamian forerunners, see p. 31.

by the adoption of writing, which reached the island before 2200 BC and was used, as elsewhere, to compile the records, inventories and accountancy needed for governmental purposes. Babylonian cylinder seals of the early second millennium are found on Crete, and then clay tablets show first a hieroglyphic and subsequently a linear version of the Egyptian script, with a good many changes and additions. These signs are incomprehensible to us, and so are the more developed varieties of linear writing which came next. These derive not more than one third of their symbols from older pictorial forms but show curious analogies with much earlier Mesopotamian and even Persian systems, which had probably become known to Crete through Syrian intermediaries. In the last years of Cretan splendour, however, this script was superseded by another linear notation, used by a new group of rulers who had come from the mainland of Greece (*c.* 1400; p. 107).

Another means by which the lords of the island, first Cretan and then Greek, asserted control over their subjects was the horse, which appears (to judge by a picture upon a seal) to have arrived before the end of the third millennium. But much more important was the unprecedented power and range of Crete at sea. Later Greeks preserved a tradition that Cnossos had possessed a maritime empire under a king or series of kings called Minos, after whom the civilisation has come to be known as Minoan today.[3]

The expansion to overseas territories was evidently, for the most part, commercial rather than political. As early as *c.* 2000 there was a colony on the island of Cythera, which is adjacent to the southern tip of the Peloponnese and can be seen on a clear day by the Cretans. Excavations are also revealing settlements on the mainland peninsula of Onugnathos (p. 99) adjoining Cythera and on the obsidian-bearing island of Thera which was the nearest to Crete of all the Cyclades, half-way to mainland Greece on the one side and Asia Minor on the other.

The Cretans moved in both these directions. On the Greek mainland, the Mycenaean civilisation initially owed much to their guidance (p. 102). Towards the east, in the same latitude as Thera, there was a strong Cretan colony upon the island of Rhodes, separated from Asia Minor by a narrow strait. Beside these narrows the colonists settled at the Rhodian harbour-town of Ialysos, which became a stage on Cretan trade-routes in both directions.

One of these routes led northwards along the Aegean coast of Asia Minor, where a further trading-centre was founded in *c.* 1600 at Miletus. A strained relationship with the local kingdom of Arzawa, which alternated between autonomy and dependence on the Hittites, is suggested by the fourteen-foot-high wall erected by Miletus shortly before 1300. Inland routes however, were poor, and the place served principally as a port of call. Southwards, too, Rhodes helped the Cretans to open up vital communications to Cyprus and the Syrian coast, where they had their own separate trading colonies at Ugarit, Alalakh, and elsewhere. Egyptian influence also, which is apparent at Crete from the beginning of the millennium, became particularly strong from 1600 onwards, conveyed by means of ships proceeding to the island by way of Cyrene or direct.

Cretan wheat was good, and barley, developed by deliberate crossings, was even more important. But neither these cereals nor the excellent local figs are likely to have been extensively exported. The timber of Crete was of interest to the Egyptians. But the island's principal products were wine and olive oil. Their cultivation had been learnt from Syria or Asia Minor during the fourth or third millennium BC, and later on vines and olive-trees must have been abundant enough to yield large exportable surpluses. Signs of both crops have already been indicated at Myrtos (p. 88), and excavations at Cnossos and another site ten miles away have revealed further presses for wine and oil. Massive jars in the palaces of Cnossos and Phaestos were probably filled with this merchandise. Greeks later said that the first olives in the Peloponnese had been brought there from Crete.

For a long time this happy picture remained unspoilt by external enemies, since they could not stand up against Cretan fleets. But the island was terribly damaged by the volcanoes, earthquakes and tidal waves of the second millennium BC. Several phases of destruction culminated in the most fearful disaster of all time. This convulsion, which apparently occurred between 1500 and 1450 BC, originated from the crater-island of Thera (Santorin), which was shattered by an eruption of gigantic size and force. As new soundings have begun to show, the tall houses of the Cretan colony on Thera were buried under heaps of ash to a depth of from twenty-five to fifty feet*. As the sea-water cascaded into the huge fractured crater, where it still remains today, prodigious explosions caused by the superheated vapours created tidal waves which devastated the entire archipelago as far afield as Crete, where even inland centres were deeply affected. In 1883 the eruption of Mount Krakatoa in Indonesia killed thirty-six thousand people, and fifty-foot waves caused destruction over enormous areas. But the crater of Thera was four times as large as Krakatoa's, and the havoc that it caused, though unrecorded because literary history had not begun, is shown by excavations to have been gigantic. The whole centre of the island seems to have blown up thirty miles into the air, and the fall-out was scattered as far as Israel. The Book of Exodus tells of a later occasion when all the land of Egypt was shrouded for three days in a darkness which could be felt.[4] When Thera exploded, a poisonous cloud of blackness and devastation descended upon the whole civilisation of the eastern Mediterranean.

Not all the ravaged Cretan settlements and palaces were able to recover.† But Cnossos – like certain other towns on smaller islands – revived on a grand scale for fifty years or more. Henceforward, however, Cnossos was a more militarised place, under the management of Mycenaeans from the mainland. Contacts had been established with them earlier, and perhaps now they took advantage of the cataclysm to establish their authority on the island.

Early in the fourteenth century all the great Cretan centres were again destroyed by an earthquake; or perhaps by an onslaught, or a series of raids, by piratical sea-marauders such as already infested the rocky southern coasts of Asia Minor and would soon make themselves felt over a much wider area (p. 85). Even after this further disaster Crete regained some prosperity and retained an important though subordinate role. But by *c.* 1150, if not earlier, the palace at Cnossos was no more.

The civilisation which thus ended had created one of the most

* One still has a perfectly preserved windowsill, with flower pots and water jars.
† Kato Zakro was neither looted nor reoccupied.

brilliant Mediterranean artistic cultures. Architecture, stone vases, pottery and seals had rapidly developed autonomy from their Egyptian and Levantine prototypes, and the gem-cutters who worked with graver, saw and drill upon semi-precious agates and chalcedonies became the most characteristic of Cretan artists. Before the end of the third millennium painters interested in the animals, fishes and flowers of the Mediterranean and its coasts were already offering imaginative variations upon the naturalism of their Egyptian masters (p. 57). A wild goat is shown, and a hind resting in a grotto. A dog hunts a deer in a wood, and a fish and octopus are seen swimming among coral-like reefs.

Soon after 2000 BC further scenes of natural life appear in increasingly bold and lavish patterns upon frescoed walls and egg-shell-thin wheel-made pottery. Some of these various styles are reminiscent, at first, of near eastern centres such as Mari. But the Cretans loved to depict scenes that they themselves knew: lions, bulls, ibexes, birds and monkeys roaming in a rocky landscape: crocus and iris and lotus, yellow roses, myrtles, palms, vetches and blown sprays of olive; or seaweed waving in the water, flying fishes and anemones and seashells and many another marine creature. Egyptian models are left behind by new perceptive subtleties of observation. The Cretans did not aim at representing natural forms for their own sake, but seized on those which appealed to an orgiastic love of colourful movement; nature is imitated, yet subordinated to a flowing overall pattern that came easily to the painter as he gradually turned the vase upon a mat. There is also a sophisticated taste for deliberate distortions, reflecting modern-seeming conflicts and compromises between realistic and abstract approaches. Natural objects are imitated, yet stylised in the interests of an inner meaning as well as a pattern. Cretan polypods and dolphins are less photographically accurate than Egyptian fishes, but they are more alive; and a Cretan cat, although less exactly represented than its Egyptian counterpart, gives a better impression of stealthy cruelty. In depicting the Picasso-like strength and directness of a bull, the passionate beauty of plants in bloom, the shimmering mysteries of underwater life, the Cretan is the master. The Mediterranean world is discovered and reproduced with impressionistic intuition.

Vessels of rock-crystal, obsidian and other difficult stones, are worked with a traditional virtuosity which again excels contemporary Egypt. The almost casual vividness and foreshortening of a relief of singing harvesters shows a singular gift for depicting a surge of activity, a dynamic mood, a momentary event. Small Cretan figures, sculptured in the round, capture the same fugitive mobility with unhampered freedom; and the recent discovery of an eighteen-inch ivory arm has hinted at larger-scale sculptures of the same kind which have so far not been found.

This radiant world of unexpected fancies, a floating, weightless place of rhythmical motion, absorbs and improves a number of ancient near eastern and Mediterranean traditions – and it also signalises their final winding up. For Cretan art is far removed from the analytical-structural logicalities which later came to be favoured by the Greeks, and by westerners after them until Gauguin and his contemporaries. At most, Crete passed on to Greece certain shapes, motifs and techniques; for example, the colouring of statuettes with gold leaf.

The artists of Crete lack the solemnity of Mesopotamia or even the more tranquil seriousness of Egypt. Yet for all their baroque *joie de vivre* they served religion, and particularly the basic religion of Crete and indeed the whole Mediterranean area, the worship of the earth-mother: who ruled the cosmos and the earth and the sea, and all that is in them (and was probably also, in large part, the cause of the apparently unprecedented prominence of women in Cretan civilisation). Here, indeed, is a theme which did descend direct from the Cretans, for it was they who taught the Greeks the forms through which the mother goddess was worshipped.

The intermediaries were Mycenae and other mainland cities.

The Mycenaeans

As early as the seventh millenium BC immigrants from Asia Minor had settled in the north-eastern corner of Greece, beside the inviting Macedonian and Thessalian plains (p. 29). After 4000, when newcomers brought a more advanced pastoral and agricultural life, Thessaly and the lowlands to its south continued to show the heaviest concentration of settlements, though they still extended also to Macedonia. These people perhaps came from Syria since their pottery possesses artistic analogies with that area, and the site of Servia, in the Macedonian hinterland, was found to contain a wheat-grain of a Syrian variety. In *c.* 2500 Servia was burnt by cruder immigrants, whose kinsmen then moved on into Thessaly. Nomadic hunters and shepherds, they were the first of a series of new occupants of northern Greece who had come down from the Danube basin via the valleys of the Morava and then the Axius (Vardar), which flows into the Thermaic Gulf of the Aegean near the future site of Salonica.

These newcomers did not, however, penetrate in substantial numbers into the main part of Greece, or if they did its first higher cultures were not due to them. For although the Morava-Axius furrow provides a breach by which gradual infiltrations are possible, they tended to lose their force, under the influence of superior cultures, before they reached very far to the south. This was because of the difficult communications of the country, which is not only fringed by mountains but is filled with them as well. The Balkan massif, which comprises the major northern barrier, turns south in the form of the high Pindus range and its continuations, which bisect the entire land.

Greek mountains 'are not huddled together in ungainly lumps but flaunt their peaks in proud independence.'[5] Yet although they are not continuous, eighty per cent of the surface consists of them, and even what remains cannot all be cultivated, since much of it is steep and stony.

> At home we have no level runs or meadows...
> Grasses, and pasture land, are hard to come by
> Upon the islands tilted in the sea.[6]

And those words about Odysseus' little isle of Ithaca were just as applicable to most of the mainland. In the tropics men spend their time weeding; in England they plant and tend; in Greece they often have to make the soil first.[7] For poverty, said a Spartan to the Persian king, had always been the inheritance of Greece;[8] and so its people had a special love for nature in its most fertile and well-tended forms (p. 189).

In addition to severely limiting the total cultivable area, these mountains produced that famous geographical fragmentation which so largely contributed to the irremediable absence of internal unity. Thessaly and Sparta and the central Arcadian plateau in the middle of the Peloponnese are wholly shut in by mountains; the plains of Athens and Mycenae have only one open side facing towards the sea. Unlike Switzerland, Greece does not divide up into valley thoroughfares but forms separate cup-shaped plains and small plateaux, enclosed and almost sealed apart by difficulties of precipitous terrain which neither politicians nor road-engineers ever seriously tried to mitigate, so that the cost of land transport was incredibly expensive.

Goats, burners of charcoal for the reduction of ores, and hewers of timber for firewood, shipbuilding and other purposes have subjected Greece to vast deforestation and consequent soil erosion, which becomes all too easy in a country of steep slopes, long droughts, few but violent rains, torrential rivers that rapidly vanish away, and crumbling rocks. In ancient times oak, fir and cypress forests covered the mountains and most of the plains, and Cape Sunium, the southernmost point of Attica, was a wooded promontory.[9] But few trees remain there any more. Indeed the process had already gone far at the beginning of history, and by the time of Plato the land seemed a mere decayed carcass with the bare bones sticking through the skin.

> What is now left of our soil rivals any other in being all-productive and abundant in crops and rich in pasturage for all kinds of cattle; and at an early period, in addition to their fine quality, it produced these things in vast quantity. What now remains, compared with what then existed, is like the skeleton of a sick man, all the fat and soft earth having wasted away, and only the bare framework of the land being left.[10]

Nevertheless, the ancient Greek countryside was still much more productive than it is today. The Greeks were only kept alive by their agriculture, and their writers constantly preach work on the land, sometimes adding idealistically, like Socrates, that such riches are the only sort worth having. Yet the extraction of this wealth was so difficult that it needed not only the hard work recommended by many moralists but ingenuity, close observation, adaptability and foresight.

In spite of the natural advantages and early settlement of the larger northern plains, it was instead the less fertile Peloponnese which began to develop advanced cultures. This was because the area, while less vulnerable to the intrusions of backward Balkan tribes, was more readily accessible to the more civilised outside world. On this deeply indented south-eastern seaboard communities were numerous, and able to maintain intensive relations not only with one another but with the older centres of eastern and Mediterranean culture – and particularly Crete. From that island it is only fifty miles to Cythera, which in turn is separated from the Peloponnesian promontory of Cape Malea by a strait which was then not more than five miles across. Accordingly this adjoining region of the mainland, Laconia the later home of the Spartans, might have been expected to be one of the earliest parts of Greece in which settlements influenced by Crete would develop. Hitherto, evidence to such an effect has largely been lacking. But the deficiency may soon prove to be misleading, because the grave seismological upheavals of *c.* 1500–1450 (p. 94) raised this seaboard of the Peloponnese by from three to twelve feet. That is to say, cities did exist on the Laconian coast – but ever since that time they have been covered by the sea. A start is now being made with the excavation of one of these submerged places on the isle of Elafonisi, which was once the Onugnathos peninsula and of all places on the mainland was nearest to Cythera and Crete. Beneath the water is a twenty-one acre town dating from *c.* 2000 (the same date as Cythera) with walls of uncut stone blocks. Subsequent discoveries in the same area may well reveal other advanced communities of even earlier date.

Laconia, then, looked down towards Crete. So also, from a somewhat greater distance, did the next promontory to the north, to which its subsequent capital Argos gave the name of the Argolid; and this was the headland which witnessed the most famous developments. Adjoining on the other side the strategic isthmus of Corinth, which like itself boasts of a rich well-watered plain, the Argolid is flanked by two deep, wide arms of the sea, the Saronic and Argive gulfs.

At the very head of the Gulf of Argos stood the town of Lerna

(Mili), controlling its farmlands and coastal approaches and drawing water from three springs. Here, shortly after 2300 BC, a fort measuring seventy-five by thirty-six feet, enclosed by a double ring of fortifications, protected a two-storey residence – probably a royal palace – walled with hard red plaster and roofed by small square fire-baked tiles and slates. The red burnished pottery produced at Lerna was derived from metal prototypes which had evidently come from Asia Minor, and that also appears to have been the origin of the people who founded the place. Their trade, however, was mainly with the islands of the Aegean.

Lerna was destroyed by fire in *c.* 2100, and it is probable that the ravagers were a group of the Indo-European-speaking peoples who invaded huge areas at this period (p. 71). They reached Greece, in all likelihood, from the north down the Morava-Axius gap which had brought earlier settlers to Macedonia (p. 97). This origin and route are confirmed by the worship of the sky-god Zeus who was destined to become the chief divinity of Greece, since his association with northern sites such as Dodona and Mount Olympus seems indicative of immigrants from that quarter. At Dodona in Epirus, a place of ancient migratory encampments where priests sleeping on the ground with unwashed feet interpreted the pronouncements of the god, his voice was heard in the rustling of the sacred oak-leaves and in the thunder which rumbles there more often than anywhere else in Europe.

After their arrival in Greece and intermixture with earlier inhabitants, the newcomers gradually began to speak a language which was the forerunner of Greek. In spite of individual detectable acts of violence such as the destruction of Lerna and other centres, the infiltrations lasted a long time, since these remote ancestors of the Greeks do not seem to have been fully settled in their homes until two centuries had passed since their devastations (*c.* 1900).

When one or several of the successive migrant waves hit the more southern regions of Greece, contact was made with a more settled population that had access to near-eastern influences. Accordingly, in imitation, the newcomers likewise developed a way of life that was agricultural rather than pastoral; and contacts across the Aegean are indicated by their wheel-made pottery, which resembled contemporary products of Troy (p. 85).

Gradually, the eastern coastlands of Greece witnessed the construction of towns far more imposing than anything Europe had seen before. One of these places, only a short distance from Lerna, was Mycenae, at the northern end of the plain of Argos eight miles from the head of its gulf. Here on a limestone outcrop, not far from the watershed leading over into the Corinthian plain, stood an easily defensible rocky citadel, possessing a good water supply and dominating the routes from north and south.

Along a flattish ridge below the citadel, lavish treasures have been found in two circles of deep shaft-graves dating from about 1500 BC. Graves of this type, built of rubble walls which originally supported a cross-beamed roof of stone slabs or clay-plastered reeds or twigs, had also been dug at Lerna and elsewhere on the Greek mainland and islands, and go back to humbler structures of earlier date in the same regions.* But they also recall, in general terms, some ancient stone-built subterranean vaults in Mesopotamia (p. 31), and invite closer comparison with Alacahüyük, Ugarit, Byblos and particularly south Russian sites, where burials show the same curious bodily posture with outbent knees.

For these dead of Mycenae, unlike the Homeric heroes who purported to belong to the place (p. 143), were not cremated. Their corpses were laid out in richly ornamented clothes and surrounded by weapons and vessels and precious works of art. The blades of their daggers are decorated with inlays in gold, silver and lead-sulphur mixtures, executed in superior techniques which owe something to various eastern originals. The contents of the shaft-graves are international and very expensive, presenting curious oscillations between intricate sophistication and tawdry vulgarity, miniature exquisiteness and monumental grandeur – between styles that are naturalistic and abstract, borrowed and original.

The habitations where these rulers lived have left no trace. But about themselves we learn something from golden masks,

* Newly excavated grave mounds in Epirus (southern Albania) may prove to be among the precursors of the Mycenaean graves.

showing broad, bearded, moustached faces which (like other aspects of these treasures) recall people of Caucasus and Iran rather than any delicate Cretan; and their tunics do not resemble wasp-waisted Minoan robes. To judge from artistic themes, the Mycenaean princes spent most of the time fighting and hunting. Their powerful armoury of weapons included new and deadly flange-hilted slashing swords of partly Cretan and partly Levantine inspiration, long rectangular and figure-of-eight shaped shields (the latter probably copied from Crete), and chariots intended for warfare on the plains. One shaft-grave also contained a special kind of whetstone that is common in northern Europe and presents one of the first indications that Mycenae, like Troy, communicated with the European hinterland (p. 85).

Yet in spite of all these traceable links with other countries, it is still impossible to discover who these rich and fierce, somewhat barbarous but culturally acquisitive rulers were, or even whether they descended from earlier settlers in Greece or had immigrated themselves.

At all events, in *c.* 1450 BC there were sharp cultural changes which suggest that they were superseded by fresh waves of newcomers. The funeral customs of the dynasties that followed were different, since they were buried in large circular chambers, sometimes free-standing beneath a cairn but more often half-underground and approached by a masonry-lined unroofed passage. These imposing tombs are surmounted by 'bee-hive' domes incorporating the process of the corbel, in which levels of masonry are laid one upon another in ever narrowing, increasingly projecting, concentric circles; the stones cannot fall because of the great weight above which holds them fast. Since graves of this type had already appeared as early as 1600 in southern parts of the Peloponnese not far from Crete, it may be that the form was influenced by circular burials on that island (p. 91). Corbelling, too, may have been of Cretan inspiration, though it is mainly a response to local religious beliefs, requiring that the rulers should be buried in permanent monumental tombs. There are two types of grave, those built for repeated use by whole families (as in Crete and western Europe), and the grander Mycenaean category of those intended for a single princely funeral. The largest among nine such tombs at Mycenae is one near the end of the series which is nearly fifty feet in diameter and height (*c.* 1350–1330). The seventeen-foot doorway is surmounted by a lintel which weighs more than a hundred tons. Such masterpieces of constructional technique could only be achieved by governments possessing large concentrations of wealth and energy.

The sites in various parts of Greece where such tombs can be found are often near harbours at the heads of southward-facing gulfs. Next, towards the end of the period of their construction, great palaces also arose at several of the same centres. One was at Mycenae itself, after which, perhaps rather misleadingly, the whole civilisation has been named in modern times. Southwards from Mycenae, upon a slight rise behind the road, was the satellite fortress of Tiryns. Now a mile away from the Gulf of Argos, Tiryns then adjoined its shores and was one of Mycenae's ports. A further anchorage was close by, and a third lay farther north upon the Gulf of Corinth, so that maritime communications faced west as well as east and south.

Another of the leading centres of the Mycenaean age was Athens. Like Mycenae, it was situated a short distance from the sea and dominated a south-eastwards facing promontory. This comprised the land of Attica, the hinge between Peloponnese and central Greece, parallel to the Argolid and separated from it by the Saronic Gulf. Athens was linked to the sea by the open roadstead of Phaleron Bay, and perhaps gained its original importance when another settlement down the Attic coast was destroyed at the same time as Lerna. The material remains of Mycenaean Athens are mostly lost beneath its subsequent grandeur, but imposing walls were apparently constructed in the middle of the thirteenth century BC; and Athens, again like Mycenae, possessed a covered stairway descending to an underground spring which lay hidden outside the walls. The importance of the place at this date can best be determined not so much by its own legends as by the leading role it evidently continued to play after the destruction of the other Mycenaean centres (p. 134). How many of the three Attic plains the city controlled cannot be discovered, but no doubt it drew most of its food from the small adjoining Cephisus valley.

Thirty-three miles north-west of Athens was the Boeotian fortress capital of Thebes; and for a time this was another of the greatest towns in Mycenaean Greece. Now partially excavated, Thebes stood on a low ridge separating two plains at the point where the route from Attica to northern Greece is crossed by another which joins the two seas, leading from the Gulf of Corinth across Boeotia to a strait separating it from the large Aegean island of Euboea. Thebes owed part of its wealth to the control of these narrows. Furthermore its plains, much more extensive than those of Attica, provided abundant and excellent grain and rich pastures for cattle and sheep; and no other area in Greece, except Thessaly, had so much meadowland and open country in which a strong breed of horses could be reared. The southern plain was watered by the River Asopus, and its counterpart contained the extensive Lake Copais, adjoined on the farther side by a wealthy fortified town at Orchomenos, which organised an elaborate drainage system in the area. But as the Mycenaean epoch wore on, it seems that these Boeotian centres were eclipsed by Athens.

Other recent excavations have revealed parts of the only important settlement of this period so far discovered on the west coast of Greece. This was Pylos, spoken of by Homer as the venerable Nestor's realm. The palace and adjacent buildings (though their identification with Nestor's residence is dubious) were situated on a narrow hill among gullies tilting deeply down towards Navarino Bay five miles away. Although there is no convenient water-supply (since the nearest fresh-water spring is across the valley), the country round Pylos produced large quantities of wine, olive-oil and corn. But the place became powerful because of its location at the beginning of a Peloponnesian land-route, where sea-traders could disembark their cargoes and avoid the perilous sea journey round the southern capes.

These, according to our present knowledge, are the principal cities belonging to the Mycenaean civilisation. Their walled fortresses, constructed of hard limestone, porphyry and conglomerate, are dominated by princely residences of a more or less uniform construction. Great stretches of the interiors were dark, but upper storeys had windows and roofed balconies.

The buildings were grouped round courtyards which were sometimes flanked by porches or loggias leading into large, strong, simple central halls with circular hearths, altars and pillars reminiscent of earlier buildings in Greece and previously Asia Minor. Like the men themselves, these halls bear little relation to Cnossos; the palaces as a whole are more axial, symmetrical and internally focused than Crete's. It is true that the Mycenaeans called upon its superior culture for their squared masonry, wooden timbers and mouldings. But they also drew on native mainland models, as well as borrowing (with cruder obviousness than the Cretans) from the east and particularly from Asia Minor with which their own way of life had much in common.

The same ambivalent attitude is shown in the small-scale Mycenaean arts, which likewise draw upon the island's traditions but do not flow nearly so freely, being concerned less with movement and more with the structural preoccupations that were to characterise the Greek art of the future. Probably this distinction of Mycenaean from Cretan styles was caused in the first instance not by any deliberate aesthetic policy but by sheer degeneration due to provincialism. Nevertheless, the methods of the Mycenaeans developed confidently along these new and different lines.

Their pottery for example, fired at unusually high temperatures, was influenced by Cretan shapes but also produced original conceptions such as the tall-stemmed two-handled wine-cups which later Greece inherited. The pots, under old mainland influences, show firmer and harsher painted contours than those of Crete. Their naturalism, too, is partially derivative but again different in effect. Earlier metalwork found in the shaft-graves had already shown quasi-naturalistic designs, and now reliefs on gold cups seem to depict scenery from the air, with rocks growing from the bottom edge and hanging from the top. The landscapes shown on pottery, too, portray plants that the painter must have seen, since they have been found in excavations; and yet the resulting pictures are at one remove further from nature than Cretan scenes. Just as those had distorted Egyptian naturalism, so the Mycenaeans moved one stage farther away, exercising a new taste and gift for simplification and abstract pattern. They liked rich, unshaded primary colours, particularly blues and reds, and used paint to brighten the floors, walls, benches, columns and beams of their palaces. While a fresco from Thebes shows women in Cretan dress, friezes at Tiryns recall centres in Asia Minor such as Alacahüyük; and recently discovered clay sarcophagi from Attica and Boeotia, dating from the last years of this culture, paint human figures and other themes in styles that echo not only Crete and Asia Minor but Cyprus and the Levant as well. The most oriental, however, of all Mycenaean arts was ivory-work, since most raw ivory came to Greece from Syria. One masterpiece in this medium is a small group consisting of two goddesses and a child, which has been interpreted as an anticipation of the later Greek cult of Demeter. The identification is not certain; but much Greek religion goes back to Mycenae.

Relief sculpture in stone is represented by warlike scenes that are Europe's first monumental and representational stone-carvings, and by Mycenae's corbelled gateway crowned by a limestone triangle which displays two lionesses confronting a central tapering column, with their paws on a waisted altar. Although this altar has a Cretan look, the design is familiar from gems and ivories of Syrian and Mesopotamian inspiration. Mycenaean paintings too show columns of a similar kind, sometimes fluted as in Egypt and surmounted by capitals which are transitional between Egyptian and later Greek forms. Such is the remarkable blend of cultures adapted by the artists of Mycenaean palaces and tombs.

As in Crete, the political relations between the main towns cannot be determined. No doubt each dominated the plainland adjoining its fortress, and Mycenae controlled Tiryns. But whether it also exercised the vague national overlordship indicated by Homer is uncertain; nor can the tradition that Athens exercised a similar loose suzerainty over quasi-independent Attic kingdoms be confirmed.

The Mycenaeans introduced improvements in agriculture and horticulture. Their outstanding cultivation of the olive is recalled by later legends and institutions of Athens (p. 188). The amount of wine they succeeded in producing, in favoured areas, is suggested by the 2,853 stemmed drinking cups found in a single room at Pylos. In addition to keeping large herds of cattle, the local princes also bred horses, and the chariots introduced by the earlier dynasties now moved rapidly along constructed roads with bridges and reinforced culverts. Use was made of formidable slashing-swords of bronze, and excavators in a fifteenth-century tomb near Mycenae have recently discovered a warrior's complete bronze armour, including a cuirass scarcely equalled in excellence until the time of Louis Quatorze. 'Occurring as it does at the very beginning of the history of metal plate-armour, it almost surpasses belief.'[11]

In order to assess and control their complex resources, the masters of these towns found the institution of writing invaluable. The linear script generally known as Mycenaean seems first to have been used in Crete, on behalf of the Mycenaean rulers who had eventually taken the island over (p. 107). Then, after 1300, this same script is found at the leading centres on the mainland, where its principal discoveries have been made at Pylos and Thebes. This form of linear writing adhered to the ancient practice of representing whole syllables by single signs, seventy being derived from linear Cretan.

Most inscriptions were incised on tablets of wet clay which were subsequently dried in the sun; while those which have remained in existence until today owe their survival to accidental preservation by the fires which consumed the palaces. The view of most scholars is that the language they transcribe is an early form of Greek and that this tongue, a branch of the Indo-European family with no close links that we can now detect, had begun to evolve in the country many hundreds of years earlier when Indo-European-speaking peoples had first arrived and mixed with earlier settlers (p. 100).

These records of the Mycenaeans, used for governmental and inventorial purposes as elsewhere, refer to the extensive and highly organised labour force which their lavish way of life might have been expected to require. But all this elaborate bureaucratic administration, while representing the climax of earlier near eastern systems, is totally at variance both with the Homeric picture of a casually feudal earlier age (p. 142) and with the talkative, comparatively unsystematic arrangements of the later Greeks. There is much information about land ownership, agricultural produce, textiles and garments, furniture and household goods, military and naval equipment. At Pylos, though the exact meaning of the Mycenaean word is still disputable, references to a wide variety of different sorts of olive-oil have been detected.

Although much of this oil was offered to the gods, a great deal was also exported. The corridor of a recently excavated house at Mycenae, equipped with heating so that the oil should not congeal in cold weather, was found to contain thirty large jars waiting to be shipped away. Nor was olive-oil by any means the only export, since cargoes sent to Egypt also included hides, timber, wine and purple-dye. In exchange, the Greek mainland received precious metals, linen, papyrus and rope.

The commercial range of the leading mainland cities was imposing. Crete had become a dependency, and its colonies at Rhodes and Miletus were taken over and flourished – perhaps the latter, in its highly strategic position on the main sea routes, was an independent state (p. 93). Subsequently, the exploitation of these coasts by the Mycenaeans became more intensive still. From the thirteenth century in particular there is evidence of their settlers or traders at an enormous number of widely distributed ports. In Cyprus for example, which developed its own lively ceramic variations, colonists from Greece opened up immensely profitable mines of copper. Mycenaean Cyprus replaced Asia Minor as the principal supplier of the metal, and Cypriot copper ingots, which served the Levant as barter currency, have been found in large quantities on a merchant-ship wrecked in *c.* 1200 BC off southern Asia Minor. Beside these coasts Mycenaean outposts multiplied, probably extending as far as Cilicia. There were also settlements in the ports of Israel, Lebanon and Syria, whose own seamen of Ugarit and Alalakh no doubt joined the local Mycenaean community in sending Greece its spices and ivory, since their own maritime activity, preparatory to the Phoenician expansion (p. 120), had now begun to revive.

Mycenaean links as far afield as Cyrene have recently been demonstrated, and more easterly connections are indicated by numerous Babylonian and other oriental seals discovered at Thebes. The Black Sea, too, may well have been explored, since the legend of the voyage made by Jason and the Argonauts seems to date back to Mycenaean times. The Golden Fleece was river-washed gold or golden grain, in either case beside the Caucasus, where rich gold and bronze objects of Mycenaean type, dating from the sixteenth and fifteenth centuries, have been found to the west of Tbilisi (Tiflis). The origins of different parts of this Argonaut tale can be variously traced to Orchomenos, Thessaly and Miletus, which had evidently already inaugurated its historic interest in the Black Sea (p. 179).

But when Jason returns from there, the story brings him back by divergently imagined river routes which dimly reflect further remarkable expansions of Mycenaean activity into Adriatic and western waters. In one version the Argo navigates the River Po (Eridanus), recalling an ancient tradition that Pylos came there for amber – which originated in the Baltic but occurs abundantly in Mycenaean tombs.[12] Recently an intermediate Mycenaean coastal station has been discovered just beyond the mouth of the Adriatic, in north-western Greece.

But Mycenae's commerce went even farther afield than that, since its merchants also called and settled in eastern Sicily and the adjoining Lipari islands. Others moreover were to be found near Taranto in the instep of Italy (soon after 1400), and upon the island of Ischia off Naples. The history of the Mediterranean has at last reached the central regions of that sea. The west, too, now comes into the picture. For the Mycenaeans wanted its metals. What they needed most, for the conversion of Cypriot copper into bronze, was tin to supplement the slender supplies available on the Greek mainland and archipelago. More could be got from Etruria and Spain and even England, and all three of these sources were now, at least indirectly, within their reach. Etruria was accessible from Ischia. Vigorous cultures which continued to succeed one another in south-east Spain knew of the Mycenaeans, or were even colonised by them, unless Troy was responsible (p. 84). Such contacts in the far west were steps of great boldness, since travellers in those waters beyond Sicily had to do without the sight of land in a pathless sea to which Aegean sailors were unaccustomed. And these sailors and traders also had some sort of commerce with more distant countries still, since from *c.* 1500 onwards their beads and curvilinear decorative motifs penetrated into France and as far as England and Ireland.

The maintenance of such communications required many

improvements in shipping; and this was the age of the slim clean-lined sea-rover, furnished, as far as their small sketches show, with new types of rigging, battle-rams, and as many as fifty oars.

Towards the end of the second millennium, however, as the whole near and middle east seethed with violent movements of population, far-reaching voyages had to be gradually sacrificed to home defence. Documents reveal, for example, that Pylos was now guarded by ten naval stations with garrisons varying in size from thirty-six to a hundred and thirty men. A fortification was built across the whole or part of the isthmus of Corinth. And the walls of the cities themselves were extended and strengthened.

But these measures were unavailing. Even if it was the Mycenaeans who took Troy (p. 85), very soon afterwards their own centres collapsed, on the mainland as well as overseas. Perhaps this was a piecemeal process that took place around 1200 or during the first half of the twelfth century BC, comprising first a progressive decline of trade and then the downfall of Pylos (presumably as a result of seaborne attacks), followed by the final completion, by sea or land or both, of a process of destruction that had already been gradually encroaching upon Mycenae and Tiryns. Athens seems to have been partially exempt (p. 134), but was now only an enclave in general chaos. This may partly have been brought about by internal or intercity strife, though unknown external marauders were probably the principal agents of devastation.

One of the great hordes now in motion consisted of a barbarous Indo-European-speaking people, the Dorians, who came like their forerunners from the north. It is possible (though it cannot be proved) that they were the destroyers of Pylos, Mycenae and Tiryns. Or the destruction may have been the work of the so-called 'Urnfield peoples' who had spread over much of Europe in the preceding centuries – practisers of cremation, the rite not of the historical Mycenaeans but of Homer's description of them. At all events the epoch had ended in a holocaust, and another age was now about to begin.

5

The Expansion of Israel, Phoenicia and Carthage

Philistines and Hebrews

In the general break-up before and after 1200 BC, one of the sea peoples that had ravaged the Mediterranean (p. 59) established itself at the southern extremity of the Levant seaboard, before it turns at a right-angle towards Egypt. These were the Philistines, who during the twelfth century subdued the Canaanite population throughout the coastal region between Mount Carmel and Sinai. The northern half of this strip was the plain of Sharon, but it was the other part, subsequently called Philistia, which contained the chief towns of their later confederacy. The principal centre, Ashdod, three miles from the sea, possessed no harbour (since the flat straight beaches of this shore had none) but commanded the road which led from Egypt and the southernmost Philistine town, Gaza, up towards the cities of Phoenicia and Syria.

It is difficult to form any objective assessment of the Philistines, because their Hebrew neighbours disliked them extremely, as abusive modern associations of the word suggest. Indeed, the Philistines were formidable rivals who reduced the Hebrews, for a time, to impotence (*c.* 1050), bequeathing to the Holy Land its historic name of Palestine, which has been given such emotive significance in modern times, first by its association with a British mandated territory and then as the designation for a hoped-for Arab state.

One of the Hebrew prophets indicated that the Philistines had come from Caphtor,[1] a term which may cover various east Mediterranean shorelands but seems to refer particularly to

Crete. Philistia certainly possessed strong links with the Cretans and even stronger ones with the Mycenaeans. Its numerous and distinctive wine-jars display locally interpreted imitations of Mycenaean styles; and the armour of Goliath, the champion of the Philistines, was of Aegean character. Although nothing of their speech and script has survived except a few proper names, they seem to have spoken a language that was not Semitic like that of their Hebrew neighbours, but wholly or partly Indo-European. However, the Canaanites who became their subjects evidently exercised a reciprocal influence, since Philistine towns generally retained their Canaanite nomenclature.

The strength of Philistia lay partly in high-prowed ships which are depicted by Egyptian artists, and partly in horses and raiding chariots, but principally in the use of iron which was produced under efficient, monopolistic control and became a common, everyday metal for the first time. The Egyptians were impressed by the huge round shields of the Philistines, and their stout swords. Iron also began to be used for the tips of ploughs, so that they could deal better with heavier soils. A further new technical aid of a different sort consisted of the camel, which was domesticated in about the twelfth century and subsequently inaugurated great caravans to Mesopotamia (p. 119).

Behind this coastal area occupied by the Philistines lay stretches of upland: the hills of Samaria, and then, farther south, Judaea, into which Hebrews, taking advantage of the disturbances after 1300, gradually infiltrated from Egypt, perhaps joining other tribes which had remained behind and associating with them in a loose confederation.

This rocky little plateau, only a thousand square miles in extent, was watered in autumn and spring by the 'former' and 'latter' rains of the Bible, but they are the least reliable and predictable in all the Mediterranean. Yet the rain-water was eked out by dew, and the Hebrews, longing for a country of their own, saw this as a 'land of hills and valleys, that drinketh water of the rain of heaven, a land which the Lord thy God careth for'; a land with corn and wine and olive, and flowing with milk and honey.[2] The bush and scrub uplands also pastured sheep and particularly goats, and in ancient times, before this pasturage and other human causes had reduced the woodlands to scrub, potentially productive soil was more extensive than it ever has been again until the reclamations of modern times. From Gezer, near the border between Philistia and Judaea, comes a limestone plaque of the tenth century BC which gives a calendar of the agricultural and horticultural year.

While not wholly invulnerable and fairly close to the main caravan routes, Judaea did not bestride them since they passed alongside on lower ground. Prophets complained that the country was too accessible to outside influences, and yet there remained at most times an element of detachment about such exchanges. The same judicious blend of isolation and accessibility was apparent in the choice of Jerusalem as the Hebrew capital. The place dated back to *c.* 2600 BC, having been founded originally, as recent excavations show, on a site south-east of the later and higher Old City, in order to guard an essential spring in the valley. A wall was built in *c.* 1800, if not earlier. Then, during the period preceding the arrival of the Hebrews, this had been one of the last surviving outposts of the Egyptians before they retreated into their own country. The Canaanite tribe that succeeded them carried out, during the thirteenth century, a major town-planning operation, constructing massive stone-filled terraces. After resisting the Hebrews for longer than almost any other town, Jerusalem was finally taken by David in about 996 BC.

It occupied a central position, controlling the main longitudinal hill-traffic through Judaea. Only eighteen miles to the south lay Hebron, where Abraham had come before the trek to Egypt, and in the other direction, by way of Samaria, it was not more than fifty miles to the Jezreel (Esdraelon) plain which broke through the hills and linked Jordan to the sea. Jerusalem too, was less than twenty miles from Jordan's extension, the Dead Sea, and scarcely twice as far to the Mediterranean. Yet the fall to the Dead Sea is a steep one, and the approach from the Mediterranean is through tortuous rocky defiles. The city is two thousand five hundred feet above sea-level, and its projecting spur of the Judaean hills is surrounded by valleys on three sides. Furthermore the network of tribes into which the Hebrews were grouped had set no mark on the place. Their kings Saul and then David (*c.* 1000–980) had suffered from the unreliability of these units, and so David rejected their holy place

Bethel eleven miles away – which excavations prove to have been sacked four times within the previous two hundred years – and made Jerusalem the capital for every tribe alike.

Pushing back or suppressing the Aramaean states to the north (p. 118), David also broke the supremacy of the Philistines, establishing a port at Joppa (Jaffa-Tel Aviv) which cut them off from the northern half of their dominions in the Sharon plain. Yet the Philistines, although patriotically minimised by Jewish tradition, taught the Hebrews horse-breeding, chariot warfare, iron working, and many industrial techniques, and contributed a number of loan-words to their language. The history of Israel, like its geography, oscillated between this externalising, cosmopolitan element and a strong opposite tendency towards separateness and introversion. It was the latter set of influences which transformed ancestral religious traditions into an intense and ethical monotheism, severing the divine from the mortal plane, in contrast with the Greeks who were already moving towards humanistic conceptions. As in the highlands of Iran, where another austere faith was created, there were people in Israel who felt a vigorous, puritanical spirit of revolt against what seemed to be Mediterranean hedonism. Since, moreover, the relationships of the Hebrews with most of their neighbours varied from suspicion to open hostility, there was no live-and-let-live tendency to recognise the religions of other peoples. No other god but their own could exist.

Later, when the Jews were scattered far and wide, these ideas meant that Jehovah did not vanish with his kings, becoming instead the first of all gods to survive his original political basis. But in the time of David, as in the same area today, religion and politics still went together, and it was amid the stirring of these explosive ideas that the Hebrews, profiting by temporary weaknesses of the surrounding great powers, now became the largest and most truly independent nation ever yet seen in the Levant.

The full grandeur of this Hebrew state of Israel developed under David's last-born son and successor Solomon, who controlled vassal states up to two hundred and fifty miles northwards as far as Hamath (Hama) which commanded the Orontes valley. The horse-drawn chariots imported to the region by the Philistines, a sign of high rank under David, had become by

Solomon's time an important factor in military power, as the presence of four hundred and fifty well-built horse-boxes at the fortress of Megiddo confirms. The large-scale adaptation of Philistine metal-working, too, is shown by excavations at Ezion-geber near the northern end of the gulf of Eilat (Akaba), which have disclosed Solomon's elaborate and unique smelting and refining plants. So as to generate the maximum heat, these metalworks were situated at a place where the wind is strongest, and woods which could supply the refineries with fuel were not too far away. Both copper and iron were amply exploited. At Cartan in the Jordan valley many bronze objects of the tenth century have been discovered, and the increased use of iron made for greater efficiency (p. 112). So also, especially in regard to agriculture, did a new and rapidly extended practice of lining cisterns with waterproof lime-plaster for the conservation and storage of rainwater.

But Solomon was not content to improve upon his Philistine heritage alone, since he also formed a mutually profitable alliance with the Phoenician port of Tyre, and gave Jerusalem a palace and temple that were largely Phoenician in character.[3] The temple,[4] built in *c.* 960 BC, comprised an inner sanctuary, a hall, and side chambers three storeys high. Craftsmen were brought from Tyre and Byblos, and timber came seaborne on floats from Tyre to Jerusalem's port of Joppa, from which it was sent up to the capital by land. In front of an entrance porch of Syrian-Phoenician style stood two bronze pillars imitated from the shrine of the Tyrian god Melkart. The scheme of decoration too, with its carved cherubim and flowers, recalled the motifs of Phoenician ivories and bronzes; and intermediaries from the same area brought knowledge of Assyria's sacred palms, which provided models for the volute-capitals used for decorative purposes throughout the realm of Solomon and his successors, as well as on the island of Cyprus. These motifs in their turn closely prefigure a form of early Greek capital which became an ancestor of the Ionic Order.

The political strength of the Hebrews rapidly declined, because after Solomon it proved impossible to maintain the national unity, and the country, already almost divided by a Canaanite enclave, split into two parts. The ten northern tribes established a new dynasty to form the kingdom of Israel, which after two changes of capital established its royal residence at Samaria, a central observation-point close to the plains both of Sharon and Jezreel. The single tribe of Judah, later enlarged by border rectifications, remained under the house of David, with its capital at Jerusalem. Both states flourished in the eighth century BC, Israel as a land of aristocrats and wealthy merchants and Judah with a more homogeneous population. Yet neither kingdom was large or strong enough to exert independent political influence, or even – for very long – to survive. In *c.* 721 Samaria was taken by the Assyrian king Sargon II. Judah, more compact, held out until 597, when Jerusalem succumbed to the Babylonian army of Nebuchadnezzar. A subsequent revolt was followed by two years' siege, at the end of which the city was captured and razed to the ground (586).

Massive deportations led to the widespread dispersion which in due course spread the influence of the Jews and their religion throughout the Mediterranean area to which, in origin, this faith was so alien. Not long after the fall of Jerusalem, however, a partial return to the homeland began when the Persians, who had succeeded to Babylon's empire, allowed forty-two thousand Jews to go back to a small area round Jerusalem. A new temple was built (516), and subsequent Mediterranean empires allowed or encouraged the existence of small local principalities of Hebrew faith, but it was not until the most modern times that a state comparable in strength with Solomon's has been re-established.

Syria and Phoenicia

The downfall of the Hittites in the thirteenth century BC caused a vacuum over a huge area. But throughout the Mesopotamian and Syrian borderlands of Asia Minor Hittite influence was not destroyed, since a group of small kingdoms formed a 'strange Hittite afterglow' which lasted for nearly five hundred years. They are often called neo-Hittite, but the Hittite-descended rulers were only a veneer over populations containing complex racial mixtures of Canaanites and many others. The survival of such régimes was due to the strength of their round or oval hill-top towns surrounded by massive walls, sometimes in two concentric circles.

Although the territories of some of these states came down as far as the Mediterranean, most of them were based on centres in the interior. Hamath regained its independence after Solomon, and precariously enjoyed freedom, even possessing several vassal dependencies of its own upon the seaboard. Another princedom, north of Hamath, included the ancient port of Alalakh (near the later Antioch) and its Amik plain, where the Luvian language of southern Asia Minor was still spoken, and written in Hittite hieroglyphs. To the north again, a further state, with its inland capital at Zincirli upon Mount Amanus, reached the coast on the Gulf of Iskenderun (Alexandretta). Round the corner in Asia Minor was yet another small principality which, after these southern neighbours had already begun to fade, temporarily established control over the historic Cilician plain. Its capital, as in earlier centuries, was probably at Adana; and neighbouring Tarsus, which was still the area's vital port and perhaps at times a capital on its own account, produced pottery reflecting influences from the Greek mainland. But even more intricate cultural blends are found some sixty miles to the north-east of these towns at two eighth century fortresses which guarded the approaches to Cilicia from either side of the River Ceyhan (Pyramus). For one of these strongholds had a bilingual inscription in linear Phoenician and hieroglyphic Hittite, and artistic objects combining Phoenician, Egyptian and also Assyrian motifs.

The Assyrians, not far distant from these lands, had been a power to reckon with for a millennium, and at intervals they reasserted their control. Yet such spectacular excursions were preceded and punctuated by periods of sharp political decline. One of these setbacks was caused by a fresh wave of Semitic-speaking immigrants or conquerors, the Aramaeans. The first identifiable peoples using those languages had been the Babylonians (Akkadians) in fourth-millennium Mesopotamia. Next came the turn of the Levant, which had successively absorbed Canaanites and Phoenicians and Hebrews; and now came the Aramaeans who, like their predecessors, spoke a west Semitic dialect. The invasion and infiltration of these originally uncouth nomads continued from the fourteenth century onwards during the next two hundred years, when the whole of the eastern Mediterranean was suffering from upheavals. Temporarily overwhelming both Assyria and Babylonia, the Aramaeans broke during the twelfth century into the central latitudes of Syria, where their tribes eventually consolidated into a series of small states bordering upon the more northerly neo-Hittite kingdoms. At first the frontier between these distinct and hostile groups passed south of Hamath through Lebanon, but then the Aramaeans conquered Hamath and Zincirli and their respective strips of Mediterranean coast, leaving the Amik valley and its hinterland as the only parts of Syria under neo-Hittite control.

The Aramaeans were landsmen, skilled in the caravan-traffic which crossed their territories. Yet these small states had no easy time in a world of larger powers. This was true even of the strongest of them, Damascus, situated beyond Anti-Lebanon in a thirty-mile-wide plain famous for its cornlands, orchards, gardens and olive-groves. First the princes of Damascus had to contend with their momentarily powerful Hebrew neighbours during the successive reigns of Saul, David and Solomon. Then Damascus became an ally of Israel and tried to resist the Assyrians. But the coalition it led against them in 853 BC was defeated at Qarqar in the neighbourhood of Hamath.

The next threat to the Aramaeans occurred during the following century, when many of their states became the vassals of a new great power formed by the rulers of Urartu. These were a people of horsemen and herdsmen, Hurrian (p. 70) in religion and perhaps Caucasian in tongue, who derived most of their art from Assyria but displayed an expertise in metal-work, engineering and irrigation which strongly influenced not only the Phrygians in Asia Minor but Greeks and Etruscans (pp. 153, 235). From their capital far to the east on Lake Van, the Urartians established protectorates over the neo-Hittite territories along the lower Orontes valley and sea-coast, and pushed south through Syria where they reduced a number of Aramaean centres.

At the end of the eighth century, however, the power of Urartu was broken by the Assyrians. These now proceeded to annex the neo-Hittite kingdoms which the Urartians had taken over – before long we hear of a ruler on the Gulf of Iskenderun being executed – while the Aramaean states resumed their efforts to maintain an independent existence. Sometimes they prospered, but it was not very long before Damascus and its allies succumbed finally to Tiglath-Pileser III of Assyria (*c.* 733), and soon afterwards a similar confederacy, under the leadership of Hamath, was overwhelmed in a second disastrous battle of Qarqar (*c.* 721).

Following the immemorial custom of the region the Aramaeans were not so much cultural innovators themselves as pickers up of other people's cultures, including a simple practical script modified from Phoenician models. And yet these were the people destined to impose their language upon the entire near-eastern world: for by the time of Jesus, who himself spoke Aramaic, this Semitic dialect reigned unchallenged as common speech over an enormous area.

West of Damascus there is a stretch of coast on which the great ports of Phoenicia were concentrated within easy reach of one another. Their inhabitants were Canaanites who had escaped absorption by the more recently arrived Aramaeans owing to the protection afforded by the Lebanon massif which rises steeply in the immediate hinterland.

Certain passes, it is true, were inviting to enemies; at either extremity of the range, for example, were rivers, the Litani (Leontes) and the Nahr el Kelb (Eleutheros), of which the flanks are inscribed by many invaders. Yet these passes brought traders even more often than conquerors along the camel-caravan routes which were beginning to open up again in the tenth century BC. And with the help of these perennial streams, each community had its own strip of cultivable land, small but fertile enough to grow vines and olives, and breed sheep and goats and cattle.

But the towns looked not so much landwards as out to sea, from their harbours on bold headlands and adjoining islets. One of these ports, the ancient centre of Byblos, remained an Egyptian base during most of the second millennium BC, but by *c.* 1100 it was obliged to change its allegiance when Tiglath-Pileser I of Assyria invaded the Mediterranean coastlands and extorted tribute. Contributions were also made by two other cities, Sidon, forty miles south of Byblos, and Arvad (Aradus), fifty miles away on the other side. This admission of suzerainty meant that the timber and other resources of the cities came into Assyrian hands. Yet during a subsequent period of stress Assyria could not maintain control.

Nor, any longer, could Egypt, since the country's imperfect recovery from external attacks (p. 59) meant that its merchant-princes trading in the Levant did not obtain much political backing from home. Early in the eleventh century, a generation after the Assyrian invasion, an Egyptian envoy Wen-Amun tells how he received little comfort from Zakarbaal, ruler of Byblos.[5] To begin with, it was difficult to obtain an interview with this prince, 'who was sitting in his upper chamber and leaning his back against the window while the waves of the great Syrian sea beat against the rocks below'. But this sea, insisted Wen-Amun, 'belongs to Amon [the god of Egypt] and his is the Lebanon; it is merely a plantation for the Boat of Amon'. However, the Byblian felt strong enough to answer, 'I am neither your servant nor the servant of him that sent you'. From now on Egypt could no longer conquer in these regions. The most it could do was to offer alliances and commercial agreements.

At this time Byblos apparently still had some sort of dominance over Sidon and Tyre. But during the forthcoming period, when Phoenicia assumed extraordinary importance at sea, first Sidon and then Tyre profited from the long maritime experience of their neighbour to take the lead themselves. Pictures of their trading ships show curved prows and sterns, and two banks of oars below a raised deck protected at the sides by shields*. The Phoenicians are said to have been the first people to navigate by observing the stars; to travel beyond sight of land; to sail at night; and to undertake voyages in winter-time.

Cyprus had been visited by Phoenician traders by the turn of the millennium, and two hundred years later it received colonists from Tyre who established tributary kingdoms based on Citium (Larnaca) beside the south-east coast, and on the double acropolis of Idalium fifteen miles inland. The civilisation of Cyprus during the next two centuries shows a strange fusion of elements from Phoenicia and Israel, together with con-

* It is uncertain whether they or the Greeks invented the two-banked system of oars (p. 157).

servative traditions still retained from Mycenaean times. This cross-fertilisation of cultures was accompanied by a strong vein of native fantasy expressed in local gold work and gaily extravagant paintings and terracottas showing scenes from daily life.

From Cyprus the Phoenicians moved rapidly, with the aid of their abundant local shipbuilding timber, into the wider inheritance of far-flung trading stations and factories left by the Mycenaeans. Phoenician commercial bases appeared on the coasts of the Aegean islands, Cilicia, Cyprus and north Africa. Their activities also extended as far as Malta, Sicily, Sardinia, and the south of France. In Spain too, there were particularly important centres even outside the Strait of Gibraltar, notably Gades (Cadiz) and the so far unidentifiable Tartessus, which like their other settlements were later taken over by Tyre's daughter-city Carthage (p. 126). The Greeks also colonised the same regions, but it seems likely that the Phoenicians, though their western Mediterranean expansion was not quite so large as used to be believed, entered this part of the sea a few years before their competitors.

The rise of Sidon ('the fishery') came suddenly in *c.* 990–980, when the victories of the Israelites under David relieved these cities from the Aramaean peril which had seemed likely to succeed earlier menaces from Assyria and Egypt. Built along the north slope of a headland a little distance from the shore, the town was not invulnerable, but there was adequate room for expansion. The port comprised two harbours, including an exposed bay on the south and a more protected northern basin formed by a low line of rocks (strengthened by a wall) extending from the end of the promontory towards the mainland.

Tyre (Sur, 'the rock'), twenty miles from Sidon, was called its daughter. Probably, that is to say, its population included Sidonian immigrants, in addition to sea-raider settlers and coastal Canaanites; for the tombs of the area show a variety of burial rites. Supported by David and Solomon, whose temple at Jerusalem was commissioned from Tyrians, these people took the lead in Phoenicia and for a time at least their king Hiram (*c.* 970–936) ruled Sidon as well. Tyre lay a few hundred yards from the mainland on the two largest of a chain of rocky islands. Hiram joined these islands together by an embankment and linked them to the coast by a mole, thus forming two excellent harbours, the northern one protected by the chain of isles and connected with the other, which was artificial, by a canal. Air and submarine archaeology have revealed partially submerged quays, and the turrets and battlements of the town appear on an Assyrian relief. In the ninth and eighth centuries trade continued to mount and multiply in the many-storeyed houses of Tyre, 'the crowning city, whose merchants are princes, whose traffickers are the honourable of the earth.'[6]

As in the most antique past, many of these cargoes consisted of the timber of Lebanon, to which the Old Testament refers in detail.[7] But an even more important export consisted of clothing and textiles coloured with the dyes which Phoenicians derived from the spiny-shelled *murex* (rock-whelk) caught in baskets off their coast. Each *murex* secreted two precious drops of yellowish liquid from which tones ranging from rose to dark violet could be extracted in boiling vats. In the absence of mineral stains, this was the only fast and firm dye the ancients possessed, because it did not need to be treated with fixatives like vegetable colourings. Since the molluscs hide during high summer and do not produce a good colour in spring, they could only be collected in autumn and winter, which was one of the reasons why the Phoenicians initiated the practice of sailing out of season (p. 120). Factories (located to the lee side of the town owing to their unpleasant smell) have left great mounds of shells on the outskirts of Tyre and Sidon, indicating the enormous scale of the exploitation.

The inhabitants of this coast may well have owed their national name of dark red or purple men (*phoinikes*) to the lucrative monopoly which transformed their robes into these colours. The materials had at first been imported ready-woven by way of the various harbours along the Levantine coast. Crete had been one of the places that sent them, but after that island's final decline the Phoenicians and Syrians imported raw wool instead, and exercised their own outstanding gifts as weavers and embroiderers.

With the aid of the fuel abundantly supplied by the adjacent Lebanese hills they also became excellent metallurgists, working and exporting silver brought from Cilicia, and copper from Cyprus; many trading-stations in the west were located with a view to obtaining the tin which was needed to convert this copper into bronze (p. 69). The Phoenicians were also famous for the techniques of gold repoussé and granulation which they had learnt from Mycenae and Egypt. And the Egyptians again – whose influence was stronger here than in northern Syria – taught them the art of converting their fine, flinty river sand into popular and exportable glass. 'The Phoenician, though he possessed an artistic bent, was less interested in art for his own purposes than for the price he could get for it abroad.'[8] Accordingly, like earlier peoples in this cultural melting-pot, he obtained his aesthetic ideas from a great number of different sources. For example the local ivory work (p. 76) synthesised Egyptian, Canaanite, Aramaean and Cypriot models into neat and delicate masterpieces which in turn gave many ideas to the Greeks. An even stronger influence was exercised by the Phoenician and Syrian alphabet, which before *c.* 800, serving a literature that is unknown to us, developed from Canaanite models into full maturity. This form of writing then spread to the Greeks, who were, however, obliged to supplement the system with signs indicating vowels (p. 150).

Assyria's recovery in the ninth century brought heavy pressure not only upon the neo-Hittite and Aramaean states but upon the Phoenicians as well. Tyre and Sidon were among the cities which bowed before the storm and paid successive Assyrian monarchs their tribute of gold, silver, fine many-coloured cloths, and ivory. Governors too were planted by Assyria in the cities of the coastland and interior alike (*c.* 742), and Tyre and Sidon, though still allowed to fell timber in the Lebanon, were taxed (amid rioting) when it came down to the warehouses. Sargon II, however, 'gave peace' to Tyre, and Sennacherib and others used its sailors, but Esarhaddon (681–669) laid waste rebellious Sidon and allowed artists to represent him holding the prince of Tyre on a leash. On the leash, too, is shown the contemporary king of the Egyptians, since now for the first time in history (though for less than twenty years' duration) one of the two main centres of near eastern civilisation, Egypt, had been conquered by the other, Mesopotamia.

Meanwhile the Assyrians were producing various institutions which subsequently, through Phoenicia and Syria, exercised much influence upon the later Mediterranean world. One such heritage was their thoroughly worked out concept of a large-scale, well-organised empire based on good communications. Fruitful innovations in the architectural field included the principle of the real semicircular (no longer corbelled) arch, which was later developed by the Etruscans and Romans; and they also drew upon types of castellated fortifications which the Assyrians had designed for towns lacking natural defences. Other buildings with a future were Assyria's porticoed palaces at its capital Nineveh and elsewhere, constructed in a monumental style owing debts to Sumerians, Babylonians, Hurrians and Hittites. These palaces, with their walls painted or covered with brightly glazed bricks, were guarded by great winged, human-headed stone bulls and lions, adapted by many a Greek artist who knew them directly or through Syrian intermediaries. And the Greeks again, followed with greater elaboration by the Romans, adopted the Assyrian device of converting the old single-scene reliefs or paintings into continuous narratives of royal campaigns or hunts. An imposing precedent was also set by libraries of tablets dealing with astronomy, astrology, geology, geography, law, religion, medicine and magic.

Assyria's position, however, began to weaken when its neighbours the Medes of north-western Persia asserted their independence in about 620. Soon afterwards, in alliance with Babylon, they jointly attacked and destroyed Nineveh. The Babylonians took over the Assyrian heritage, and six years later ejected an Egyptian army which had again penetrated from end to end of the Levant. This victory, at Carchemish, was won by the king's son Nebuchadnezzar, who during his own subsequent reign achieved unprecedented grandeur in the new buildings of his capital. He also captured Tyre, which fell after a siege of thirteen years (*c.* 571), whereas Sidon apparently gave in without a struggle and was consequently restored to its ancient position as the chief Phoenician town.

Yet when the overthrow of Babylon by the Persians brought to an end the vast phase of near eastern history which Mesopotamia had dominated (539), Sidon and Tyre displayed greater powers of survival than their master. For, although they too passed into the Persian empire for more than two centuries, they continued to provide the conquerors with seamen and fleets.

Carthage and the west

Shortly before and after 800 BC, the Phoenicians began to develop their trading posts into colonies. The most important of these settlements were in north Africa, where the 'New City' of Carthage (Kart-Hadasht) was established by Tyre. The traditional foundation date was 814 BC – and the earliest cemetery burials so far discovered go back at least as far as the eighth century. Probably the purple-beds in the neighbouring Gulf of Tunis, which enabled Phoenician settlers to practise the principal industry of their homeland, contributed to their choice of the site. But this, like their other early foundations, was also well chosen to safeguard vital points along the maritime lifelines to the west (p. 128). Carthage's exceptional importance, however, was due to its position at the narrow waist of the Mediterranean, which is only seventy-five miles wide at this point.

Situated on a peninsula in the recesses of the Gulf of Tunis, the place was well protected from the hinterland, and among its several beaches a southward-facing bay behind a small headland provided a spacious and sheltered port. This was later augmented by two artificial harbours which have been identified with lagoons lying north of the bay, just over half a mile from the citadel hill. Carthaginian houses normally had two storeys but sometimes as many as six,[9] with internal courtyards and almost windowless outside walls as in Arab and African cities today. Since well-water was only available eighty feet below ground, many of the dwellings also possessed their own cisterns for the collection of rain.

Thirty miles north-east was the other leading Phoenician foundation of Utica (Henchir bou Chateur), on rising ground beside the opposite bank of the River Medjerda (Bagradas). The river mouth, which has now moved five miles away, was then adjacent; and indeed both Utica and Carthage may at one time have been islands.

For a century or two these places were simply colonies of Tyre, but then, apart from nominal and decreasing ties, they became independent both of Tyre and of one another. But Utica, though jealous, was soon much less important than its neighbour. The populace of Carthage was allowed a share of the profits and remained sluggishly non-political, while the government owed stability and strength to the tenacious, cautious ruling class which controlled its republican system.[10]

Under this guidance, before the middle of the seventh century BC, Carthage had taken over and greatly extended and reinforced Phoenician trading posts and settlements all over the Mediterranean. Like their predecessors, the Carthaginians chose to plant 'emporia' – carefully spaced-out anchorages on offshore islands and promontories or at river estuaries, with populations of not more than a few hundred people apiece. Preference was given to locations possessing a good source of fresh water, natural salt-pans, and if possible a limestone outcrop to provide masonry and accommodate the community's rock tombs. And there must, above all, be a suitable sheltered beach, however little, on which traders and settlers could draw up their rounded, keeled, high-bulwarked merchant ships, or the long war galleys with figureheads of Carthage's frightening gods.

Like the Phoenicians, these seafarers wanted metals from Spain; and indeed this became the most vital of their needs. But to sail due westwards in that direction along the unwelcoming African coast was to risk a lee shore and hostile current. The Carthaginians also hoped for supplies from Etruria far up the west coast of Italy. But neither Etruria nor Spain were accessible without bases on the islands which lay upon the intermediate sea-routes, namely Sicily, Sardinia, Corsica and the Balearics.

Bases in Sicily were again essential to control the narrow strait beside Carthage, so that the western Mediterranean could be closed to all incursions from Greece and the Levant. Along the western tip of Sicily, which was nearest to Carthage, there were already several Phoenician settlements. After Greek settlers from other parts of the island had tried to expel them (*c.* 580), the Carthaginians openly intervened in the island and assumed leadership of the Phoenician colonists. Thenceforward, for three disturbed centuries, in spite a heavy defeat by the Greeks at Himera (480), it remained their cardinal policy to retain this Sicilian foothold.

The principal Carthaginian port in the island was at Motya, a polyglot town of many-storeyed buildings which may have served as models for later tenements on the Italian mainland. Motya, near the present Marsala, stood in a sheltered bay on a small low off-shore island which an artificial mole connected to a long, rocky, mainland peninsula beside a small coastal plain. Recent excavations have revealed an inner dock with a canal. Motya was well placed as an intermediary with Etruria, and so were other Carthaginian towns nearby; while, round the corner, this same purpose was even clearer at Panormus (Palermo), where a roomy basin terminating in a small inner harbour, recessed and protected from westerlies, faced directly north towards Italy.

On Sardinia, from which the Carthaginians obtained supplies of lead, they inherited and developed four ports, three of them on promontories: Nora, near the southernmost point of the island, dated back to a Phoenician foundation soon after 800 or even earlier. As for Corsica, Carthage imported its wax and honey, but the island was chiefly significant because of its proximity to the Etruscan mines of Elba. When, therefore, Greeks from Phocaea tried to settle at Aleria (Alalia) on the Corsican east coast opposite Elba (p. 173), the Carthaginians and Etruscans opposed them with a combined fleet which, although defeated, inflicted such severe losses on the Phocaeans that they had to leave (535). The two allies were on sufficiently good terms to form a joint community on the Etruscan coast at Pyrgi, and Carthage also had a colony a little farther north at S. Marinella, fifty miles from Rome with which the Carthaginians are believed to have signed an early treaty (509). The victory of Aleria benefited them more than their allies, since it strengthened their hold over Corsica. Using that island as a base they were able to remain in touch with Phoenician ports and off-shore islets of southern France – a Phoenician temple was the origin of Monaco – though Greek Massalia remained in general control of the area (p. 173).

Far more vital, however, was Spain. On the way there was the Balearic island of Ebusus (Ibiza), which the Carthaginians occupied (*c.* 654–653 BC) so as to keep the Greeks away from this stepping stone to all the Spanish wealth. For the exploitation of Spain's silver, copper and tin were as necessary to the existence of the Carthaginians as if the mines had been located a few miles from the city. On the south-eastern coasts of the peninsula, the Carthaginians took over and greatly enlarged a Phoenician settlement at Malaca (Malaga), which had a deep harbour protected by a cape and hill from natives and recurrent floods. Commanding a hinterland valley route that led to a gap in the Sierra Nevada, Malaca made and sold oil from the olives of the Guadalmedina estuary plain, and exploited the neighbouring salt pans in order to pickle and export fish. Forty miles farther east, at Sexi (Almunecar), recent excavations have unearthed Egyptian jars pointing to trading relations with the east during the ninth century BC. A settlement by the Phoenicians soon followed. For they and their Carthaginian offspring were the people – although the Greeks quickly became rivals (p. 171) – who first opened up the Mediterranean from end to end, making it a civilised lake.

Moreover, at a very early date they passed through the Strait of Gibraltar into the Atlantic – a hard thing to do unless a levanter (east wind) is blowing. Gades may well have been founded before 800, no later than Carthage. Concentrated upon the northern extremity of what is now a peninsula linked with the shore by sedimentation, but was then an island athwart the mouth of the Guadalete river, this city was under Carthaginian occupation from *c.* 600, but exceptionally retained a merchant fleet of its own. Gades had easy access to the mines of southern Spain. So did another Phoenician harbour-town, which lay farther away still but may have been as old as Gades and even more important. This was Tartessus, which became an independent ally of the Carthaginians until its destruction (perhaps by them) in *c.* 500. The people of Tartessus knew of Ireland and Britain, and the gold treasures found in south-west Spain may have come from them. The site of the place, hitherto unidentified, has been variously assigned to the Huelva area or to some point on the Guadalquivir (Baetis) river, either near Seville or lower down at the estuary.

Here, then, were two Phoenician and Carthaginian ports beyond the strait, which was closed to Greeks and described by them as the end of the accessible world.[11] The Mediterranean now came to be called the Internal Sea in contrast to the Atlantic, of which the discovery began. It is now widely accepted that in *c.* 600 a Phoenician expedition sponsored by Egypt circumnavigated Africa, sailing down the Red Sea and returning after just under three years;[12] and the Carthaginians, as they tightened their control over Spain, later used its coast as a base for further feats of Atlantic exploration.[13]

In its own country too Carthage had established a dominion larger than any previous Mediterranean state, except Egypt in the same continent. The immensely long, sinuous north African shoreline is different from most other Mediterranean seaboards because of the inhospitable character of its abrupt cliffs and dunes, and the shallowness of its bights and coves that are not true inlets. Furthermore these coasts are so completely cut off on the land side by the Atlas mountains and Sahara desert that Tunis, Algeria and Morocco are called the Island of the West. The greater part of their surface suffers from violent unstable conditions of drought, and the maritime areas tend to be both unhealthy and insecure. But a Mediterranean climate exists in certain inland regions with heavy soils well-watered by rainfall and suitable for continuous cultivation. In particular the country that is now Tunisia, where the barriers recede farthest from the sea, has large alluvial pockets, and the longitudinal basin of the river Medjerda (Bagradas) which empties its waters into the Gulf of Tunis is notably rich in natural phosphates. Among the products of this valley are the heaviest wheat crops of the ancient world and an abundance of olives, as well as vines and varied fruits including dates imported from the east. One of the outstanding techniques of Carthaginian farming, which Mago's handbooks on husbandry derived from the Greeks and handed down to the Romans, was dry-farming in areas of limited rainfall, comprising methods of treatment designed to conserve the natural moisture of soil for which no irrigation was available.

By the fifth century the Carthaginians had taken over the entire twenty thousand square miles of this Tunisian plain, thus acquiring a territorial empire and abandoning the traditional Phoenician policy of concentrating on maritime outposts. For the sake of these new rich lands and their cultivators,

Carthaginian religion shifted its emphasis from the Tyrian city-god Baal Hammon to the earth-goddess Tanit, akin to the ancient fertility deities. Reports, elaborated in Gustave Flaubert's *Salammbo*, that babies were burnt alive in sacrifice to these divinities have been confirmed by infant remains now discovered in a Carthage sanctuary. The spirit of this gruesome faith, which was unaccompanied by any original artistic manifestations, consisted of submissive weakness before the overwhelming, capricious power of the gods. A primitive, persistent impulse demanded that the maintenance of their protective, fertilising activity must be guaranteed by continuous supplies of human blood.

Although the Carthaginians never obtained a secure footing on the interior plateau, it was they who handed on the products of Africa to the Mediterranean world : not only agricultural techniques, but gold, ivory, wild beasts and especially slaves. Such cargoes were transmitted by the settlers whom they planted at many points along the coast. These colonists were allowed to intermarry with Berbers and other natives of these areas, generating mixed races of descendants who prospered as seamen and farmers and gave Carthage an effective mercenary force of light infantry, expert in ambushes or raids and capable of enduring conditions of extreme heat. Use of the Barbary horse, for which the Atlas plains were well suited, enabled Carthage to push westwards into what is now Algeria and Morocco and eventually to enlarge their dominion in Spain to an extent that made a clash with Rome inevitable (p. 263).

PART TWO
The Greeks

6

The Homeric Age

The revival of Greece

By about the twelfth century BC Dorian invaders or immigrants from the Balkans had infiltrated Greece down to its southernmost extremity (p. 110). But the old picture of their overwhelming the Mycenaean civilisation and introducing Greece to cremation and iron must be regarded with caution. In the first place it is not certain that they were the destroyers of the Mycenaeans (p. 110). Secondly, cremation originated not with the Dorians (who in any case did not all adopt the custom) but from Asia Minor where the rite had been practised for a long time; nor for that matter was it wholly unknown in Greece even before the Dorians. The hypothesis that the Dorians introduced iron into the country is equally mistaken, since this had already come to Greece from elsewhere (p. 74). And besides bronze, which Greece had inherited from earlier times, was still preferred, and this alloy, with its tin component presumably provided by local finds, continued for a long time to be the favourite material for weapons. From the eleventh century BC onwards iron objects begin to appear in Greece and Crete, but the metal was greatly inferior to the tempered product of later times. The *Iliad* mentions a lump of iron won as a prize at games, and Athena in the *Odyssey* appears in the guise of a ship-master carrying a cargo of shining iron to barter for copper from Cyprus. Iron was still rare, and its advent, although full of significance (p. 112), was no immediate revolution; nor was it due to the Dorians.

Indeed, the only material innovation that can at present be attributed to the Dorians is a simple style of dress consisting of a modified blanket, with a new sort of large violin-shaped pin at the shoulder. In the field of ideas and religion, however, they carried further the revolution initiated by earlier Indo-European-speaking inhabitants, continuing to superimpose upon the old earth-mother cults, as Plato noted,[1] the worship of the sky-god Zeus and his attendant deities, who now increasingly became the patrons of Hellenism.

Although the Dorians submerged large areas of Greece, not every region was affected. The ancient Mycenaean shrines of Delphi and Delos continued their historic careers. There was also a strong tradition, which may well be correct, that Athens repelled the newcomers; and the descendants of its Mycenaean population preserved independence. This city, therefore, may well have been a focus for the transmission of many Mycenaean customs and legends to later generations of Greeks. Athenian society did not, it is true, proceed to develop along Mycenaean lines. But that was partly because of the extensive influx of refugees from many afflicted areas, who intermarried with Athenians and created a new racial and cultural situation, exemplified by the simultaneous coexistence of cremation and inhumation rites. These displaced persons also helped to give Attica the largest population of any part of Greece,[2] and during the tenth century BC Athens, protected by its mountain barriers, became the strongest mainland state, in addition to retaining a measure of the sea-power which it had no doubt already possessed in Mycenaean times (p. 103).

At Athens, then, there was already a substantial basis on which to raise the city of the future. Most other towns, however, had to be built up from almost nothing. While waves of invaders and roaming bands were battering down the earlier cultures of Greece and fracturing its old tribal and clan organisations, the normal units were humble, isolated villages of related families, grouped together to hold down their serfs.

When resources grew a little larger, the next step was often for groups of adjacent villages to join together as single city-states.[3] This was what people believed had earlier happened at Athens. But the development or revival of this sort of amalgamation over a wide area was due to the Dorians, who found that only the fusion of their scattered villages could assure the impregnability and permanent mobilisation that were needed to maintain their dominance. In the north-eastern Peloponnese they fortified the double citadel of Argos, which inherited traditional institutions of nearby Mycenae, such as the earth-mother's hill-shrine now renamed after Hera. Argos retained control over a wide area until the eighth or seventh century BC, when the overlordship passed to another Dorian foundation, Sparta, near the south-eastern extremity of the peninsula. Already famous for its bronze-works and iron-mines, this region of Laconia, after suffering from catastrophic incursions of the sea caused by an eruption, had again become thickly inhabited after *c.* 1300 when more northerly regions were collapsing. During the twelfth century, there was another marked decline; and this may have been due to the initial impact of the Dorian incursions.

Sparta was situated on the River Eurotas, twenty miles from its south-coast estuary. This upper basin of the river was healthier than the marshy coastal lowlands, which were left to the subjugated earlier inhabitants, the Helots, to till. For while other Greeks satisfied their land-hunger by emigration and colonisation, the Spartan method was conquest, and so thorough was this that for over eight hundred years the city itself remained without walls or protection. Located on a mound which raised it above flood-level, the place was easily accessible on all sides. Like a few other sites in Greece, it was mainly chosen as a natural focus of communications, and in particular as a base not for defence but for punitive reprisals, in which blows could be struck out quickly in any direction. Though the mountains of the Peloponnese separated states, they could not hold up Spartan armies, and the ruling class maintaining this constant vigilance (which eventually developed into a terrifying discipline) always dwelt at the central point of Sparta itself and were forbidden to work at agriculture or any other civilian profession. Plato approved of the existence of such superior leisured classes dependent on a subject population, but his assumption was that the leisure would be available for education and politics (p. 203), at which the Spartans of historical times did not excel. In early days however their horizons were wide. At the beginning of the second millennium BC this corner of Laconia had already contained vigorous communities, owing to its proximity to Crete (p. 99); and already in the ninth century the links between the two countries were being restored, since Crete was colonised by Dorians from the Peloponnese.

Most of the city-states that now rose to importance were

centred upon citadel-towns, standing at some distance from the coast in order to ward off marine invaders. Such eyries were still favoured even when a convenient seaboard location was available,[4] and a particular preference was felt for mountain spurs or slopes ascending suddenly from the plain. These citadels were reminiscent of Mycenaean times, but now the walls enclosed not only the fortress but the whole urban population, whose houses and market-places were established on the level ground at the foot of the acropolis.

Usually also there was a pocket of fertile land within reach of the town. Yet most of these dependent areas were extremely small. Corinth and Chios had rather over three hundred square miles; the Boeotian city-states, apart from Thebes, averaged only seventy. Only three city-states possessed more than twenty thousand citizens – and only one of these, Athens, was on the Greek mainland, the others being in Sicily (p. 168). Sometimes fragmentation reached ridiculous lengths. The island of Ceos (Kea), close to the southern extremity of Attica, is only twelve miles long and six across – about the size of the Scottish island of Bute, or just over twice Manhattan Island; and yet these limited dimensions included no less than four separate city states. But the ancients saw no objection to such miniature dimensions. 'Better,' says a poet, 'a small city perched upon a rock than all the splendour of Nineveh.'[5] So long as a city-state can grow without losing its close-knit unity, said Plato, it should be allowed to grow – but no further, and that meant very little.[6]

The city-states of Greece, as contemporaries recognised, produced the finest achievements that civilised man had ever hitherto attained. They also evoked deep patriotism; exile from one's city was a terrible thing, as the poet Theognis knew.

> Cyrnus, I have heard the voice of the crane crying shrilly.
> It comes to me with its message that it is time
> To plough. It sets my black heart beating
> That other men have my fields with all their flowers.[7]

It was his own plot of land and his own city-state that he missed, not his country. For Greece was not a country. Its farmers, like those of Egypt and Mesopotamia, gradually aquired a surplus of wealth, but they did so without moving on to any wider political fusion. Geographical fragmentation had a lot to do with this, and helped to make self-sufficiency a leading aim. But geography does not explain everything, for although Greek urban civilisation failed to flourish in large lowland areas such as Thessaly and Macedonia, which had been earlier centres of progress, roots were often not struck in mountainous regions either. Moreover, there was no physical barrier between, for example, Corinth and Sicyon, and yet they remained independent; city-state boundaries did not invariably correspond with natural divisions. But the deliberate siting of the earliest towns away from the coast helped to isolate them, and so did the absence of common road-building. This separatism provides the reason why Zeus is ascribed such a large number of adulteries. The new chief god, who transcended the individual city states, had to be associated with their already existent and different local goddesses, so that he could be regarded as the father of their legendary children.

This lack of political unity also led to disastrous inter-city strife which was renewed for century after century. One of the earliest recorded historical events (*c.* 700 BC) was a bloody and protracted war between two city-states on the island of Euboea, Chalcis and Eretria, which lay only ten miles apart and were fighting for a tiny strip of plain. 'Strife,' said the poet Hesiod, 'is wholesome to men,'[8] and war was described as the first and most natural source of income, 'to procure wealth for the city from her foreign enemies'. Plato exalts this into a general law, stipulating that 'every city is in a natural state of war with every other, not indeed proclaimed by heralds, but everlasting'.[9] Long after Crete re-emerged as a Dorian country, the citizens of one of its most trivial city-states, Dreros, were still required to take an oath of hatred about their neighbours: 'I shall never be well disposed to the people of Lyttos by any device or contrivance, neither by night nor by day, and I shall strive as far as lies in my power to do ill to the city of Lyttos.'

Nevertheless this political decentralisation, and the local patriotisms which it engendered, provided a great competitive stimulus to artists. Already in the eleventh century BC a surprising new art, full of promising seeds for the future, showed itself in the construction and design of Greek pottery. Investing old Mycenaean shapes and patterns with fresh stability and reducing them to their formal fundamentals, this novel style displayed an invigorating, dynamic tautness, tension and rational proportion, achieved no longer by hand-drawing but by compass and multiple brush. In these 'small, bleak, thrifty designs'[10], Greek art had somehow been born; and it achieved a measure of uniformity, since vases of this sort, showing local variations, are found from Thessaly to the Argolid and then across the Aegean, with Athens, less poor and isolated than other areas, probably taking the lead.

From about 900 BC the initiative was again seized by the Athenians, when a ripe Geometric style accentuated the logical synthesising qualities of these experimental versions. The designs now incorporated a host of patterns – swastikas, zigzags, cubes, maeanders, keys and rings. Early in the eighth century, the repertoire is enlarged by the addition of animals, birds and rosettes which show dependence upon Syrian models (p. 160), since the wares of the two countries had begun to be exchanged again. Moreover a great future is hinted at by the appearance of human scenes, not woven into the ornament as in Celtic and other styles, but standing outside as separate units and compositions. It was still Athens which showed the greatest mastery of such inventions, but the less sophisticated pottery of certain Aegean islands, including particularly Euboea, contributed to the revival of artistic contacts between Greece and the east; and the refined products of Corinth at the strategic isthmus had wider influence still, reaching as far as Ithaca in the Ionian Sea.

The first identifiable Greek temples (*c.* 850–750) are just thatched, propped, timber cubicles, impoverished cottage versions of Mycenaean halls. But the far more developed ceramics industries, from all those centres, deny the name of Dark Age which our lack of information compels us to attach to the epoch.

The early Ionians

A little before 1000 BC there began a large eastward movement of mixed populations from Greece to the coasts and offshore islands of Asia Minor. This 'Ionian migration' was probably a result of the Dorian conquest of large parts of Greece, which had deprived many of the previous inhabitants of their subsistence. The migration was a joint, gradual achievement of numerous communities; but Athens' later claim to have been its leading spirit is corroborated by the resemblance of its dialect and festivals to those of Ionian foundations, and by the retention in their social system of the four names for tribes that were used at Athens. The Mycenaean refugees who had flocked to Athens could not return to their homes and were obliged by shortage of land to migrate somewhere else, and the whole enterprise needed the sea-power and leadership which the Athenians, who seem to have avoided the disasters that overtook other Mycenaean centres (p. 134), were able to provide. Moreover, after the long journey there were potentially hostile populations which could only be dealt with by well-organised determination. The newcomers ejected or subjugated the people who lived on the land they wanted, and chose sites on islets and peninsulas which guarded them against reprisals.

This west coast of Asia Minor had begun to play a prominent part in history during the third millennium BC, when Troy had a brilliant independent career. From *c.* 1500 Miletus, Rhodes and other centres had been prosperous Cretan and Mycenaean trading posts and settlements, and Ephesus was probably the capital or chief port of an Asian state that varied between autonomy and dependence upon the Hittites (p. 86). Now, however, this shore was gradually opened up along its whole length.

Four parallel rivers, the Caicus (Bakir), Hermus (Gediz), Cayster (Küçük Menderes) and Maeander (Menderes), flow down westwards from the lofty plateau to an utterly different country beside the Aegean. This seaboard is an alluvial, thoroughly Mediterranean territory which possesses greater potentialities for cultivation than Greece, being richer in olives and noted for its fruits and vines and vegetables. Not far away stand the islands, again fertile, highly individual and often of considerable size, 'like the backbone of an ass crowned with savage woods'.[11]

The valley-routes, extensions of continental trunk roads, sent down foodstuffs and metals from the interior, and supplied cattle and wool and goat's hair to the textile works which soon led the whole of Greece. The climate of this coastal strip was regarded as the best in any Greek land.[12] Its winters are milder than those across the Aegean, and the total annual rainfall is greater. The droughts brought by summer are not catastrophic, and sea breezes remain brisk. Climatic conditions are particularly good in the central portion of the shoreland, opposite Attica, to which the Athenians and their fellow immigrants came. For this country of Ionia suffers neither from the somewhat excessive cold and wet experienced along more northerly stretches of the coast nor from the heat and dryness that prevail farther south; so that climate and fertile soil alike must have contributed to the decision to make this the region of the earliest Greek settlement.

The southernmost town of the area was Miletus, where the first Ionian successor of the Cretan and Mycenaean settlements has lately been shown to have possessed a city wall and three-storey houses. The town stood on a peninsular headland at the entry-point of the Latmian gulf, which was then not the freshwater lake which the Maeander's silt has made it now, but a capacious Aegean inlet. There was good farmland in the neighbourhood, and the new foundation, like Ephesus across the river, soon began to take a greater interest than its predecessors in the trade-route up the Maeander valley, which is the one easy thoroughfare up to the high plateau. It was probably Miletus which in due course inaugurated the tenth century pottery found at more than half a dozen of these Ionian sites.

The fact that the Milesians, although they were one of the communities retaining Athenian tribes, also claimed partly Cretan origin,[13] indicates that they formed some connection with the population originating from that island whom they found at the place on their arrival. But Homer (who knows of no Ionian city except Miletus) peoples it with native Carians, whose males the Greek settlers slaughtered, appropriating the widows for themselves.[14] Accordingly the Milesians of historical times were of even more mixed race than the descendants of other colonists, and spoke a peculiar version of the Ionic dialect.

Only twenty miles from Miletus lay the isle of Samos, where pottery of mainland types is found from at least 900 BC, and the shrine of the earth-goddess, Hera, according to recent excavations, goes back almost to the same date. Samos and another large and important island, Chios, some forty-five miles to the north-west, controlled the longitudinal Aegean coastal route.

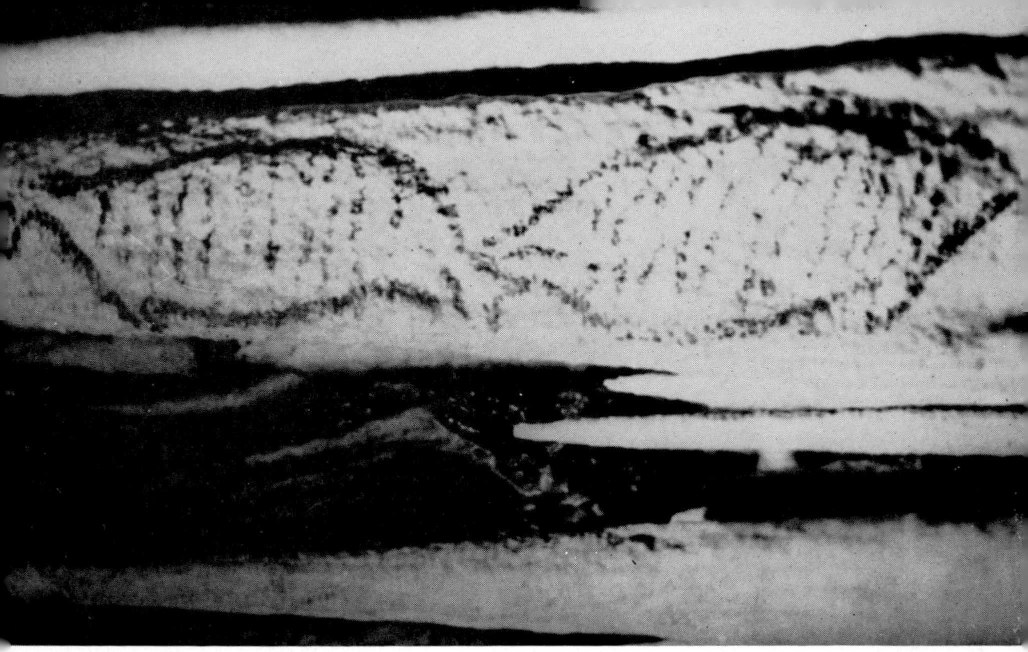

1 From the cave of Nerja, behind Malaga in south-east Spain: painting of the Old Stone Age which may represent dolphins: if so, their earliest known representation

2 The caves of Mount Carmel (North Israel): a vital point at which comparatively advanced cultures reached the Mediterranean in the tenth millennium BC

3 From Jericho, seventh millennium BC. The beginnings of portraiture: a human skull, features modelled in plaster, and cowries inserted in place of eyes

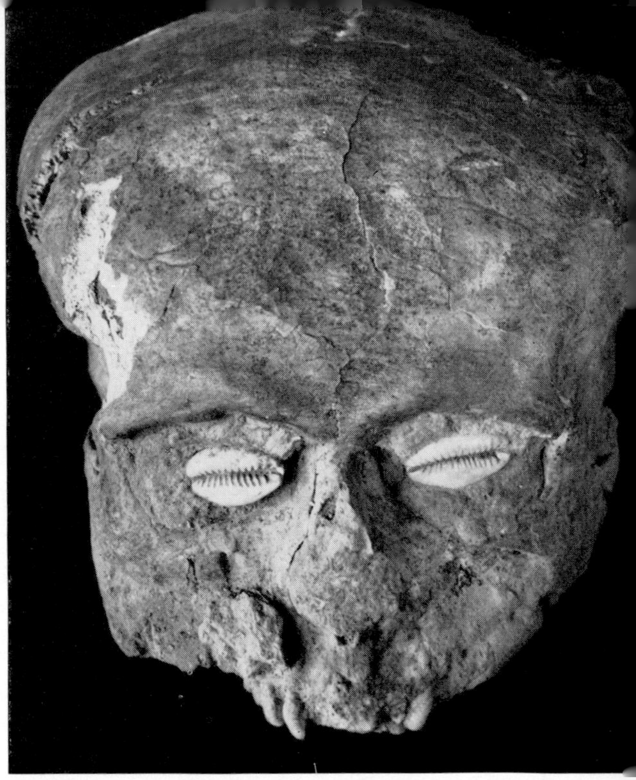

4 Ritual leopard dance; fresco on the wall of a shrine at Çatalhüyük (Asia Minor). Early sixth millennium BC. These are the earliest paintings hitherto found on man-made walls. Two further layers of pictures were subsequently superimposed

5 The wild ancestor of emmer wheat (*triticum dicoccoides*)

6 Cultivated emmer wheat (*triticum dicoccum*). An early stage of emmer, of the seventh or sixth millennium BC, is found at Jarmo in N. Iraq and Çatalhüyük in Asia Minor. (It was cultivated in Britain until the sixth century AD)

7 Cultivated einkorn wheat (*triticum monococcum*), developed from the wild *triticum boeoticum* of the uplands, has come to light at Çatalhüyük, where bread wheat (*triticum aestivum*) was also grown

8 Spelt is a form of wheat (*triticum spelta*) which may not have been grown until the second millennium BC

9 Wild barley was developed into the tougher two-rowed variety which was replaced by the six-rowed form in the irrigated alluvial plains

10 Landscape in Cilicia (south-east Asia Minor), one of the key territories of the ancient Mediterranean. A pass and strategic hill near Adana, on the way to the Taurus mountains in one direction and the fertile plain in the other

11 Basin with spout from Khirokitia, southern Cyprus, made of volcanic stone (andesite). Sixth millennium BC. The decoration is probably inspired by basket work, and the two holes show that the basin was repaired in ancient times

12 The goat: provider of food, but also major contributor to the deforestation of the Mediterranean zone. Here the victim is the evergreen Barbary almond (argan) in semi-arid southern Morocco

13 The River Nile: by far the greatest river that flows into the Mediterranean: creator of the first national state upon its shores, because of the united effort needed to organise irrigation

15 Sennefer, the Chancellor of Queen Hatshepsut and King Thothmes III: an example of the Egyptian hieroglyphic writing

14 Flint knife from Gebel-el-Arak in Upper Egypt, within reach of the Red Sea. Fourth millennium BC. The ivory handle shows a water battle between boats of Nile and Tigris type (below and above respectively)

16 Model of ship of Queen Hatshepsut (fifteenth century BC), based on reliefs at Deir-el-Bahari. These vessels represent the climax of Egyptian ship-building, but their lack of keel and of strong ribs made them unfit for the open Mediterranean

17 The sanctuary of Thothmes III at Karnak (fifteenth century BC). The granite piers are decorated with the country's symbolic plants: in front the lotus of Upper Egypt (its volutes perhaps foreshadowing Ionic capitals); behind, the papyrus of Lower Egypt

18 Cedars of Lebanon, survivors of the forests which attracted invaders from early Egyptian times: by Edward Lear (1812–88), who painted and sketched many regions of the Mediterranean

19 These obelisks in an enclosure behind the temple at Byblos in Phoenicia represent divine presences and exemplify the Semitic tendency to dispense with images

20 Storage jars and tombs beside the Mediterranean at Byblos

21 A goddess of the early third millennium BC from Mari, a city which, although far to the east on the middle Euphrates, exercised a strong influence on Mediterranean culture

22 From Jabbul, near Aleppo: the head of a statue believed to represent a god of the Hurrians, the people who contested the control of the eastern Mediterranean with the Egyptians after 1600 BC

23 Hittite soldiers at the battle of Kadesh against Rameses II of Egypt (*c.* 1286 BC). From a relief at Karnak

24 Ivory plaque of a goddess with two goats from Minet el Beida, a port of Ugarit (Ras Shamra) in Syria. Thirteenth century BC. The flounced skirt and bare breasts recall Aegean customs

25 Ivory plaque from Megiddo above the Valley of Jezreel. Thirteenth or twelfth century BC. Adopted by Egypt, the winged griffin is closely paralleled on Mycenaean ivories, and was later modified in Greek art

26 Tyre seen from the air. The small harbour on the left is the old northern port. Behind it, linking what was formerly an island to the mainland, is the isthmus first formed by Alexander's siege mole (332 BC)

27 Detail from the Harvesters' Vase from Haghia Triada, Crete, sixteenth century BC. In this procession of farm workers a vigorous new human touch has appeared in Mediterranean art

28 Figure, twenty-nine inches high, from Amorgos, one of the Cyclades islands which possessed extensive deposits of marble as well as the emery which was needed to fashion it. Third millennium BC. These statuettes foreshadow the statuary of later Greece

29 The maritime artistic themes of the Cretan sea-empire, *c.* 1450 BC

30 A god from Zincirli behind the Gulf of Alexandretta, *c.* 850–700 BC. This border-line 'neo-Hittite' area maintained a mixed culture that exercised much influence on Greek art

31 Giant storage jars for corn and olive-oil have been found in considerable numbers at Cnossos, as elsewhere in Crete

32 The temple-palace of Kaparu at Tell Halaf (Gozan) in North Mesopotamia. Ninth century BC. A blend of Hittite, Assyrian, Phoenician and Aramaic styles that made its way to the Mediterranean and affected its culture

33 Jug from Citium, south-eastern Cyprus. This sort of painting of the eighth and seventh centuries BC shows a vivid, fantastic blend of Greek and Phoenician influences

34 Inscription from Tell Qasile, Israel's port near modern Tel Aviv, on the northern edge of Philistine territory. *c.* 700 BC. Such were the Semitic scripts which were adapted by the Greeks

35 Bronze tripod cauldron, from Altintepe in east Asia Minor. Urartian work (early eighth century BC). Similar or identical objects were used by Greeks, Etruscans, Phrygians and Celts

36 The silt constantly washed down by Mediterranean rivers has meant that many of them now enter the sea many miles from their former mouths. In ancient times the Cayster (the modern Küçük Menderes) debouched at Ephesus: today its mouth is far away

37 Olive grove near Sparta. These tenacious evergreens, the foundation of Mediterranean life, are capable of surviving for many centuries

38 J. M. W. Turner (1775–1851) painted the myth of Dido building Tyre's colony of Carthage, which long rivalled the Greeks and then the Romans for the control of the Western Mediterranean

39 The art of the Carthaginian empire. A statuette from the Nurra in Sardinia, an island which has had a long tradition of such work. A man in a pointed cap is raising his hand in blessing. Eighth or seventh century BC

40 Ivory statuette of the later seventh century BC, probably made to decorate a lyre. The eyes and pubic hair were inlaid. The technique of Syrian ivory-work is united with the Greek feeling for pattern. Found on the island of Samos

41 Athenian clay figure vase of a kneeling youth binding a fillet round his hair, *c.* 530 BC. Greek art has now partly emancipated itself from Eastern models

42 The Trojan Horse, which contained Greek warriors and according to epic tradition enabled the besieging army to capture Troy. A clay wine jar of the later seventh century BC, recently discovered on the island of Myconos

43 Sphinx from Naxos, now at Delphi; early sixth century BC. The Greek sphinx (which appears in the myth of Oedipus) is a complex product of traditions from Egypt and the Levant: the Egyptian sphinx was male but the Syrians turned him into a female.

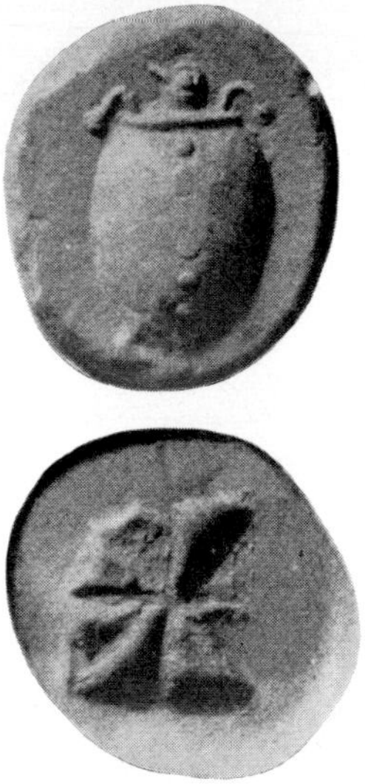

44 With Assyrian and Syrian stamped metal discs as precedents, coinage originated among the Lydians of west central Asia Minor in the seventh and sixth centuries BC. The lion's head is the mark of the royal paymaster

45 The use of coins spread from Lydia to Ionia and the islands of Greece. One of the most widespread early Greek coinages consists of these 'turtles' of the commercial island-city of Aegina

46 A king of prosperous Cyrene, Arcesilas (probably Arcesilas II the Cruel, *c.* 560 BC), sits on board ship and watches bales of merchandise being weighed and stowed. Paintings on a cup from Sparta, which maintained close relations with Cyrene

47 Doric temple at Segesta in north-west Sicily, left unfinished in *c.* 416 BC at the time when the city appealed to the Athenians for help against its enemy Selinus. After the Athenian failure, Segesta appealed to Carthage instead

48 Ionic capital from the temple of Artemis at Ephesus. The Ionic order, which mainly evolved on the coasts and islands of Asia Minor, derives from Egyptian and Levantine floral prototypes

49 The capitals of the latest of three Greek architectural orders, the Corinthian, beginning in the fifth century BC, are decorated with acanthus leaves in the tradition of the Egyptian papyrus and lotus capitals. This specimen belonged to a building at Carthage

50 The basic Mediterranean cult and myth: the earth-mother Demeter with her daughter Kore (Persephone) who vanishes beneath the earth for four months of the year. From Eleusis, where their Mysteries were enacted. Mid-fifth century BC

51 Syracuse coined triumphantly, with the head of its city-goddess Artemis Arethusa, after it had overwhelmingly defeated the Athenian invasion. The artist Cimon signs his name on the head-band. *c* 410 BC

52 Philip II of Macedon, before putting an end for ever to the importance of the city-states, coined on the weight standard of his Greek neighbours so as to facilitate trade. *c* 359 BC

53 Chased gold stag, the centre-piece of a Scythian shield, from Komstromskaya in the Kuban. Seventh–sixth century

54 This remarkable head, of about the fifth century BC comes from Ilici (Elche) near Alicante on the eastern Spanish coast, in an area where Greek, Phoenician and Carthaginian, and native Iberian traditions met

55 The Feñon de Ifach, south of Alicante: near the frontier between the Greek and Carthaginian sectors of eastern Spain. (The tall plant, an American agave, is an eighteenth-century importation from Mexico)

57 A portrait of one of the Sarmatians who in later Greek times displaced the Scythians north and west of the Black Sea. Silver-gilt armour-boss from Herastrau, Roumania

56 Helmet from Veii, Etruria, probably used as a cover for a cinerary urn. Before 700 BC. These bronze products of the so-called Iron Age have affinities not with Greece but with the Danube region.

58 Part of an Etruscan painting in the Tomb of Hunting and Fishing at Tarquinii. Beneath a flock of wild ducks a fisherman is casting his line amid leaping dolphins. Later sixth century BC

59 This fortress town of Saguntum beside the Spanish coast was an ally of the Romans. Its capture by Hannibal in 219 BC precipitated the Second Punic War which gave Rome the control of the western Mediterranean

60 Antiochus III the Great (223–187 BC), ruler of the huge Seleucid successor-state that was formed from part of Alexander's empire, who failed in his attempt to challenge Rome for the supremacy of the eastern Mediterranean

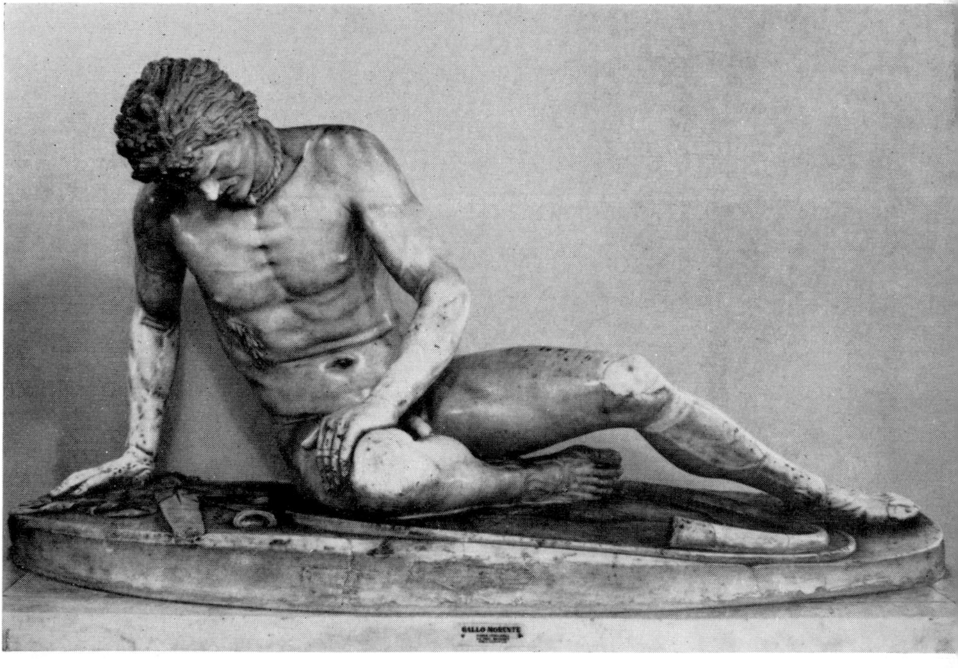

61 The Dying Gaul. Marble copy of a bronze statue of the School of Pergamum (western Asia Minor) dedicated there after Attalus I (269–197 BC) had repelled the invading Galatians (Celts)

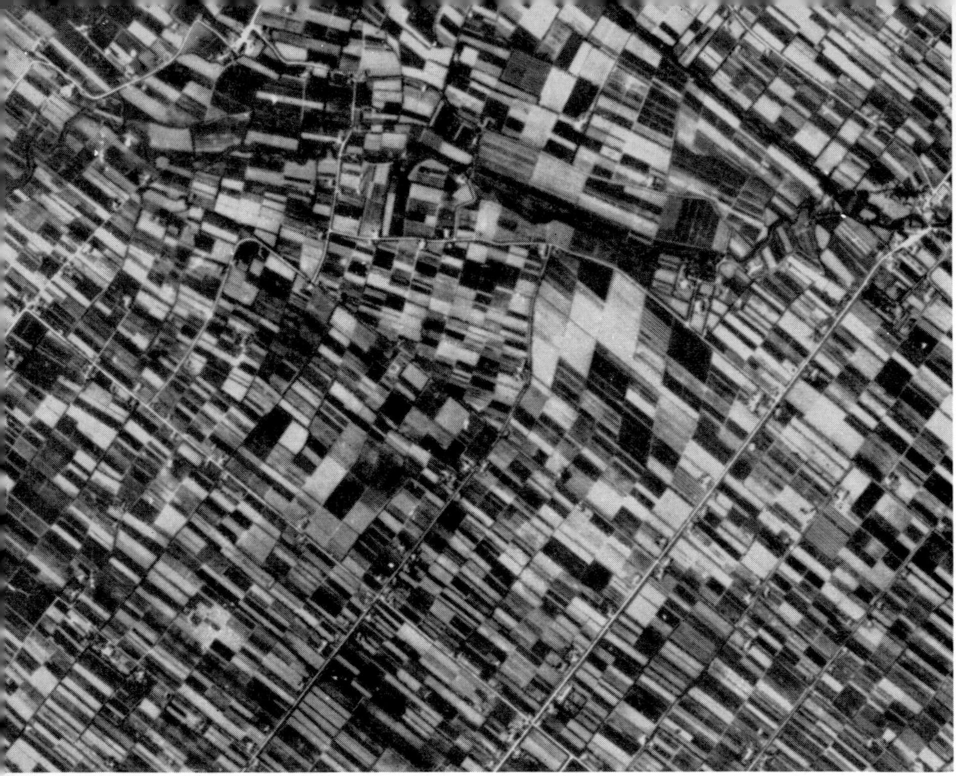

62 The Po plain became more and more vital to Roman wealth and power. 'Centuriated' landscape near Cesena (south of Ravenna), showing roads which still preserve the Roman grid system used to divide up the fields

63 Claudius and his wife Agrippina the younger (the mother of Nero) honour one of the most venerable Mediterranean cults, that of Artemis (Diana) of Ephesus whose archaic statue is shown (DIANA EPHESIA). AD 50–4

64 The Roman emperor Hadrian (AD 117–38) conceived a progressive view of the regions of the empire as individual entities. He proclaimed himself the 'restorer' of these territories – in this instance Spain, where he was born (RESTITVTOR HISPANIAE)

65 The sea-front of the great palace at Salonae (Split) in Dalmatia, built by Diocletian (AD 284–205) for his retirement. Drawing by Robert Adam (1728–92)

66 Roman warships – probably fast light Liburnian 'destroyers' – moving across a harbour. Fresco from the Temple of Isis at Pompeii

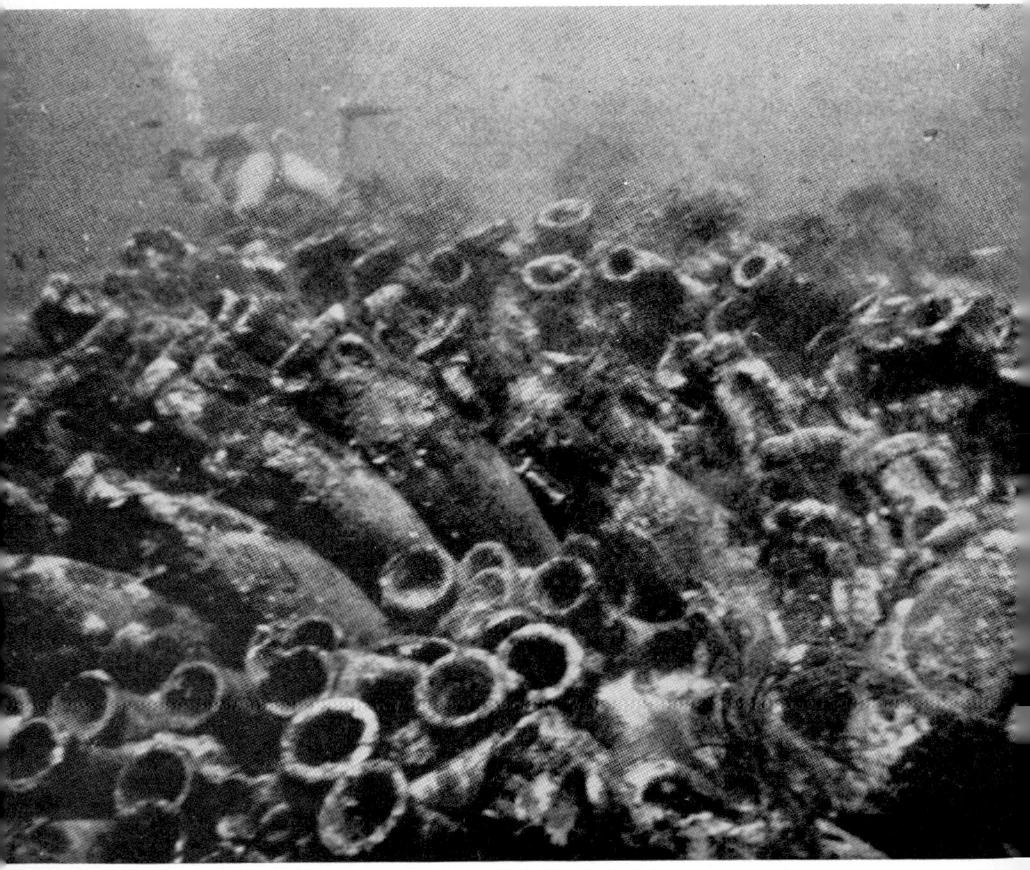

67 Mediterranean commerce greatly expanded under Augustus – but remained hazardous. A trading ship wrecked off the Ile du Levant (Hyères). When found, some jars still contained remains of tunny bones and molluscs in fish-sauce

68 Imaginative wall-painting of an Italian harbour from Stabiae (Castellamare) in the Bay of Naples, showing ships, wharves, quays, warehouses, markets and columns crowned by statues

69 The sea-front of an Italian mansion of the early empire. Painting at the house of Marcus Lucretius Fronto, Pompeii

70 St John the Divine on the Aegean island of Patmos, by Nicolas Poussin (1593–1665), supreme among all the artists who have had their own visions of the Mediterranean scene

71 Mosaic from Thabraca (Tabarka, N. Tunisian coast) depicting a Christian basilica, *c.* AD 400. North Africa, which had provided many great Latin writers, now played a leading part in church affairs

Beyond Chios was the third great isle of Lesbos. This, together with the adjoining mainland coast as far as the Troad, belonged to a different area of settlement, Aeolis, colonised mainly from Boeotia and Thessaly which lie directly across the Aegean. Conservative and secluded, the Aeolians possessed a fertile agricultural belt terminating in rough hills. These inhibited contacts with the interior, but certain inland connections were established through Cyme (Nemrut) on a river estuary at the head of a bay, where the main coastal route turns inland along the Hermus plain's northern edge. Although the motherland of many little Aeolic towns, Cyme was slow to exploit its position, preferring to leave maritime trade to the Lesbian city of Mytilene. Yet it was said to be a Cymaean who first brought tin from an island somewhere in the west, and this was also the place from which Cumae in Italy, the Helleniser of Rome, derived its name.

The Aeolians, then, settled to the north of Ionia, and on the other side appeared an offshoot and overflow from the Dorian invasions of the mainland, again coming from the parts of Greece which involved the shortest journey by sea (*c.* 900 BC). These sources included Argos and its neighbours, whose colonists arrived on the islands of Cos and Rhodes and spread to the adjacent mainland coast of Caria, except for Cnidus at the south-western tip which was one of the few settlements made by the Spartans.

But it was neither in this new Doris nor in Aeolis that the new civilisation flowered. The centre of the advanced culture lay between those two regions, in Ionia. Although the Ionian cities were politically separate and diversified in race and interests, they possessed the unity of shared beliefs and combined to worship Poseidon at the shrine of the Panionion, which possessed a sixty-foot-long altar now identified on the promontory of Mycale beside Samos. This common patriotic faith was also focused upon the little island of Delos, half-way between their old homeland and their new. There people from all the Ionian cities met in festival to celebrate a holy place they inherited from much earlier times and now revered in the name of Apollo, a god of non-Greek name who became the most Greek of all.

Many are your temples and wooden groves, and all peaks and towering bluffs of lofty mountains and rivers flowing to the sea are dear to you, Apollo, but in Delos do you most delight your heart; for there the long-robed Ionians gather in your honour with their children and shy wives . . . the men and well-girded women with their swift ships and great wealth.[15]

It was for these athletic and musical festivals, which were among the most impressive phenomena of aristocratic early Greece, that during the ninth or more particularly the eighth century poetic genius transmuted old, orally transmitted poems into a new idiom and spirit embodied in the continuous written narratives of the Homeric *Iliad* and *Odyssey*, on which all subsequent culture and education in the ancient Mediterranean world were based.

The Ionians were well qualified to understand, collect and hand on these ancient lays because one of their principal homelands, Athens, had remained in a position to conserve its Mycenaean past (p. 134). Besides, the new Ionian towns themselves still lived among raids and migrations or their disturbed aftermaths, which kept alive the spirit associated with legendary heroes of the past.

Like other epics of the Trojan cycle, the Homeric poems purport to tell of the age when Troy allegedly fell to the Mycenaean Greeks not far short of half a millennium earlier (p. 85). Yet the air of feudal individualism in the *Iliad* and *Odyssey* is startlingly irreconcilable with that epoch's bureaucratic elaborations as revealed by the archaeologist's spade (p. 107). For while the poems describe objects and techniques and places and events from those earlier times, and others from darkly seen intermediate periods, what they really illuminate is an exalted version of eighth-century Ionia and its aspirations. The recurrent sensitive touch, tactful speech-making and candid individualism are products of contemporary Ionian sophistication, and although a Homeric hero will often call upon the gods, the humorous cynicism displayed in their treatment is another reflection of the attitude which, for all their love of religious festivals, the Ionians adopted and later carried on into their philosophical systems (p. 176).

The *Iliad* and *Odyssey* are each the work of an outstanding poet; or they were written by a single great poet at different stages of his life, 'a genius who exploited three existing conditions: love of the past, love of festivals, and the alphabet'. For the recording and survival of the Homeric poems would have been impossible if an alphabet had not been recently imported from the east (p. 150). The contents of the work, too, include a good many echoes of ancient Asia. Achilles and Patroclus of the *Iliad* are a heroic pair of companions like Gilgamesh and Enkidu in a Mesopotamian epic which circulated widely in Asia Minor (p. 152). Menelaus' loss and recovery of Helen recall an epic of Ugarit (Ras Shamra) telling how Keret won back his beautiful bride. The circumstances, it is true, have little in common, and the comparatively jejune earlier tradition has become incomparable poetry, but there were evident transmissions of thought, ideas and poetical methods.

The elusive blend of resemblances and differences can be seen from a comparison between the *Iliad*'s story of cremations such as that of Patroclus and customs practised by the Hittites.

> The Hittite and Homeric rituals have the following points in common: (1) the body is burnt; (2) the pyre is quenched with potable liquids; (3) the bones are dipped or wrapped in oil or fat; (4) the bones are wrapped in a linen cloth and a fine garment; (5) they are placed in a stone chamber (this does not apply to the funeral of Patroclus); (6) there is a feast. On the other hand, they differ in the following respects: (1) the Homeric warriors place the bones, wrapped in fat, in a golden urn, which is not mentioned in the Hittite ritual; (2) in the Hittite ritual the bones are placed on a chair or a stool; (3) the Hittite 'stonehouse' is apparently complete in itself, whereas the Homeric warriors raise the barrow over the grave; (4) the magical operations are peculiar to the Hittite ceremony, the athletic games to the Homeric.[16]

The differences are considerable; and yet the similarities still suggest some association, however indirect this may have been. Such links could have been gradually forged on many occasions during the second millennium BC. But the real Mycenaeans had not been cremated at all, but buried, and probably the main connection with the east dates from the time of the final compilation of the *Iliad*, when, as the adoption of the alphabet so clearly showed, communications with the Levant had been re-established.

In the *Odyssey* poetic genius takes another form, but here too there are clear eastern analogies. The visit of Odysseus to the underworld follows a tradition which again goes back to the Mesopotamian epic of Gilgamesh, or to a work which was the ancestor of them both. Moreover, Gilgamesh, like Odysseus, is shipwrecked, and builds himself a raft, and meets Siduri who resembles Circe.

Contemporary Ionia on the other hand, or the contemporary ideal of an Ionian, is detectable in the poet's picture of the mythical Phaeacians, who enjoy dancing, music and comfort, and, after their daily farming and herding, like hot baths, clean clothes, good wine and comfortable beds. Yet, strangely enough, the author of the *Odyssey* chooses to ignore the city-state, although it was fully developed in Ionia when he wrote. To him towns are no more than fortified settlements, and the new conception forms no part of the poetic picture which he draws. Presumably he found it prosaic.

In other respects however the *Odyssey* is abreast of contemporary life, and in particular the poem exhilaratingly reflects current widenings of the Mediterranean horizon. This sense of wonder, love of adventure, and directness in human relationships have deeply affected the course of subsequent literary history. So has the poet's regard for personal initiative and ingenuity in solving a baffling situation – here was the versatile Complete Man who remained one of the lasting ideals of the Mediterranean world.

But what the *Odyssey* conveys above all else is the zest and thrill of the salt sea itself. The Mycenaeans had sailed far and wide, and this love of the sea descended, at least in faint memories, from them. Yet it is not of their epoch that the *Odyssey* chiefly speaks. For its completion dates from a new age, in which contacts were even more far-reaching, intellectually explosive and cosmopolitan; and, although the guise is legendary and antique materials are introduced, the spirit which the wanderings of Odysseus reflect is the spirit of the Mediterranean world during the poet's own time.

The sea

Greece is only one-third the size of Italy, and one-sixth as large as the Iberian peninsula, and yet the Greek coastline of two thousand six hundred miles is considerably the longest of the three. The Aegean, with its numerous ports and easy communications, is a bridge rather than a barrier, since among this dense scattering of islands no ship can ever be more than forty miles from shore. The absence of tides made it unnecessary to wait for flood-water or build sea-walls or locks, and facilitated the frequent beaching that prevented hulls from becoming foul through constant immersion in warm water. So long, here, was the reach of the naval arm that the Greeks won and lost most of their major wars at sea. They knew very well that the Mediterranean was their life-blood; the indented coast and the barrenness of the land combined to make them seafarers. 'Farewell, dear sea', said the epitaph of Eretrians who fell in far-off Media,[17] and Xenophon's men, after wandering in the same alien continent, were overwhelmed with a peculiarly Greek joy when they saw the Black Sea again from above Trebizond.[18]

Aeschylus speaks of the multitudinous laughter of waves;[19] but they could not be relied upon to laugh. The god of these waters, Poseidon, might be soothed by Odysseus, but not for long.

> Still I can give him a rough ride in, and will!
> Brewing high thunder heads, he churned the deep
> With both hands on his trident – called up wind
> From every quarter, and sent a wall of rain
> To blot out land and sea in torrential night.
> Hurricane winds now struck from the south and east,
> Shifting north-west in a great spume of seas.[20]

Winds are capricious and fitful, changing and dropping quickly, and causing bewilderment with their incalculable cross seas and eddies in confined water. During the summer, strong dry blasts veering round from the north come with clear skies from the land-mass of Eurasia. Telemachus in the *Odyssey*, sailing southwards from Ithaca to Pylos through the Ionian Sea, found this wind very agreeable;[21] yet it was also a north-north-easter off Cape Malea which began all Odysseus' troubles.[22] Besides, this prevailing summer wind was complicated by a brisk alternate play of coastal breezes. As the water is warmer than land by night and cooler by day, air gets displaced after sunrise and sunset; and breezes blow off the shore in evening, and off the sea at dawn.[23] The Greeks only liked winds right astern, or nearly so. They were fine seamen, but in the same way as good soldiers fear battle Greek sailors entertained a justified suspicion of the sea – and Odysseus, according to the poet, as much as anyone else, for he knew its perils only too well.

Some of these dangers came from pirates, lurking in narrow creeks and inlets.[24] All early nautical activities had taken place under the shadow of this menace; and indeed the profession of pirate had been regarded as quite honourable.[25] To avoid being caught at sea after dark it was better to beach the ship and use it as a citadel and rampart during the hours of sleep. Odysseus' men mutinied because at nightfall they were not allowed to make for land and rest.[26] The Phaeacians were mythical because they did not share the fears of ordinary seamen. They had no need to, since their ships sailed magically without pilots to steer them.

In real life, there remained the terrors of storms and pirates; and of hostile inhabitants lying in wait behind the shore. Archilochus paints a grim picture of shipwreck on the Black Sea coast in the seventh century BC:

Slammed by the surf on the beach
Naked at Salmydessos, where the screw-haired men
Of Thrace, taking him in,
Will entertain him (he will have much to undergo,
Chewing on slavery's bread)
Stiffened with cold, and loops of seaweed from the slime
Tangling his body about,
Teeth chattering as he lies in abject helplessness
Flat on his face like a dog
Beside the beach-break where the waves come shattering in.[27]

To sail upon these waters, declared Sophocles, was marvellous and perilous;[28] an awesome destiny which was at best a purge of human ills, and an obvious metaphor of troubles for the ship of state.

I cannot tell what wind prevails:
From this side rolls a mighty sea,
From that the next: between them we
Ride where our black ship sails,

By the huge tempest strained and worn;
Water is swilling round the mast,
The sail is riddled with the blast
And flapping, holed and torn.[29]

These menacing expanses are not the placid mirrors of tourist posters. Everything that touches them partakes of torrent and tornado;[30] 'and between the sun's burning rays, air currents cut in that are as hard as the edge of a scythe.'[31]

When traders had begun to venture forth again after 800 BC, Hesiod felt obliged to include a sailing section in his poetic calendar. But although he had crossed the narrows to Euboea (p. 150), he hated the idea of leaving land at any time, and indicated that the Aegean was only safe for less than two months after the summer solstice.[32] Thereafter,

The blasts of the winds are blowing
From every direction.
Then is no time to keep your ships
On the wine-blue water.[33]

Later Greeks were sometimes prepared to go on sailing until the poor visibility of November, and took to the sea again when the first fine days arrived in early spring. But they were slow to follow the enterprise of the Phoenicians in sailing out of season, and harbours were consequently chosen regardless of winter gales, but with a view, instead, to protection from the north winds of summer.

In spite of much speculation then and ever since, it was already pointed out in ancient times that the journeys of Odysseus cannot be located on any real map.[34] The earlier part of his voyage, from the island of Tenedos off Troy as far as Cape Malea, was within the realm of determinable geography, and the land of the Phaeacians, Scheria, may echo something of Corcyra (Corfu) in the Ionian Sea. But after that come vague regions to the west of Greece, traditionally identified with south Italian coasts; and although mistaken in his belief that the Black and Caspian Seas were linked with ocean, the poet's similar assertion regarding the Mediterranean suggests that the Strait of Gibraltar was not unknown to him.

Some of his sea-lore may have come from the Phoenicians,

and other parts from stories handed down from the days of Crete and Mycenae. But the wanderings of Odysseus must surely also echo the experiences of Greek sailors who were again, at this very time, exploring the unknown or forgotten western Mediterranean, and his story reflects the wider geographical and economic horizons which marked the first steps in Greek colonisation (p. 167). Odysseus himself, as he draws inshore to the land of the Cyclopes, notes the possibilities with a sharp prospector's eye.

The *Odyssey*'s pitch-tarred, red-prowed, undecked ('hollow') ships[35] are often regarded as archaic descriptions of the past, but they no doubt draw many features from contemporary vessels. Merchantmen like Odysseus' own vessel were broad-bottomed, with the concave bows of an American clipper, and depended mainly on their single-masted square sails, with oars only fulfilling a subsidiary role because freightage would never have justified oarsman's pay. A drawing of *c.* 1100 from the small town of Pylos which survived its Mycenaean splendours shows an undecked warship with a small fighting platform for the lookout and a few others in the abruptly rising prow, and a slightly larger platform aft for helmsmen and captain. Twenty oars were normal, but the literary tradition suggests that fifty-oared craft, with twenty-five rowers a side, may already have existed as well. The length of the ships described in the Homeric poems probably did not exceed forty feet, but the fifty-oared variety must have been more than twice as long, which was about the limit for propulsion by a single bank of oars. These larger ships no doubt carried soldiers and archers to conduct replicas of land battles at sea. But a cup of the later ninth century BC depicts a novel warship of faster appearance, with low straight hull and keel-beam prolonged to form a pointed ram. Henceforward sea-fights were no longer mere land-fights transferred to the water, but victory would go to the quickest and most skilful crew.

Yet for all his seafaring skill Odysseus, unlike his heirs imagined by later writers, loved the soil of his native Ithaca, though it was only a rocky little island and owed everything to its command of sea-routes. The poet of the *Odyssey*, too, glories in the sea, but this only makes him appreciate land all the more. For the first time the glories of Mediterranean landscape and scenery are brought into human consciousness. There are rich meadows and clear springs; the wedding couch of Zeus and Hera is a bed of clover, crocus and hyacinth. But above all nature is loved in its relation to humanity, and like so much else in the epics this strikes the keynote of the Greek experience that was to come (p. 189). Nature harnessed by man is the ideal, in the rich, well-tended, neat orchards and gardens of the Phaeacians and Calypso. Even the after-life itself is like a lush Garden of Eden.[36]

7

Greek Civilisation Enriched and Diffused

Hesiod and eastern ports

It was because of the alphabet, as well as poetic genius, that the Homeric poems advanced so gigantically beyond their formula-remembering predecessors (p. 143). For the most decisive of all Greek borrowings was their adoption and modification of the eighth-century Phoenician writing (p. 123). As it stood, this script was unsuitable for the Greeks since it possessed no vowel-signs, which they needed to express word-endings and to differentiate between many words containing identical consonants. A remedy, however, was suggested by several unwanted letters of the Semitic alphabet, which were turned into vowels; and by *c.* 720 the Greek alphabet was fully established.

Variant forms are at first found at a number of different centres. But the very archaic alphabet of the large island of Euboea, off the Aegean coast of central Greece, probably provides the Levantine link, since the people of its city, Chalcis, played an active pioneer role in a Greek trading establishment at the Orontes mouth which transmitted many eastern institutions to the homeland (p. 152).

Euboea was also relevant to the poems associated with the name of Hesiod, which like the Homeric epics were perpetuated through the medium of the alphabet. Hesiod came from Boeotia, but he claims to have visited Euboea across the narrow strait[1] and won a poetic competition at funeral games in Chalcis. Moreover, there existed a tradition that writing had first been brought to Greece by Levantines visiting Boeotia;[2] and Hesiod, who was acquainted with the wine of Byblos,[3] may have possessed contacts of this sort.

The principal surviving Hesiodic poems, the *Works and Days* and *Theogony*, which have come down to us in forms dating from *c.* 700, breathe a more sober and earthbound atmosphere than the Homeric cycle, and indicate a division between the two schools that may have started a century or two earlier. The *Works and Days* is a rendering of one of the wisdom texts which had long been common in Egypt.[4] But the particular shape which it adopts is that of an agricultural almanac, like certain ancient Sumerian compositions[5] and a tenth-century farming calendar found at Gezer on the borders of Israel (p. 113). The *Theogony* on the other hand gathers together ancient tales about the early gods who first controlled the universe. Some of these stories, notably a myth of the sky-god consuming his own young, seem to echo Egypt, and there are also Egyptian parallels to the tale of the first woman Pandora which appears in both Hesiodic poems. These Egyptian analogies, if they are not too general to be relevant, could have been introduced by Greek traders who had now begun to visit Egypt (p. 163).*

In essence, however, the *Theogony* is a hymn of praise to Zeus, and that is a genre which had received its classic expression in the Babylonian *Enuma Elish*, an epic of creation designed mainly to celebrate the glory of the youthful god Marduk. Passages from the epic, which dates from *c.* 1125–1050 BC, have now been found in northern (Turkish) Mesopotamia on a site which has also disclosed parts of another Babylonian work, the *Epic of Era* of perhaps *c.* 860 BC, containing a list of god, king, noble, singer and scribe closely paralleled in the *Theogony*.[6]†

The next links in the chain, those between northern Mesopotamia and Greece, are traceable in Cilicia and north-west Syria. Cilicia is an especially likely intermediary or part-source, since Typhoeus (Typhon), the monstrous enemy of Zeus in the *Theogony*, is attributed by other poets to caves in that region, where pottery discovered at Tarsus shows that this ancient town was fulfilling its role as transmitter.

There is also a specific link with the coastal land immediately

* Greek mock-epics of animals go back to Egypt's strip-cartoons, and the Greek novel is partly derived from its romances of travel and other themes – an early example, *The Dream of Nectanebus*, being a translation from the Egyptian.

† Also of Mesopotamian origin were Aesop's Fables, which started life as a popular Assyrian collection of animal stories, and the *Ninus Romance*, one of the prototypes of Greek novels, which is a tale of a legendary King of Assyria.

bordering upon Cilicia. For the primitive Hesiodic story of how Cronos, at the prompting of his mother the Earth, castrated his father Ouranos, resembles the epic of Kumarbi which had been translated or freely adapted from Hurrian by the Hittites (p. 73). There too, very much as in the Greek story, occur the impregnation of the earth-goddess, emasculation of the sky-god, birth of a goddess like Hesiod's Aphrodite, and swallowing of a stone in substitution for the god's offspring; and the struggle with the monster Ullikummi is comparable to the episode of Typhoeus. Moreover, an alternative Greek version actually sites the conflict between Ouranos and Cronos at Mount Casius beside the Amik valley just to the south of the Orontes mouth; and that neo-Hittite territory (p. 117) is precisely where the Hurrian-Hittite epic had deliberately located the story. In spite of many differences, Hesiod's stories of divine origins and parricides evidently owe much to the perpetuation of these myths in that corner where Syria and Cilicia meet.

One link is provided by the *Epic of Baal* from Syria (*c.* 1400–1350), since its picture of a young divinity relying on special weapons to vanquish his enemy foreshadows the Hesiodic account of Zeus' suppression of successive rivals. This was found at Ugarit (p. 77), but an even more important intermediary for all these westerly movements was the place now called Al Mina, on the high south bank of the Orontes mouth. The age of the settlement cannot be determined, since a change in the course of the river has washed away all its history before the ninth century. The earliest finds of Syrian pottery date from then, but by 750 BC the Greeks had established an important settlement at Al Mina which, although the port was low-lying, unhealthy and liable to floods, continued in existence for four hundred years. The place has been very plausibly identified with Posidium, an ancient harbour town known to have existed in this Syro-Cilician borderland. While various great and smaller powers strove for the control of the interior and established successive overlordships over the coast, the Greek community at Al Mina was one of the principal centres which tapped and passed back home the various resources of the east, including objects of trade, cultural achievements, and a variety of oriental religions; and similar roles were performed by other coastal sites where pottery of the same types as those found at Al Mina have been identified.

The earliest of the Greek pottery from Al Mina had originated in Euboea, which has also, as was suggested, been credited with some of Hesiod's oriental lore and, above all, with the initiative in acquainting Greece with the Levantine alphabet. This script may well have been learnt at Al Mina, where the early traders included a large proportion of men from the enterprising harbour-city of Chalcis, though seventh-century finds indicate that by then Corinthians and east Greeks had taken the lead instead.

From Phrygia to Corinth

Another area which continued to play an important part in diffusing eastern influences throughout large parts of the Mediterranean area was Asia Minor.

The leading position established there by the Hittites had to some extent been taken over by the Phrygians, whose invasion from the Balkans was one of many movements which disturbed the area during the thirteenth and twelfth centuries BC.[7] This horse-rearing aristocracy, perhaps belonging originally to a Thracian tribe, established their capital in the very middle of the peninsula at Gordion (Yassihüyük), which four centuries later was so rich in crops and cattle and precious metals that the name of the Phrygian king, Midas, whose dynasty were buried in grandiose thickly timbered tombs, became proverbial.

Gordion imported bronzes by the road from Assyria, and particularly bronze cauldrons from Urartu (p. 118). Moreover, although the Phrygian kingdom stopped two hundred miles short of the Aegean, it passed on many of these objects to the Greeks. It also handed on the Phrygian version of the ancient Anatolian worship of the earth-mother, which during the eighth and seventh centuries BC took root and developed extensively in Greece, supplementing traditions which already existed there from earlier epochs. A male deity of the Phrygians, Dionysus (Diounsis), probably came to Greece not from them but from the kinsmen they had left behind in Thrace. A further Phrygian gift to the west, though we no longer have any knowledge of it, was a rich musical heritage; and another, of which likewise no examples have come down to us, was a highly active textile industry, from which the coastal Greeks benefited by importing woven materials and Phrygian slaves trained to copy them. The language of Phrygia, which is now undecipherable, was written in letters bearing a close resemblance to two varieties of the alphabet that appeared very early among the Greeks, and were presumably obtained from Phoenicia or Syria like theirs.

Early in the seventh century BC Gordion was devastated by wild Cimmerians from the Lake Van area, who ravaged large areas as far as the Aegean coast and showed the civilised world the power of nomad cavalry. Although the culture of Phrygia soon revived, its political power vanished and was mostly taken over by the Lydians, whose country lay farther west and was therefore in much closer contact with Greece. These people used an alphabet somewhat similar to those of the Phrygians and Greeks to write their language, which seems to be a late-surviving remnant of an Anatolian group of Indo-European tongues.

The historian Herodotus, who regarded the Lydians as the colonisers of Etruria (p. 233), also described them as the first people who ever became travelling salesmen. They revived and improved the old Hittite and Phrygian trade-routes to the east and particularly to the readily accessible west. Their capital Sardis, at the edge of a well-watered plain only forty miles from the Aegean, dated back at least to the third millennium BC, and had been resettled before 1100. The place possessed a massive citadel and not far away were magnificent royal graves. Engineers, political refugees, business men and bankers came to Sardis, and until King Croesus fell to the Persians (546 BC) it was the financial capital of the near eastern world. The Lydians inherited and developed the textile industries of Phrygia, its religious ceremonies in honour of the earth-mother, and its taste for music. But they were more influenced by Greek than by oriental art; and they also had many things to offer in exchange. These included gaily patterned fabrics, excellent cooking, scents, purple rugs, smart hats and jewellery, and painted gables (perhaps of Phrygian origin) from which those on Greek temples may have been derived.

Another of their contributions to Greek civilisation was coinage. Since the most ancient times Egypt had regarded gold as the principal medium of exchange, and the Sumerians had possessed temple treasuries which became safe deposits and then banks. These and other peoples conducted trade by means of metal pellets, lumps, ingots, rings and bars.[8] The early Greeks adopted similar methods of reckoning, and in some parts used iron spits. But true coinage was brought into existence by Lydia. The first stage in this evolution of currency was incision by a punch or iron nail, as a time-saving measure to guarantee fineness or weight and enable the man who had made the mark to know the same piece of metal again. Next, with Assyrian and Syrian stamped metal discs as precedents, designs began to be cut in the surface by intaglio dies. This vital step was taken by Lydia. Apparently the first of these designs was a lion's head conveying the authority of the Lydian king Ardys (*c.* 640–630), giving pieces the character of standard coins (*staters*) that was subsequently confirmed by the occasional appearance of a monarch's name. This new currency was at first made of electron, the 'white' gold mixed with silver washed down by the River Pactolus from the mountains through the market of Sardis. But since values were based on gold content, which in this alloy visibly fluctuated, Croesus (whose gold refinery, with 300 small basins, was found in 1968) instead devised a bi-metallic series including some coins made of pure yellow gold and others of silver.

Although liable to be passed in trade, these earliest issues were primarily intended not for that purpose but for official payments by the state. Their recipients no doubt included Greek mercenary soldiers who had hired themselves out into Lydian service. By one means or another the coins poured into Ionia, where the Greek cities were under strong Lydian influence which, despite Milesian resistance, was now becoming transformed into a benign form of control.

Before 600 a group of these Ionian cities, including Ephesus, Miletus, Phocaea, Chios and Samos, began to imitate the Lydian coinage. One of their earliest pieces, issued apparently by Ephesus, is inscribed with the name of a certain Phanes who may have been either a governmental functionary or a private merchant. But the official nature of subsequent coinages was indicated by city-arms of lion, bee, seal and sphinx.

Such guarantees of value meant that a trader no longer needed to search for a man who was ready to barter with him direct; economic mobility and fluidity were greatly increased. These easily transportable coins served far more effectively than any previous medium to convey wealth, accumulate capital, and encourage division of labour. Coinage generated money-changers who began to draw up contracts, accept funds for safe keeping, and make loans available for increased output or services.

And so money gradually transformed Greek society. Manufacturers were able to make cheap goods, and, as people began to own possessions and travel about more, a conscious effort to gain financial advantage entered Greek life. But credit was seldom allowed to outrun bullion resources, and the country had too few resources to grow rich. Nor, above all, were riches distributed evenly, since poverty hampered the circulation of currency. The loans now needed in an increasingly competitive society were only available at very high rates of interest, which resulted in mortgages and the enslavement of debtors.

These perils created by the monetary revolution became increasingly apparent when coinage spread to the west shores of the Aegean. Here the primacy belonged to Aegina, commandingly situated in the Saronic Gulf across from the Ionians. On this poor island, with little of its own to sell, landowners were less important than merchants, who became distributing agents for the entire surrounding regions. Consequently, the earliest European coins were the silver 'leather-backed turtles' from the Aeginetan mint.

But very soon these were superseded by large issues of silver bearing the winged horse Pegasus. This was the currency of Corinth, which established a commanding position at the crucial moment when Greece was becoming wide open to external contacts. The Mycenaeans had made only limited use of the geographical situation of the place, which possessed unique qualities. For the isthmus dominated by Corinth controls communications not only between northern Greece and the Peloponnese but between the eastern and western seas, the Aegean and the Adriatic. Adjoined by the citadel of Acrocorinth, a sixteen hundred foot high flat-topped hill that overlooked the isthmus and its land approaches, the lower parts of the city were two miles from the Gulf of Corinth. On the gulf itself stood a port, Lechaeum, to dispatch and receive western traffic, with Perachora on a promontory for incoming seafarers unable to complete their journeys before night. Another harbour, Cenchreae, faced eastwards into the Saronic Gulf of the Aegean. Assisted in this spectacular fashion by natural advantages, Corinth had taken the commercial lead by 700, and retained it for more than a hundred and fifty years.

It also took the initiative in naval construction, since its long, low, lean warships with tapering rams were probably the first Greek craft to place their rowers at two levels with superimposed banks of oars.* This navy gained a strong position in the Ionian Sea by a victory in *c.* 664 which established the Corinthians on Corcyra (Corfu) beside the north-western extremity of Greece, where their colonists now supplanted a settlement from Eretria in Euboea.[9] The principal town of Corcyra has an anvil-shaped harbour which faces the mainland and controls the narrow coastal strait, so that the island became the natural starting-point for ships sailing on to farther trading-stations up in the Adriatic Sea and across to Italy. Corcyra broke away from the Corinthians during the sixth century, but meanwhile it had helped them to establish supremacy throughout the waters between the Greek and Italian shores.

This supremacy was made possible not only by better ships, but by a new type of heavy infantrymen (hoplites) whose purpose was to protect and extend their own city-state, and to land at overseas bases. Their arms and armour, which were completed in gradual piecemeal fashion during the seventh century, consisted of a bronze helmet, breast-plate and greaves, a large elliptical bronze shield, a heavy nine-foot thrusting spear with an iron head, and an iron sword. Such were the soldiers who fought all the major battles of the Greeks, and won the Persian wars. Cavalry were impracticable except in Thessaly and Boeotia owing to inadequate pasturage, but it seems strange that a light-armed type of infantry fighter was not developed for the country's rocky terrain. The reason for this was that few states could survive the loss of their crops for more than a year at most, so that the principal objective was the capture of the

* It is unknown whether the Phoenicians anticipated them (p. 120).

enemy's agricultural plain and the retention of one's own. Accordingly, the new equipment was designed for fighting on the level ground.

Precedents for helmet, corselet and greaves could all be traced back to Mycenaean Greece rather than to oriental kingdoms, for which they would have been too hot. But the big shield resembles those of Assyria and Urartu, regions which taught the Greeks so many of their metalworking techniques. Tradition ascribed the invention of the outfit as a whole to Euboean Chalcis, which meant 'the place of bronze' and produced the finest iron swords as well. But hoplite equipment and tactics evolved most rapidly and completely among the three leading military powers of the Peloponnese, Sparta, Argos and Corinth. At Corinth especially, a whole series of vase paintings shows how important, even at a maritime centre, this type of warfare had become. One of the principal forms of hoplite helmet, appearing with other arms in *c.* 700, was named after the city, and some fifty years later its artists displayed troops operating in the characteristic mass formation (phalanx) for which, so far, there is no evidence from earlier eastern states.

Such military improvements were likely to attract particular interest at Corinth, where a new régime headed by autocrats (*c.* 657–582 BC) aimed, for the first and only time in the history of the city, to create a land empire. 'Tyrants' of this type also seized power at neighbouring cities, such as Sicyon on a spacious high tongue of land overlooking the gulf between two river-gorges, and Megara whose fertile plain on the south side of the isthmus was so narrow, and cramped by Corinth, that many of the population set sail to establish colonies elsewhere.

Mycenae's successor Argos had already experienced a strong-armed monarch earlier in the seventh century, but the Corinthians (who perhaps brought him down) were the first to be governed by a new kind of ruler who held dictatorial powers and aimed at popular appeal. The leading commercial centres were the places where republican governments succumbed to these tyrannies, because the distress and debt accompanying prosperity had caused the proletariat to welcome this displacement of the upper classes, whose supremacy was, in any case, beginning to be undermined by written legal systems (p. 193), open law-courts, and internal clashes between old landed property and new mobile 'wealth which confuses birth'.[10] The tyrants also made efforts to ensure that their hoplites, the better-off middle class whose ideal was no longer a spectacular duel but collective steadiness, should cease to feel excluded from privilege; and the new coinage stimulated craftsmen, traders and artisans.

Although such methods released creative forces in every sphere, Corinth did not often produce the sort of distinguished individuals who abounded among the Athenians. However, the second of its three autocrats, Periander (*c.* 625–585), was an exception, because he was the most powerful man in the whole Greek world. It was he, moreover, who enabled his city to exploit to the fullest degree its unique double-faced destiny when he spanned the whole three miles of the isthmus by the construction of a convex limestone road close to where the Corinth Canal runs today. On its twin parallel grooved tracks, wheeled trolleys drawn by oxen conveyed warships and freighters from sea to sea, the latter often with their cargoes still aboard.

Corinth's expansion coincided with the maximum infiltration of eastern materials and ideas, which thus spread far and wide through its agency. Such oriental influences appear most clearly in the greatest of the city's exports and arts, its pottery; and of this something will now be said.

Greek art and the east

Greeks used clay pots for various purposes that would now be served by glasses, tins or barrels. But most of these receptacles were intended to hold wine, water, oil, scent and other liquids. The Greek habit of diluting wine with water (p. 188) called for special shapes: two-handled covered vessels for temporary storage, large bowls for mixing, and ladles for transferring the mixed product into jugs. Cups, deep or wide and shallow, ranged in size from large ceremonial vessels, passed round guests reclining at a dinner party, to small containers of olive-oil and scent suspended from the wrist by a string.

The functional part played by these various ceramic types within the Mediterranean pattern of life proved not a hindrance but an encouragement to artistry. Clean and vigorous contours were produced by a long established craft tradition working on a perfectly adapted material. Clay from sedimentary deposits of

Greek riverbeds exhibited wider variations of fineness than near eastern counterparts, possessed a sufficiently low content of lime to resist crumbling, and at its best contained the right proportions of grit-dust to prevent crackings or shrinkages in the kiln. When a lump was left to stand in the Greek climate, evaporation soon created a paste just stiff and soft enough to knead. Colour varied with the length and intensity of firing, but most Greek ceramic clays, although capable of producing contrasts, were reddish owing to the presence of iron oxides.

The painting of pottery was an ancient art handled with unparalleled skill by the Greeks. 'In nearly all their painting we can discern under the lively forms of men and animals a geometrical skeleton through which the design acquired a special neatness and balance, and satisfied the Greek desire for an intelligible, dominating order.'[11] Greek pots were intended to be seen in groups, standing on stone pavements in the sun. Their sharp, clean drawing and unglazed brightness relied on Mediterranean light to mitigate what in dimmer climates might have seemed, when they were new, too colourful effects.

These possibilities were exploited by the Corinthians in a remarkable series of styles which started in the later eighth century, reached their climax early in the sixth, and continued to hold the field until the lead passed to Athens in *c.* 550. The clear bright clay of Corinth, coated with a glossy pigment, could be given a purple, red or orange lustre, and decorated with silhouettes engraved by a technique of incision which had not been employed for more than a thousand years. Almost from the outset artists evolved a swirling, curvilinear riot of design, persuading natural shapes into polychrome calligraphic formulas like the crowded textures of fine stuffs.

These patterns were principal features of the orientalising movement which the revival of Syrian communications diffused throughout Greece. The models for Corinthian ceramics, however, were not other pots, since few of any quality were being produced in the Levant. But numerous motifs were inspired by the details of bronzes and sculptures and ivories and probably textiles (now vanished) from many near eastern regions. Monsters abound; the Greeks of this age, like Hesiod, felt a need to represent the world's untamed quality which had been symbolised for many centuries by representations of the ancient goddesses surrounded by beasts. The Corinthians long continued to prefer animal designs – goats, deer, dogs and birds – to the human scenes that were coming into favour elsewhere. Lions, too, only a memory in Greece itself though still lurking in Macedonian forests,[12] are reproduced in both Assyrian and north Syrian (neo-Hittite) guises. But the latter is the style which predominates, since the eclectic fusion that was now reaching Greece came largely from the Levantine harbours exporting Syrian and Phoenician ivories. The Corinthian sphinx, for example, is female, because this Egyptian symbol of the king had been given a change of sex by Syrian artists. Occasional Egyptian motifs, however, are still found; but they are greatly modified and stylised. And indeed none of these representations look very like oriental works. They are the borrowings of genius which adopt techniques and iconographies only in order to transmit them to a different, livelier atmosphere and a new world. 'Whatever the Greeks take over from foreigners,' said a writer who may have been Plato's secretary, 'they change by making it into something finer.'[13]

The Greeks were saved from the 'sophisticated senility' of this more ancient art by their good sense, aided by a rapidly growing native tradition. Perhaps they were lucky that their comparative obscurity and remoteness from the east caused the infiltration to take place rather slowly. Its onset may perhaps have retarded the Greeks in the development of their specific talents for pattern, draughtsmanship and monumentality. And yet, by becoming available at at time of crucial susceptibility to formative influences, this oriental influence decisively enriched their technique. It also provided a challenging stimulus to the intense cerebral aesthetic activity which was needed to absorb what the east had to give and then build upon it the true originality of the future.

Some of the finest Corinthian pots are tiny scent and unguent bottles of the mid-seventh century, fashioned and painted with a miniature, discreet delicacy which was not equalled until eighteenth century rococo. It was in those years before 600 BC that Corinth reached its commercial zenith, flooding the west with its products and reexporting Egyptian terracottas, amulets and scarabs in exchange for Sicilian wheat and Etruscan metal. Corinthians also penetrated into the interior of the Balkans, and their cargoes reached all the Greek cities of Asia Minor except Miletus, which produced its own rival ware of yellow-coated reddish clay, charmingly painted with silhouettes and textile-like narrative designs (p. 175). The trade of the Corinthians was liable to be intercepted by outlying competitors, of whom their own dissident colony Corcyra was one. But their extraordinary central position long enabled them to outface all rivals.

This rapid development of Greek pottery was paralleled by the evolution of sculpture in clay, stone and bronze. The little figures which had long been carved in many parts of the country assumed a new sophistication in a sharply outlined Boeotian bronze of early seventh century date. Samos, too, provides an ivory statuette of a kneeling youth (*c.* 610) which perfectly unites eastern techniques with the Greek sense of form.

Many of the small figures of the period already have Greek faces, alert and angular, but these were at first combined with the wig-like hair and forward-thrusting forearms of Syrian and neo-Hittite statuettes of mother-goddesses. Cyprus, which was an outpost of Syro-Phoenician culture (p. 120), perhaps played a part as intermediary, since already by the eighth century its figurines were appearing upon more westerly Aegean island sites. But Greece did not need the Cypriots to transmit oriental ivory traditions, since it was already aquainted with them through direct contact with Syria itself.

The Ionians had inherited Crete's delight in surface pattern and vivacious movement, and the Syrian feeling for soft, rounded plastic forms. But the sculpture of Samos and its Milesian neighbour is also beginning to show the classic Greek interest in man for his own sake. Yet, as befitted a people which sought to explain the world by purely intellectual means (p. 175), this process was combined with a fascination for mathematical lines. The use of hard materials in any case necessitated such a preoccupation, but the Greek artist revelled in it, since he was launched upon his task of amending nature's disorder by his own sense of form.

A major step was taken along these paths when sculptors of the seventh and sixth centuries BC introduced the epoch-making novelty of large-scale statues. The first examples to be made of durable materials seem to have come from the archipelago of the Cyclades, where the availability of good marble and emery scraping-tools had long proved incentives to sculptors. Soon after 600 Samos, to which tradition ascribed a pioneer role, produced a more than life-size female image which is of a curiously rounded shape because it imitates a clay idol turned on the potter's wheel.

Just at the time when sculptors in various parts of Greece were tentatively launching upon these new paths, they came into contact with the specific influence they needed. For it was now that Greeks first had an opportunity to see the unfamiliar, massive statuary of Egypt.

After the catastrophe of temporary capture by the Assyrians, the unity of Egypt had been restored by King Psammetichus (Psamtek) I (*c.* 663–609 BC). Establishing a capital at Sais in the north-western part of the delta, and nostalgically copying native artistic styles that were two thousand years old, the merchant-kings of this dynasty ruled with the help of a Phoenician fleet, Carian and Lydian mercenaries, and Ionian 'men of bronze' with the new hoplite equipment (p. 157). As a retirement pension, he established his Greek soldiers in two frontier stations, on either side of the delta's eastern arm.[14]

Meanwhile trade developed, and later in the century thirty ships from Miletus entered the Nile mouth near its western end and built a fortified station, 'the Wall of the Milesians'. Not long afterwards the Egyptians allowed the formation of a permanent Greek harbour and market-town at Naucratis, linked by a canal to Sais which was ten miles away (*c.* 620?). An emporium like Al Mina, Naucratis had four warehouses adjoined by their own temples, and soon began to make its own pottery and terracotta to send home corn and probably papyrus and linen, in exchange for silver and other products.

Welcomed by King Amasis (568–525), who married a Greek woman from Cyrene, this overseas extension of Greece obtained significant privileges, since ships brought into other mouths of the Nile were obliged to send their cargoes on to Naucratis in barges. The first Greeks to settle there came from the Asian seaboard and Aegina, but in due course the place housed merchants from as many as twelve cities. The consequence was a considerable flow of traders and other visitors between Egypt and Greece, which thus had every opportunity to learn of Egyptian achievements such as monumental stone statuary.*

In architecture, too, the seventh century witnessed the beginnings of something much more ambitious than anything that had been seen since Mycenaean times. It was again Egyptian influence which taught Greece the post-and-lintel formula of stone buildings with columns and capitals surmounted by horizontal entablatures (p. 54). But the Greeks, in their more moderate climate, felt able to turn the Egyptian temple inside out, so that the columns were now in the open air, where they assumed added importance. Moreover, the low Greek gable, with its projecting eaves designed to throw off snow or rain, goes back to beginnings in a less balmy country: the uplands of Phrygia and Lydia have been suggested as its place of origin (p. 154). The Greeks who first imported the feature were said to belong to Corinth, where the seventh-century invention of large, heavy terracotta tiles demanded the abandonment of the much steeper pitch inherited from early thatched roofs.

The Doric Order, with its comparatively plain capital consisting of a convex moulding surmounted by a flat square slab, was the first to develop. In eighth- and seventh-century shrines, columns were still made of wood, and a number of permanent features in later stone temples seem to point archaistically to these wooden origins. But now, since the heavy tile roofs needed a stronger support, regular courses of masonry were revived and used for the lower parts of the Heraeum at Olympia (*c.* 590) and then, ten years later, for entire walls at Corcyra.

The cushioned capitals and fluted columns of such temples are reminiscent of Egypt, and the bright contrasting red and blue paints that ornamented the stucco-covered high parts of the buildings likewise recall the near east. Egyptian, too, with Assyrian and Levantine infusions, are the combinations of lotus, papyrus and palmette which appear in these coloured decorations, and it was Egypt, again, which inspired monumental vistas such as the processional way at Miletus' great shrine of Apollo at Didyma.

Yet the results, at their best, were masterpieces of proportion far superior to any of the near eastern models. Elaborate,

* For debts to Egyptian literature, see p. 151.

refined skill was employed to exploit the effects of the Mediterranean sun as it picked out every angle and fluting. The ruins that have survived today, and reconstructed versions in soggy northern climates, do not enable the effect of these ever-changing contrasts of light and shadow to be recaptured; and the luminosity within the porticoes necessitated a delicacy of modelling unimaginable in countries where the sunshine is weaker. Another Mediterranean feature is the contrast between strong light and darkness on the actual threshold of the shrine, where the dilated pupils of visitors peered through the penumbra at the vast statue round which the building had been planned.

Against the majestic verticality of columns uprising from the earth their richly painted, sculptured, horizontal crowns set up a strong tension by their defiant differentiation from the Mediterranean landscape. The contrast makes a planned, composite, active impact upon the senses, and formidably active and dynamic, again, is the intellectual, conceptual process whereby all the themes borrowed from earlier civilisations have been transformed. This analysis and synthesis of environment and prototype bear an unprecedentedly powerful stamp of the human mind: the temples of the Greeks, like their other masterpieces, are consummately human.

The second main architectural Order, the Ionic, ran to greater sizes. Preliminary colonnaded structures were followed by huge, elaborate constructions put up late in the seventh century BC at Samos and Smyrna, clearly after examination of the many-columned Egyptian temples which Naucratis had made known (p. 163). The Ionic style, like all eastern Greek art, differs from Doric because of its even stronger taste for colourful, superficial decoration. Column capitals were at first bell-like, with spiral scrolls, which began by branching upwards and outwards but were then rolled flat and linked together so that their horizontal burden could be carried by a broader surface.

The designs of these capitals included semi-abstract stylisations of the overhanging leaves of the palm-tree or lotus. They had appeared in the Doric Order also, but the Ionic ornament is more lavish. The decorative forms imposed on this basically functional architecture draw upon the repertory of flower and plant patterns which throughout the near east had graced minor arts, adorning the legs of chairs and tables or even decorating ivory fly-whisks. A pattern based on an alternation of eggs and arrow-heads comes from Egyptian designs of lotus flowers and buds; a favourite form of fan-shaped palm-leaf, on the other hand, derives by way of Syria from the Mesopotamian 'Tree of Life'. And indeed the Greeks, with their love of geometry, tended to prefer the highly schematised plants and flowers of the Levant to the more literal luxuriance of Egypt. But on one occasion a Mesopotamian palm-leaf grows out of an Egyptian lotus; and this effectively symbolises the freedom artists felt to play conjuring tricks with their models and to change or abstract them out of all recognition.

Colonies in the west

Early Greek commerce was a matter of private, separate individual voyages by shipowners who lacked capital, depended on whatever loans they could raise, and captained their own small ships at sea. Such were the men who journeyed to the outer parts of the Mediterranean carrying pottery, textiles, ironwork, leather goods, jewellery and works of art, and bringing back corn, wool, timber, dried fruits, salt fish, metals, hides, amber and ivory. But all this took many years to achieve. There also came a time when these traders, like similar Mycenaean and Phoenician travellers, were supplemented or replaced by voyagers prepared to settle down at these distant spots. People emigrated from Greece because there was no longer enough land for its population to cultivate. The main objective of most emigrants, therefore, was to find coastal lands occupied by inhabitants backward enough to eject, and then to establish agricultural settlements on the land thus vacated. They were farmers; although, inevitably, their new foundations also led to increased trade, augmented by piracy and the collection of tolls. But the first colonies were organised by the land-owning aristocracies of homeland city-states as a remedy for agrarian unrest – as places to send landless second and third sons. And so the colonies, too, began as republics like the places from which they came. 'Colony' is a misleading term; even if a few mother-cities such as Corinth had more proprietary ideas, these colonies were mostly independent from the start. The Greek word for them means 'away-home' (*apoikia*).

The diffusion of these new settlements round the Mediterranean and Black Seas was a huge, gradual, adventurous explosion, taming seas and winds as the Egyptians and Babylonians had controlled rivers and nomad peoples domesticated deserts.[15] When Europeans of a later date colonised north and south America, nearly every beginning of a colony ended in disaster; one in three of the Pilgrim Fathers was dead within a year. It was probably the same with the Greeks. At Abdera in Thrace, for example, we hear of the first two expeditions being wiped out by the natives, and only a third massive migration of Ionian refugees from the Persians taking hold. The vital function of preventing clashes and encroachments between the many colonising city-states was taken over by the pan-Hellenic oracle of Apollo at Delphi, which amassed a unique corpus of information and advised many prospective settlers on appropriate sites and cults.

The main wave of agrarian colonisation was preceded by certain very far-flung foundations which seem to have been guided by commercial rather than agricultural aspirations. For these intrepid colonists had their eye on the rich metals of Etruria (p. 235); and so they landed along the coast of the Tyrrhenian Sea. And yet the new settlements could not be planted nearly as far north as the mines, since they must remain well outside the area of Etruscan control. Early in the eighth century BC, therefore, the Euboean towns of Chalcis and Eretria collaborated with Aeolian Cyme in Asia Minor to send settlers to the island of Pithecusae (Ischia) which lies just beyond the western extremity of the bay of Naples, a hundred and fifteen miles away from Etruria. Offshore islands of this kind had already been favoured by the Mycenaeans and Phoenicians, and Mycenaean vases are found on Pithecusae (p. 109), which contained fertile strips as well as gold deposits within its eighteen mile circumference. But above all, the island's little circular lake with its narrow entrance was one of the best Mediterranean harbours for small boats, well placed to launch raids or impose tolls on rivals attempting the Etruscan transit trade; and this was a matter of which the colonists had experience, since at home these same Euboeans had been accustomed to levy tolls on the use of the narrows which separated them from the mainland.

By *c* 750, however, volcanic eruptions made it necessary to leave Pithecusae, and the Chalcidians (whose relations with the Eretrians on the island had become strained owing to warfare at home) joined the Cymaean settlers in a move to the Italian mainland, where they founded the colony of Cyme (Cumae) on a site two miles north of the bay. This place, which had already been visited by Greek traders, was not very well off for cultivable soil, but its fortified hill enjoyed the protection of a marshy hinterland and had access to a sandy beach on which ships could be drawn up. The bronze-workers of Cumae, pupils of their mother-city Chalcis ('place of bronze') and of Urartu whose cauldrons occur in local finds (p. 118), later became the teachers of the leading metal industry of Capua in the interior of Campania; and the Cumaeans were also destined to play a very large part in the introduction of Greek civilisation to Rome.

From about 730 BC onwards colonies of a more normal, agricultural kind occupied all the coastal alluvial plains of eastern Sicily and south Italy. Sicily was strategically as significant to Greeks as to Phoenicians and Carthaginians (p. 126). Sufficiently large to form a tempting prey, small enough to hold out elusive hopes of political unification, the island has always provided 'a history of settlement, a history of men who found themselves new homes in a strange land'.[16] Between the Semitic-speaking and Greek communities constant friction developed, but generally the former were restricted to the western areas, nearest to Carthage, while Greeks colonised the eastern regions which likewise lay opposite their own home country. Sicily surpasses all Mediterranean islands by its productivity and variety, and in the extreme contrasts between barren interior and fertile plains and coastal tracts. The vale of Enna was the stage for the fertility myth of Persephone, and to its north-east rose the volcano of Etna that has erupted a hundred and forty times in twenty-five centuries and enriches the island's limestone core with abundant layers of decomposed lava. To the south of the mountain is one of the few perennial flowing rivers, and although there is a four-month summer drought, favoured areas have rain at all seasons. In spring, this usually falls at the right time for growing wheat, which yields remarkably heavy crops.

The enterprising people of Chalcis, who had taken the lead on the west coast of Italy, also figured prominently in the earliest Sicilian colony. This was Naxos (Capo Schiso), which took its name from the Aegean island associated with Chalcis in the foundation (p. 174). This first settlement was just below Etna, whose snow-laden peak was a surer mark for navigators even than Cape Cod for newcomers to America. Naxos was on a headland site, almost a peninsula, near a stream and a small inland valley which was conveniently cut off from the perilous interior but sufficiently fertile to warrant the choice of a bunch of grapes as the colony's emblem.

The men of Chalcis and their colony Naxos went on to new places, expelling native populations and establishing themselves at two harbour-sites, Catana and Zancle – later called Messana (Messina) – which served the most important farming areas on the island. The latter foundation was also partly the work of Cumae, naturally interested in controlling this strategic passage where the two halves of the Mediterranean meet in a narrow strait of swirling eddies and formidable blasts, from which Zancle's semicircular port was sheltered by a projecting spur.

According to tradition, it was only one year after the foundation of Naxos that the Corinthians moved farther down the west coast and colonised Syracuse, ejecting a native community and perhaps associating with themselves a smaller contingent from Chalcis. Syracuse, destined to become the most populous city in the Greek world, stood on the side of a deep bay, partly closed by an island which was to become the site of a citadel and – joined to Sicily by a mole – dominated the entrance to ports on either side. The Syracusans took the lead in a flourishing mercantile society, and their silver coinage was particularly abundant and spectacular.

Other Sicilian foundations during the next century and a half culminated in two south coast foundations, Selinus ('wild celery') with its huge temples, and Acragas (*c.* 580) established by Rhodian and Sicilian colonists on an elevated plateau two and a half miles from the sea, at the edge of undulating vine and olive country. But Greek Sicily mainly derived agricultural wealth from its position as the principal grain-producing and exporting country of the Mediterranean area. In addition to the cities on the coast, air photographs have now revealed large numbers of inland settlements which participated in this activity.

After Greeks had begun to found colonies in eastern Sicily, they saw they must also control the mainland bank of the Straits of Messina. So the Chalcidian settlers at Zancle became founders or part-founders of Rhegium (Reggio Calabria) on the Italian side of the narrows. Soon, however, another set of colonists appeared in Italy, the Achaeans. In spite of their glorious Homeric name this people had played an undistinguished part in their own poor homeland of the almost harbourless northern Peloponnese. But now they founded significant settlements on the Gulf of Taranto which is the instep of Italy, with the double intention of occupying rich agricultural soil and exploiting the overland route across the toe of the peninsula, so that cargoes could be moved by road between the Tyrrhenian and Ionian seas without having to pass through the treacherous Messina Straits. The first of these colonies was Sybaris (*c.* 720), which transported goods across the isthmus for Milesians and Etruscans alike. But the site was primarily chosen because of an adjoining plain rich in wheat, vines, and pastures for cows and sheep, and a river employed for the washing and dyeing of wool; beyond were mountains providing wood, resin and wax. A by-word for all this wealth, Sybaris only survived two hundred years before suffering total annihilation from its neighbour Croton (510 BC). The river was diverted to obliterate the vanquished city, which archaeologists now hope to uncover again from beneath twenty feet of alluvial soil. Croton had performed the cruel act under the influence of a politico-religious brotherhood founded by the mystic and mathematician Pythagoras after his migration from Samos. The destructive conquerors issued coinage imitating the design of a bull which Sybaris had placed upon its fine intaglio-style currency; while Metapontum, farther along the same wide gulf, likewise showed the source of its wealth by depicting an ear of corn.

In *c.* 700 Achaeans had moved northwards, perhaps from Sybaris, and established Posidonia (Paestum) on maritime flats only fifty miles short of Cumae, whose trade with Etruria the new foundation was intended to challenge. Although Posidonia is unusual in possessing no acropolis, its impressive dimensions can be seen from surviving temples of sixth and fifth century date.

Another participant in this colonising activity was Sparta (*c.* 706), which sent a group of war-time bastards to occupy Taras (Taranto) on the northern coast of the gulf which bears its name. The citadel rock of Taras stood on a triangular tongue of land between an outer bay and a capacious inner basin which was the finest harbour in southern Italy. Its people proved stronger than their Achaean neighbours, and made great profits from their orchards, fisheries and murex, which was used to dye the adjoining products of the best sheepdowns in the peninsula.

Taras also sent out settlers of its own to colonise the heel of Italy, and maintained contacts not only with Corcyra, just across the Ionian Sea, but with trading communities far up into the Adriatic on either side of the mouth of Italy's largest river the Po, which had long attracted commercial activity. On the north side of the delta, sixth-century objects have been found at Adria, where Greeks traded with the Eneti who inhabited the present Venezia; and excavations at Spina on the south arm, where Greeks and Etruscans together occupied street-canals upon a line of isolated coastal dunes (p. 242), have brought to light huge numbers of vases.

In *c.* 638 BC a Samian merchant called Colaeus – an involuntary explorer like Leif Ericsson on the coast of America – was blown so helplessly off his course from his native island to Egypt that he actually passed through the Strait of Gibraltar to the Phoenician port of Tartessus on the Atlantic (p. 121), from which he brought home an immense treasure of silver. Nevertheless, the Greeks proved unable to assert their interests in southern Spain against the Carthaginians. They were more successful, however, in staking out an alternative route to the country by way of France. Greek pottery of the later seventh century has been found in Gaulish villages at the mouth of the Rhône, and enterprising mariners of the small Ionian town of Phocaea, travelling in packs of fifty-oared ships, established a colony in *c.* 600 at Massalia (Marseille) – three low hills, within a circuit of only a mile and a half, on a small steep limestone peninsula beside a sheltered basin. Protected by a marsh and flanked by streams, the settlement was deliberately placed forty miles away from the debouchment of the Rhône to avoid the silt borne by anti-clockwise currents. Moreover, the cold, blustering, dry mistral wind which whistles down the valley from central Europe in winter and spring is kept off by a substantial headland.

Throughout the sixth century Massalia received many imports from Ionia and eastern Greece. Nevertheless, the place did not grow rapidly at first. For although rain is comparatively plentiful, the neighbouring Gaulish cornland was poor, and the site was hemmed in by mountains which hindered expansion and disqualified Massalia from becoming a suitable capital of the region. Besides, like early Montreal and then Winnipeg, it lay on the very outskirts of a barbarous world, with no civilisation to its north. Before long, however, Massalians started to penetrate this unknown region by taking over the river-traffic of the Rhône, which although its full, current-ridden waters are not easily navigable above the delta, provided an all-important northward gap. Thus began the historic process of penetration through the complex of internal river routes which France is the only Mediterranean country to possess. In exchange for corn, amber, and tin, the wine amphoras of the colony found their way far inland at an early date, and Greek artistic masterpieces of the later sixth century have come to light as far afield as the Seine.

Moreover, the exuberantly plastic, rhythmically patterned, curvilinear art of the Celts, though lacking the Greek interest in the human body, was largely inspired by the palm-leaves, tendrils and plant-designs which began in *c.* 500 to reach Gaul and the Rhineland, not only from the Etruscans (p. 235), but also on the wine-jars of Massalia. These Greeks, it was later observed, 'taught the Gauls a more civilised way of life.[17] Abandoning their barbarous habits, they learnt to till the fields and cultivated the vine and olive. Their progress, in manners and wealth, gradually gained such momentum that it seemed justified to describe Gaul as part of Greece rather than Greece the coloniser of Gaul.[17]

In addition to these inland approaches, Massalia dominated

the land-route between Spain and Italy, where there was a tradition of a sixth-century Massalian treaty with Rome. The mother-city Phocaea failed to establish itself against the Carthaginians and Etruscans in Corsica (535), but on the south coast of France Carthaginian and Phoenician outposts were superseded by a whole monopolistic network of Massalian settlements. Greek in derivation, as a result, are names such as Monoecus (Monaco) with its formerly Phoenician temple, Nicaea (Nice), Antipolis (Antibes), Agathe (Agde) on a rocky islet tied to the mainland, and towards the Pyrenees the white limestone promontory of Leucate jutting out from a coastal lagoon.

From there the line of Massalia's foundations was extended into Spain, where trading journeys resulted in the establishment of Emporiae (Ampurias) on an islet just offshore from a native town. In direct rivalry with Phoenicia and Carthage, Massalians and Phocaeans pushed colonies southwards down the Spanish coast as far as the latitude of the Balearic islands, and their last outpost, the westernmost of all Greek settlements, was nearly as far as Phoenician Malaca. From Ilici (Elche) near Alicante comes a sculptured, mitred, bejewelled woman's head, once polychrome, which illustrates the creative impact of archaic Hellenism on local Phoenician and native Iberian cultures, and shows that there was a vigorous Greco-Spanish as well as a Greco-Scythian and Greco-Etruscan art (p. 181).

Ionia and eastern colonies

This remarkable role of Phocaea in the west is one indication of the major part played by the Ionians in the mighty expansion of Mediterranean horizons during the period. The Ionian homeland on the coast of Asia Minor lay partly upon the highly individual and distinctive islands (p. 140). To the north, Aeolian Lesbos, on which Mytilene was the largest town, had longstanding designs upon the Dardanelles route. In the opposite direction, Dorian Rhodes revived and maintained its historic trading links. But the most important of all were two islands between them, Chios and Samos, which formed part of the twelve Ionian states. Chios, which produced corn, figs, gum-mastic and what was generally regarded as the best Greek wine, served as the financial centre for a large area, and although its government soon turned to democratic institutions and lawcourts (*c.* 600), this remained one of the rare Greek examples of a society which not only used slaves but was mainly based on slavery (p. 201).

Nevertheless it was a poet of the island, Ion, who wrote a hymn to Opportunity, 'the youngest of the daughters of Zeus'. But this might have come even better from the people of Samos, who were the outstanding opportunists of the Greek world. Their island not only provided a port of call for the Levant trade, including the bronzework of eighth-century Urartu, but was the Asian terminal of the principal all-weather route to mainland Greece. With its circular 'frying pan' of a harbour, Samos was the most strategically valuable island in the Aegean and the key-point of every ancient naval plan. Its sumptuous Heraeum was the largest of all sanctuaries and glittered with dedications, its young men were famous for their fashionable clothes,[18] and the rich landed class remained influential until late in the fifth century BC.

But this aristocratic régime was sharply punctuated by the 'tyranny' of Polycrates (*c.* 533–522), who had been installed by a fellow autocrat at Naxos, the island which was joint coloniser of the Sicilian settlement of the same name. Although Naxos had momentarily become the richest centre in the Aegean, Polycrates outdid his Naxian patron on a majestic scale. Maker and breaker of treaties with Egypt and Persia, he became the first Greek to organise the ancient occupation of piracy on a grand scale, and the one Mediterranean ruler of his day who understood that sea-power, if effectively employed, could rival large land forces. His harbour-mole and water-tunnel, engineering portents a century ahead of their time, show how the Samians excelled in applied science and experiment. Its people also settled far and wide, and their ambitions were bound to conflict with those of their all too close neighbours, the Milesians. Polycrates imported their thoroughbred sheep and did his best to interfere with the markets of Miletus, which retaliated by closing them to all people from Samos.

There were also significant mainland cities, such as Smyrna, half-Asian Ephesus which retained active communications with the interior, and Phocaea, the Greek Amalfi which had replaced Cyme as a colonial founder. But Miletus was still more important than any of them, as it had been already nearly a thousand years earlier. Soon after 800 the Milesians built a fortress with walls twelve feet thick; then they crossed their gulf and annexed the lower end of the Maeander plain. A new acropolis and harbour of about the sixth century, revealed by recent excavations, were probably in part the work of a 'tyrant' Thrasybulus. Allied with Periander of Corinth, he profited from internal strife between Milesian farmers and a powerful merchants' guild to establish a dictatorship, which subsequently broke up into civil war lasting for two generations (*c.* 580). But the strength of Miletus, capable of surviving these convulsions, was its woollen and textile market, designed with the help of Phrygian and then Lydian slaves to supply the fine tissues and many-coloured embroideries of Phoenicia and Syria. An important and widely distributed class of pots now ascribed to Miletus (p. 162) reflects and adapts some of the oriental motifs which round about the year 600 inspired Ionian sculpture also.

Very soon afterwards further eastern influences, again after undergoing local transformations, figured largely in the thought of the versatile prodigies of the same city who have been described as the first Greek philosophers. Their conclusions were derived from myth and priestly formula and geographical and astronomical lore inherited from Syria, Mesopotamia and Egypt. But the Milesians used this mixture of unscientific and quasi-scientific material to formulate, for the first time in history, a limited number of principles from which they deduced truths in accordance with rigorous intellectual processes. Sometimes, indeed, this cerebral approach led to an over-logical disregard for the actual data of experience. Yet often, too, these were respected. The inquisitive minds of the Milesians were directly stimulated by their far-reaching experiences and cultural borrowings and travels. The spirit was later summed up by Euripides, who declared 'happy is he who has knowledge that comes from enquiry, and surveys the unageing order of deathless nature, of what it is made, and whence, and how.'[19]

The earliest of these half-logical, half-religious thinkers, Thales, originated metaphysics by suggesting that all material substances, however different they may seem to our senses, can be reduced to a single basic material. His enquiry into the nature of the universe began from Hesiod's assumption of its unified control. This had been founded on eastern elements (p. 151), and Thales, who was reputed to be half Phoenician, had learnt his astronomy and geometry from Babylon and especially Egypt. Although the story of his prediction of a solar eclipse (585 BC) must be rejected, since even his Babylonian masters could not have foretold this precisely enough at so early a date, Thales' theory of the earth riding upon the waters is paralleled in the Egyptian myth of Nun, and the idea of its formation from water may have come from the silting of the Nile, which was one of the many Egyptian phenomena brought to the knowledge of the Greeks by their new contacts with that country (p. 163).

Anaximander, on the other hand (*c.* 546), who believed the earth to be freely suspended and eternally moving in space, was more Babylonian in his ideas, although this heritage had again come down to him, in part at least, through Greek works such as the Hesiodic poems. He also contributed greatly to Mediterranean studies by drawing up the first map of the inhabited portions of the earth. His younger contemporary, Anaximenes, was the first man to conceive the cosmos as governed not according to a moral but a physical law. Quantitative changes, he maintained, are able to produce qualitative effects also, because of rarefaction and condensation, of which the importance was suggested to him by a pressure process for the felting of woven materials which the textile-minded Milesians had seen in Scythia (p. 181). In the same spirit Xenophanes of Ionian Colophon felt obliged to reject traditional myths because of his belief that all things originated from earth and water, supporting this materialism by the observation or report of such things as sea-shells found upon hills, and the impressions of fish and seaweed upon rocks. Ionians of this frame of mind were also much preoccupied with the weather which played such a large part in their explorations, and this interest made them keenly aware of sunshine and storms and rainbows and the transformations that swept continually over their horizons. The philosopher who incarnated this consciousness of change was Heraclitus of Ephesus (*c.* 500). He saw the world as a harmony of opposites – the same sort of attunement of tensions as appeared in the bow and lyre, and seemed particularly natural to the Ionians who lived on the borders of the Greek and Asian worlds.

From shortly before 600 until Persia replaced benign Lydia as suzerain (546–540) and the destruction of allied Sybaris (510) diminished western trade, the Ionians and especially the Milesians were at the height of their remarkable prosperity. Markets were available all the way from Spanish Tartessus to Naucratis in Egypt and Posidium in Syria, where Ionian wares, together with those of Corinth, reigned supreme. Except in those regions of the west where Carthage claimed the heritage, the Phoenician was now outclassed.

> He saw the merry Grecian coaster come,
>   Freighted with amber grapes and Chian wine,
>   Green, bursting figs, and tunnies steeped in brine –
> and knew the intruders on his ancient home,
> The young light-hearted masters of the waves.[20]

This trading gave an impulse to colonisation, which was very attractive to the small separate Ionian enclaves, sandwiched between the sea and an alien interior without enough land to feed their growing populations. The lead was taken in spectacular fashion by Miletus. The brisk coastal and ferry traffic that must always have been maintained by that city led to the astonishing total of ninety colonial foundations, of which more than half have been verified. To these settlements Miletus provided a proportion of the colonists, the majority of ships and leaders, and a large part of the necessary knowledge of sea-routes and local conditions.

The greatest effort was devoted to the Black Sea area and its approaches. Although Mytilene had taken up positions astride the Dardanelles, and other cities too were active in the area, Milesians settled at Abydos within the strait during the seventh century BC, and then became the first colonists along the Sea of Marmara. The most successful and perhaps the earliest of these colonies was Cyzicus (Bandirma), a large natural harbour on a broad-headed offshore island joined by bridges to a point on the mainland commanding an inland route. The badge of Cyzicus was the tunny, which figured largely in its economy. This fish played a more important part than any other in the diet of ancient Mediterranean peoples. It could be preserved for long periods in olive-oil, and the Greeks, who unlike the Homeric Achaeans[21] ate a lot of fish,[22] chased tunnies into shallow waters to be dispatched by harpoons, and placed outlook towers on headlands to watch their movements. Although the Mediterranean is far poorer than the Atlantic in plankton and therefore in fish as well, shoals of tunny are found in winter as in summer on almost every coast. But especially large groups move together from the Black Sea every year and then congregate in the central Mediterranean at the end of May, before dispersing north again or proceeding westwards into the Atlantic. The Sea of Marmara is a natural creek for trapping these large, fat, nutritive fish.

At the other end of that sea was the fifteen miles long Bosphorus. The Greeks who first settled in its neighbourhood came not from Miletus but from the small town of Megara, whose narrow homeland made emigration a necessity. And so Megarians sailed through the Aegean and Sea of Marmara to the Bosphorus, where at the beginning of the narrows they founded Chalcedon (Kadiköy) on the Asian shore (*c.* 676?). A Persian later called this the 'city of the blind' because its founders had failed to notice the superior advantages of Byzantium, the future Constantinople on the opposite side. But Byzantium's strategic position evidently interested them less than the good grain of Chalcedon – and perhaps also its greater security from Thracian incursions. Nevertheless it was not long afterwards that the Megarians occupied Byzantium as well. The traditional year is 660; and recent discoveries of pottery date from before 600.

Compared by a medieval chronicler to a three-cornered sail bellying in the wind, the place was situated on the point of a promontory bounded on the south by the Sea of Marmara and on the north by the navigable Golden Horn. This deeply recessed, riverless and therefore non-silting backwater, sheltered from northern gales by a wind-break of hills, had already been a ferry-station more than six centuries earlier. It was an ideal and indeed inevitable halting-point for ships before or after they tackled the Bosphorus, with its wind-lashed currents from the Black Sea that zig-zag seven times through the strait from corner to corner and finally to the headland itself, swirling past the

Golden Horn but filling it with the wealth of fish to which its epithet may be owed. 'By sea,' said the Greek historian Polybius, 'Byzantium commands the mouth of the Black Sea so securely that no trader can sail in or out without its consent. And since the Black Sea contains many of the commodities required by other peoples for their way of life, the Byzantines enjoy complete control over all these supplies.'[23]

Yet it was not the Megarian founders of Byzantium but the sailors of Miletus who worked their way through the currents of the Bosphorus out into the stormy Black Sea. The Greeks did not call it Black but *Euxeinos* or hospitable; either in a hopefully flattering reversal of an earlier name *Axeinos*, 'inhospitable', or perhaps through a corruption of a Semitic or Iranian word meaning dark or north.

The legend of the Argonauts may reflect explorations of the sea as early as the second millennium BC (p. 109). By 800 or soon after, Ionians and other islanders knew something of the tribes and curiosities on its shores (p. 146), and the Homeric poems show some vague acquaintance with its southern seaboard. But first-hand information did not come until the seventh century, when this north-eastern region was the only maritime area within Greek reach which still remained unexploited.

The opening up of all this wealth was almost entirely the achievement of the Milesians, who converted the Black Sea into a semi-private lake. More than half of their settlements were planted upon its coasts or approaches, and their traders were preeminent throughout the whole region. The tons of grain, smoked fish, cattle skins, furs, honey, wax, gold and amber – and the human freights of slaves – shipped out from the Black Sea every year were largely carried by the ships of Miletus and paid for by its business men and bankers. The importation of Black Sea corn made it possible to turn more and more to specialised production. Nor did the ships need to travel empty to the Black Sea, since they could carry cargoes of olive-oil and wine for the settlers, who still ate and drank in the Greek way.

On the rolling well-watered ridges of the Black Sea's Asian seaboard, the Milesians found not only extensive woods but abundant timber for ship-construction. This coast had been settled by many earlier civilisations, but recent excavations at its central point, Sinope (Sinob), suggest that Greek colonisation did not begin until shortly before 600. Although Sinope possessed a fertile garden strip, communications with the interior of Asia Minor were poor. But the place stood at the Black Sea's waist, where the crossing to the Crimea, with its rich resources of grain, was shortest; and Sinope's peninsular anvil-shaped harbour was a half-way house to iron mines farther east. Closer to them was its daughter city Trapezus (Trebizond, Trabzon). This formed the terminal of the northern land-route to Iran, which Greeks began to use during the sixth century.

Sinope's foundation approximately coincided with the first appearance of further settlements to the west of the Black Sea, in what are now Rumania and Bulgaria. An attraction to explorers in this region was the Danube, which provided a natural channel for trade and was easily approached from the fertile Dobrogea beside its marshy delta. The first Greek colony, Istros (Histria), was near the mouth, and less than fifty miles from the river's great curve before it approaches the sea. Built on a low hill which is now part of the mainland but at that time stood on a peninsula or island, Istros was at first only a little settlement of one-room stone houses, living on delta fisheries (*c.* 600). But before long the productive corn-growing hinterland was opened up, and proximity to the Danube crossing supplied a brisk river trade and gave access to gold and silver in the mountains beyond the other bank. Farther down the coast, on a peninsula at the southern (Bulgarian) extremity of the Dobrogea, recent underwater explorations have begun to reveal another prosperous city at Bisone, which later vanished from view owing to its inundation as a result of an earthquake.

There were also Milesian colonies of about 600 BC where the Russian rivers debouch into the Black Sea. These are the immense, invaluable streams flowing one after another from the edge of the forest zone down through the east European plain, all the way between the Carpathians and the Kuban.

The inhabitants of this region, the Indo-European-speaking Scythians, had probably come originally from the Volga steppe, driving before them the Persians and Medes into the Iranian lands that became their homes. During the later seventh century, however, the Medes forced them to return across the

Caucasus, and Scythians streamed back into the southern regions of Russia. Their unique artistic talents are illustrated by fantastic blends of naturalism and stylisation. The resplendent royal tombs of their various kingdoms depict rams' heads, eagles, lions, boar, deer and fishes in styles which fuse earlier Eurasian nomadic traditions with Median, Assyrian, Urartian, Anatolian and Greek motifs.

The country in which they had now settled or resettled was an inexhaustible storehouse of raw materials. Originally mounted head-hunters whose diet was meat and milk, many Scythians learnt to profit by the agricultural wealth in their midst and turned to the cultivation of corn in the 'black earth', the flat, deep Ukrainian and Moldavian plains, extending inland for twenty days' journey. The climate is not Mediterranean because more rain falls in summer than during the winters, which are dry and hard. But when the thaw ended, strong horse-teams ploughed the soil while it was still damp and sticky, and made it produce massive quantities of grain. The surpluses were shipped down by river to the Black Sea ports, together with hides, furs, timber and slaves, and exchanged for Greek manufactures and oil and wine. 'Greek wine-jars take the place of the Tsar's vodka flasks in a Siberian encampment or gin bottles in an African kraal'; and the coastal plains of Russia had been drawn into the Mediterranean world for many centuries to come.

The earliest settlement established by Miletus to tap this huge market was probably Tyras (Belgorod), on a headland overlooking the shallow estuary-gulf of the river of the same name, now the Dniester. Where the next big rivers towards the east, the Bug (Hypanis) and richly meadowed Dnieper (Borysthenes), merge as they near the sea stood Olbia, the northernmost and wealthiest Greek colony. Ships could be drawn up along the right bank of the Bug, and the settlement, built on a carefully laid-out plan, prospered from its fisheries and above all became the greatest of all markets for exporting grain.

Meanwhile Milesian goldsmiths at the place were collaborating with native talent to produce a Greco-Scythian art which is as remarkable as that of another fringe region, Etruria*. The early history of Olbia also displayed another analogy with Italian developments since, as at Pithecusae (p. 167), there had

* Compare also Spain, p. 173.

first been a settlement on an offshore island, or possibly a peninsula. This was Berezan just outside the river-mouth, where Milesian newcomers had joined or superseded a native community. The mainland site of Olbia to which they subsequently moved was better placed to tap the hinterland traffic of the inland waterways, and enabled them to penetrate up the Dnieper as far north as Kiev and the Pripet marshes. These and the other south Russian rivers, with their long history of earlier cultures, are great upcountry arteries, like the Rhône and its French network of streams: but on a far larger scale, since no other region in the world possesses a concentration of rivers of such quantity and size.

Before the seventh century ended Greek traders had passed right through the Black Sea into the remotest corner of the Sea of Azov (Lake Maeotis), more than three weeks' journey beyond the Danube. The two stretches of water are separated by the Crimean peninsula, in which a number of Milesian and other colonies were founded on parts of the coast where erosion harbours of Mediterranean type provided shelter for small craft. The principal concentrations, however, were upon the strait (Cimmerian Bosphorus) which connects the two seas, separating the Crimea's Taman promontory from the mainland north of the Caucasus. Among a number of Greek settlements on either side of the narrows, the most important was Panticapaeum (Kertch), the city destined to become the capital of a Bosphoran kingdom rich from gold and the grain it sold to Greece. Panticapaeum, on the commanding Taman headland above the strait, possessed a harbour – better than it is today – and good fishing facilities, and ready access to the excellent cornfields of the Crimea's south-eastern coastal strip, which enjoys cover from the cold north winds.

Finally prospectors and then colonists from Miletus penetrated to the farthest extremity of the Black Sea, where the mineral and agricultural wealth of the Caucasus was within reach. On this coast, where seventy – or some said three hundred – languages could be heard in a single small-town bazaar, the Milesians were establishing themselves before 500 BC; but already a hundred years earlier the goods found in Caucasian tombs had borne witness to the existence of an important sea-route running from one end of the Black Sea to the other.

The spirit of this whole activity was summed up by Hecataeus of Miletus (*c.* 500 BC) in his *Journey Round the World.* Writing mainly about Mediterranean territories and narrating their history, the work describes towns and peoples, plants and animals, products and harbourages. There were two parts, one comprising Europe and the other Asia. The Asian section included Egypt and Libya; for Greeks lived there also. The settlers at Naucratis and other Nile delta markets did not possess independent city-states of their own (p. 163), but there were fully-fledged farming colonies on the fertile Mediterranean plateau and seaboard of Cyrenaica. The earliest and most important of these was Cyrene, on the heights overlooking a sacred spring at the unusual distance of twelve miles from the sea. The colonists at Cyrene produced corn, dates, and wool. The silphium plant, too, which grew only in Cyrenaica and is now extinct, was exported far and wide both as a food-seasoning and for medicinal uses that contributed to the reputation of Cyrene as a medical centre.

Its first settlers, soon supplemented by others, came from the nearest parts of the Greek world, Crete and Thera in the southern Aegean (*c.* 630). Milesians did not, therefore, have matters all their own way. Nor did they at the northern extremities of the same sea, since there as in Italy the pioneer coloniser was Euboean Chalcis – which gave its name to the three prongs of Chalcidice pointing southwards into the sea from Macedonia. This triple headland provided an obvious area for settlement, being only a hundred and twenty miles from Chalcis, and the nearest place to Greece which was not already preempted by irremovable occupants. For the scarcely Hellenised hinterland belonged to semi-barbarous Macedonian princes, who could not prevent the Greeks from planting their colonies. These concentrated upon the south-west faces of the promontories, which were sheltered from the north winds by coastal ridges and enjoyed a Riviera-like climate. Consequently Torone (*c.* 710), together with other foundations established by more than one mother-city on the Macedonian shore and islands, gained a special reputation for wine. The wood and pitch of the area also attracted attention, and the former came to play a prominent part in Athenian policy (p. 200). Along the coast, adjoining the populous, turbulent states of Thrace, were other colonies, one of them Abdera which overcame a shaky start involving two

Ionian settlements (*c.* 650–500). The people of Abdera retained a reputation for thick-headedness. But that was somewhat belied by its production of two leading philosophers, Democritus who learnt his atomic science from Leucippus of Miletus, and Protagoras who declared, in terms worthy of this great story of exploration, that 'man is the measure of all things'.

Greek colonies in the eastern Mediterranean and Black Sea were not usually so large or imposing as those in Sicily and southern Italy, and they did not usually start so early. Yet they represent an equally remarkable diffusion of the Greek way of life over enormous areas, and they helped greatly to stimulate inquisitiveness, breadth of mind, and no-nonsense observation. Miletus played the largest part, and it was the Milesian Hecataeus who had the characteristic confidence and arrogance to declare: 'I write what I believe to be true, for the stories of the Greeks are manifold and seem to me ridiculous.' Fantastic tales could nowadays be checked; his compatriots had penetrated to countless places, and the size and range of the observable world had been vastly enlarged.

8

Athens and Alexandria

Greek crops and natural beauties

The climate of Greece suffers from a pretty severe summer heat. Rainfall practically gives out for two months in the north and for four in the Peloponnese, and worst of all in its eastern regions. Summer winds are strong, but where they are hot or non-existent there is a tropical climate; the Thessaly plain has the same mean July temperature (90°F.) as Seville, and everything dries up. Moreover the country is poorly served by rivers. Most are winter torrents that roar and erode, and then vanish; the very largest, Achelous in Aetolia, was only navigable for twenty-three miles. Canals and tunnels assumed such importance that they were often attributed to the divine Heracles, who was also said to have drained the marshy plain of Tempe.

The least useful of these irrigated areas were utilised for pasture. In Greece, this was not an alternative use for cultivated soil, but the function of a different piece of ground not good enough to be sown or planted, consisting of fenlands and river meadows for cattle, and artificial fields (where possible) for the higher-cropping oxen and horses. Sophocles tells of a shepherd who adopted the ancient custom of moving his flocks to higher ground during the summer (p. 28). Towns paid tribute to goats and cows by adopting them as their emblems, the latter being an echo of the days when payments were made in such animals. Nevertheless the Greeks, unlike the legendary meat-eaters of Homer, ate fish more often than red meat (p. 178), and when meat came their way the general lack of rich pasture meant that it was usually pork.

The better soil, though still reluctant, was keenly and laboriously cultivated, and in spite of all trading expansion the fundamental activity of the Greek world continued to be agriculture. During prehistoric times the country's principal crops had been wheat and barley, beans, figs, and peas. But in historic epochs came the characteristic triple Mediterranean pattern of cereals, wine and oil, expressed by the myth of Anio priest-king of Delos, whose three daughters could by the grace of Dionysus each grow one of these products at will. Vegetables, too, did not cease to be important, since small-holdings aimed to produce a balanced variety for the local market. But corn, wine and oil were paramount.

Corn, however, is less prolific than in more northern countries. Normally only wheat was made into bread, though inferior soils were more suitable for barley (p. 22), which was not baked but kneaded into porridge. The best and heaviest wheat was the spring crop of Boeotia, but the only part of the country which produced a margin for export was Thessaly: and the major city-states of Greece were continually concerned to increase their supplies.

The seasonal pattern varied from place to place. Cyrenaica had harvests in three different regions at different times – along the sea, up in the hill-country, and on the plateau farther south. In Attica, fields were ploughed three times a year to keep the upper layer loose. The first of these operations took place in spring, and then after the summer harvest the land was cross-ploughed with a lighter share, and finally during the autumn it was ploughed again in the original direction as a preliminary to sowing. The Greeks were deeply moved and excited by the myth of Demeter and Persephone, celebrated in the Mysteries which seemed to compare the ever-recurring gladness of the earth to the joy a Greek felt in the beauty and vigour of human youth. From the harvest until the sowing, while the grain was stored in subterranean silos, plant-life had the longer of its two annual periods of rest, and people were at leisure for other matters; but Persephone was lost to her parent, for she had departed to Pluto and the regions beneath the earth. The Mysteries, celebrated at Eleusis near Athens, enacted the ever recurring sorrow of her loss.

> Where the Great Mother, mourning for her daughter
> And beauty-drunken by the water
> Glittering among grey-leaved olive-trees,
> Has plucked a flower and sung her loss.[1]

But then in October, amid fervid rejoicing, the corn-maiden and corn-mother were reunited.

After the sowing, relatively mild winters meant that seeds were not displaced by heavy thaws which would have followed a deep frost. When the hoe, in February or March, had cleared away weeds and made a roughened surface that would prevent the water from running away, wheat and barley ripened more quickly than in northern climates and were ready for cutting in May or the beginning of June, before the soil dried out. The poetess Sappho, like other Greeks, found the ripe corn beautiful; and she describes the evening moment when

> The cornland glows
> With light upon its thousand blooms.

Mediterranean agriculture has changed little since ancient times, not so much owing to primitive conservatism as because new techniques have proved inapplicable to these soils. For example, even the largest ploughs retained a light and almost toy-like appearance. Best made of holm-oak for the beam, oak for the share, and laurel or elm for the pole,[2] they penetrated only about four inches into the soil, because heavier ploughs would have exposed the loosened earth to erosion by summer wind and winter flood. Crops were usually threshed by sticks or the hooves of oxen, and it was not until the later periods of Greek history that scientific attention was devoted to labour-saving devices (p. 218).

Again, until a three-crop rotation was invented (p. 256), half the cornland was always lying fallow. During this fallow year, the soil was manured by use as pasture, and ploughed. Fallow was wasteful, but dry-farming methods, involving constant hoe and spade work in spring and summer, were gradually learnt from the near east. Another means of overcoming land-shortage was the interculture of grain between olive-trees and between vines. The roots, being at different soil levels, do not compete for water, while the increased density of vegetation raises winter ground temperatures by several degrees and protects terraced slopes from erosion.

Vines may once have grown wild in Greece, with their seeds

distributed by migrating birds, but cultivation began at a very early date (p. 108). Bushes were trained low along the ground, sheltering it from the summer heat with their leaves. The Greeks improved the culture of the vine by careful hoeing and above all by summer pruning, which largely determined the quality of the fruit and next year's wood.

And so the grapes swelled in late summer, and during September Greeks had to interrupt their summer-long devotion to politics or war in order to heap the ripened fruits into baskets and bring them to be trodden on floors of wood or stone. The first product was best, and best of all the juice squeezed from the grapes by their own weight. Then, after presses had extracted a second yield, the must was stored for six months to ferment in huge pottery jars.

The *Odyssey* writes of viticulture with loving appreciation,[3] and by the time the poem was written, although the Greeks long continued to obtain its choicest wines from Thrace and other lands, they themselves already had widespread vineyards; though none of them were very large, since the broken, tumbled countryside did not favour standardisation or mass-production. Like Mediterranean peoples now, the Greeks were not heavy drinkers, still less drunkards. Yet wine, exalted as the vehicle of inspired communion with the god Dionysus, was a basic feature of their lives. They usually mixed three parts of water with two of wine. This may have been because the wine was stronger or nastier than ours, or because, during the summer at least, more liquid had to be absorbed to counteract loss of body moisture. Another practice which causes surprise today was the freedom with which wine was blended with other products. The addition of ashes and lime neutralised excessive acid and assisted maturing. Porous wine-jars were lined with pitch for the flavour. Honey, still the chief sweetener in the absence of sugar, was also added on occasions, and so were myrtle-berries, almonds, thyme, goat's milk, sea-water and the dip of a red-hot iron. Modern Greeks still mix resin with their wine.

The olive was likewise native to Greece, though, in historic times at least, its major importance in the economy only dates from the sixth century BC. However, it had been cultivated in much earlier times, particularly by the Mycenaeans (p. 106), and legend told of

that hallowed coast where Athene broke
Forth the primeval pale branch of olive,
Wreath of the bright air and a glory on Athens
shining.[4]

The holiest thing in all Attica was the archaic olive-wood image of the goddess Pallas Athena in the Erechtheum. She was the patron of patient craftsmanship, and of the peace that the slow-growing olive-trees needed and symbolised.

On these plains,
Our sweet grey foster-nurse, the olive, grows
Self-born, immortal, unafraid of foes;
Young knaves and old her ageless strength defies
Whom Zeus and Pallas guard with sleepless eyes.[5]

Another important item in Greek diet was the fig, whose early shoots are compared by Hesiod to the footprint of a crow. Figs were eaten more than any other fruit by the Greeks, whose attribution to them of a Carian origin may well be justified since Asia Minor is one of the westernmost of the countries to which they are indigenous. Capable of bearing two or three crops a year, and possessing broad rough deciduous leaves which lose little moisture by evaporation, they were always a cheap and staple food. The juicy sub-acid pomegranate too, which the prophet Mahomet later described as a purge for envy and hatred, was native to the middle east. But the pears and plums of Greece were indigenous, and so was the apple described by Sappho,

The sweet apple which reddens upon the topmost bough,
Atop on the topmost twig – which the pluckers forgot
somehow –
Forgot it not, nay, but got it not, for none could get it
till now.[6]

Odysseus, too, had revelled in luscious orchards. And yet all such Greek enjoyment of fruits and other natural products was clearly related to the edible benefits that they gave to man. Such are the quinces and ripe grapes admired by the sixth-century poet Ibycus, and Pindar's meadow loaded with golden fruits,[7] and Aristophanes' picture of

Figs and olives, wine and myrtles,
Luscious fruits preserved and dried.[8]

But the Greeks liked nature for one other reason besides its practical benefits, since they also possessed a special fondness for sacred, secluded enclosures of trees and water:

The glade where the grass is still,
Where the honeyed libations drip
In the rill from the brimming spring.[9]

Such groves were revered for religious reasons, and loved for their contrast to the parched lands of summer. This was the spirit in which Mesopotamians and Persians had grown parks out of their oases, and it was in imitation of Persia that magnificent pleasure gardens were made at Syracuse.[10] The depiction by artists of these verdant horticultural masterpieces, which later became so fashionable (p. 218), had perhaps begun already in classical times, though if so the paintings, like other wall-pictures, have not survived.

With wild nature, on the other hand, affinities are rare and specialised. Except as providers of timber, forests bored the Greeks, or frightened them as places of horrid visitations by Dionysus, while the only mountains described as beautiful are those of the legendary Atlantis. In most literature and art there is a noticeable absence of such background. There are isolated and tantalising exceptions, as when Alcman of Sparta illuminates the hues and shapes of land and sea by a sudden poetic flash:

The hills have fallen asleep.
O'er cleft and crag
One quiet spreads,
O'er rocks that face the deep
And stony torrent beds.[11]

And although flowers were chiefly appreciated (as they had also been by the Egyptians) for the garlands and bouquets they made for mankind, two hymns written by unknown early poets in honour of Apollo and Demeter show a deep love of blooms and blossoms for their own sake. There is likewise deep pathos in Sappho's

wild hyacinth flower, which on the
hills is found,
Which the passing feet of the shepherds for ever
tear and wound,
Until the purple blossom is trodden into the ground.

Aristophanes, too, in the lyrical passages of his masterly fifth-century comedies, hears the plane-trees whispering, and calls upon the clouds to visit their wide domain.

Come from old Ocean's unchangeable bed,
Come, till the mountain's green summits we tread,
Come to the peaks with their landscapes untold,
Gaze on the Earth with her harvests of gold. [12]

Yet here again there is a difficulty; for gold and green do not seem interesting descriptions of colour. The reason for this is that the Greeks measured colours not in shades like ourselves but in different qualities of light: 'a bright colour is nothing but light's continuity and intensity'[13] Light was what gave Athens its epithet of 'violet-crowned': the strange luminosity that throbs in early autumn upon Mount Hymettus, at the instant before the sun goes down.

It would, indeed, have been strange if such alert people had not shown keen insight into certain aspects of nature. And yet it remains a second-best to man. Homer's wealth of exact, detailed natural descriptions is particularly devoted to similes illustrating human affairs; and when a character in tragic drama appeals to the Mediterranean or mountainous scene around him, this is not because its beauties are loved, but because the speaker despairs of humanity. Such is the cry of Philoctetes, abandoned on the island of Lemnos.

Caverns and headlands, dens of wild creatures,
You jutting broken crags, to you I raise my cry –
There is no one else I can speak to.[14]

The Greeks discerned a bond of sympathy between man in his helplessness and the elemental forces of nature, but it was not until later that they began to seek in it a reflection of their daily moods (p. 224).

Meanwhile Euripides (*c.* 485–406) is the Greek poet of classical times who comes the nearest to modern feeling in his sympathetic, almost mystic, susceptibility to wild nature.

> By the blue and shining lake
> Where the grasses trail, I hung
> My purple robes in golden rays of sunlight,
> Spreading them upon the shoots
> Of bulrushes.[15]

Yet even Euripides sees the natural world not quite as something of normal interest, but rather as a symbol of the fierce asceticism, far removed from ordinary human qualities, which Hippolytus dedicates to the virgin goddess Artemis.

> My Goddess Mistress, I bring you ready woven
> This garland. It was I that plucked and wove it,
> plucked it for you in your inviolate Meadow.
> No shepherd dares to feed his flock within it:
> No reaper plies a busy scythe within it:
> Only the bees in springtime haunt the inviolate
> Meadow.[16]

Such are the declarations ascribed to abnormally isolated or desperate men. Other Greeks did not aim at privacy in their poetry or their lives (p. 203), and did not therefore turn to nature for spiritual reinforcement. 'The classic is apt to take us to a scene and leave us amid its beauty, the modern is determined that we shall be thrilled with the proper emotions.'[17]

This man-centred attitude, which found nature less significant than human beings, is clearly defined by Socrates. For, taxed by his friend Phaedrus with a strange ignorance of the rustic environs of Athens, he is reported to have replied: 'forgive me, my dear friend. You see, I am fond of learning. The country places and the trees won't teach me anything, and the people in the city do!'[18]

The zenith of Athens

The humanism to which those words of Socrates bear indirect but powerful witness belonged to a society where people loomed far larger in the landscape then ever before; and not only people but individuals. Long ago, there had been a revolution increasing human rights far beyond any precedents. For from about 650 BC onwards, the Greeks had begun to be given laws which could be written down, seen by all, and criticised if they seemed unsatisfactory. Such legislation was not, of course, new in itself, since an impressive system, protecting the poor against extortion had already appeared in Sumeria during the third millennium BC, and similar measures were incorporated in a Babylonian code. But that, like the more developed Assyrian system which followed, still envisaged the law as a means of maintaining a just divinely appointed order. In eighth-century Babylonia, however, when the discovery of cosmic periodicities led astronomers to regard the seven planets as the ultimate authority, god was demoted in favour of law, which henceforward became an end in itself, fastened both by Persians and Greeks to an absolute standard of morality independent of divine ordinance.

Such a standard was personified in *Eunomia*, described by Hesiod as one of the three sisters 'minding the works of mortal men'.[19] This was the political creation of the aristocracies who still controlled cities: a gospel of social discipline and service, in which responsibility corresponded with privilege. Although at some places this aristocratic order broke up temporarily into autocracy (p. 158), other centres found lawgivers who successfully prolonged the stable conditions of oligarchic government, or helped society to shift its basis peacefully from birth to wealth, or gave their names to gradual processes of codification which served the same ends.

Poets quoted the view that money makes the man,[20] and at Athens Solon, appointed 'archon and reconciler' to end civil strife (*c.* 592–591), noted that the richest 'have twice the eagerness that others have'.[21] Although Solon did not aim at popular appeal with the blatancy of Corinth's tyrants (p. 158), his purpose, like theirs, was to do something for everybody. He attracted popularity by seizing the island of Salamis from Megara, and placed agriculture on a profit-making basis so that Attica was henceforward able to produce a surplus of its excellent oil for export purposes. The chief Athenian offices of state were still reserved for the nobility, but agitation among the rising middle class, which had now become essential to the army, was met by admitting the rights of all citizens to a share in the government through participation in a redefined Assembly. Their responsibility in the administration of the law was also acknowledged, and a humanised code rescued poor people from misery and fear by abolishing bondage for debt.

Yet in spite of the fine balance of these measures, three-cornered strife soon broke out again, between the nobility who felt that things were moving leftwards too fast, the 'country people' (poor clansmen and labourers) who considered that progress was not rapid enough, and the intermediate artisans or guild members who were content with the safeguards of Solon's constitution. As elsewhere, such dissensions led to a revolution which brought a 'tyrant' into power. Under this able man, Pisistratus, bases were secured on the vital north-eastern route to the Dardanelles, as well as in the strait itself. Gold, timber, flax and pitch became available from Macedonia, and grain, livestock and slaves from Thrace; and Solon's economic policy, combined with a judicious reconciliation of classes, was continued so effectively that Corinth, which had provided the model for autocracy and mercantilism alike, was superseded by the Athenians as a commercial power.

One of their principal instruments for achieving this result was a superb new sort of black-figured pottery, which after spectacular polychrome experiments reached its climax in the years after 550. The new technique employed as a background the natural surface of smooth-textured red, buff or orange clay from the local river Cephisus, exploiting particles or processes which provide a brilliant sheen. The painting upon this surface, executed within sharp incised outlines, is an equally glossy, rich black pigment of almost indestructible strength. As foreshadowed by earlier Attic vases, the themes to which the novel method is devoted are no longer Corinth's animal patterns but human scenes drawn from myths, portraying selected incidents in engraved detail.

Human, too, or human beings ideally interpreted, are the boys and girls portrayed by talented Attic sculptors during the later sixth century BC. The main visual purpose of Greek art, which was to communicate the beauty of the human body in the spirit of Pygmalion's mythical statue that came to life, is already clear in this relatively immobile and archaic guise. The frequent use of bronze instead of porous stone, though its intrinsic value doomed statues to eventual destruction, made it easier to free their limbs and particularly their arms. The influence of Ionia, dominant in Athenian fashion under Pisistratus, is reflected in the delicate robes of girls, whose sculptors' signatures suggest that they came from the coasts of Asia Minor; and more easterly influences are apparent in the custom by which these statues are brightly painted, like the vermilion-tinted images of Mesopotamia.[22] Borders of dresses were patterned in green and gold, lips became red, and the yellow tint that had already been given to hair on Cretan ivories appears again (p. 96). (Renaissance sculptors, too, would no doubt have coloured their statues in the same way if the paint had survived on the ancient works which were available for their study.)

After the death of Pisistratus (527 BC), his family, like the descendants of other tyrants elsewhere, could not long maintain their position, and Cleisthenes decisively modified the constitution of Athens in the direction of democracy (*c.* 508–507). His aim was to destroy the electoral influence of hereditary clans, with which henceforward the commercial elements represented by the guilds were to be placed on an equal footing. This was achieved by dividing Attica into a new system of small geographical constituencies (demes) in which no distinction existed between one citizen and another. After Solon a sort of threefold party system had developed (p. 194), but Cleisthenes' constituencies were grouped in three new regions designed to represent the principal interests of Attica; handicrafts and capital, fisheries and mining, pasture and timber. Each deme elected a fixed number of members to a Council of Five Hundred, so that all Athenians, whatever their birth or wealth, had equal voting power. A check, however, was still placed on democracy, in this careful system of balances, by granting both the Council and the state officials responsibilities considered appropriate to their experience.

Such was the Athens which found strength, during a rare, crisis-born union of Greek cities, to play a leading part in resisting the most serious invasion that the country ever had to face.

The invaders were the Persians, an Indo-European-speaking community which had first become known in the south-western regions of the country now bearing their name. From the middle of the sixth century they had successively conquered their former suzerain Media, next Lydia and its Ionian subjects, Cilicia, Babylonia, Syria, Israel, remote Transcaspia, and then Egypt (525) which consequently passed for many centuries into alien hands.

The Achaemenid dynasty who seized and ruled this empire had developed a particularly thoroughgoing form of autocracy because their country, fringed by hostile, envious tribesmen on many sides, needed efficient forms of protection and internal organisation. The military superiority of the Persians was due to able generalship, mobile archery, and (according to the historian Herodotus) the healthy climate and hardy conditions which produced their manly pastoral peasantry. He adds, however, that the Persians were 'of all mankind the readiest to adopt foreign customs, good or bad'.[23] They inherited and refined upon all the traditions of ancient Iran and Mesopotamia; and when Darius I (522–485) built his palace at Susa, he employed the products or workmen of all the lands he had conquered.

The whole of Asia Minor was now in Persian possession; never before had any power achieved a durable conquest of the entire peninsula. Its subjection was sealed by the construction of the fifteen hundred mile Royal Road, the successor of Assyrian, Hittite, Phrygian and Lydian routes and the ancestor of those of Rome, which could convey a mounted man all the way from Sardis to Susa in the greatly reduced time of fifteen days. But this unification of Asia Minor was a most damaging blow to the Greeks, because it meant, as Lydian supervision had never meant, the detachment and loss of all those cities of the west coasts and islands which formed so important a part of the Greek community.

Darius next decided to invade Europe. His first objectives were the Scythians beyond the shores of the Black Sea, because they were intimately related to his enemies on the Asian steppes. With Scythia gone, these Asiatic nomads could be taken in the rear, and then he would be free to tackle Greece. Darius' Samian engineer bridged the Bosphorus with pontoons, but the vast design petered out in failure (513–512) and Greece was given a welcome pause. Yet the Persians left a large army in Thrace and remained masters of its straits, and the danger came nearer when Athens, joined by Eretria in Euboea, sent help to the Ionians who had organised a large-scale rebellion against Persia (498–494). The revolt, led by Aristagoras of Miletus, was suppressed, and the consequent destruction of his city and the massacre, enslavement and deportation of its people formed grim landmarks in Mediterranean history, and caused shock and horror throughout Greece. Henceforward, the Ionian navies in the Aegean were replaced by Persia's Phoenician fleet.

For the Greeks, hampered though they were by collaborators and a neutral Delphic oracle, the time had now come to put into effect (though only for the briefest duration) the sense of common nationality which had been slowly increasing during the centuries. Darius' invasion (490) was designed in the first instance to punish Athens and Eretria, but both this enterprise and the subsequent expedition of Xerxes were primarily intended to conquer the Greek mainland, since without its annexation the western borders of Persia's empire remained unstable and insecure. The epic battles that saved Greece have done more than anything else to hand down to history a specific image of the European and Mediterranean world opposing Asia, in sequel to the legendary victory of west over east in the Trojan War which every Greek knew from the *Iliad* (p. 142).

Darius was repelled by the Athenian infantry at Marathon. But then, ten years later, the army of Xerxes streamed for seven days over his Dardanelles bridges, made of 674 ships joined by cables of Egyptian papyrus (480). Heroic, suicidal Spartan resistance at the Thermopylae pass, and a successful confederate naval action at Artemisium beside the Euboean strait, delayed but did not turn back the Persian advance, and Athens was evacuated and occupied by Xerxes. The Peloponnesians wanted to withdraw the Greek fleet to the Corinthian isthmus and await the Persians there. But Themistocles, by threatening Athenian mass withdrawal to Sicily and Italy, persuaded them to fight between the island of Salamis and the Attic coast. In order to neutralise the superior speed, height and manœuvrability of Persia's Phoenician ships, they had to be enticed into the narrow neck of water.

The Persian fleet, in a perpetual stream,
At first appeared invincible; but when
Their numbers in the narrows packed and hemmed
Grew dense, they cracked their oarage in the crowd,
And smote each other with their beaks of brass,
And none might help his fellow.[24]

And so the invasion suffered irretrievable disaster. The successful vessels of the Athenians, supported by those of their neighbour and recent enemy Aegina, were more stoutly built and less affected by swell than the Phoenician ships, and carried crews who excelled in boarding after the massive three-pronged rams had driven home. These famous triremes were equipped with outriggers supporting a third bank of oarsmen, arranged in echelon so that as many as one hundred and fifty oars could be used. Such a system, which made ships much more powerful and gave better headway against contrary winds, had probably been introduced on a small scale in *c.* 525 but was not extensively developed until the 480s. As a base for the new Athenian fleet, Themistocles had already supplemented the open Phaleron roadstead by the Piraeus (493–492), where a new town built on a recently evolved geometrical plan was grouped round three harbours including a large landlocked basin. The Salamis fleet was paid for by the fortunate recent discovery of a rich vein of silver at state-owned Laurion in Attica's metalliferous eastern coastal range, the richest Greek mining territory ever to have been exploited.

These battles were followed by the crowning glory of Plataea in southern Boeotia, where a land-force in which Spartans and their subjects were predominant finally ejected the Persians from Greece (479). Plataea, like Marathon, seemed to confirm the wisdom of a strategy based on heavy infantrymen (p. 157), and Themistocles' plans for building up naval supremacy for Athens were consequently impeded. But although he himself was eclipsed in *c.* 470 by a pro-Spartan opposition party, his policy gradually prevailed, since the rest of the fifth century saw a persistent Athenian attempt, by naval means, to form a larger Greek political unit than had ever been seen before.

During the forty years after the Persian Wars, Athens increased the number of its allies among the city-states to two hundred, distributed throughout Greek waters and including outposts in the west. At first, these confederates were formed into a voluntary League of Delos, of which the purpose was joint defence against Persia. Contributions to the league, assessed according to means, could be paid either in money or ships. Most allies wished to offer monetary contributions, but Athens preferred them to give ships, which she herself controlled and manned, thus mitigating Athenian unemployment. Soon, however, cities were coerced to join the league, and rebellious members experienced the use of force. Increasingly the confederacy assumed imperial form, with military service made obligatory and constitutions and jurisdiction dictated by Athens. Compulsion became more and more frequent as Athens, seeing the total store of wealth to be limited, resorted to increasingly predatory methods, while the allies correspondingly resented every encroachment upon their autonomy. Athenian seapower and alliance with Megara also created bitter hatred among its jealous neighbours, the Corinthians (460), and from the next decade onwards, under the guidance of Pericles, attempts to remain friends with Sparta were likewise quickly abandoned.

For now came the time when Athens, protectively linked with the Piraeus and Phaleron by fortified long walls, used the funds of its confederates to plunge into aggressive imperialism on many fronts, even undertaking an unsuccessful expedition against Persian-controlled Egypt. Aegina was reduced to subject status, and Megara and Boeotia temporarily subjugated. But then, weighed down by enormous expenditure, the Athenians negotiated a five years' truce with Sparta and, following a vain attempt to summon a Pan-Hellenic congress, made peace with the Persians (448). These decisions meant that Athens must forgo eastern expeditions and evacuate what it had seized on the mainland. Instead, however, citizens were sent out to form colonies in the modern sense – settlements subject to Athens – on Euboea and other islands and the Dardanelles. Imperialism was not to be renounced, and Pericles, whose oratory secured him repeated annual reelections to one of the city's ten policy-making annual generalships, did everything to strengthen the fleet. 'How,' he contemptuously remarked, 'can mere farmers, with no knowledge of the sea, achieve anything worthy of note?

. . . Your naval resources are such that your warships can go where they please.'[25]

The use of Athenian money, weights and measures was enforced throughout most of the empire, and dangerous revolts were crushed. In an age of improved communications and closer relations with the western Greeks (p. 166) imports included meat, nuts, cheese, sails, incense, carpets and ivory. Timber for shipbuilding was vital, but an even bigger business in Athens was the import of grain from the Black Sea (p. 182). The government took stringent measures to encourage and protect this traffic, and ten times in every year the Assembly's attention was officially directed to the question of corn.

The Corinthians, however, still refused to accept Athenian supremacy at sea, and induced the principal land-power, Sparta, to join them*. The consequent Peloponnesian War (431–404) had scarcely started when Pericles died, but the hostilities, immortalised by Thucydides, dragged on for a long time, since the protagonists, with their shifting patterns of allies, found it difficult to come to grips. A Spartan attempt to cut Athens off from its timber-supplies in Thrace was followed by an uneasy peace (421–416). But then the Athenians responded to an appeal from Sicily – in whose grain they were interested – by launching an ambitious expedition which Syracuse catastrophically defeated. Many of the Aegean allies of Athens revolted, cutting off supplies of Black Sea corn, and nine years later a final battle on the Dardanelles destroyed the Athenian fleet protecting this lifeline. The war was over, and Athens' attempt to create and maintain a Mediterranean empire had been defeated.

The Athenian way of life

The grain which so greatly influenced the conduct and result of the Peloponnesian war was needed by Athens so as to feed its excess population. In the time of Pericles the whole city-state may have comprised forty thousand citizens and a total free population of about one hundred and fifty thousand, of whom nearly half lived inside the city itself. Slaves, who had always existed in ancient societies, perhaps totalled seventy thousand –

* Thucydides rightly declares, however, that the basic cause of the war was the hostility between the great powers Athens and Sparta.

rising to more than twice that figure in the following century – and mostly came from the hinterlands of Asia Minor, Thrace and southern Russia. We hear, at this period, of no manufacturing industry employing more than a hundred and twenty slaves, since large-scale agricultural slavery was never common in Greece, and slaves were not much use to a small farmer since they ate almost as much as they produced. Yet the demand for labour outran the free supply in the state mines at Laurion, where numerous slaves worked in appalling conditions. It was not until the next century that liberal opinion increasingly dwelt on their human rights.

Among those, on the other hand, who were free and held citizen status, the confidence inspired by victory against the Persians had stimulated the growth of a more thoroughgoing democracy at Athens. State offices were converted into salaried posts, and although business was filtered through the Council of Five Hundred ultimate decisions rested with an Assembly in which every citizen could speak and initiate motions. This was not representative government but a democracy in the most direct and literal sense; and the country where this profoundly significant institution was invented must now be described.

By the diminutive standards of Greece, the thousand square miles of Attica, fifty miles long and up to thirty broad, represented a relatively large unit. Its interior is studded by a loosely-jointed system of mountains and hills, which divide up the land into a number of not wholly disconnected compartments. The shoreland was indented and favoured coastal navigation and fishing. At the opposite extremity was the hill-country, a land of woods and scrub, pasturage, goatherds, woodcutters and charcoal burners. And between hills and coast were the plains from which Attica derived the grain and vegetables and fruit on which it lived. The main sections of the plainland were the Cephisus valley adjoining Athens; a narrow alluvial plain behind Eleusis, eleven miles north-west of the city; and an eastern plain between Mounts Pentelicon and Hymettus. Yet even this fertile red-clay area, the largest, measured less than eight miles across.

Since there were no moist valleys and few upland meadows or expanses of grass, conditions were unfavourable for stock-breeding. As elsewhere in Greece wheat only could be grown on the best pieces of soil; otherwise the crop had to be barley. In spite of the fame of a certain brand of fig, Attic orchards as well as vineyards were mainly of secondary importance. For most crops the annual ill-distributed rainfall of sixteen inches was barely adequate. Besides, this is the most exposed of all Greek lands to the dry north-eastern winds which blow violently and dustily for 164 summer days. Damper draughts coming from the west and south-west are vaporised over the burning plains; the location of Attica in the rain-shadow of mountain ranges makes it the driest part of Greece (p. 185).

The land is a hard one, and the difficulty of wringing subsistence from it demanded and rewarded tough, quick, intelligent enterprise. The long shoreline invited seafaring and curiosity, and made access to older civilisations easy, but not too easy. Although climatic explanations of character must be used with caution (p. 310), these longlasting north winds and unbroken hours of sunshine dispelled humidity and lassitude and made for liveliness and swift changes of mood, while sharp changes of temperature discourage fatalistic resignation.[26] In ancient times the cameo-clear landscape of Attica, and its crisp, buoyant, atmosphere more limpid and translucent than any other sky this side of the Red Sea, were already appreciated for their tonic encouragement of a perceptive clarity of mind (p. 208).

Sky and scenery were never far away, because life was mostly lived out of doors. The winter, lasting from January to March, was too short for anything approaching comfort to be attempted in the houses, which were still made of sun-dried brick on stone or rubble foundations. While the women cooked, their husbands, if they were there, had to lie down so as not to be choked by the smoke. But more often they went out, and Assemblies, Councils, lawcourts and the endless discussions by Socrates and by Plato's Academy continued to be held out of doors throughout the winter. After that, there were interruptions by agriculture, but when the corn had been harvested in May or early June, time was found for the elections, because the citizens were back home and the roads, such as they were, had dried. Moreover, if cities had not begun to make war against each other before the corn-harvest, they could do so thereafter until the September vintage.

They were, indeed, all too likely to do so, because the very conditions that tautened Greek minds over-stimulated nervous people, who were numerous, and the reverse side of all this mental activity was an argumentative quarrelsomeness. Another result of the out-of-door life was that personages had to court the public gaze and plunge openly and unrestrictedly into social intercourse without any of the formal isolations that seclude important people elsewhere. Like the Spanish honour of Lope de Vega and Calderon, the code of the Greeks was concerned with what the neighbours would think; and another consequence of spending so much time out of doors was exceptional inquisitiveness. Lawsuits, conducted in such an atmosphere, were noisy, and sacrificed expert opinion and legal science to the excitements of the theatrical presentation of a case. In the Assemblies, too, so much depended on immediate impact. For everything had to be transacted by people meeting together; to do otherwise was the ultimate barbarism.

> Cyclopes have no muster and no meeting,
> No consultation or old tribal ways, . . .
> Indifferent to what the others do.[27]

In Athens, said Pericles, 'even those who are mostly occupied with their own business are extremely well-informed on general politics – this is a peculiarity of ours: we do not say that a man who takes no interest in politics is a man who minds his own business; we say that he has no business here at all.'[28]

The loud say consequently possessed by every citizen sometimes meant that a burst of eloquence could carry away a whole gathering into united, impulsive action. And yet, at the same time, the very fact that any and every man could have that say made the Greeks individualists to a degree unknown in any previous epoch. This individualism was formulated in the maxim that man is the measure of all things. Protagoras, who made the pronouncement, implied that voices may understandably be raised against each other, because no absolute truth can be discovered; all disputes have two sides, and can be argued in two ways. And they were – with such prompt articulateness that no man had time to brood on what he was going to say. The flashpoint was low, and either one's own or one's opponent's view was quickly acted upon, with violent, immediate repercussions. 'The Athenians,' said a man from Corinth, 'are by nature incapable of either living a quiet life themselves or of allowing anyone alse to do so.'[29] They felt a reverential admiration for the Mean – because it was so often beyond their grasp.

Such was the small community which, within the space of less than three generations of this fifth century, excelled at tragic drama, history, philosophy, sculpture, architecture and painting. This simultaneous, classic achievement in so huge a variety of fields was startling and unequalled (p. 315), and the Athenians, fully conscious of their exceptional role, felt impelled to imperial enterprises because such a wonderful civilisation, and the leisure required for its continuance, could not be maintained without wealth. And they were inspired by the added belief, idealistic among some though no doubt cynical among others, that this was all being done for all Greece: because, as Pericles reminded them, Athens was an education for the entire country.

In writing of earlier Greek culture this book has endeavoured to detect whatever eastern influences were apparent, and then to note the specific Mediterranean contributions. Now, the first part of the analysis is no longer directly relevant. It is true that when Socrates (d. 399) began the process, interpreted by Plato, of applying serious critical and philosophical thought to questions of morality and conduct, he is in a direct line of descent from the Ionians and their eastern heritage (p. 175). Yet that heritage has been completely absorbed and is only rarely perceptible, while his debt, on the other hand, to the talkative, enquiring atmosphere engendered by the immediate open-air day-to-day life of Athens is much more obvious. The tragic dramas of Aeschylus, Sophocles and Euripides declare their eastern inheritance more clearly, since the myths with which they are concerned contain a large quantity of elements as oriental as the sphinx encountered by Sophocles' Oedipus. Yet these debts, again, although recognisable, are thoroughly assimilated; classical Greece has completely absorbed its gifts from the east and made them its own.

Besides, Greek tragedy owes most of its essential character to its location in the Mediterranean area. For one thing, seeing that the plays were performed at festivals of Dionysus in early spring and late winter, their structures and themes contain, embedded in the subtlest poetic sophistication, many deliberate echoes of old tribal choric dances and songs in honour of Dionysus, including the Chorus itself which is so strange to modern theatre-goers. Moreover, the whole character of the tragedies is as deeply affected as the rest of Athenian life by the Mediterranean climate, since – like the discussions of Socrates and Plato – they were performed in the open air. This made Greek drama totally different from the modern theatre. Scenery had to be very simple, and actors used padded clothes and padded thick-soled boots and masks and speaking tubes. Audiences, numbering up to thirty thousand people, mostly sat so far away from the stage that neither facial expressions nor subtle gestures would have been visible. 'What the audience watched was something more like a distant group of coloured and moving statuary than a group of actors in our sense . . . the dramatist had to rely for his effects almost entirely upon the mere word.'[30] And since actors were few, and spectators could not have followed more than three speaking parts together on the open-air stage, the dramatist had to avoid under-plots and devote himself to making a single simple story as profoundly dramatic and intense as he could. Moreover, this story was already known to the audience: so that attention was still further concentrated on the actual language of the poet, which accordingly, in these peculiar Mediterranean conditions, brought the flexible, rich clarity of Greek to its highest point.

In architecture, again, the eastern contributions had been thoroughly absorbed (p. 164). The last of many transformations of the flowered column-capital which Greece had taken from the east was the decorative creation of the Corinthian Order, sheathed by two tiers of slender leaves, at first somewhat vague and unspecific in character, and then clearly depicting the foliage of the acanthus plant. From *c.* 450 BC the acanthus is found on gravestones and minor architectural features, but the huge principal role of this Corinthian ornament still lay in the future. For this was, instead, the age in which the old Doric and Ionian Orders attained their culminating achievements.

In the imperceptibly curving, hallucinatory subtleties of the Doric Parthenon (447–432), as in the myths of contemporary tragedians, the immense conflation of past near-eastern influences has been totally assimilated and transfigured. More than any other Greek temple, the Parthenon sets a dominant human stamp upon its landscape. In ancient times the dominance was more emphatic still, since the decorated parts of the building shone with vigorous colours (p. 164), and uncoloured portions such as the columns had not acquired today's golden patina but gleamed with the original whiteness of the marble they were made of. This most monumental of all materials, marble, had replaced coarser, softer stone on temple façades from *c.* 525 BC onwards, and proved perfect for the sharp edges and precise outlines of these buildings. The quarries of Mount Pentelicon, twelve miles north-east of Athens, produced finely grained, densely crystalline, glossy marble which could be chiselled into iron-hard knife edges and sharply moulded and undercut reliefs, responsive to every changing nuance of brilliant light and shadow.

Sculptors, on the other hand, who likewise designed most of their products for the open air, preferred the coarser but more malleable and exceptionally translucent marble of Paros, one of the islands of the Cyclades where marble had first been used to make works of art; this material has clearly visible crystals and a creamy surface which darkens to the colour of pale smoke. The Greeks added painted tints (p. 195), but these gained in subtlety during the fourth century when they began to rub the surfaces with beeswax, which subdued the glare of the fresh-cut stone while retaining the play of light over its crystals.

Parian marble was already employed for the sculptures of Apollo's temple at Olympia (*c.* 468–456), which stands at the turning-point between severe, archaistic, glassy formality and the full classicism that was approaching. It was at this tense, equivocal moment that an artist created the Olympian Apollo, from whose gesture and expression – or lack of expression, hinting disquietingly at unspeakable potency – the grandeur of the god of Hellenic order flashes forth. Yet, even so, this is still a grandeur which does not belong to another dimension of the universe. For the culminating point of Greek art is man, though, in statues such as this, he is raised to the most exalted of all possible levels.

The same message is conveyed with ripe fluency by Pheidias, whose deeply shadowed Parthenon reliefs (447–432) develop the previous century's experiments in over-all friezes into the innovation of depicting scenes from human life. They are more human than the Olympian sculptures, though the humanity is still ideal and not real; this is the maturity of that strange blend of idealism and close observation which characterised fifth-century art. And although its artists had fully absorbed what the orient and Crete had to offer, their most grandiose manifestations, at least, were still a good deal closer to those traditions than can easily be divined today, when we no longer have the huge gold- and ivory-plated wooden statues of Pheidias' Olympian Zeus and Athena Parthenos or Polyclitus' Argive Hera, monumental works not intended, like most Greek sculpture, for the open air, but flickering huge and uncanny from the penumbra of their shrines.

In pottery, too, a new red-figure technique evolved from *c.* 530 onwards perpetuated and enhanced the supremacy which Athens had gained in this field. While improving on the graceful shapes created by their forerunners, potters now sometimes left the painting of their vases to separate artists. These reversed the process of the black figure style (p. 194), leaving the human forms in the natural reddish surface-colour instead of painting them black, and covering the backgrounds with black paint instead.

At the same time, the incisions which had outlined the earlier designs were replaced by drawing, in long springy sweeps which gave greater freedom and flexibility. Towards the end of the sixth century painters had made the historic discovery of foreshortening, and the last murals of Polygnotus of Thasos (*c.* 470–460) seem to have abandoned rigid base lines in favour of a new *trompe l'oeil* plasticity which is repeated, as far as convexity permits, on red-figure vases and others elegantly painted upon a white ground. The next generations experimented in novel transparencies of clothing and lively facial treatments, and shortly before 400 Apollodorus of Athens is reported to have given an illusionistic depth to his wall-panel paintings by subtle graduations of colour and shadings of human figures.

Living at a time of explosive, continuous cerebral explorations, these artists achieved that supreme control over their various media which is described as classical. Vision had been liberated from conceptual bonds to the limits permitted by intellectual and aesthetic idealism, and the aristocratic taste and elegance characteristic of earlier Athenian art was now strengthened by a new, firm synthesis between control and passion. These achievements owe something to the scenery and climate of Greece (p. 202). 'The extreme lucidity of its atmosphere gave the Attic landscape a variety of outline and a delicacy of colour which made it a natural school of art.'[31] Already abnormally susceptible to line and form, artists were perpetually stimulated and challenged by what was all around them. The predominant dull-green and hard grey-white hues of this landscape may have struck cold, to a people who loved brightness, and impelled architects and sculptors to add strong counteracting colours, but the clean strong light imposed a discipline which made the eye see things in contours and reliefs much sharper than the evanescent nuances of the north.

This, then, was the classical Athens which long captivated Europe and then north America, and provided the basis of their education and inspiration. Such, too, were the surroundings which the transforming gaze of Wieland, Hölderlin, Goethe and Schiller made into a legendary mirage of escape from this narrow world into a time and place of perfect harmony and order, full of noble simplicity and serene grandeur, controlled in emotion and balanced in thought. 'I shall go over my old ground,' cried Byron, 'and look upon my old seas and mountains, the only acquaintances I ever found improve upon me.' And he even broke through the legend into reality, by setting out on his last journey to free the Isles of Greece from despotic domination.

> Eternal summer gilds them yet:
> But all except their sun is set.

Philip, Alexander and Alexandria

The fourth century gradually initiated a phase of substantial Greek land-empires, each controlling many city-states which retained self-government in local matters but lost their independence.

The first of these larger units was formed in Sicily. There Syracuse defeated the Athenian invasion (p. 200), but its next enemies were the Carthaginians on the west coast, for now the ancient friction (p. 126) broke into open war. Carthage captured Himera (avenging a defeat there seventy-one years previously) in addition to Acragas which ranked second among all Greek foundations (405). Refugees flocked in to Syracuse, where Dionysius I, a mule-driver's son, spent seven years building up a political and military machine to prevent the Carthaginians from extending their rule over the whole of the island. At home, Dionysius obliterated the democratic system in favour of dictatorial rule, which he maintained for nearly four decades. His method of government was a blend of outward magnificence and savage oppression. Hated by the rich, whom he ruthlessly taxed and intimidated by secret police, he was supported by the proletariat and liberated slaves, as well as by intellectuals including Plato who visited him from Athens (387).

On the military side, Dionysius formed a powerful fleet of over three hundred ships, including a new and much imitated sort of vessel with four or five rowers pulling at a single oar. He also improved siege-craft by novel catapults that were employed to capture Carthaginian Motya (398). Although unable to hold on to this gain, he penned the enemy into the western extremity of Sicily (392) and throughout the rest of the island controlled not only Greeks but the native interior, which he was the first to subdue. This 'Ruler of Sicily', as he called himself, then proceeded to invade the toe of Italy as well as forming numerous alliances in other parts of the peninsula. Dionysius also ravaged Elba and Etruscan Caere, occupied Corsica and perhaps even parts of the Adriatic coast, and suppressed the pirates who abounded in that area.

Syracuse, lying athwart trade-routes from all four points of the compass, was now the largest city in Europe, with a population of more than half a million. The state it controlled was the first important political creation of the Greeks in the west, and the largest they had ever formed anywhere; next to the king of Persia, Dionysius was the strongest power in the Mediterranean world. By the time of his death (367), however, he had not fared too well in a further prolonged war with Carthage, which in the end defeated his ambition to found a central Mediterranean empire. More ground was lost under his successors, until a moderate democracy set up by the Corinthian general Timoleon (344–337) regained a measure of prosperity.

On the Greek mainland, during the greater part of this period, the city-states had continued to fight one another with inconclusive results. First there were thirty years in which the Spartans, having won the Peloponnesian War, unskilfully endeavoured to found an empire, owing such success as they achieved to Persia which dictated a general King's Peace (387–386). Then the Athenians, recovering from their defeat in the Peloponnesian War, reasserted not only their cultural supremacy – epitomised by Plato, Aristotle and the sculptor Praxiteles – but also their central commercial position, and launched a second attempt to found a league. Ostensibly less tyrannical than the first, this was largely concerned with the provision of sufficient corn for the city, a task requiring banking, shipping and wholesaling activities which were largely left to Syrians, Phoenicians, and Greeks from Asia and the west. Athens also reached an understanding with Sparta about their relative spheres of influence (371). But there followed a period in which Thebes defeated the Spartans and became the leading city-state for the first time in a thousand years under its talented military leader Epaminondas, whose death in battle, however, extinguished this shortlived attempt (362).

Exhausted and at the mercy of any strong power, Greece now gradually succumbed to the Macedonians who inhabited its northern borderlands. Spanning the modern Greek, Yugoslav and Bulgarian frontiers, Macedonia was a land of stalwart peasants and horse-riding squires, who had retained their primitive Homeric society in view of the continual necessity for defence against wild Illyrian and Thracian tribesmen. The country was vulnerable to their incursions because the Balkan mountains, though descending steeply towards Greece, are approached from the north by gradual slopes which invited invaders.

The Macedonian kingdom exercised suzerainty over extensive plateaux enclosed by high mountains. But its nucleus was the twenty to forty mile deep coastal plain of the rivers Haliacmon and Axius at the head of the Thermaic Gulf, where Salonica was later to form the radiation-point of continental routes. These alluvial flats contained stretches of cultivable, cereal-exporting soil, as well as pasture for large herds of horses, cattle and sheep; while the forests of the neighbouring uplands, far more abundantly supplied with many kinds of wood than they are today, comprised the chief source of lumber for the eastern Mediterranean world.

The kings of Macedonia claimed Greek origin, but the people as a whole possessed more Thracian and Illyrian blood and long remained outside the cultural sphere of Greece, speaking a language which, although containing some words borrowed from the Greeks, was for the most part unintelligible to them.

Sometime after 700 the Macedonians migrated from the western highlands to the fringe of the plain, above which they established their first capital at Aegae (Edessa, Vodena), strongly placed beside orchard-country containing sites that had been occupied from remotest antiquity (p. 29). Soon afterwards, they moved downwards into the coastal area (*c.* 640), where the kingdom was knit more tightly together during the fifth century by a series of able kings.

These people felt little affection for the major Greek city-states which treated them as pawns in the political game, and still less for the settlements these had planted right beside the nucleus of Macedonia upon the three-pronged peninsula of Chalcidice (p. 183). After the Peloponnesian War, the colonies banded together in a flourishing independent Chalcidian League, with its capital at Olynthus upon a coastal hill between the peninsula's western and central headlands. The excavations of Olynthus reveal a new type of early fourth-century residence, combined with three shops to form a single block. The houses were roughly square in shape and divided into two parts, one of which is a long narrow room facing southwards (away from the prevailing wind) through a small colonnade on to a square interior courtyard. The better Greek dwellings of the past had sometimes possessed small courtyards and porches, to give shade in summer and catch the winter sun, but the scale of these new plans shows an incipient decline of the classical idea that private residences should be squalid and all effort concentrated on public buildings.

However Olynthus, like the rest of the Chalcidian League,

was among the victims of King Philip II of Macedonia (348). Another flourishing port taken over by the league, though well outside the Chalcidice, had been Pella, which now likewise fell to this overwhelmingly able ruler, and became his capital. Its site, rediscovered recently on a low hill near the Axius, is now twenty-three miles inland but was at that time joined to the sea by a navigable river and lake. Excavations have revealed town walls six feet thick, a thirty-foot-wide convex road, a water-supply maintaining a drainage system, and large houses with Ionic colonnades and floors made of pebbles formed into mosaic designs.

The Macedonia which Philip ruled from Pella was much larger than ever before. He had annexed the Strymon (Struma) valley and the neighbouring gold and silver mines of Mount Pangaeum, and compelled his Thracian neighbours to accept the Hebrus (Evros, Meriç) as a frontier (it is the boundary between Greece and Turkey today). By a series of attacks from inner lines, the mountainous tribal hinterland of upper Macedonia was also brought under control. The powerful, centralised kingdom created by Philip served the Aegean and Adriatic for nearly two centuries as a bulwark against the nomads of central Europe.

This achievement had become possible because Philip was the leading general of the day and made his army more formidable than any the Mediterranean world had ever seen. Heavy cavalry, exceptionally well-trained, transformed land warfare by operating in wedge-shaped formations of his own invention, and the Macedonian infantry, drawn up in a phalanx of novel flexibility and depth, were armed with spears or pikes twice as long as those carried by the Greeks. Philip also gave increased mobility to his fleet by adding small, very fast single-banked ships like those used by his Illyrian (Liburnian) neighbours for their Adriatic piracy.

The mortal peril from this new power, which the danger and downfall of Olynthus clearly foreshadowed to the city-states of Greece, was brilliantly expounded by the greatest of Athenian orators Demosthenes: but in vain since, after a measure of unity had at last belatedly been achieved, Philip triumphed at Chaeronea in Boeotia (338). The days when city-states of the mainland could act as major political powers were at an end.

Instead, they were formed into a federal League of Corinth consisting ostensibly of Macedonia's allies but in hard fact its subordinates.

At the beginning of the fifth century the Persian invasions had sought to secure political repayment from the Greeks for their vast and varied cultural borrowings from the east. Now Philip's son Alexander III the Great (336–323) repaid the debt in a very different sense by expanding Mediterranean Hellenism over gigantic areas of the east. After briskly securing Macedonia and its new southern appendages in Greece, he undertook the task he had inherited from his father – the destruction of Persia's power. In a unique land-Odyssey extending over only half a decade (334–329), Alexander conquered the whole empire. The first decisive battles, taking place in three successive years, were all fought on the Asian shores of the Mediterranean – beside the River Granicus (Çan Çayi) where it debouches into the Sea of Marmara; on the Issus plain between Cilicia and north Syria; and at Tyre which stood siege for seven months and was obliterated. Such was the end of the Phoenician sea-power which had first served Egypt, then became great in independence, and finally provided Persia with its navies. 'And Tyrus,' prophesied a Hebrew after the event, 'did build herself a stronghold; and heaped up silver as the dust, and fine gold as the mire of the streets. Behold, the Lord will cast her out, and he will smite her power in the sea; and she shall be devoured with fire.'[32]

The Macedonians pursued king Darius III eastwards to Gaugamela east of Mosul, where a final decisive battle brought the Persian monarchy to an end and its entire territory under the control of Alexander. Next he extended his frontiers as far as Rusian Turkestan and the Punjab. Intending his régime to be a partnership between races, he had assumed the kingship of Persia (as well as Egypt and Babylonia), and the Persians were again his models in the conciliation of regional cultures and local sanctuaries. This policy, however, caused dissatisfaction among his Macedonian associates, and the vassal city-states of Greece did not like having to treat him as a god. Greeks were accustomed to attribute a quasi-divine status to past heroes and benefactors, but this was an extension of the same idea to a living man; and Alexander, portrayed in semi-godlike fashion by the sculptor Lysippus of Sicyon, may well have formed a mystic belief in his own divine mission.

Outstanding as a commander, especially in handling the heavy cavalry he had inherited from his father, Alexander was more liable to criticism in the economic field because his release of the Persian treasure caused the prices of wheat, barley and wine to be doubled, and the cost of oil to increase more steeply still. On the other hand he displayed exceptional insight by using the land he had conquered to found a large number of new Greek cities. This colonisation helped to bring about the preeminent result of his career – the gradual extension of Greek civilisation to millions of people dwelling in huge areas of the east. Already before the middle of the fourth century a tendency to emigrate from the Greek mainland had become apparent, and the Athenian orator and educationalist Isocrates reminded the Mediterranean world of a concept which was no stranger to Syria and the east when he observed that 'men are called Greeks more because they have a part in our culture than because they come of a common stock'. Now, during the Hellenistic Age that followed Alexander, the various Greek dialects were destined to diminish and amalgamate with the *koine*, the uniform, hugely widespread common tongue of the Greek translation of the Old Testament (Septuagint) – which was made in Egypt from *c.* 280 BC – and then of the New Testament as well.

Alexander reputedly founded seventy Alexandrias, as far afield as Herat and Kandahar in Afghanistan and 'the Remotest' (Eschate) on the River Syr Darya (Jaxartes) where the Tadjik and Kirghiz republics of the Soviet Union now meet – more than twenty-three hundred miles east of the Mediterranean. Most of these settlements were mere forts; but others had a larger destiny.

The greatest among all these Alexandrias was in Egypt (331), established by the conqueror on the site of an ancient village, and enlarged, after his empire had split up, by the dynasty of the Macedonian general Ptolemy I Soter (d. 282 BC) who seized Alexander's body by fraud and built it a mausoleum in the new city. Alexandria stood at the border of the western desert just beyond the Nile delta, on a narrow limestone strip between the sea and the coastal lagoon of Lake Mareotis. This foreshore was not liable to become silted up, because the prevailing easterly current along the coast carried Nile sediment in the opposite direction. Shelter from north winds and waves was provided by a double barrier, comprising the Pharos island and a parallel ridge of reefs farther out. That narrow island, half a mile long, lay three-quarters of a mile out to sea, opposite the urban strip. Between Pharos and the mainland (now linked to it by a mole) were twin harbours of the anvil-shaped formation long familiar in the east, but exceptional for their large dimensions. These harbours, each with a small closed annex opening from its inmost point, consisted of a large natural eastern basin, now protected by huge breakwaters, and an artificial counterpart on the western side. This was linked by a canal to Lake Mareotis, which formed an even more spacious harbour with ample room for the Nile traffic which entered it through a further canal from the delta's western arm.

On the island, Sostratus and other architects designed for Ptolemy I and II the largest of all ancient lighthouses, which gave warning of the approach of hostile fleets, guided friendly vessels into port, and helped them to sail away on the offshore breeze which rises along this coast after dark. Only a few stones of the lighthouse survive today, but descriptions and representations on coins suggest that it stood in a colonnaded court and towered nearly four hundred feet high in three diminishing tiers of local limestone, marble, and reddish-purple granite from upper Egypt. The square bottom storey, which was pierced by numerous windows and rose to nearly half the structure's height, comprised a huge central hall which may have contained hydraulic machinery designed to lift fuel to the higher levels. The middle tier, occupied by a single or double spiral staircase, was octagonal, and above it an open circular top storey supported a cupola upon eight columns. This apex of the building was illuminated at night by a fire of resinous wood, whereas by day, apparently, a huge polished steel reflector reflected the sunlight and sent heliographic messages.

The massive, efficient port facilities of Alexandria, including stone quays and lines of warehouses, provided for the simultaneous reception of one thousand two hundred ships, and stimulated an enormous trade which absorbed traffic that had previously gone to Athens, Corinth and Rhodes (p. 225); from

Alexandria to Rhodes a fair crossing took only four days. The Alexandrians were far from self-sufficient, since they imported all their timber, metals, horses, wool, purple, marble, fine wines, spices, salt fish, pickled pork, honey, cheese and olive-oil. Yet their exports were far more important, owing to the enormous size of Egypt's corn-crop, which made the country the largest grain-producer in the whole Mediterranean area, exceeding, as time went on, even Sicily and Tunisia. Alexandria also provided the world with papyrus and was the principal distribution-centre for linen and eastern spices. Other exports included glass, woollen goods, scents, ivory, goldsmiths' work and luxury articles generally; while cheap goods were made as well, for exchange over the land frontiers with African tribesman.

The city stored water in a unique chain of underground cisterns, and was surrounded by a wall which from the outset made Alexandria larger even than Ephesus or Miletus. Its ambitious layout, on the site of the present town-centre, displayed a rectangular plan bisected by a hundred-foot-wide latitudinal street which was crossed by a second major thoroughfare. On the eastern harbour stood the royal quarter, including the tombs of Alexander and the Ptolemies, the Museum (university), and the library of which leading poets, Apollonius Rhodius and Callimachus, were director and employee respectively. The palace of the Ptolemies nearby was not a massive edifice on the pattern of older monarchies but a Greek juxtaposition of clustered halls and living rooms. By 200 BC this had become the greatest city of the known world: a papyrus later declared that it *is* the world.[34] A dazzling whiteness came from stucco surfaces made of the gypsum which gleams like snow along the coast to the west of Alexandria; and beneath the gypsum was everywhere solid stone. The place could not be burnt, noted a Roman general, because none of its buildings were made of anything that would burn.[35]

What was inflammable, instead, was the population. For this was no unified city-state but the cosmopolitan royal capital of a variegated kingdom, and although the ruling class were Macedonians and therefore culturally more or less Greeks, there were also other, separate, communities belonging to different nationalities. Prominent among these were the Jews of the Dispersion (p. 116), whose residential area was situated behind the palace. A millennium later, the Arab conqueror of Alexandria reported: 'I have taken a city of which I can only say that it contains four thousand palaces, four thousand baths, four hundred theatres, twelve thousand greengrocers and forty thousand Jews.' Although this was an epoch in which most barriers were down, the Greeks and Jews of Alexandria always remained enemies, not for commercial reasons since the Jews were not yet prominent as traders, but because of insuperable differences of religion and temperament.[36] From the second century BC onwards many Macedonians and Greeks intermarried with Egyptians; and so the bulk of the population of Alexandria 'did ultimately fuse into a more or less homogeneous mass, turbulent, crazy for shows, sarcastic and sometimes hostile towards the dynasty.'[37]

This house of the Ptolemies, descended from Alexander's general, produced tenacious men who achieved a satisfactory relationship with the ancient vested interests of Egyptian priesthood and temple, though they made the old Egyptian mistake of wasting money and energy on the Levant (p. 59). Ptolemy II (282–246) established an economic system in which state control went farther than ever before. Except for the lands of Alexandria, Greek Naucratis, and a new centre of Hellenism in upper Egypt called Ptolemais, the whole of Egyptian soil belonged to the monarch. The kings likewise owned nearly every means of production throughout this country of ten million people, and controlled virtually all commerce on a monopoly or percentage basis. Their nationalised industry of vegetable oils was protected by a 50 per cent tax on imported olive-oil; and as corn-merchants they outdid even the rulers of the Crimean Bosphorus (p. 182). The Ptolemies, it was complained, had started treating their people's possessions as their own.[38] The bureaucracy which enabled them to do so was destined to provide valuable guidance to the Romans, but under Ptolemies of the second century BC its oppressiveness and diminishing honesty caused desperate men, reduced to destitution, to start riots and flee into the marshes.

In contrast to these increasingly depressing surroundings was the superb research performed in the Museum and library of Alexandria. The Greeks of this epoch, on the whole, were philosophically minded theoreticians rather than scientists, excelling particularly at mathematics, in which the greatest of all ancient writers on the subject, Archimedes, was a Syracusan, but Euclid, who superseded all previous geometricians, came from Alexandria. Archimedes also directed himself to practical applications, since he developed a water-screw, and there were men at Alexandria like Ctesibius who invented a water-clock and a catapult worked by compressed air; while botanists were much influenced by the practicality of Theophrastus of Lesbos, who was not superseded until Linnaeus more than two thousand years later – and his teacher Aristotle of Stagirus, the founder of biology and zoology (d. 322 BC). If ever, asserted Aristotle with true naturalist's passion, 'the facts about bees are fully grasped, then credit must be given rather to observation than to theories, and to theories only if what they affirm agrees with the observed facts.' Although few if any other Greeks were capable of the full rigours of this approach, such, nevertheless, was the spirit which lay behind a host of advances by Alexandrians and their contemporaries. Treatises on agriculture, for example, invented and passed on to Carthage and Rome the scientific principles of land use, while cultivation benefited not only from Archimedes' water-screw but from the importation through Alexandria of eastern irrigation machines, improved sickles, stronger ploughs with metal shares, and a form of hand-mill which represented the first important new use of rotary motion since the invention of the potter's wheel.

There was also a greatly increased tendency to specialisation, which had been alien to the classical age. Benefiting by this sort of expertise, Ptolemaic Egypt adopted livestock from Arabia, Sicily and Asia Minor, special fig-trees from the same peninsula, and seed-corns and high-quality vines (trained in novel styles) from Greece and Syria. Poets celebrated the calm and spaciousness of the pleasure gardens of Alexandria, which were improved versions of royal parks elsewhere; and a new and more intimate concern for natural beauties, apparent also in contemporary poets (p. 224), was mirrored in the work of a second-century Alexandrian painter called Demetrius. The impressionistic scenes he was said to have made fashionable were still, no doubt, largely settings for human figures, but their disposal, in the picturesque religious enclosures long admired by Greek writers (p. 190), represented a step towards landscape as an autonomous interest in its own right. There was, moreover, a close relation between this *rapprochement* of art to nature and a contemporary taste for descriptive fiction, which linked the ancient Egyptian romances, now translated into Greek,[39] with the novels which were to form the principal reading matter of the Greco-Roman world (p. 295).

Meanwhile the members of the Museum pursued their studies in a cosmopolitan atmosphere free from political or religious direction. Alexandria was the central point of scholarship as no city has ever been again,[40] and the learning of Greece, Egypt, Mesopotamia and Persia was collected and fused for later transmission to the west and north. Such, for example, were the various models from which Alexandrians first contrived a modern calendar, complete with Leap-Year. An intense new interest in foreign parts, which had become far more accessible in this age of wider horizons, meant that much of the best research was devoted, like Sostratus' lighthouse, to the improvement of maritime communications. The 'Coast Pilot' of the Carian Scylax the Younger is the oldest known guidebook to the entire Mediterranean (*c.* 350). Then, after Pytheas of Massalia had discovered that tides were caused by the moon and not the sun, a director of the Alexandrian library concluded that a ship sailing west from Spain would eventually reach India. This was Eratosthenes of Cyrene (d. 194 BC), who also measured the diameter of the earth correctly to within fifty miles, and may be regarded as the creator of scientific geography, which is a typical invention of this increasingly expert phase of Mediterranean development.

Syria and the Aegean after Alexander

Far larger than the kingdom of Ptolemy was a second successor-state of Alexander, which the dynasty of another of his Macedonian generals, Seleucus I (d. 280), established from the Indus to the Aegean, with a final western outpost in Thrace (*c.* 240). Grappling with overwork and separatist movements, Seleucids endeavoured with some success to preserve thirty million subjects from anarchy, to raise their standards of living, and to permit wide autonomy in their cities, which were theoretically the king's subjects but enjoyed freedom as an act of grace. Like

Alexander, these monarchs envisaged a Greco-Persian character for their composite dominions, but they laid particular stress on an extensive inflow of ex-soldiers and other Greek immigrants. This policy cost them, ultimately, the cooperation of the Iranian element, but it also meant that the main Seleucid contribution to civilisation was the establishment of many new Greek cities as well as the revival of old ones. The location of these colonies reflected the dual Asian-Mediterranean basis of the empire, which depended jointly upon Mesopotamia and north Syria. The capitals created by Seleucus I in these lands became two of the most important cities in the world. One was Seleucia on the Tigris a little north of Babylon, and the other, Antioch, stood fourteen miles inland from the Mediterranean, beside the River Orontes and the Amik plain which had for many millennia been a nucleus of advanced civilisation (p. 25).

In *c.* 300 Seleucus transferred 5,300 Macedonians and Athenians to Antioch from a neighbouring settlement which they had occupied seven years earlier. The new foundation gradually collected four quarters with separate walls, the first occupied by the initial settlers, the next filled with the native inhabitants, and the others housing further colonists added in the third and early second centuries BC. The city was presided over by a statue of Fortune, who was much revered in these anxious times. The sculptor, Lysippus' pupil Eutychides of Sicyon, made the goddess personify Antioch itself, with a figure representing the Orontes at her feet; the group was set up above the river under the open sky, and its originality lay in a complex three-dimensional composition intended for appreciation from any angle.

Syria must already, at this time, have been manufacturing the woollen goods which were later a leading export, but Antioch was a city less of industry than of commerce. Besides enjoying easy contacts with Tarsus and Asia Minor, its site commanded a route eastwards to the not far distant Euphrates crossing, which the Seleucids linked by road with their second capital on the Tigris. Antioch's Mediterranean port, fourteen miles to the west, was another new foundation, Seleucia in Pieria, built on a defensible hill site by a bay just far enough north of the Orontes mouth to avoid its silt. This was only an open roadstead, where sea-going ships discharged cargoes into lighters to be towed up the river, but it served the whole Mediterranean. Seleucia also housed the burial-place of the dynasty, 'rising gloriously from the sea in terrace after terrace up its great cliff, and worshipping a conical stone come down from an older world'.

Farther south, upon the middle stretches of the Orontes, the torrid foundation of Apamea was used by the kings to stable their horses and the elephants whose deadly initial impact upon cavalry had been learnt from Alexander's north Indian opponent Porus. A few miles west of Apamea was Laodicea on the Sea (Latakia), the port for the wines of north Syria which at this time were bracketed equal to those of western Asia Minor as the finest in the world.

For a hundred years the coast of Syria and Israel, that ancient source of enmity between Asiatic and Egyptian powers, was disputed between the Seleucids and Ptolemies. Finally, however, Antiochus III the Great asserted Seleucid control (*c.* 200–197) and brought his empire to the height of its prosperity. Moreover Egypt's possessions in Asia Minor, which had rivalled and alternated with those of the Seleucids amid long and crippling wars, constant changes of suzerain, and a variety of city-foundations that continued Alexander's expansion of Hellenism, likewise changed hands.

But the expulsion of the Egyptians from Asia Minor still did not give the Seleucids control of the whole peninsula, since during the previous century their realm, too, had contracted in these Aegean borderlands. The Seleucid capital of Asia Minor was Sardis where the Lydians had formerly reigned, but the breakaway was led by Pergamum (Bergama), a hill-fortress rising above the fertile valley of the Caïcus fifteen miles east of the Aegean. At first its surrounding territory had been ruled by a vassal of the Seleucids, but Eumenes I (263–241) with Egyptian assistance had thrown off their sovereignty, and his son Attalus I (241–197) asserted his claim to the title of king and gave his name to the dynasty that followed. Pergamum's port on the Aegean was enlarged, and a new outlet was added on the Sea of Marmara. At a time when the prosperity of the Greek mainland had diminished (p. 223), the rulers of Pergamum rapidly increased their wealth by exploiting and developing silver mines, grain production, stock-breeding and a woollen textile industry. Another local manufacture was parchment. The skins of animals had long been employed as a medium for writing, but now a new process was developed (? *c*. 196–180), so that eventually, several centuries later, this took the place of papyrus as the principal writing material of the western world.

The Pergamene state was governed by a strong monarchic régime which was a less elaborate version of the Egyptian system, with a Greek bureaucracy and extensive slave labour. The kings made great efforts to transform Pergamum into a city worthy of their ambitions, and Eumenes II (197–160) built up his royal capital on a magnificent series of arched terraces. The city was attractive to tourists and invalids because of the neighbouring shrine of the now fashionable god of healing, Asclepius, and it gained fame also from the principal sculptural school of the day, which produced skilful baroque works making a novel and spectacular use of light and shade.

Pergamum now proceeded to play a vital part in the politics of the Mediterranean region. Among other cities which passed under its control from Seleucid or Ptolemaic hands, Ephesus was preeminent as a transit centre, gaining steadily on its rival Miletus. Yet Miletus, too, still maintained distinction, since its wool remained the best in the world, one of its explorers sailed as far as the Aral Sea, and the city, reconstructed after Persian destruction and then again by Alexander, was adjoined by a spectacular new temple at Apollo's Didyma shrine which rivalled the temple of his sister Artemis at Ephesus. Priene, nearby, was a *tour de force* applying fashionable geometrical principles of design to a hillside, which was covered with public buildings and houses planned round courtyards (p. 211).

The kings of Pergamum owed their prestige mainly to their defeats of Celtic (Gaulish) invaders and devastators of Asia Minor, whom Attalus I succeeded in penning into the central area, named Galatia after them. The process of warding off these massive hordes had been started in Europe when Antigonus II Gonatas (283–239) defeated twenty thousand Gauls and thereby asserted his claim to Macedonia, traditional bastion of

Hellenism against the north. Once installed as its king, he defeated his neighbour and rival, Pyrrhus of Epirus, who had risen rapidly to power but then exhausted his resources by forays in Sicily and southern Italy. Antigonus was one of the few monarchs of the ancient world who nearly put philosophy into practice, and his formulation of monarchy as 'glorious slavery' – hard work that seems glorious to the world – gave many hints to the later propaganda of Roman emperors, and was emulated in earnest by Marcus Aurelius.

The realm taken over by Antigonus had been strengthened by the new foundations of Alexander's officer Cassander (d. 297). These included the town which he called after his wife, Thessalonica (Salonica), an amalgamation of twenty-six small communities beside the Thermaic gulf, in a marshy area which was now drained and made into a focal point of Balkan communications. The military and naval power of Macedonia was strengthened by Demetrius I the Besieger (d. 283), the founder of the Thessalian fortress of Demetrias, which commanded most of Greece. This formidable condottiere also competed with the Ptolemies in creating ever larger catapult-carrying ships with seven or ten men to the oar, and even larger models with echeloned formations of rowers.

Inheriting these advantages, Antigonus controlled most of the city-states of the Greek mainland, though they retained internal self-government. And yet the air was also full, belatedly, of blue-prints for cooperation between one such city and another, and two formerly backward areas on either side of the Corinthian Gulf now took the lead in turning theory into practice and forming close confederations between cities. These were the Achaean League (280–146) covering most of the Peloponnese except Sparta, and the Aetolian League which occupied Delphi (*c.* 290) and within seventy years had dominated the whole of central Greece outside Attica.

At a time when the wealth of Greece was declining in relation to neighbouring lands, the cultivation of its soil became more sophisticated. There was an ominous growth of latifundia, large stretches of tillage and pasturage cultivated by increased numbers of slaves. But technical methods, such as the use of fertilisers, improved in efficiency, and farmers studied the nature of the soil more carefully, sometimes superseding the old two-field system by a much more productive three-staged process of rotation. Olives numbered at least twenty-seven varieties, mills and presses for extracting their oil were re-designed, knowledge of grafting methods became advanced and widespread, and in the years round 300 BC citrus fruits and melons were introduced into Greece from the east.

Pure silk remained out of reach of Greek manufacturers because they did not discover the Chinese method of unwinding the cocoon, but instead a substitute silk now began to be manufactured. The people of the island of Cos, off south-western Asia Minor, possessed silk worms and carded and spun their pierced cocoons into a coarse kind of silk, feeding worms on the leaves, not of the Chinese white mulberry, but of a black variety which grows wild in Asia Minor and its offshore isles. A second type of robe was made from another sort of worm which lived on the oak and ash trees of Cos.

The same island produced the distinguished medical school of Asclepius (going back to Hippocrates, d. 399 BC) and the pastoral poems of Theocritus (d. *c.* 250), an emigrant from Syracuse who lived for a time at Alexandria but made his principal home at Cos. The rural poetry which he invented for nostalgic readers living flat, drab urban lives looks at natural beauties more closely and appreciatively than had been the custom hitherto (p. 191). Theocritus expresses an unfamiliar sensibility towards nature in its more delicate and sweeter aspects and moods. He loves the country's shade and sounds, the wind in the pines and the blackbird's song. Often cheerful and sunny but sometimes sombre, at times almost Wordsworthian in his sentimental bond with the surrounding world, he admits the Mediterranean landscape, in its own right, as an active element in the poet's consciousness.

> Heartsick, I wish I were the bee
> That, blundering, buzzes its way into your cave
> Past the ivy, the fern that hides you from me.[41]

When Theocritus is in Alexandria, he longs for the hills and streams and meadows of other Mediterranean lands. Written in a broad but literary Doric – one of the last dialects to survive the general assimilation – his pastoral inventions owe debts to his native Sicily, home of the legendary father of this type of poetry, Daphnis. But, in so far as his convention recognises any local setting, the closest links of Theocritus are with Cos, where he describes a walk in the noonday heat, 'when even the lizard sleeps upon the stone wall'. With its high double mass of sheer rock, its silk-bearing trees, and a central lowland of soft marls and sands rich in grain and vegetables and pastures and vines, the island epitomises the varied elements in the Aegean scene. Cos is the homeland of the poet Philetas, whom Theocritus acknowledges as his master.[42] Their contemporary Apollonius Rhodius of Alexandria, in his *Argonautica*, likewise shows a deep sensitiveness to the natural scene; and later bucolic poets speak with novel pleasure about the sound of the waves, or like painters and sculptors see Mediterranean rusticity with a new descriptive directness, sometimes blended with traces of the 'pathetic fallacy', so beloved of later European poets, which endows nature with human feelings.[43]

Cos shared a flourishing wine trade with Rhodes, but in other respects the Rhodians exceeded their smaller neighbour in importance. Indeed, during the centuries that followed Alexander, no other Greek community equalled Rhodes in activity, resources, and influence. At its northern tip, a single city-state had been made out of the three which had fulfilled a historic role for over a thousand years (408). Surviving a Persian occupation and a famous siege by Demetrius I the Besieger (305–304), the island retained full independence, and its prosperity received impetus from Alexander's conquests, which gave unrestricted access to Cyprus, Cilicia, Syria and Egypt. The Rhodians also benefited from Alexander's destruction of Tyre, shortlived though this proved to be, and succeeded in diverting to themselves a considerable part of the Black Sea corn traffic of Athens, just as they also aspired to its role as a centre for philosophers.

A substantial income was derived from 2 per cent import and export duties levied on passages through the strait, and jars of Rhodes found as far afield as Persia, the Crimea, the lower Danube, Africa and Italy included wine and oil that were not necessarily home grown. For Rhodes, with its position on the main passage-way of the eastern Mediterranean, even outdid

Alexandria, for a time, as the supreme receiving and dispatching centre. The Rhodians were also leaders of international banking exchange, and laid down the first organised code of maritime law, which was later partially taken over by Romans and Byzantines and Venetians in turn.

Naturally enough, Rhodes was also prominent in the ship-building advances for which this age was notable. Riggings and steering-gears were improved, and the new bowsprit sail made the navigation of large craft so much easier that captains were more prepared to sail direct across the open sea instead of hugging the coast. Rhodes, however, preferred not to construct the largest variety of vessel with which Macedonia and other great powers were experimenting, but concentrated instead upon those with four men to an oar which were the fastest type of major ship and consequently best adapted to their favourite tactics of manœuvring for a ram. They also added a new device, consisting of containers of blazing fire slung at the ends of two long poles which projected from the bows (*c.* 190 BC). The fleet, small in size but unsurpassed in quality,[44] was unique for the perseverance it devoted to keeping down the piracy that was rampant in the eastern Mediterranean. Closely guarding the shipping channel between the island and its mainland possessions, this Rhodian navy carried out its city's policy of supporting the freedom of the seas and balance of power against one imperialist after another. When Rhodes had been gravely damaged by an earthquake (225 BC), an unprecedented compliment came its way: for not only many small Greek states, but all the major ones as well, sent contributions towards its recovery.

From its concave hill, looking out like a great auditorium upon a crescent bay, the town faced northwards across the strait to Asia Minor. With eight miles of landward walls Rhodes was more spacious than any Greek city except Syracuse and Athens. The five partly or wholly artificial anchorages added up to the best equipped port in the Aegean world, and inspired a Rhodian to write a treatise on *Harbours*. Three of these basins, of capacious size, were formed out of indentations on the more sheltered eastern side of the cape; and adjoining their elaborate works was a large and complex navy yard protected by a strict security system. Air photographs have revealed the rectilinear plan of the city, with its uniform houses and thoroughfares which were famous for retaining their decorative aspect from every visible angle. The three thousand statues with which these streets were adorned included the highly accomplished products of the Rhodian school itself, of which the most famous was the Colossus, a statue of the city's patron-god the Sun carved by Lysippus' pupil Chares of Lindus to adorn the harbour, though not, as was later believed, to bestride its opening.

The local boast was that every Rhodian citizen was worth a warship in himself;[45] but to become a citizen was not easy. For although dependencies on the coast of Asia Minor were admitted to the full franchise, Rhodes stood out against the liberal tendencies of the day by allowing no foreigner citizenship – and excluding them from participation in its trade. On the other hand this was also the nearest ancient approach to a welfare-state, compromising ingeniously between the interests of the citizen body as a whole and the ruling class, whose sponsorship of social services and other popular measures helped to ensure that the large cosmopolitan, nautical proletariat never made trouble.[46]

This was particularly unusual, since the third century BC inaugurated a time of economic difficulties which threatened to disrupt the whole Mediterranean world. Currency depreciations (*c.* 300), causing people who received the debased coins to believe they were not getting their due, meant that the price-increases which had started under Alexander continued at an alarming, ever steeper rate, ruining people with fixed incomes and making it impossible for the poor to pay for their food or rear their children. As the resources of the great Mediterranean powers were frittered away by constant warfare, the rich managed to hold fast, but the gulf that divided them from most of the population became continually wider. From 270 BC onwards, there was an ever-increasing army of desperate, penniless men, and disturbances and outbreaks of unrest became more and more frequent. These were caused not only by 'free' poor but by slaves, whose numbers sharply mounted as destitute vagabonds, displaced persons, prisoners of war and people captured by pirates all fell into the slave-traders' clutches.

Consequently, one of the most important places in the Aegean world was its principal slave-market. This was situated at Delos, the central island of the Cyclades archipelago, which had long attracted many visitors for the less unsavoury purpose of pilgrimage to the shrine of Apollo. Early in the third century BC, under the influence of the rapid economic developments of the nearby Asian coast, Delos also became the hub of the entire Aegean corn-trade, and the headquarters of an archipelago confederacy. Monuments erected on the island show how the powers vied with one another to have a stake in the place. Antigonus Gonatas of Macedonia, for example, erected a portico four hundred and ten feet long, an early instance of the long colonnaded shelters of which Greek cities were now becoming very fond. During the last phase of all before the entire region fell into the hands of the Romans, Delos was destined, with their encouragement, to take over the commercial supremacy from Rhodes throughout the eastern Mediterranean (p. 270).

PART THREE
The Romans

9

The Etruscans and the Beginnings of Rome

The Etruscans

Italy's central position in the Mediterranean is a call to self-assertion. Though somewhat withdrawn from continental turmoils, it is a joint, not a barrier, between the eastern and western portions of the sea, open to maritime channels on every side. Moreover, an elongated peninsular shape provides a shore-line that is second only to that of Greece in length: there is one mile of coast for every fifty-nine square miles of land, whereas Spain, for example, has one to one hundred and forty-five.

At least three-quarters of the country consists of hills, rising up to the harsh ribs and vertebrae of the Apennines which curve from the Ligurian seaboard across towards the Adriatic, and then back again to the toe. The four plains into which these mountains divide the mainland are greatly superior to anything in Greece for size and fertility alike. There is the Po valley in the north, which remained for a long time outside Italy. The lowlands of Etruria and Latium, bisected by the Tiber, stretch for eighty miles along the western coast. Next comes Campania, where the Greeks had outposts beside the bay of Naples. And then finally, to the south, are the warm, well-watered maritime districts which Greek colonists intensively occupied and developed.

Rome enjoys two thousand four hundred hours of sun during the year, while London only has one thousand three hundred. Yet Italy, except for torrid areas beside the southern fertile strips, is exceptional for its relatively temperate and humid climate, which facilitated land-utilisation on a scale that no other Mediterranean country had ever been able to attempt. In comparison with other parts of the world, these plainlands seemed 'full to overflowing of all that is serviceable and gladdens the heart'.[1]

The first Italian pastoralists and farmers, short, slight and long-headed, had come to the south-east of the peninsula, travelling across the Adriatic from the Balkans. Then, early in the third millennium BC, settlements were being built on piles by the swampy Po and lakes. Later newcomers, including round-headed immigrants from across the Brenner, introduced the smelting of copper, and from *c.* 1600 BC further new arrivals who had traversed the Venetian passes practised cremation, built timbered, platformed, moated houses on dry land, and linked their Po valley concentrations not only with summer settlements on higher ground but with important offshoots in metal-producing Etruria, where they worked in bronze (p. 235). They also made a dark burnished pottery and used amber imported from the far north (p. 84).

Then, perhaps in *c.* 1200 BC, a population of mixed cultures and origins, who knew iron and fashioned masterly engraved bronze work somewhat reminiscent of the Aegean, occupied the same villages and created others over wide areas of the middle and lower Po valley, south Etruria and Latium, with outliers in eastern Italy and southern Campania. According to a custom which originated in central Europe, the ashes of their dead were consigned to urns, which are usually in the shape of two cones with the flat ends placed together, but in Latium instead form little models of the huts in which the living people dwelt. Perhaps the people who practised these rites were joined by elements from the sea raiders who were active at this time in the east (p. 58).

Such elements combined with later Greek and oriental influences to make the culture of the Etruscans. This was a vigorous, derivative, and yet in certain respects original civilisation, which flourished in what is now southern Tuscany and northern Lazio, covering a territory of two hundred miles from Arno to Tiber and extending inland as far as the Apennines. The notoriously enigmatic people of this land of Etruria, who called themselves Rasenna, were no doubt mostly descendants of earlier settlers in these regions, with perhaps sufficient new immigrants added from time to time to justify the ancient tradition that the Etruscans came from the east. But 'the real problem is not where they came from, but where the various elements came from that went into their making'[2] – not as physical human beings but as significant participants in Mediterranean civilisation. One of the earliest phases of this process could possibly have originated from Lydia, since that is the region of Asia Minor specified by Herodotus as the original homeland of the Etruscans.[3] But whether this Lydian connection comprised actual immigrations or merely cultural movements, it still would not explain the undoubted oriental features in their culture, since Herodotus was writing of a mythical period (*c.* 1300–1200) four or five centuries before those features appeared in Etruria or even originated in their own Asian homelands. Perhaps Herodotus was right about the Lydian influence, but should have placed it in the early first millennium BC. For the existence of eastern links in that subsequent epoch is demonstrated not only by artistic parallels but by inscriptions from the north Aegean island of Lemnos which show that its people spoke a language resembling Etruscan.

The nature of that language, however, is at present still as speculative as the question of racial origins. During the seventh century BC the Etruscans adopted an alphabet of twenty-six letters, probably derived, with necessary adjustments, from the Greek script which came to Italy through Chalcidian settlers at Pithecusae and Cumae (p. 168). However, our forty bilingual inscriptions in Etruscan and Latin do not enable us to decipher the tongue in which they are written, or even to determine whether its linguistic family is partly or wholly Indo-European.

Etruria is one of the most varied regions in Italy, containing an intricate diversity of reliefs, soils and land-uses which embody in an extreme form the fragmentation imposed by the neighbouring Apennines. Many of the sandy bays, which once followed one after another between rocky headlands, have now been filled with silt, and shores that were densely inhabited have become a forbidding wilderness. The silt was the product of erosions caused by the ravages of goats and charcoal-burners, and above all by the removal of huge quantities of timber for ship-building and fuel, and the consequent deforestation which released millions of tons of irreplaceable top soil (p. 5).

Indeed it is impossible to decide what was the 'natural', original, vegetation in parts of Italy where these changes have been taking place for so long. The country mostly has a dual vegetation pattern, comprising both the evergreen oaks resistant to Mediterranean conditions and the deciduous varieties characteristic of more northern countries; but which of these two types arrived on the scene first is disputed. At any rate ancient Etruria was covered by oaks of both sorts, and by dense forests of beech. The Etruscans loved these lands and coasts and lakes for their hunting and fishing.

> Tall are the oaks whose acorns
>   Drop in dark Auser's rill;
> Fat are the stags that champ the boughs
>   Of the Ciminian hill;
> Beyond all streams Clitumnus
>   Is to the herdsman dear;
> Best of all pools the fowler loves
>   The great Volsinian mere.[4]

But there was also fertile land in abundance. Because of the Apennine screen and the proximity of the Tyrrhenian Sea, which is deeper and warmer than the Adriatic, western Italy has a winter temperature five degrees higher than the east, and many Etruscan towns were carefully sited to derive the maximum benefit from the cultivation of their horse-drawn ploughs. At first the staple diet of the area was unhusked emmer wheat made into porridge. But the more refined sort of wheat, subsequently developed for bread-making, was said by the Romans to be the best in the world, its ear weighing a quarter as much again as those of the richest Greek crops in Boeotia. The country became identified, as time went on, with the characteristic triad of wheat, vine and olive, combining them in the interculture which is still typical of Tuscany today. It was probably Greeks from south Italy who introduced the vine, and subsequently the olive as well (p. 256).

The city-states of Etruria were traditionally twelve in number, though recent air photography has shown that every hill in the country which had natural defences on three sides possessed an Etruscan town. To compensate for poor river communications, there were good roads capable of carrying heavy traffic. These permitted the states to send delegates to an annual religious gathering at the shrine of the goddess Voltumna, which has not yet been identified. Yet in spite of this measure of joint activity the Etruscans almost completely lacked political cohesion; their geographic fragmentation, or the temperament of the people and of their monarchs and subsequent republican governments, made them even more incapable of united action than the Greeks.

Nevertheless the cities, whether in collaboration or singly, adopted a very active policy at sea, sending out adventurous fishing and trading fleets, gaining a formidable reputation as pirates, and combining with Carthage to keep Corsica, opposite the Etruscan coast, out of Greek hands (535). The northern promontory of that island is only thirty miles from the island of Elba, with its abundant iron mines from which the Etruscans derived a great part of their strength. This iron of Elba was collected and smelted at the mainland town of Populonia, perched on an eminence towering seven hundred feet above a natural harbour; for this was Etruria's principal coastal city.

Its metallurgical activities, recalled by huge slag-heaps in the vicinity, enabled the Etruscans to become great iron-workers like the peoples of Asia Minor and Urartu who during the eighth and seventh centuries BC, directly or by Greek intermediaries, introduced them to this craft (p. 118). Populonia also imported copper, zinc and tin from other parts of Etruria and produced zinc and lead in its own immediate neighbourhood. These comprised almost the entire mineral wealth of Italy, and were the only substantial mines in the entire central Mediterranean area.

Nor far away rose the even higher hill of Vetulonia, now nine miles from the sea but in those days almost upon its shore. This walled town, with its vast surrounding necropolis, was reputedly the place from which the Romans copied the insignia they adopted for officers of state.[5] In addition to supplies of metals from its immediate neighbourhood, Vetulonia was rich in imported gold and silver, and before 700 BC had brought in bronze cauldrons from Urartu that provided models for local workers.* But then sand and silt filled up the adjacent harbour, and now the place has become just another 'worn-out little knot of streets shut inside a wall'.[6]

This northern region of Etruria, behind its maritime bases, consists of the well-watered, wooded foothills of the Apennines. The southern part is a very different terrain of alluvial, volcanic plains and hills and furrowed valleys. During the seventh century BC the cities upon these southern extremities of Etruria increasingly took command. They had already had a long history; indeed Tarquinii, forty miles north-west of Rome on a stream-girt hill near the sea, may have been the oldest of all Etruscan towns, and excavations show continuous growth from a village that must be regarded as pre-Etruscan (though when the transition came is hard to say) to the city which became one of the richest in Etruria. This abundant wealth is demonstrated by an early bronze industry, supreme until *c.* 650, and then, a century later, by splendidly painted cemeteries on neighbouring hills. And Tarquinii was reputed to have given the Romans their Etruscan dynasty which had the same name as the town.

A rival town nearby was Vulci, eight miles from the sea. Beneath the citadel's steep cliffs flows a river which is joined by tributaries running below two other sides of the hill. Burials start soon after 900 BC, and two centuries later a high degree of prosperity is revealed by huge numbers of imported Greek vases, as well as by glorious local traditions – including a story that Vulci, like Tarquinii, had provided a king to early Rome. The bronzework of the town was exported as far as Greece and central Europe, and Vulci possessed a fertile plain which after centuries of subsequent desolation is now cultivated again as in ancient times.

On the other side, Tarquinii is separated from Caere (Cerveteri), twenty-five miles to its south-east, by the extinct metalliferous Tolfa volcano, which gave first the one place and then the other its greatest prosperity. Caere stood on a rocky spur looking across the Maremma coastal plain to the sea, and beside it were cemeteries of much architectural grandeur and

* Urartian cauldron-mounts with designs of female-headed birds and bulls' heads are found in Etruria as in Greece. For similar cauldrons in Phrygia and Capua, see pp. 153 and 247.

diversity. For this city, rising out of ancient beginnings, had become by 600 BC the greatest and most outward-looking city in Etruria, and one of the most important centres in the whole Mediterranean world. Caere possessed several ports from which it policed the seas, including Pyrgi (Santa Severa) where recently discovered bilingual inscriptions on sheets of gold indicate the existence of a Phoenician community. The name of one of the other harbour-towns, Punicum, is equally suggestive; it was the joint efforts of Etruscans and Carthaginians which kept the Greeks out of Corsica (p. 173). And yet among the approximately twenty-five thousand inhabitants of Caere there were also groups of Greek residents, since of all Etruscan cities this was the most interested in trade with Greece, as well as with Cyprus, Syria and the east. It was largely due to Caere that Etruria was more than half Hellenic in culture (p. 240).

A little inland from Caere there is a steep rise to a volcanic plateau, and on its edge stood Veii, surrounded on three sides, in characteristic Etruscan fashion, by ravines. The grandeur of Veii did not come suddenly, for as elsewhere there had been continuous building since early in the first millennium BC. But the place began its greatest days soon after Caere (*c.* 550 BC). Veii was superior even to Rome, twelve miles away, in the size and fertility of its cultivable lands, and it was largely through these that the city became prosperous. This agricultural success was due to the arts of irrigation which the Etruscans learnt, directly or through Greeks, from Assyria and Urartu (p. 118), and which, like much else, they passed on to Rome (p. 246). Veii conserved water in cisterns replenished through shafts leading from the rock, and the flow of its river moats was regulated by lengthy tunnels. Moreover, for several miles northwards the valleys, which would otherwise have been too waterlogged for cultivation, were drained by an elaborate honeycomb of artificial channels. These measures could not have been undertaken without abundant man-power and a central authority at Veii strong enough to coordinate arrangements with the owners of all the various lands involved.

At the end of the sixth century, however, the simultaneous threats of Rome, piracy and silting, combined perhaps with the exhaustion of coastal mines, meant that Tarquinii, Caere and Veii declined in importance and power. The supremacy passed instead to places farther inland, and of these the most famous was Clusium (Chiusi), standing seventy miles from the coast on an isolated hill overlooking a Tiber tributary, the Chiana. Its fertile valley grew white wheat and served as a corridor through central Italy. But Clusium owes its fame to the half-legendary Lars Porsenna (of disputed origins) who a little before 500 BC championed the exiled Tarquin's cause and temporarily seized control of Rome – or, according to the patriotic Roman version, was narrowly thwarted by Horatius at the fateful bridge.

The widely spreading Etruscan cities of the dead, filled with graves of enormous variety, recall cemeteries built in Syria, Crete and Greece during the second millennium BC, but add their own façades, domes and cubic designs, for which the closest analogies come from Greco-Scythian graves of the Crimea and elsewhere in south Russia (p. 182). In these tombs of the Etruscans, by which the architectural splendours of Mycenaean burials are at last exceeded, jutting eaves reproduce Phrygian and Lydian prototypes in exaggerated form, and these are again recalled by the spreading gables of temples (p. 154). Their roofs were loaded with a colourful riot of brilliant painted terracotta ornaments, and the buildings, chiefly made of wood, were given high stone bases and deep porches which could not have been made on the mainland of Greece. At first these shrines look like little houses, but towards the end of the sixth century temples of grandiose size, designed by architects who seem to have been highly esteemed, began to be erected in the cities of the Etruscans. Where they particularly excelled, however, was in the construction of arches, of which they learnt part of the principle from Assyrian and Urartian models and conceivably also improved their technique, according to recent discoveries, by reference to Greek southern Italy. Surviving city-gates are mainly or entirely of later date, but the constructional methods can already be seen in early sepulchral monuments and irrigation tunnels. Etruscan private houses, of which we can learn something from the tombs made to resemble them, seem to have introduced a form of central hall, uncovered or with an opening over a rainwater tank, which later became the *atrium* characteristic of a certain type of Roman house (p. 279).

The sculpture and painting of the Etruscans are provincial

versions of Greek styles, but the provincialisms show creative originality to an even greater extent than other fringe arts such as Greco-Scythian or Greco-Iberian. The numerous Greek models that were available included thousands of vases which came in by sea, or from Greek colonies such as Rhegium in Calabria where factories existed for their reproduction. Moreover, as their Phrygo-Lydian gables suggest, the Etruscans were not by any means immune to the orientalising trends which contributed so much to early Greek art. On the contrary, Etruria not only absorbed all of these influences, though without much of the critically stern process of modification to which they were subjected by Greece, but from 700 onwards supplemented them by its own direct contacts with northern Syria and Phoenicia, Asia Minor, Urartu and Assyria. Etruscan artists were born imitators, and the large resources of their country enabled them to imitate prolifically. But they also greatly exceeded the Greeks in a special taste for parody and the grotesque, and possessed an uninhibited, unsubtle love of colour which attracted them to spectacular eastern designs and precious materials. But this was only part of a marked Etruscan preference for energetic simplification which, like mannerism and baroque two millennia later, deliberately denied and distorted its classical models – and gave them a new and curious quality.

Etruscan sculpture, for example, showed little concern for ideal abstractions or refinements, but infused its realism with a touch of exaggeration in order to make a vivid lifelike impression. The tendency is already apparent in seventh- and sixth-century funerary urns from Clusium which are surmounted by almost caricatured portrait-heads – the ancestors of one persistent element in the Italian portrait tradition, resembling in the economic spontaneity of their technique a remarkable series of statuettes made by contemporary Sardinians. The Clusium figures have their hands joined in prayerful poses learnt from neo-Hittite states of north Syria (p. 116). Soon afterwards, however, this style gave way to hair-braids and shoulder-locks reminiscent of Assyria. But then at Veii, which became the leading centre of Etruscan terracotta sculpture, an Apollo and other masterpieces of the decades preceding 500 BC show strong Ionian inspiration. Yet there is also an un-Ionian element of coarseness. This is partly due to the original position of these colourful striding forms, which stood high up on temple roofs and were meant to be seen from afar. But there is also a sense of force and effortful strength which is an original, provincial, Italic contribution. In Etruria, as elsewhere, large size bronze statuary has survived in a few fine specimens only; but in one single city, Volsinii, the Romans found as many as two thousand statues of bronze.

Etruscan metalwork started with Urartian and even Mycenaean echoes, and passed on to astonishingly lavish and expert repoussé and granulation jewellery techniques learnt from the Phoenicians, whose precious objects were imported and appear abundantly in Etruscan tombs. However, a curved ritual horn of Etruria, the *lituus* later adopted by the Romans, goes right back to far earlier copper trumpets of Asia Minor such as have now been found at Alacahüyük (p. 81). Etruria also borrowed Egyptian and Mesopotamian themes. But this sort of delicate granulation had become fashionable in the Greek east also, and as Etruscan goldwork reaches its peak in the sixth century BC the prevailing canon of beauty, although modified by local flamboyance, is basically derived from Ionia.

This no doubt applied to Etruscan painting also. But here the Ionian link is harder to identify, because the tomb architecture of the country, though partially dependent on Mycenaean and other near eastern models, was of a type quite unfamiliar in Greece. Greek painted panels on other kinds of building (which have not survived) no doubt exercised an influence on techniques, yet this remained a peculiar Etruscan *genre*, inviting original treatment. In the Tomb of Hunting and Fishing at Tarquinii (*c.* 520–510), the paintings of flowers and foliage and flying birds and dream-like sea-scapes show a gayer exuberance and fresher attention to nature than have hitherto been discovered among Greeks of that time. The recently discovered Tomb of the Olympiads, on the other hand, luxuriates with formal inventions elaborated with imaginative originality from the animal friezes that Greeks had adopted from the east. Influenced by the pottery (and no doubt murals) of Ionian centres such as Miletus, the Etruscan artists were encouraged by the peculiar medium of this funeral architecture to add a strong individuality of their own.

During the period when these paintings were made, Etruscan artists achieved their greatest work; and then came stagnation and decline. That is to say, the correspondence of this art with the styles of the Greeks was restricted to their archaic period, since at the slightly later date when Athenian canons of classicism became paramount the Etruscans, driven from the international scene (p. 248), were no longer in a position to draw upon current Greek fashions. Their classic age, then, was the Greek archaic age; and the Greek classic age could evoke no further response from them.

At about the same time their attitude to life, or rather death, changed also. For even if their intense concentration on funerary monuments had always contained a morbid element, at least the desire for the dead to have protection, sustenance and a pleasant, comfortable time had evoked an art reflecting what was evidently a festive, sensuous, dance-loving life on this earth, in which women took a greater part than among the Greeks (p. 202). But in later times their art dwelt instead upon horrible monsters of the underworld; a defeated Etruria had been overwhelmed by the terrors of death. Irrationality and superstition prevailed, and while Greece was turning to philosophy, geometry and physics, the Etruscans concentrated instead on divine revelation and direct communion with the dread supernatural forces. The period of their creative art was at an end.

The expansion of Etruscan power

During the sixth century BC the Etruscan cities established a second homeland comprising a successful group of settlements in the rich valley of the Po (Eridanus, Padus) beyond the Apennines. Alone among European rivers flowing into the Mediterranean, the Po is navigable for a considerable distance. It receives a double allowance of rain and melted snow, from the Alps and the Apennines alike; and the rains of autumn and spring are supplemented by further downpours in summer. So the Po provides no less than 38 per cent of the total run-off of all Italian rivers, and in contrast to the peninsula itself the supply of water is actually excessive. The local flora is less Mediterranean than central European; and this region did not form part of Italy until the first century BC.

Although the Etruscans possessed trading connections as far as the Alps and even beyond, the marshy Po is a divider rather than a unifier, and its southern and nearer bank was where their towns were concentrated. This area, now part of the province of Emilia, had known intensive settlement and cultivation since early times (p. 232). From twenty to forty miles wide, it includes a narrow belt of firm plateau country, built up by the sediment and gravel of tributaries between the Po swamps and clay foothills, with access over the Apennines into Etruria. Along this arable, well-watered strip, market towns strung out from west to east beside the tributaries served hillsmen and plainsmen alike. Although the streams tend to wilt in summer and flood in winter, this was an agricultural zone of a richness and variety which Roman writers never ceased to praise.

Bologna retained its importance as one of the main points of transit along the edges of the Po marshland (the later Via Aemilia) and from peninsular to northern Italy. During the centuries after 1000 BC the place continued to take the lead in commercial and material advancement, its relations with Italy resembling those of the Ohio-Mississippi basin with the Atlantic seaboard before communications were fully established. Soon after 550 BC, whether by warlike or peaceful methods, this crucial point fell to the Etruscans, who founded the new city of Felsina outside the earlier town. From that centre they overran the whole area, probably establishing a loose federation of about a dozen city-states on the pattern of the mother country.

One of the earliest of these foundations was Marzabotto, established on the pass between Felsina and Etruria to secure the new territory's southern communications (*c.* 500). The third of the main Etruscan cities beyond the Apennines lay fifty miles east at Spina, which is now far inland but then presided over the head of the Adriatic on one of the seven mouths of the ever-changing Po. There were Greeks at Spina (p. 171), but by the end of the sixth century this strategic location on the sea-route down to the Mediterranean, enjoying riverside cornlands, good northern communications and lagoon fishing, had also tempted a substantial Etruscan community to the place. Although Greeks had fought and would again fight Etruscans off the west coast of Italy, they had reason to cooperate with one another on the east coast, both against pirates and against

Greek states which periodically tried to control the lower opening of the windswept, stormy Adriatic sea. Accordingly, the gold and terracotta objects found in the huge waterlogged cemeteries of Spina include products which come not only from Athens and the Greek colonies of southern Italy, but also from Etruscan workshops at Vulci and Clusium.

Spina stood on a line of coastal dunes between lagoons and the sea. Its warehouses and dwellings, like those of its successors in Venice and Ravenna nearby, are shown by air photographs to have been built on wooden piles and platforms according to a rectangular plan, marked out by the canals which Etruscans knew so well how to build. Here such channels were particularly necessary since the danger of flooding, from which Venice is still suffering today, was continuously heightened by the filling up of the river bed with mountain silt; the lower reaches of the Po are always above the level of the surrounding plain, and would have flooded the place permanently if left alone.

The expansion of the Etruscans in these northern areas was paralleled by a southward drive. Just beyond the Tiber which formed their lower limit, a semicircle of hills is dominated by volcanic Mount Albano, fifteen miles from the sea, which covered the plain's impermeable clay with porous soil rich in phosphates and potash. After its craters ceased to erupt in *c.* 1000 BC, cultivation, though still challenging, became potentially profitable, so that the Alban slopes were now the kernel and richest part of Latium; and groups of shepherds gradually moved into the area, establishing villages on the bluffs that jutted out among the tall beech copses.

These people were Indo-European-speaking lowlanders, offshoots from a group of about fifty loosely federated Latin tribes practising the new customs which had begun to take shape in Italy just before the first millennium BC (p. 232). Soon afterwards other hills a few miles farther north were occupied by the Sabines, mountaineers belonging to a second collection of peoples speaking a distinct but related Italic language. Then these sets of migrants began to move from the hill-fringe down on to the rolling scrub-covered lower plateau, with its marshy valleys leading towards what was then a heavily wooded coast.

At the same distance from the sea as Mount Albano, these Latins and Sabines came to a deep trough of the Tiber, and settled beside its left bank on the steeply sloping Seven Hills or hillocks, a hundred to two hundred feet high, cut off by ravines (once tributaries) from each other and from the main hinterland. This site of Rome was well watered, well protected, adjacent to fertile land, and accessible to useful winter pasturage. The place stood on the most central and best of the three chief cross-routes of Italy, potentially dominating the main line of communications along the whole of the western and more populous flank of the peninsula. An early beginning to exploit these advantages was made when the occupants of the site, moving alongside riverbanks which provided much easier routes than they do now, assumed control of the valley as far as the sea, and in the opposite direction pressed inland to a point seventeen miles farther upstream, where recent agricultural developments have disclosed a convergence of ancient paths leading from the mountains towards the coast.

The Tiber, which is the largest river in the peninsula of Italy and possesses the widest drainage area, comes to the last of its ford and ferry points at Rome. This crossing spanned the final stretches of firm ground where the river turns and breaks through the low range to reach the marshy coastal plain, becoming navigable and finally debouching at the only approximation to a natural harbour for many miles in either direction. Equidistant from Reggio and Turin, Rome is nearer the country's centre than London, and equals it as an internal port and focus of roads.

It was perhaps half a century before the city's traditional foundation date (753 BC) that Latins and Sabines came beside this riverbank and established their separate villages (or revived previously existing ones), like those which preceded the Etruscan cities a little farther north. Soon after 600, the Etruscans extended their dominion to include Rome, which was now a unified town. Perhaps, as legend recorded, the Latins and Sabines had merged a short time previously, or it may instead have been the Etruscan overlords themselves who amalgamated the separate hill-top villages.

In any case Rome, which had previously been the westernmost bastion of the Latins and Sabines against Etruria, now became an Etruscan outpost against the two Italic groups. The marshy Forum valley, which the villages had jointly used as a burial-place, was already inhabited by the seventh century BC, and by 575 it was drained with the skill characteristic of its new masters and became the new town's main square. The 'Wall of Servius Tullius' is later, but traces of town walls that have lately been identified may belong to this date.

The dynasty from Etruria which had seized the place, represented in literary annals by two kings named Tarquin, employed the precipitous Capitoline hill as their citadel, built a large temple of the sky-god Jupiter (Tinia) and gradually raised Rome to equality with Caere and Veii.

Virgil's legend of a Trojan immigration under Aeneas perhaps echoes a real landing of refugee sea peoples on the coast of Latium (p. 232), or it may symbolise some other of the oriental elements which figured so strongly in Etruscan culture and were present also at Rome: for instance it now seems that the Phoenicians and Carthaginians possessed an anchorage there, just as they did at the ports of Caere. Or the Trojan story may merely be one of many myths designed to work Rome somehow into the heroic traditions of the past. Another aspect of the *Aeneid*, its tale of Greeks (Arcadians) who lived at Rome even before the newcomers from Troy, may again be mythical in itself, yet it faithfully reflects the fact that influences from that quarter were so strong that a later Greek historian could actually call his compatriots the founders of the city.[7] One town which may have served as an intermediary was Satricum (Conca), for example in the transmission of the cult of Castor and Pollux (Polydeuces) which was established at Lavinium, fifteen miles from Satricum in one direction and Rome in the other. But a great many Greek institutions were passed on to Rome direct from the colony of Cumae which succeeded Pithecusae (Ischia) just north of the bay of Naples (p. 168).

The Latin alphabet, too, included letters which closely resembled equivalents in the writing of Cumae. Nevertheless it was probably through Etruria, which had already borrowed the script of Cumae, that the Latin-speaking peoples acquired this alphabet, subsequently adapting it to their own requirements. And indeed the story that the elder Tarquin was himself a Greek from Corinth[8] confirms (either in factual or legendary guise) that many Greek institutions came to the Romans in this way, through Etruscan intermediaries. For Caere and Veii were both in the immediate neighbourhood of the city; and recent air photographs have revealed a very early route connecting it with Veii.

Rome was not, it is true, wholly Etruscan, because the greater part of its population was of the same mixed stocks as had been there before the Etruscans came. And yet the very same thing might have been said of Rome's Etrurian neighbours too. The only significant difference, seen by the hindsight of history, is that the Etruscan language did not finally take hold at Rome, which remained its own kind of 'explosive mixture of Greek sulphur, Etruscan saltpetre and charcoal from that ancient wood of prehistoric Italy'.[9]

But the Etruscan element, including all its eastern ingredients, was very strong. Proper names, architecture, engineering, art and ceremonial, all show that during the greater part of the sixth century BC, and perhaps until *c.* 450 BC, the place was virtually as Etruscan as Caere and Veii – and certainly as much so as several other neighbouring places in this borderland which, although Etruscan origins were ascribed to them, were likewise Latin in their speech.

At Rome, as elsewhere, the Etruscan rulers greatly encouraged agriculture. The heavy-soiled cornland, with hardy species of coarse emmer wheat or spelt as its staple crop, was irrigated like Etruria. Although shepherd life was partially giving way to cultivation, the pasture-land on the river, which had been the town centre in the days before the Forum, continued to serve as an important market for cattle. Moreover, the rulers of Rome asserted their claims to collect the salt deposits at the Tiber mouth and trade them to central Italy. An outpost of Veii which had existed for that purpose was destroyed. Patriotic Roman tradition attributed this event to a pre-Etruscan epoch,[10] but the destroyers may well have been the Tarquins, who were surely not always on good terms with this embarrassingly close neighbour, Etruscan though it was. There was a strong tradition that Rome not only demolished Veii's salt collecting station but had already by then, before the period of Etruscan rule, founded its own port, Ostia. This is again unlikely, but archaeologists may well some day find an Etruscan

Ostia in one of the unexplored sectors east of the modern or ancient towns of that name.

A similar sixth-century date can probably be attributed to Rome's first wooden bridge, which connected the heart of the town to a fort in Etruscan territory across the river.

This bridge also carried much trade from Etruria and Rome to regions farther south. For, although maritime communication in that direction were poor, Rome was linked with more southerly centres by two low cols which provided a route between Mount Albano and the Apennine foothills leading into the valley of the Liris (Garigliano). The mouth of that river was outside Latium; it lay in Campania, which extended from that point onwards for nearly eighty miles past the bays of Naples and Salerno. Fanned by moist south-west winds, the spongy volcanic earth of this extensive plain is rich in phosphorus and potash, and retentive enough of water during the summer drought to escape the exhaustion which finally overtook the soil of Latium. Campania was the chief granary of mainland Italy, yielding from three to six times the national average and furnishing in some districts as many as three crops of grain every year.

The centre of these fertile lowlands was Capua, a road junction on the River Volturno (Vulturnus) sixteen miles from the Mediterranean. Pushing southwards into this region, the Etruscans made Capua into a city of their own, famed for its terracotta roof tiles and bronzework, including large cauldrons which, though based on models from Urartu (p. 118), were made of copper imported from Etruria and forged by techniques taught by the Chalcidian settlers of neighbouring Cumae. It was probably also from Capua, through Samnite intermediaries (p. 252), that the Romans learnt the appalling Etruscan practice of gladiatorial games.

From there, the Etruscans extended their domination over all or most of Campania. If they came by land, their route may have brought them either down by the Liris valley or along the coastal strip, which was marshy but lent itself to naval support. If, on the other hand, they arrived by sea, it is uncertain whether they landed in the north or south of Campania. Nor is it known when the Etruscans assumed control of these territories.

Recent excavations at Capua and elsewhere suggest that penetration had begun by *c.* 650 BC, but the greater part of the Campanian plain probably did not pass into Etruscan hands until the following century was well advanced.

If that is so, then the region did not fall to the Etruscans until the very moment when their central power was contracting or beginning to collapse. Although they had successfully joined with Carthage in keeping the Greeks out of Corsica, revenge was soon obtained by their settlers in Campania. For in *c.* 524 the Etruscans were defeated in a land-battle by Aristodemus of Cumae, and fifty years later a maritime defeat off the same town, at the hands of Hiero's Syracusan fleet, put an end to their southward expansion altogether. Twenty years later Syracuse expelled the Etruscans from Corsica and Elba, and at some stage during the same period a confused series of moves and counter-moves, heroically distorted and simplified in legend, led to their final ejection from Rome. Before 420, Samnites of the Campanian hinterland had taken Capua (p. 252). Next, soon after 400, the Etruscan settlements in the Po valley were destroyed by invading Gauls (p. 250). After all these disasters only their original homeland now remained to the Etruscans, and the long grim duel which ended in Rome's destruction of its obvious rival Veii initiated a period in which these cities too collapsed piecemeal within the course of two centuries.

The renown of Etruria, said Livy, had 'filled the lands and the waters from one end of Italy to the other, from the Alps to the Straits of Messina'.[11] But like the Greeks, and unlike the Romans, they never achieved anything approaching unity. As Virgil's choice of an exiled king of Caere, Mezentius, to be the *Aeneid's* conventional tyrant is intended to suggest, they must have lacked the capacity to become popular masters, so that when crisis came their subject peoples allowed and encouraged them to fall.

10

The Republic Unites the Mediterranean

The unification of Italy

The replacement of Rome's Etruscan overlords by an aristocratic form of republican government, during the late sixth or fifth century BC, led at first to a period of impoverishment and insignificance.* And yet gradually, in the course of the next two hundred years, this small city-state absorbed the entire peninsula of Italy. The only precedent for the political unification of a whole Mediterranean land had been provided by the Egyptians, and Italy's amalgamation produced even more far-reaching results owing to the diversity and central position of the country.

Although of mixed origins, Rome had joined the loose group of Latin communities which were settled into seven hundred square miles of land south of the River Tiber. By 500 BC about a dozen of these towns were left, including Praeneste (Palestrina), Tibur (Tivoli) and Tusculum (near Frascati), all of which still dealt with their Roman neighbours on more or less equal terms. In the face of common danger from all sides, this equality was admitted by a treaty establishing common private rights between the citizens of Rome and any Latin city (*c.* 493); and thereby, in a small way, the principle by which Rome ultimately united Italy was already laid down.

Joining forces with its Latin neighbours, Rome defeated the Sabines whose ancestors had played a part in its own foundation (*c.* 449). But many years were needed (*c.* 498?–304) to wear down their more backward and turbulent relatives who had

* Though isolation was not complete, p. 277.

been displaced from their homes in central Italy by population pressures – and now occupied the hills to the east and south-west of the city, from which they looked down covetously upon the grain, fruit, vegetables, and winter pastures of Latium. These peoples included the Aequi, who fortified Mount Algido at the extremity of the Alban hills (until *c.* 431) and penetrated as far as Praeneste and Tusculum; and the Volsci who moved west from the Liris valley and reached the Latin seaboard, occupying Antium (Anzio) and making it their principal town.

In the north, too, the Romans were engaged just as heavily, grappling with the cities of Etruria which had now become their enemies. After a setback (*c.* 477), they finally conquered their wealthy and powerful neighbour Veii (396).

> Veii of old had monarchs of her own,
> And in her Forum stood a golden throne.
> Now in her walls the plodding shepherd's horn
> Sings, and amid her bones men reap their corn.[1]

The destruction of Veii led to further annexations which made Rome the largest state in the area; a century of warfare had doubled its territory. Veii fell because the Etruscan cities failed to stand together, and because they were weakened by successive incursions of Celtic Gauls, first into Etruscan territory in northern Italy, and then far into the homeland itself. One such marauding force disastrously defeated the largest army the Romans had ever mobilised on the River Allia (Fosso Bettina) (*c.* 390). Although the Capitoline citadel may have held out, the rest of the city suffered a brief occupation until the nomad Gauls could be bought off.

These devastations had shown how vulnerable small places were, and the ensuing generation saw Rome grow into a much larger town than any of its neighbours. For although anarchy following the Gaulish invasion had at first induced the Latin League to assert itself against their humiliated associate, the Romans succeeded in annexing Tusculum and driving a wedge from their more compact base through the middle of the scattered confederacy. Then, after fighting and negotiating with the Etruscans had secured the northern frontier, a further war against the Latins resulted in the dissolution of their league and incorporation of its smaller members into the growing Roman state.

Seven of the larger towns, however, were dealt with individually on the principle of divide and rule, and allowed to remain as ostensibly equal allies. The Romans also showed themselves to be less exclusive than some contemporary Greeks in the extension of citizen rights. Incorporated Latins became full citizens, and individuals could obtain its franchise by residing at Rome: citizenship was worth having, and it was attainable. This policy of prudently fostering mutual interest and sentiment may have been owed partly to inadequate siege-craft, which made it difficult to enforce more vigorous methods, but it was also a signpost to the future successes of the Romans. They were fortunate, too, because these early external dealings were with peoples who shared their cultural background and were surrounded by the same acute external dangers, which made them relatively amenable to voluntary incorporation.

One significant step, which seems to have occurred shortly before the final dissolution of the Latin League, was the earliest development of Ostia as Rome's port. Whether the tradition of a much earlier foundation was correct or not (p. 246), a party of Roman citizens was sent out during the later fourth century to settle upon the site. Silt washed down the Tiber, from the eroded hillsides and fields of central Italy, has now pushed the Mediterranean far away.

> The marsh birds breed in her bay,
> And a mile to the shoreless westward,
> The water has passed away.[2]

But in those days the rectangular fort established at Ostia stood on a flat coastal spit backed by a defensive landward belt of marshy lagoons. For centuries this was scarcely a harbour, but a mere roadstead on the open coast. Not being a manufacturing centre, Rome had little to send down to its port, but Ostia could receive overseas imports of foodstuffs, which were then transferred to lighters at the river mouth and towed up to the capital by oxen. However, until a naval and then commercial base was developed in the third and second centuries BC, the principal role of Ostia was to protect Rome from maritime attacks – replacing Etruscan Caere which had formerly policed the seas but was now no longer trusted (p. 237).

This sort of fortified outpost was a new departure, but before the 260s eight other colonies of Roman citizens had been established up and down the seaboard, including Antium which in Volscian hands had served as a base for pirates. But these citizen colonies were only small coastguard stations of about three hundred people, whereas foundations of a second category could comprise as many as six thousand. These were the 'Latin colonies', which had first all been south or south-east of Rome, but gradually extended over a much wider area. They included increasingly large numbers of Roman citizens – including surplus members of the city proletariat – but there were Latins too, since these were joint Roman and Latin communities. Colonies of such a type, which proved invaluable to Roman expansion, were sited at strategic locations or centres of communication such as river crossings, road junctions, harbours, openings of mountain passes, and points commanding frontier areas. Self-governing except in foreign policy, the towns guarded and consolidated battle gains, prepared the way for further advances, and pegged down or encircled tribes whose loyalty was in doubt.

The subjugation of Latium by the Romans caused them to covet Campania which lay beyond. By 400 BC the Etruscans had been superseded in nearly all this fertile plain by a number of tribes, including the Samnites – warlike peasants and farmers (perhaps distantly related to the Sabines) whose Oscan language, named after earlier immigrants, resembled Latin in its grammar, but was written from the fourth century onwards in a version of the Greek alphabet of Cumae (p. 168). Expanding from the landlocked central Italian plateau, where they lived in semi-isolated, loosely associated hillside communities, the Samnites were impelled downwards into more fertile lands by the same economic pressures which had attracted other waves of mountain peoples into the plainlands of Latium farther north.

Along with many other parts of Campania, the Samnites annexed its chief Etruscan town, Capua, and the leading Greek colony, Cumae (*c.* 425 BC). Nothing came of a defensive alliance with the Romans, and appeals they received from desperate Campanians met with a favourable response which resulted in the first Samnite War (?*c.* 343–341). The aftermath of these obscure campaigns witnessed the transfer of Capua from the Samnites to Rome, which derived important influences (including Etruscan gladiatorial games) from its civilisation (p. 247).

These influences reached the Romans along two roads, built by engineers who borrowed methods and techniques from the great road-builders of eastern empires and their Etruscan heirs. The more inland thoroughfare, partially completed by *c.* 370, was the Via Latina. Replacing old tracks by fitted blocks of lava, this road ascended from the Tiber valley to the low col of Mount Algido and then followed an easy reverse slope into the Liris valley, maintaining from there onwards an average distance of twenty miles from the sea until it came to Capua. The second of the roads linking that city with Rome was the Via Appia, which crossed the southern foothills of Mount Albano and continued close beside the coast. Before long there were widespread extensions of this strategic all-weather road system, which imperiously surmounted all obstacles and contributed outstandingly to the passage of culture and gladiators in one direction, and government in the other.

The Via Appia was built during the second Samnite War (328–304). This had begun with an attack launched on Fregellae in the Liris valley by the Samnites, who then shatteringly defeated twenty thousand Romans and allies at the Caudine Forks, somewhere between Beneventum and Capua (322). But the victorious army could not take Tarentum (p. 259) or the cities of Apulia, and were prevented from occupying Lucania. When a third war followed (298–90?), alliances with invading Gauls failed to save the Samnites from the steadiness and efficiency of the Roman legions. The unwieldy phalanx had been replaced by formations suitable for hill warfare, which fought in open order and were equipped with throwing javelins instead of thrusting spears; and generations of incessant, desperate fighting had taught commanders how to exploit the advantage of Rome's inner lines against a divided or loosely organised enemy.

The Romans were now masters of central and southern Italy. By 260 BC their confederacy extended over 52,000 square miles, a larger dominion than that of any contemporary Mediterranean power except the distant Seleucids. From the Tyrrhenian to the Adriatic sea, nearly a million people in the middle latitudes of Italy had been enrolled into the Roman state as full or half citizens paying a direct capital tax assessed on means. The allies of Rome who were not incorporated in this way – well over a hundred old and new Latin colonies and Italic tribes – were mostly situated upon either flank of the central belt, in northern Etruria and Umbria on one side and the Samnite and Apulian highlands on the other. These communities, which provided just over half Rome's total military force, rarely had any say in determining peace or war, but paid no direct taxation.

This union incorporated a number of features from Greek models, but the difficult communications and linguistic diversities of Italy outside Latium led Rome to avoid their various contemporary experiments in federalism. Although tribal sentiments were discouraged, patriotic feelings towards cities and localities remained: Cicero, for example, forgot he was a Volscian, but liked his native Arpinum. In spite of this intense particularism, however, the Italians felt a less profound attachment to political independence than most Greeks. Without more than an occasional rebellion, the peoples of the peninsula were prepared to give up complete autonomy in exchange for the unprecedented Pax Romana. The Latin language gradually wore down mutually incomprehensible dialects, and an exceptional Roman talent for law, which had already long ago produced a written code (*c.* 450), was another factor which contributed to the creation of a common Italian culture.

The cultivation of Italy

Like any Greek, and like the Etruscans who were their agricultural teachers, early Italians loved their land not for its beauty but for its productiveness. Later Romans knew very well that this was what had first made their civilisation possible.

> Then barbarism vanished: then orchards were planted,
> And fertile gardens drank the nourishing streams.[3]

The origin of Roman greatness was deeply rooted in the cultivation of the soil.

> This was the life which once the ancient Sabines led,
> And Remus and his brother; this made Etruria strong;
> Through this, Rome became the fairest thing on earth.[4]

So said Virgil, but he also repeated the reminders of Hesiod, many centuries earlier, that for all Italy's potential wealth, farming remained a perpetual challenge that needed all possible energy and skill.

> For the Father of agriculture
> Gave us a hard calling: he first decreed it an art
> To work in the fields, sent worries to sharpen our
> mortal wits,
> And would not allow his realm to grow listless
> from lethargy.[5]

One of these worries was the weather, for the Italian climate, though supreme in its glory and variety, yields to no other Mediterranean land in violence.

> Oft have I seen a sudden storm arise,
> From all the warring winds that sweep the skies:
> The heavy harvest from the root is torn,
> And whirled aloft, the lighter stubble borne . . .
> And oft whole sheets descend of sluicy rain,
> Sucked by the spongy clouds from off the main.[6]

Italian rivers also, like the torrents of Greece, can be temperamental and dangerous enemies.

> Trunks of trees come rolling down,
> Sheep and their folds together drown.
> Both house and homestead into seas are borne,
> And rocks are from their old foundations torn,
> And woods, made thin with winds, their scattered
> honours mourn.[7]

Yet in spite of all such hazards the economic life of ancient Italy continued to be dominated by the land. There was no greater source of wealth or safer investment; and most people lived outside the towns. Three ploughings from different angles made by light ploughs, preferably of elm, lime and beech,[8] doubled the quantity of moisture the soil retained during the dry summer months. And so during the years when Rome was building up its confederation, the coarse emmer wheat which most people had been eating was partly superseded by the more highly evolved bread wheat (p. 234), and porridge was partly replaced by baked bread. Then, during the second century BC, the improved methods of production (p. 223) discovered in Greek lands now spread to Italy. Although large areas were turned over to grazing (p. 258), other parts of the country found that foreign wars stimulated rather than hindered the cultivation of cereals. The concentration of ownership enabled corn seed to be more skilfully selected; spiked sledges of Carthaginian pattern were used for threshing; and the ancient biennial fallow[9] may sometimes have been replaced by a threefold system including restorative courses of leguminous plants.

And yet, all the same, the grain grown in Italy was still not nearly enough. Rome's rapidly increasing population needed extensive imports, and its government, like that of imperial Athens, directed very careful attention to securing the overseas territories that could provide them.

Wild blue grapes still grow in some of Italy's brambled ravines, but it was probably Greek colonists, directly or through Etruria, who first familiarised the country with their cultivation (p. 234).* From *c.* 350 onwards this was considerably extended, and vines were trained on elms, oaks, poplars, fig-trees, reeds and occasionally olives, or grown on frames of forked stakes and horizontal cross-pieces.*

After 200 BC vine growing began to spread even more rapidly when the new large estates distinguished between different vintages, taking trouble to vary the conditions of fermentation and preserve wines for the twenty years that were sometimes needed to attain maturity. Italian wines were sweeter and had more body than those of Greece, and Pliny the Elder, differentiating between fifty kinds (and ninety varieties of grapes), proclaimed the home product's supremacy with lyrical patriotism.[10] On the Apulian Tavoliere plain, before it fell into desolation (p. 258), air photography has identified a mass of vineyards, complete to the last tree-pit and trench. A particularly high reputation, however, came to be attached to the vast terraces

* A wrecked hundred-foot vessel of the second century BC found underwater off the south coast of France contained perhaps fifteen or twenty thousand gallons of wine sent by the Italian Greeks, with the best quality on deck and lesser brands in the hold.

of volcanic Latium, where the wine of Setia (Sezze), thirty-five miles south-east of Rome, enjoyed the greatest esteem.

The cultivation of the olive likewise extended northwards gradually from Greek southern Italy, but it was again not until the second century BC that olive-production increased in Italy on a substantial scale. 'Nature did not desire us to be sparing in the use of oil', said Pliny.[11] And yet just when the Italian market was growing, supplies from Greece had diminished, so that more must be grown at home. Olives were ideally suited to the large estates of an absentee owner, since the production of a cash crop needed little additional effort except at harvest-time when hired free labourers were called in to supplement the slaves. The same land might also be used for grain-growing or sheep-grazing, and capitalists who cultivated olives could afford to wait for slow but profitable returns, which were forthcoming even from inferior land.

> A stubborn soil and inhospitable hills,
> When the clay is lean and the fields are strewn
> with stones and brushwood,
> Delight in the long-lived olive.[12]

Provided drainage was adequate, olives throve in Italy whether soil was dry and calcareous, or was tenacious clay, or clay and gravel mixed. Pliny knew fifteen especially good varieties, and four types of press worked by beams or screws. Sabine olives became famous, and so did those of the rolling hill-country of Picenum (Marche), but the principal olive groves were in Apulia and Campania. On the dry, sheltered Apulian coastal strip south of the River Ofanto (Aufidus), there is again today a continuous olive grove stretching southwards for a hundred miles. But the finest quality of all (which now comes from Lucca) was grown by Venafrum in the Volturno valley where Latium, Campania and Samnium meet.[13]

When external contacts developed during the third century BC, many of the new plants and fruits that had been introduced into Greece came on to Italy. These included apricots, lemons and melons; and other new importations were sesame, several species of clover, lucerne (originally from Persia), radishes, flax, beetroot, cherries, peaches, almonds, chestnuts, walnuts and quinces, and certain types of fig and plum. Varro, on whose first century BC handbook Virgil poetically drew, acclaimed Italy as one great orchard.[14]

Varro's manual was the successor of a line of agricultural handbooks, based on local knowledge but ultimately going back to Greek and Carthaginian studies, such as the twenty-eight books of Mago which were translated from Punic into Latin by a decree of the senate. Cato the Elder's book *On Agriculture* (*c.* 160 BC) details every item of equipment needed to set up a farm, indicating where they can all be got in Italy.[11] Cato still admires the ancient type of farm supervised by the proprietor and his family and worked by household dependants, and in the north and elsewhere this system flourished as never before (p. 269). Nevertheless, he also indicates that in other areas displacements due to foreign wars had caused the old allotments of from five to thirty acres, operating on a subsistence basis, to be replaced by large cash-crop ranches of more than three hundred.

This changeover to large properties caused improvements in corn production (p. 256), but it also meant that huge regions abandoned this in favour of pasturage. For Cato, in the southern areas with which he deals, advocates grazing as the most profitable use of land. Since climatic conditions favour the beeches, oaks and chestnuts that provided their food, pigs had long been ubiquitous, and Latin had no less than seven names for them. But now there was increased demand for wool; more mutton and beef were being eaten, and clover and lucerne were grown as fodder. In Italy as elsewhere in the Mediterranean, livestock, being easily transported, had long been a characteristic form of wealth; the Latin word for money means sheep, and oxen had been engraved on the rectangles of bronze that served as early Italian coins.

Yet suitable pasture land was scarce, and could only be increased by encroachment on cultivation. And so Apulia, Calabria and Etruria, like the recently acquired Sicilian and Sardinian provinces, were transformed. Particularly remarkable was the growth of latifundia in the largest plain of the peninsula, the Tavoliere. One of the densest concentrations of population in prehistoric Europe, this sixty mile long and thirty mile deep coastal belt of Apulia was thoroughly converted to pasturage during the later Roman republic. A top layer of limestone grew rich rank grass to feed horses and produce sheep with the softest and most delicate wool. But since rainfall is scantier than anywhere else in Italy, all vegetation withers, and according to the very ancient Mediterranean practice of transhumance the sheep and goats (the animals best suited to this peripatetic existence) were driven up to crop the short wiry grass of the Apennine plateau (p. 15). The territories of many Apulian towns included valuable summer pasture on their hilly fringes, and a thousand animals might easily travel a hundred miles twice in every year. This dual pasturage can still be seen in Apulia, which after centuries of ruin is now recovering.

Victory over Carthage

The expansion of Rome's confederacy created difficulties with the Greek colonies in south Italy, and these culminated in an inevitable clash with their leader Tarentum (Taras). During the later fourth century BC the modern democratic government of this prosperous commercial and maritime power had made a treaty with the Romans in which the latter agreed not to sail eastwards into the Gulf of Taranto. Yet in 282 the Greek city of Thurii, situated inside the gulf near the earlier Sybaris, was hard-pressed by Lucanian tribesmen (related to the Samnites) and appealed to Rome for help. When the response, after some deliberation, took the form of dispatching a military and naval force, Tarentum attacked them both, and sought help from the adventurous half-Greek Pyrrhus of Epirus, who crossed the narrows and landed with twenty-five thousand men. But in spite of spectacular successes with his barbed-wire phalanx and elephants, Pyrrhus failed to dislodge the Romans. He next proceeded to Sicily, which since the virtual elimination of the natives as an intermediate power had witnessed a straight fight between Greeks and Carthaginians. But Pyrrhus' efforts to expel the Carthaginians from Sicily (278–276) were no more successful than his endeavours to keep the Romans out of the Greek regions of Italy.

So Carthage stayed in Sicily, and Rome in southern Italy. But they had at least agreed with one another that the Strait of Messina should be the boundary between them; and under the impact of Pyrrhus a further agreement was reached (279). When the Carthaginians garrisoned Messana itself (the former Zancle, now Messina), they were technically in the right since this was on the Sicilian side of the narrows. Yet Rome's Greek allies in south Italy understandably detected a threat to their safety and commerce; and the government of Messana itself (a collection of Italian mercenaries) appealed to Rome. The result was the first Punic War (264).

Its most extraordinary feature was the enterprising decision of the unseamanlike Romans to challenge Carthaginian naval supremacy by the creation of fleets of their own. Built of the timber in which Italy was richer than Carthage, and equipped with novel grapnels that enabled the eighty legionaries on board to cross over to enemy ships, the new Roman vessels gave a good account of themselves against a somewhat passive enemy strategy, but suffered enormous destruction from storms which their navigators were too inexperienced to master. Nevertheless, Rome persisted in performing prodigies of naval construction; and the last of a series of naval battles, fought off the Aegates (Egadi) islands, led to total victory after twenty-three years of unprecedentedly exhausting warfare.

Although leniently treated, Tarentum lost its special position in south Italy, which was partly taken over by a new, spacious and sheltered port settled by Roman and Latin colonists in the heel of the peninsula at Brundusium (Brindisi) (246), almost at the closest point to the Greek coast across the Ionian Sea. As regards Sicily, Roman war aims had expanded from the limited purpose of expelling the Carthaginians from their eastern coastal towns to the idea of conquering the entire island – which no earlier power had ever managed to do – so as to be able to seize all its resources of grain. With the exception, therefore, of the Syracusan kingdom which was left independent, Messana which remained an ally of Rome, and the former Carthaginian city of Panormus (Palermo) which was allowed privileged status to trade with Campania, the Romans now annexed almost the whole of the island. For the first time in history it had become an appendage of the Italian peninsula; and by the early years of the second century BC large quantities of grain were being sent to Rome.

Yet Sicily did not become part of Italy, and its cities were not incorporated into the Italian confederacy. Instead they were compelled to pay direct taxation to their new rulers, and the island was made into the first overseas province which Rome had ever possessed. Many of these communities had long been accustomed to paying taxes of such a kind to other masters, but for the Romans this was indeed a novel course to take:

> "It was chosen perhaps without much thought of its implications or possible consequences, but in time it revolutionised the whole conception of government and changed the leader of an Italian federation into an imperial power which ultimately dominated the civilised world."[16]

Moreover, once the new system was established, its extension rapidly followed. Faced with a perilous rebellion among its highly cosmopolitan mercenary troops, Carthage had to hand over Sardinia and Corsica, which were combined to form a second Roman province (227), the two islands being respectively well furnished with corn and well placed on sea-routes of commercial importance.

The Romans also began to push their frontiers northwards beyond the farthest borders of Etruria. A proposal by the democratically minded politician Gaius Flaminius (232) that lands south of Ariminum (Rimini), confiscated from the Gauls, should be distributed among the Roman poor aroused conservative opposition, but also induced his compatriots to look at these border territories with a new and acquisitive attention. After the last Gaulish army ever to cross the Apennines had been wiped out (225), the possible advantages of the Alps as a frontier began to be clear (p. 268); and an expedition across the Po, into terrain where even the Etruscans had scarcely ventured, was led by Flaminius himself. The ancient centre of Mediolanum (Milan), at the junction between the Alpine valley paths and other routes fringing the marshy plain, temporarily came under Roman control, but this region was still too distant and unsafe for the establishment of colonies. Six thousand settlers, on the other hand, were planted to guard either side of the Po, at the route-junctions and crossing points of Placentia (Piacenza) and Cremona; and the road from Rome, which had hitherto reached as far as Spoletium (Spoleto) in central Italy, was reconditioned under the name of the Via Flaminia and extended northwards, not yet as far as the Po itself, but right up to Ariminum where Italy still officially ended.

At the same time a logical but potentially aggressive extension of interest led Rome to concern itself with the opposite shore of the Adriatic across from Ariminum. Its inhabitants were Illyrians, who were similar to the ruder tribes of Thrace. During the first Punic War, however, an Illyrian chief called Agron, whose capital was at Scodra (Shkodër, Scutari), had built up a considerable kingdom extending from Dalmatia to the Ionian strait opposite Italy's heel. Agron's widow and successor Teuta annexed Epirus and further territories down as far as the Gulf of Corinth. She also provoked Rome by the ancestral Illyrian pursuit of piracy, and her capture of Corcyra (Corfu) brought down upon her a Roman fleet and army which landed and compelled her to capitulate. Teuta retained her crown, but Rome annexed one hundred and twenty miles of what is now the Albanian coast, at the narrowest neck of the sea where the north wind is not too severe to permit the cultivation of vines and olives. This step by the Romans implied a claim that the Adriatic Sea was within their sphere of interest; they were now within close reach of Macedonia and the mainland of Greece.

But before the consequences of this inflammable proximity were reached, significant events occurred in the western Mediterranean. Utterly alienated from Rome by its seizure of Sardinia and Corsica (p. 261), the energetic Carthaginian Hamilcar Barca proposed to establish an empire in Spain which would restore the fortunes of his country and destroy Roman power. The influence of Carthage in Spain had been considerably encroached upon by the sea power of Greek Massalia (Marseille) (p. 173), but Gades (Cadiz) and a surrounding strip remained in their hands, and using this as his base Hamilcar conquered or reconquered central and eastern Spain as far north as Capes Ifach and Nao, in the latitude of the Balearic islands. The Spaniards, famous for their physical endurance, proved useful for the Carthaginian army, and so did their finely tempered thrusting swords, products of the immensely rich mines the Carthaginians had now acquired (p. 265).

Since the natural contours of Spain favour roads on a peripheral rather than a radial pattern, the chief route ran along the

Mediterranean coast, and on this seaboard a fortress headquarters was established near the limits of Carthaginian occupation at the White Promontory (Alicante), beside lands which recall the most fertile regions of north Africa.

But when Hamilcar was drowned, his son-in-law Hasdrubal, moved his capital south in order to be nearer Africa and the mother city. The site which he chose was on the edge of 'a menacing landscape, a heave of bare hills, quite dry and bare ... shadowless and treeless, choked with dust, scorched with sun'.[17] Yet his foundation New Carthage (Cartagena) stood on a peninsula commanding one of the best harbours in the world and was sheltered from land attacks by a lagoon, while nevertheless having access through the Segura valley to the silver mines in the interior. But although Hasdrubal had moved to a more southerly capital, he pushed the frontier of Carthaginian Spain far to the north. Even if not every intervening tribe was conquered, his armies advanced up the coast half-way from Cape Nao to the Pyrenees, stopping only at the River Ebro (Iberus); and there may have been some sort of understanding, at least among themselves and conceivably also with the Romans, that this river was to be their frontier. Then Hasdrubal was murdered (221), and Hamilcar's son Hannibal took over.

But one town over eighty miles south of the Ebro still resisted Hannibal, and that was Saguntum, which appealed to its alliance with Rome (220) and so brought the two great powers into a new confrontation. Now is the time when the outstanding historical writer about this period, the Greek Polybius of Megalopolis (*c.* 203–*c.* 120 BC), chooses to begin his *Universal History*, since it seemed to him the moment at which the story of the Mediterranean world had for the first time become organic, unified, and inextricably interconnected in all its parts. [18]

Having demanded the surrender of Saguntum in vain, Hannibal proceeded to capture the city – feeling that, since Rome was strangling the Carthaginians at sea, hostilities could not in any case be long delayed. And so the Romans, after they had sent Carthage an unacceptable ultimatum, declared war. All their plans, however, were upset by Hannibal's decision to sacrifice his Spanish base and invade the Italian peninsula. Since the Mediterranean was closed to him, he approached the country by land, and – though accompanied by elephants, which were now a normal component of Carthaginian armies – managed to cross the Alps. Joined by a large part of the Gallic population in northern Italy, he utterly defeated three major Roman armies, north and south of the capital (218–216). But his attempt to encircle the city failed, since most of the confederates in central Italy supported their hard-pressed kinsmen. Roman generals also operated successfully in Spain, preventing the dispatch of Carthaginian reinforcements by sea; and Hannibal's enlistment of Philip v of Macedonia, who was annoyed by Rome's Adriatic annexations, produced only limited results (215–205). Meanwhile south Italy had been less loyal to Rome than the rest of the peninsula. But revolts at Syracuse, Capua and Tarentum were all put down, and a relieving army which had at last reached Hannibal across the Alps was overwhelmed. Scipio Africanus, who shared some of Hannibal's military genius and commanded soldiers superior to any the world had ever seen, drove the Carthaginians out of Spain (206), and then during successive years landed first in Sicily and next in north Africa. Although Carthage, as recent excavations show, was now protected by fortifications built across the narrow part of its isthmus, Hannibal was forced to return and organise its defence; but in vain, since the Romans, assisted by the defection of the enemy's Numidian cavalry, won a final victory not far away at Zama (202). By the peace signed in the following year, the Carthaginian state was allowed to retain a territory roughly corresponding with the modern Tunisia, but became a mere tribute-paying 'ally' of Rome.

Carthage was also obliged to accept the loss of its Spanish possessions. For the victors formally annexed the greater portion of the country (197), dividing it into two provinces because of the difficulty of maintaining unified communications. One of the provinces, Further Spain or Baetica, consisted of the southern part of the country, as far west as the present Portuguese frontier, including the rich Guadalquivir (Baetis) valley which was navigable by sea-going vessels for a hundred and forty miles from its swampy Atlantic mouth as far as Italica (near Seville) and then by boats up the well watered Corduba (Cordova) plain. Here was good soil for olives, cereals, vines and figs; already in ancient times Pliny considered the olives of this 'second Italy' next in quality to those of the Italian homeland.

Corduba was situated near the entrance of a pass across the Sierra Moreno (Montes Mariani) which protected south Spain from the winds of the Atlantic and the plateau. Extending for three hundred miles alongside the Guadalquivir, and as far as the parallel Rio Tinto where there were huge deposits of copper ore, these rugged mountains had also supplied gold and silver since very early times, and were rich in lead, iron, quicksilver and cinnabar. In spite of many difficulties of exploitation, Spain became during the second century BC the most important metal-producing country in the world. From beginning to end the Romans perhaps mined twenty-one million tons of ore from the Rio Tinto alone, extracting twelve hundred thousand tons of copper.

The eastern part of the Sierra Morena crossed from Further into Nearer Spain. That province comprised the Mediterranean coast down to a point south of New Carthage. It also extended deep into the interior, where the inhabitants were unaccustomed to foreign rule; but the Romans had learnt from Carthage the routes by which the slow task of 'pacification' could be started, and they were welcomed by Greek colonies such as Emporiae (Ampurias). Climatically this was a highly varied territory, ranging from drought to the rains of north-east Catalonia, and from complete barrenness to extreme productivity. Wine and oil were exported from Barcino (Barcelona), an open roadstead sheltered by a hill from the north winds, protected by a fortress, and linked with the mountains by a branching road. Fragments of jars which were once filled with these Spanish exports are still heaped high on a mountainous refuse dump at Rome. Other harbour towns mobilised to swell this trade included Valentia and particularly Tarraco (Tarragona), producer of the best wines. This former Iberian settlement which had served as the Roman headquarters during the second Punic War, now supplanted New Carthage as the capital, since despite deficiencies as a harbour its position two hundred and seventy miles up the coast meant closer contacts with Italy. New Carthage also enjoyed easy access to the Ebro valley, which could only be navigated for twenty miles upstream but was bordered by routes leading up to the iron, silver and gold mines of Osca (Huesca) on the flanks of the Pyrenees.[19]

The conquest of the Mediterranean completed

After the Romans had annexed a strip of the Albanian coast (229), they were likely to be involved before long in eastern Mediterranean affairs. In 217 a Greek warned his compatriots of a 'cloud rising in the west' – whichever side won the second Punic War, the Greeks would lose the right to make war against each other! And when Philip v of Macedonia, egged on by an Illyrian exile, was persuaded to help Carthage in its fight, the involvement had begun.

The result of Macedonian participation was inconclusive, but Philip's subsequent aggressiveness in the Aegean inspired Rhodes to join the Aetolian League (p. 223), Pergamum (p. 222) and perhaps Ptolemaic Egypt and Athens, in taking the ultimately fatal step of appealing to Rome (201). The motives of these associates were various. Rhodes and Athens needed peace for their trade; the Rhodians disapproved of any one power becoming a potential threat to the freedom of the seas, and saw Philip but not the Romans in this light. Aetolia had become habitually hostile to its Macedonian neighbour. Pergamum and the Egyptians were afraid of being hemmed in, because the Seleucid Antiochus III – who was in the process of conquering southern Syria and Phoenicia from Egypt – had an understanding with Philip about their partition. This made the Romans, to whom Antiochus was evasive, amenable to suggestions by their war-party that a similar coalition could be directed against themselves. Accordingly Rome, despite its exhaustion from the very recently concluded second Punic War, responded to the appeal by declaring war on Macedonia.

And so Titus Flamininus, though not yet thirty years of age, became the first Roman ever to land an army in Greece.[20] Two campaigns in Macedonia and two in Thessaly gave him decisive victory, and the Macedonians, although saved from abolition by their role as a defence against barbarism, were compelled to surrender the three 'fetters' or key fortresses of Greece, namely Corinth, Demetrias and Chalcis. For Flamininus, at Corinth's Isthmian Games, proclaimed the freedom and autonomy of all city-states (196). But the Greeks were too weak and divided for this popular gesture to become effective, and its principal result was a constant succession of grievance-bearing deputations to the Roman senate. Neither entirely altruistic nor entirely cynical, the act of liberation was intended as a form of defensive imperialism, a protectorate over Greece for the mutual benefit of both parties. For the present all Roman troops evacuated the country; yet a declaration couched in such terms was open to tougher interpretations by subsequent politicians.

Antiochus III now crossed over to Europe and invaded Thrace. Since parts of its coast had once belonged to earlier Seleucids, 'this seemed to him the recovery of the last piece of his heritage; but in the eyes of the Romans, Thrace could only be the first stage of an invasion planned to drive them from Greece'.[21] After inconclusive diplomacy the Aetolians, who felt that Flamininus' universal autonomy had deprived them of deserved rewards, invited Antiochus to become a second 'liberator' of the city-states on his own account. Advised by Hannibal who had been exiled from Carthage, he accepted the challenge and traversed the Aegean. But his army was defeated by the Romans, who then (for the first time) moved a force over to Asia Minor, and with the help of Rhodes and Pergamum won a decisive victory at Magnesia ad Sipylum (Manisa) (190). The phalanx of the Seleucids, inflexible and unguarded on its flanks, proved no match for Roman legions. The Seleucid empire remained a force in Asian affairs, but the defeat brought an end to its pretensions as a major Mediterranean power. The Egyptians, too, had earned Roman disapproval, since they were linked to Antiochus by an alliance; and in any case internal rebellions diminished their role in international affairs.

That is to say, all the three major successor states to Alexander's empire were eclipsed, and there was consequently a certain inevitability about their final disappearance during the following century and a half. As far as its traitorous reputation permitted, Pergamum took the place of the Seleucids; but the ascendant star was Rome, since naval disarmament clauses in the treaties with Philip and Antiochus had almost made the Mediterranean a Roman lake.

Yet there were still weak points in this unification of the sea; and one of the weakest was far nearer home, in what is now north Italy, between the inner gulfs of the Tyrrhenian and Adriatic Seas. During the second Punic War many Gauls in the

Po valley had associated themselves, actively or passively, with Hannibal. Cremona and Placentia at the crossing had been successfully defended against him; but after his withdrawal Placentia succumbed to a Gaulish attack (*c.* 200). The Romans now conducted a series of punitive expeditions across the Po and established control from the left bank up as far as the Alps, with Mediolanum as their principal headquarters (194). They had briefly occupied these regions before the second Punic War (p. 261), and now they did so again on a permanent basis. An important step had been taken towards making the Alpine barrier into the frontier it looks.

The new lands were not, however, incorporated into Italy, and no new province was formed; the area was to remain a militarised border zone. The reason why Rome hung back from making all Italy one was because the Alps are not so impregnable as they seem. Although Petrarch said they warded off the cold, the wind and the barbarian, a long tale of prehistoric penetrations had shown that the range is not an impassable, isolating obstacle. Easy gradients on the northern flanks encouraged invaders such as Hannibal; 'there is no need', said Polybius, 'for gods or heroes to help someone cross the Alps.' The lowest landward pass, the Brenner, had been in use since remotest antiquity, the others were gradually occupied by the Romans to pacify the highland peoples, and there were practicable passages where the mountains came down to the sea on either side.

Each new spring flood brought the Po valley a new sedimentation, rich in plant food. The climate of the basin is not wholly Mediterranean (p. 6), since the settling of cold Alpine air produces sharp and prolonged winter frosts which makes it impossible to grow olives; and most rainfall occurs during the summer half-year when heated air rising from the plains is chilled in the upper altitudes. Yet this blend of mid-European and Mediterranean conditions, assisted by the draining of the swamps either side of the Po, made the soil singularly productive; already by *c.* 150 BC there was a glut of wheat on both the river banks.[22]

Using Genua (Genoa) as a base, the Romans waged a long series of campaigns against the hardy tribes on the mountain heights of Liguria, above the headwaters of the Tyrrhenian Sea (201–154 BC). Many steps were also taken to strengthen earlier acquisitions immediately to the south of the Po, where the valleys of its tributaries descend from the Apennines (p. 242). Though even this area was still not declared part of Italy, existing colonies were strengthened, three thousand settlers were sent to the ancient regional capital of Bononia (Bologna) (189), and further colonies were established at Parma and Mutina (Modena), attracting Italians who had been displaced from their former homes by the large slave ranches (p. 258). A new road the Via Aemilia (187), after which the modern province takes its name, linked all these centres to Ariminum and onwards along the Via Flaminia to Rome. The construction of the Aemilian Way, passing through a more temperate and therefore muddy zone than earlier Roman roads, raised new problems which the engineers proceeded to solve. On either side of this thoroughfare was a great network of agricultural reclamation and colonisation, consisting of forty or fifty thousand plots of between five and thirty acres each, elaborately marked out in geometrical gridded formations. Such allotments, like similar Roman schemes for thousands of miles all over the Mediterranean area, constituted a drastic, artificial, human imposition upon nature, of which the full dimensions only become apparent since the introduction of air-photography.

It was time for the Romans to turn to what is now north-eastern Italy. As in other Alpine territories there were menacing tribesmen, and here also are the lowest, shortest and easiest mountain passes which tempted them to break in. But the Romans' flank was protected by the friendly Illyrian-speaking Veneti. Their centre had first been the river-port Ateste (Este) on the Atesis (Adige) near Greco-Etruscan Spina. But a change in the course of the river left the place high and dry (*c.* 500), and the Veneti moved their capital to Patavium, the modern Padua, on the Brinta (Brenta). As a permanent bastion on this frontier, Rome founded an unusually large Latin colony (p. 252) on the Adriatic head-waters at Aquileia. Access to the sea (which has now moved farther away) was provided by a deeply cut channel leading into a lagoon. Since the town adjoined the entrance to an easy and strategic pass and was also the terminal of a northern route, it became a focus for trade routes bringing Italy the iron and lead of Alpine and Danubian lands.

But the main function of Aquileia was to keep fierce mountaineers out of the Venetian plain. With this in mind, many ex-soldiers were chosen to be settlers, and for the same purpose land-grants were increased to fifty or even a hundred and forty acres in the hope of attracting substantial farmers who could if necessary mobilise their workers to form a garrison. Protective duties very soon had to be assumed against the Illyrian Istri, who lived in the peninsula named after them. These tribesmen, who had already attracted hostile Roman concern forty years earlier, were provoked by the foundation of Aquileia into raids which resulted in their suppression and annexation (178–177). Before very long, the olives of the fertile Istrian strip were equated with those of Spain as superior to all others except those of metropolitan Italy itself.

Independent Greece was now approaching its final convulsions. When Philip v of Macedonia died (179), his son Perseus temporarily extended the country's prestige, championed oppressed democrats, and annoyed the Pergamenes who now aspired to Aegean predominance. In the Roman senate a strong imperialistic group insisted on intervention against Perseus, who was defeated and captured (168); and Macedonia was divided into four puppet republics.

This was the first time that the Romans had abolished one of the major successor states of Alexander. A prince ruling at Scodra was also defeated, and such parts of the east coast of the Adriatic as the Romans had not already occupied now passed into their hands and were divided into three subject zones of Illyricum (167). Revolts in the piratic islands and creeks continued at frequent intervals, but starting from Dyrrhachium (formerly Epidamnus), a well-protected harbour town on a fertile stretch of the Albanian coast, a major road was built across the Balkans to Thessalonica, and then onwards towards the Dardanelles.

The Rhodians' pro-Roman record did not avail them, after their disappointment with their ally's supposed ingratitude had induced them to withhold help against Perseus – they had offered mediation instead. Rome regarded this as impertinent, and prompted by its merchants (who were eager to stop paying Rhodian transit dues) allowed Athens to set up another island, Delos, as a duty-free port. Its superior attraction to Italian and other business men virtually put an end to the prosperity of the Rhodians, whose harbour receipts fell by 85 per cent. They could no longer afford to check piracy, which flourished as never before.

At this juncture the Romans arrested many peoples in various Greek territories who were suspected of subversive opinions, and sent them to Italy. Among those deported was the historian Polybius (p. 263), penalised for the unsatisfactory attitude of his Achaean League during the war against Macedonia. Nevertheless, his own long, intimate political and military experience left him an admirer of the Romans. Inspired by the city's epic rise and stable institutions, he saw its protectorate over Greece as logical and irresistible: the year when Perseus fell seemed the culmination of a unique, epoch-making period of fifty-three years during which a single power, for the first time in all history, had unified the Mediterranean world.

Polybius gained the friendship of the cultured Roman statesman Scipio Aemilianus, who encouraged his work and took him on widespread travels. Polybius returned to Greece in 150 BC at about the time when the other deportees of seventeen years earlier, if they had survived, were also allowed to return to their cities. Shortly after their return, however, a revolt in Macedonia induced the Romans to abolish its four republics and annex the whole country. This was the first new province to be created for over fifty years. During that period Rome's insufficiency of staff and administrative organs, combined with a mistrust of distant commands, had made its rulers reluctant to extend the areas under their direct control. But now they took the plunge.

The annexation of this historic kingdom was a sharp departure from the old policy of leaving Greece free and ungarrisoned. 'According to Livy,' Gibbon remarked sarcastically, 'the Romans conquered the world in self-defence.' Or at least it could be said of earlier periods that each successive Mediterranean annexation had originated from the response to a local appeal. But now the political and moral atmosphere was sharply deteriorating. Exploitation abounded, generals and governors had become more callous and corrupt, and there was increasing impatience with Greek quarrels and complexities. Finally Corinth, on the grounds that it had violated the sanctity of Roman envoys, was attacked and destroyed (146), an event which shocked the world. The Achaean League was also dissolved, and replaced by a subject-province of Achaea which comprised most of southern Greece. In case democratic governments in the cities might be revolutionary, they were all abolished in favour of groups of propertied collaborators. Any reality of Greek independence was now at an end.

The year that Corinth fell also witnessed the end of Carthage, after a desperately fought three-year war. Under strong provocation the Carthaginians had attacked their western neighbour Numidia, thus infringing the treaty with Rome; and the penalty was paid. Stormed and demolished by Scipio Aemilianus, Carthage was ploughed over, sown with salt and cursed, and its immensely wealthy corn-producing hinterland became a new Roman province of Africa, supplementing and exceeding Sicily as a source of supply for the imperial capital.

An even richer territory, the western part of Asia Minor, was likewise annexed when Attalus III, the last monarch of Pergamum, insured against social upheaval by bequeathing his kingdom to the Romans.[24] They accepted the heritage and created their sixth province, under the name of Asia. Lacking, however, the financial machinery to collect the immensely lucrative taxes of the area, the Roman government instead farmed these out to joint stock companies formed by a rising class of financiers who were not members of the senate but had almost become their equals in power. Corporations of this kind paid a fixed total to the state – and whatever they could collect over and above that sum was their own. The tax-collectors to whom they entrusted the levy tried to bring all public as well as private property within their range, and incurred great unpopularity among the cities which had to suffer their iniquitous extortions.

The past decades had brought about great changes. Rome gained a foretaste of eastern luxury when it captured huge booty from the Galatians in the 180s, and now the destruction of Corinth and Carthage in one and the same year was a terrible twofold landmark; while the provinces of Africa and Asia had multiplied the national wealth many times over, transforming the whole character of the state. And yet this structure, for all its massive dimensions and resources, suffered from such grave internal tensions that sometimes it seemed likely to explode and crumble apart. During the third century BC the gulf between rich and poor throughout the Mediterranean area had greatly widened, and there was wave after wave of proletarian outbreaks and class warfare (p. 227).

The rebels were inspired by various visions of egalitarian Utopias. These ideal pictures, together with Stoic doctrines of human brotherhood, helped also to inspire the advisers of the Gracchi, two young Roman noblemen whose efforts to better the agrarian and social position of Italy resulted in their deaths (133, 122). The same heady mixture of miseries and ideals also plunged Asia Minor into precisely the sort of revolution that the last king of Pergamum had feared, since after his death an illegitimate prince rose against the new Roman masters with the support of Asiatics, down-and-outs, and slaves.

The rebellion was stamped out, but everywhere a vigilant watch on slaves remained continually necessary. Revolts had occurred at intervals since the beginning of the century, but now the situation was much worse since many thousands were employed upon the huge Italian and Sicilian ranches, in material conditions a hundred times worse than domestic slavery. These 'expendables' represented an acute danger against which their masters, oscillating between violence and weakness, were on permanent embattled guard. In spite of all such measures, however, a rebellion in Sicily (135) attained such terrifying proportions that a separatist slave-state was briefly established.[25] A second horde of slave insurgents (104–100), who tried to take advantage of Rome's involvement with German invaders (p. 274), needed seventeen thousand legionaries to stamp them out, and the Thracian Spartacus (73–71) collected ninety thousand gladiators, slaves and desperate men whose terrorisation of all Italy was the worst threat since Hannibal.

Nevertheless, the Romans remained great moralists, and while all this was going on they and their Greek subjects and allies found many philosophical justifications for Roman rule. Like the revolutionary theories that opposed them, these attempts owed a lot to the Stoic belief that life must be seen solely in ethical terms. But that categorical imperative, which had earlier appealed to a Macedonian monarch (p. 223), was rather too rigid and bleak for people engaged in Roman public life, and for their benefit Panaetius of Rhodes (*c.* 185–109 BC), a protegé of Scipio Aemilianus, relaxed the doctrine by conceding the merits of the sort of imperfect progression *towards* virtue to which even a Roman official might aspire.

Then another Rhodian resident, the Greco-Syrian Posidonius from Apamea on the Orontes (*c.* 135–50 BC), took a similar new look at the Stoic Law of Nature by which all men are brothers in the Cosmopolis or world-state (p. 273). Yes, he said, and that world-state, embodying all peoples and reflecting the divine commonwealth, is no Utopia to be sought through revolution, but the empire of Rome itself. These suggestions were gratefully and patriotically accepted by Cicero (*c.* 106–143), who, employing an idea that has always been found convenient by conquerors, declared the rule of the best over inferior peoples to be a natural relationship which is as advantageous to the one party as to the other.[26]

Meanwhile such few parts of the Mediterranean as still remained free were gradually brought under the Pax Romana. Trouble with the Ligurians on the borders of Italy and Gaul was dealt with by settling ex-soldiers in a fortress at Aquae Sextiae (Aix en Provence). Then, after the reduction of adjacent tribes, southern France as far as Vienna (Vienne) and Tolosa (Toulouse) was constituted into a province (121). This was done largely in order to protect the communications of Rome's Greek ally Massalia, which was left as an independent state. The newly acquired territory possessed no strategic frontiers to north or west, but controlled most of the Rhône gap and the Durance and Isère valleys that offered access to Alpine passes and Piedmont. An agricultural and strategic colony of Roman citizens (a new precedent in a non-Italian area) was founded near the farther extremity of the newly annexed territory at Narbo Martius (Narbonne), commanding a Pyrenean pass which was linked to the Rhône valley by the Via Domitia. But the new province did not remain at peace, for it was invaded by masses of German tribesmen, whom the great military innovator Marius finally beat off at Aquae Sextiae (102).

Marius also ejected further hordes from Italy itself. But now the principal danger in the peninsula came from within. For the ancient, carefully planned balance of privilege and right which had long provided the basis for Roman rule was breaking down. A short-sighted senate's ungenerous policy towards extensions of citizenship caused increasingly widespread discontent; and finally the expulsion of all non-Romans from the city, followed by the murder of the confederates' spokesman, precipitated a desperate struggle (90–89). This was known as the Marsian War, after the central Italian tribe which took the initiative in demanding the Roman franchise.[27] Its more southerly allies the Samnites, on the other hand, did not mean to share Rome's privileges, but to break its power altogether, as they had failed to do two centuries before. The loss of Aesernia (Isernia), ninety miles south-east of the capital, meant that the two main groups of rebels were no longer divided. Capua stood firm, but other cities of Campania, Lucania and Apulia fell into Marsian and Samnite hands. Elsewhere the Romans resisted with varying success, but an end to the war was only achieved by conceding the main issue for which the more moderate among their enemies had fought. For all free men in Italy and 'Gaul' south of the Po (Emilia) were now granted the status of Roman citizens.

There was only one more challenge to Roman power in the Mediterranean, and that came from the Black Sea country of Pontus in Asia Minor, beyond the frontiers of the Asian province. Its partially Hellenised Iranian King Mithridates VI, after twenty-five years spent in enlarging his territory, seized the opportunity of Rome's preoccupation with the Marsian War to invade Greece and Macedonia. The hatred felt for the Romans and their tax collectors and business men caused many cities, including Athens, to join this cause, and in Asia he instigated the massacre of eighty thousand Italian citizens. Rome's generals Sulla and Lucullus were unable to dispose of him, though the neighbouring monarch of Bithynia, important for its extensive ship-building timber, left his kingdom to Rome. Pompey, however, dealt with Mithridates in two stages. First he triumphantly revived large-scale Roman naval activity in order to overwhelm his slave-raiding pirate allies, who had been operating from the narrow inlets of rocky western Cilicia; and then he moved with equal success against the king himself, who fled to the Crimea and committed suicide (63 BC).

In the same year a solemn though largely symbolical event in Mediterranean history took place when Pompey annexed the last, strife-ridden little remnants of the Seleucid empire in Syria. Jerusalem too, which for nearly a hundred years had been the capital of a nationalist priestly house, the Maccabees, was taken by storm, only to be handed back to one of the princes as a subject state. The thoroughgoing involvement in the Levant which the Romans had now accepted meant that they must move their frontier forward to the Euphrates and assume responsibilities on the other bank against the Parthian empire, which soon afterwards destroyed a Roman army (53 BC).

For most of this century Rome's generals had increasingly asserted a semi-independent status for themselves and their armies, and now a dictatorial committee of three assumed control of the empire (60–59). One of these triumvirs, Julius Caesar, taking advantage of an even balance of rivalry between the tribes of Gaul, pushed the borders of Rome's possessions northwards so as to include the whole of the country to the Rhine (58–51), which was much farther from the Mediterranean than any previous frontier. Then, at an early stage in a series of victorious campaigns against Pompey which made him sole ruler and dictator, Caesar extended Roman citizenship throughout all territories between the Po and the Alps (49). Soon afterwards these lands were incorporated as part of the homeland of Italy itself, to which they contributed great numbers of soldiers and abundant resources.

That was in the time of the civil wars which followed the murder of Caesar (44), and as this period of convulsion finally drew to a close many rich communities of the eastern Mediterranean were temporarily ruined owing to the demands of Roman generals for billeting, requisitions, bribes, gifts, honours and entertainments. The last of Alexander's succession-states, Egypt, retained its great riches; but now this too fell to the Romans. Ptolemaic Egypt had long been more or less dependent upon them, but its last monarch, Cleopatra VII, after establishing herself on the throne with Caesar's help, extended her dominions to something like their old grandeur with the support of her new lover Antony, who as member of a second triumvirate controlled Rome's eastern provinces. Antony and Cleopatra, however, were decisively defeated at sea (31) off Actium in north-west Greece by Caesar's grand-nephew Octavian, the later Augustus. In the following year they killed themselves, and Egypt became part of the Roman empire. So great was the country's wealth that Octavian gave it a special status in the empire, under a governor who was responsible to himself personally, with the special task of channelling all this revenue into his private treasury. Although certain parts of north Africa, like the kingdom of the Crimea and other states, were left for a time as semi-dependent protectorates of 'client' status, the conquest of the Mediterranean by the Romans was now complete; and the decisive resources of its ancient eastern countries were in their hands.

The arts of the Republic

During the two and a half centuries in which Rome had become involved with Greece, the famous reversal had occurred, and captive Greece had captured her conqueror.[28] This was the second wave of Greek influences which had poured into Rome. The first impact had been received at a very early date, from colonies such as Cumae and through many Etruscan channels. And even after that the ejection of the Etruscan overlords had not meant that contacts with Greece completely ceased. For example, after their capture of Veii (396), the Romans dedicated one-tenth of the spoil to Delphic Apollo; and soon afterwards the wall built round the city in *c.* 378 BC was inscribed with masons' marks which suggest the employment of Greek contractors. Furthermore a sort of Doric dramatic sketch or farce, acted and sung in the Greek towns of south Italy, was Italianised in Oscan towns of Campania such as Atella (after which it took its name), and achieved early popularity at Rome.

But then during the first Punic War the Roman soldiers in Sicily saw for themselves the luxurious court life of Syracuse and the amenities of a Greek city. And so when the war was over their Victory Games (240) staged Latin versions of Greek tragic and perhaps comic plays written, produced and acted by a Greek or half-Greek prisoner of war, Livius Andronicus from Tarentum. Not long afterwards two Italian writers, the comic dramatist Plautus from Umbria and Ennius the Calabrian 'father of Roman poetry' (d. 169), adapted Greek genres and metres to the totally different, far less subtle, more crudely vigorous Latin language and spirit, producing works which employed Greek prototypes to achieve thoroughly original effects. This paradoxical originality through imitation remained the keynote of Roman literature, spreading rapidly to other regions of the Mediterranean, notably north Africa which produced a more Hellenic sort of Latin writer of comedies in Terence (d. *c.* 159). This was the same sort of transformation as Greece itself had achieved six centuries earlier, when its literature and art likewise had drawn heavily upon external models in order to achieve results of an entirely individual nature.

This second Roman draft upon Greece was strongly resisted by nationalists and die-hards such as Cato the Elder (d. 140 BC). Yet when Crates of Mallus in Cilicia, the librarian at Pergamum, lectured at Rome on Greek rhetoric (168 BC), he attracted great attention, and despite official disfavour the Greek educational pattern was adopted by Romans. Hellenism was also pervading other branches of life. It was in imitation of Greece that Rome had created a national coinage (*c.* 269), subsequently based on the silver *denarius* (*c.* 212) which became the first general currency of the Mediterranean world. As Rome began to grow far richer (p. 272), a port established for its service at Puteoli (Pozzuoli) (194), a former Greek colony on the bay of Naples, expanded rapidly and within the next seventy years became second only to Delos as a harbour,[29] receiving all Rome's imports and particularly grain from Sicily and Africa.

Since Puteoli also contained the principal factories for producing iron weapons and implements, while Capua likewise maintained its metal-working traditions (and specialised in kitchen utensils), Campania now outstripped Etruria as Italy's industrial centre. Outside the peninsula the main commercial ports of the late Republic included Aquileia on the inmost Adriatic; Panormus in Sicily; Narbo and Arelate (Arles) in Gaul; Gades and Tarraco in Spain; Alexandria, Cyrene, Utica and Cirta (Constantine) in north Africa; Piraeus, Ephesus and Delos in the Aegean; and Seleucia and Laodicea in Syria. Privileged communities of Italian businessmen settled at all such places, and there was a new intensive trade in cheap mass products. Bills of exchange, improved versions of Mesopotamian bearer-instruments of nearly two millennia earlier, encouraged this circulation and distribution, and harbours and docks were rebuilt and enlarged to deal with the increasing flow.

The many Greek influences now penetrating into Rome included architectural and artistic currents, for which Puteoli and other Campanian centres again provided the channels. In private houses at Pompeii nearby, the old Etruscan *atrium* and its symmetrical adjoining rooms had already been adorned with Greek colonnades since *c.* 300 BC; residential Herculaneum adopted a Greek town plan; and Greek-style bathrooms were first seen in Capua during the second Punic War.

The influx of Greek influences again blended with Etruscan traditions to produce the first signs of a Roman pictorial and sculptural art. Paintings depicted victorious battles and religious scenes, and the beginnings of a national portraiture appeared. The sculptors were Greeks or Hellenised orientals, but they modified Greek styles in order to catch the spirit and formidable facial appearance of their Roman patrons, and early portraits also owe something to the Roman custom of preserving and displaying the death masks of ancestors.

The city itself saw its first new temples made of Greek marble (*c.* 146 BC) instead of the coarser local stones; and Greek decorative motifs were also introduced. Nevertheless Etruscan and Italian traditions still showed in the very distinctive two-dimensional appearance of these temples, planned for priests or orators to command assemblages of people from high platforms. Other public buildings included rectangular roofed halls (basilicas), which displayed the influence of Greek columned halls (*c.* 184) but were treated by Romans and Italians in a new way as adjuncts to the market-place or forum, in which people met together for social, commercial and judicial purposes. Greek models were again combined with local precedents and talents by Roman builders of the first high level aqueducts (144 BC), and these in turn, combined with the visible examples of Etruscan drains and culverts, provided lessons and hints for the arches which soon afterwards began to appear in the construction of bridges.

The situation during the second century BC was one in which the rejection of Greek architectural orders was inconceivable, and yet great advances were made beyond their essentially horizontal and vertical principles. For even the poor vestiges that remain are enough to show that there was remarkable experimentation in the use of domes and vaults. This was made possible by the discovery of concrete, an invention drawn from Italy's own soil and shore which enabled Romans, or the foreign architects they employed, to advance far beyond what Greece had taught them.

Structural adhesives of sand, mixed with lime and water, had already been well known in parts of the pre-Roman Mediterranean world (p. 90), and at about the time of the first Punic War Greek colonies introduced these techniques into southern Italy. Next, soon after 200 BC, it was discovered that a much superior material existed in a sandy earth which occurred in various regions east and north of Rome but is called pozzolana because of its particular abundance at Puteoli (Pozzuoli). This is a finely pulverised volcanic product of cinders and clay, found in thick beds consisting of chunks and pebbles easily reduced to an exploitable form. When lime was added in a kiln, a glassy ingredient in the pozzolana turned the mixture into an exceptionally consistent and cohesive concrete which has not been bettered as a mortar and binding material until the discovery of Portland cement.

The molten mass was poured over an 'aggregate' of builders' waste, chips of stone, brick and marble, to which pumice could be added if lightness of weight was an important factor. These inexpensive admixtures gave size and substance to the concrete, which dried out more quickly than ordinary lime-mortar and set the whole conglomerate into a compact, monolithic mass, highly resistant to strains and stresses, almost indestructible even under water, and exerting no lateral thrusts.

> Who could sufficiently marvel [said Pliny] at the fact that the most inferior portion of the earth's substance (which in consequence designated dust) on the hills of Pozzuoli encounters the waves of the sea, and as soon as it is submerged turns into a single mass of stone that withstands the attacks of the waves and, especially if it is mixed with broken quarry-stone from Cumae, becomes stronger every day?[30]

Indeed this 'pit sand' was the same as the volcanic dust already used for moles and jetties at Puteoli itself. The availability of such an invaluable waterproof material for harbour works may well have been one of the chief reasons why the Romans in the second century BC established their port at Puteoli instead of the more sheltered adjoining basin of Neapolis. At Rome, pozzolana was already to be seen in buildings of *c.* 130 BC, though its potential for eliminating the problems of designers and stone-cutters was not fully explored until the construction of the imperial arches and vaults and domes, culminating in the Pantheon – which Greeks could never have achieved.

11

The Imperial Sea

Imperial culture and landscape

The imperial recipe of Bread and Circuses is well known; Augustus (31 BC – AD 14) and his successors were thoroughly aware that the only way to keep the huge population of Rome quiet was to give them ample food and entertainment. Enormous quantities of cheap free grain were fed to this parasite city. Land transport was too costly to mobilise the cereals of the European continent, but the traditional sources of Sicily and Tunisia were called upon, and now Egypt also was able to contribute a supply which kept the capital in corn for no less than four months of the year. 'It was artfully contrived by Augustus', said Edward Gibbon, 'that in the enjoyment of plenty the Romans should lose the memory of freedom.' The second part of the panacea, entertainment, is given great prominence in the Testament of Augustus, who lists his numerous shows, including many of the bloodthirsty gladiatorial displays which were Rome's worst heritage from Etruria.

He also undertook immense transformations of the physical appearance of the capital, boasting that he had found a city of sun-dried brick and left a city of marble. There had, it is true, been some Greek marble before, but now large parts of the city shone dazzling white with the product of the Carrara quarries; and before long all the numerous coloured marbles of the Mediterranean were to be seen at Rome.

Augustus' creation or restoration of many temples, and his construction of Apollo's resplendent shrine on the Palatine Hill, formed part of the service regarded as needful to preserve his own popularity and the people's morale.

Another feature of this policy was the distribution of his own sculptured portraits far and wide. In keeping with the dual character of his patron Apollo, who was the brilliant god of Hellenism and yet also deity of Rome, the Greeks and Asiatics who made these portraits achieve a subtle fusion of Hellenic and Italian elements. Their technique fits into the continuously evolving portrait styles of the later Greek world. But the facial features are noticeably Italian (p. 279), and they express an imperial idea – human and yet suggesting something more – which is neither purely Greek nor Roman but both. Equal successes were registered by designers who for centuries made striking and varied heads of rulers for the great coinage which now circulated from end to end of the empire.

The same subtle blend of Rome and Greece pervaded the presentation of the ruler by those outstanding writers whose support Augustus was fortunate and clever enough to mobilise: Virgil, Horace, Propertius, Livy and Ovid. Virgil (d. 19 BC), above all, becomes specific in his belief that the new order demands a complete reconciliation and harmony between the two major cultural elements in this new and unprecedented unity of the entire Mediterranean region.

Such writers of the Augustan age also show a greatly increased appreciation of the natural glories of their shores and plains and hills. This deeper insight, a direct continuation of trends already seen among the later Greeks in Alexandria and elsewhere, was brought to marvellous perfection by Virgil's *Eclogues*, which raised the tradition of Theocritus of Cos to a new pitch of intensity. The medium of the Virgilian pastoral was an elegantly stylised, harmoniously arranged Arcadia, which fuses with north Italy where the poet was born, Campania where he lived, and Sicily where the pastoral originated.

> Happy, happy old man. Here, among friendly streams
> And holy springs, you will find dark leaf-shaded coolness.[1]

All the abundant resources of the Latin language are devoted to depicting, and dressing in a veil of Greek literary tradition, the nostalgic beauties of this bitter-sweet, sensuous place of imaginative escape.

Although Roman poets, like the Greeks of recent but not of earlier centuries (p. 224), had become alive to the fascination of wild nature, they carried on the classical preference for lush landscapes assisted and transformed by man. Indeed, Virgil's *Georgics*, in form, were actually an agricultural handbook, descended from unmistakable examples of the same genre (p. 258) but transfigured into a poetic evocation of central Italy, a timeless panorama of the farmer's tasks in a sunny, temperate Mediterranean land. True to the spirit of Hesiod, Virgil does not attempt to conceal the laboriousness of this life, and yet writing of peace during the anguished civil wars that preceded Augustus' sole rule he profoundly contrasts the glory of the farmer's world with the disturbances of cities.

If the poet had lived longer, he intended one day (or so he hinted) to write another long poem on gardening. For this ancient Egyptian, Babylonian, Syrian taste was dear to the Romans. Even the name of their goddess of love, Venus, had originally meant a garden of herbs;[2] a well cultivated piece of land is 'fine Ceres and love and Bacchus together'. And so the *Georgics* dwell lovingly on a Cilician ex-pirate's small plot at Tarentum.

> He laid out a kitchen-garden in rows amid the brushwood,
> Bordering it with white lilies, verbena, small-seeded
> poppy;
> His the first rose of spring, the earliest apples in autumn.[3]

But this allotment was indeed a modest affair in comparison with what the Italian countryside could show. Already during the second century BC many of the old practical vegetable gardens had grown into something more ambitious. In Greek-influenced Campania the small cloistered bowers of Pompeii skilfully interpenetrated private houses and framed them in axial vistas. In due course current advances in horticultural science spread to central Italy – with Syrian gardeners to see to them. The parks of Lucullus, Pompey and Caesar, interspersed with the statuary needed to make an Italian garden complete, were magnificent, poetical creations. As for the imperial palaces that followed, they outdid Egypt, Babylon or Syracuse (p. 190). The collection of separate, scattered buildings that comprised Hadrian's 'Villa' at Tibur (Tivoli) was disposed with a highly sophisticated sense of landscaping and water-design (AD 126–34). The country houses of private individuals, too, in which groupings of laurel, plane and pine alternated with flower-beds and geometrically clipped myrtles, were artfully planned to suit changing seasons and to command spectacular views.

There was also novelty in the feelings which led Cicero (d. 43 BC), perhaps echoing recent Greeks, to express a love for gardens as stimulants to thought.[4] This viewpoint implied a relationship between nature and human beings which would have been quite alien, for example, to Socrates. Virgil, too, saw the countryside as the source of a deeply satisfying peace of mind, and his contemporary Horace developed the same theme of tranquil corners of nature which are places of inspiration and repose for the man fortunate enough to dwell in them,

> Beneath some spreading ilex shade
> On some green bank supinely laid.[5]

Horace loved his farm amid the beauties of the Sabine hills, because it soothed his soul and formed a necessary, beloved background for his leisure.

> You'd praise the temperate air. And think of this: the kindly
> Bushes bear wild plums and cherries, the oak and ilex
> Delight the cattle with their acorns, me with their shade.[6]

His fountain of Bandusia,[7] too, in its dark hollow of rocks beneath the overreaching oak, held special magic for the Mediterranean and near-eastern world in which fresh water was a theme for poetry and longing. Such, perhaps, was the spirit, blurred somewhat by an imperial lack of moderation, in which the emperor Domitian (AD 81–96) arranged for the courts and gardens of his Palatine residence to include at least fourteen pools and fountains. And the glade of which Petronius tells, in one of the poems which diversify his picaresque novel of Campania, recalls that nature was also a place for amorous pleasures.

> It seemed a place for love; whereof in witness sang
> The woodland nightingale, the swallow from the town,
> Through violets and grass, all calling as they flew.[8]

In consequence of such new ideas, a taste for word-paintings of flowers or trees, lyrical and declamatory or precise and realistic, had already become habitual among people of intellectual and artistic tastes at the beginning of our era.[9] And then, towards the end of the first century AD, the Romans' appreciation of their Mediterranean surroundings was made more articulate than ever before in the younger Pliny's unsentimental, observant affection for the beauties of air, water, light and foliage. The source of the Clitumnus,[10] for example, a beauty-spot a dozen miles from Assisi, seemed to Pliny to warrant a detailed description; and the woods and fresh flowers and spreading plains of the upper Tiber, where Etruria and Umbria meet, are brought before us with a sensitive clarity unknown in earlier literatures. There, at Tifernum (Città di Castello), Pliny possesses a property, and he is intensely concerned to make the most of its delectable environment.

One room looks on to the small court with the four plane trees, another on to the meadow, and a third faces the vineyard and has an uninterrupted view across the sky. . . . The riding-ground is planted round with ivy-clad plane-trees, green with their own leaves above, and below with the ivy which climbs over trunk and branch and links tree to tree as it spreads across them.[11]

Then in the later years of Rome (? *c.* 307), a nostalgic Hymn to Venus, on the occasion of her declining festival at Enna in Sicily, strikes a disturbing, unprecedented note of sensuous romance.

The heavy teardrops stretch, ready to fall,
Then falls each glistening bead to the earth beneath:
The moisture that the serene stars sent down
Loosens the virgin bud from the sliding sheath.[12]

Such were the forerunners of the innumerable writers of later Europe who have found in these glories of Italy the culmination of their hopes and dreams. Petrarch (d. 1374), a friend of Sienese painters interested in landscape (p. 289), was the earliest gardener in a modern sense, and the first person since the ancients to express an escapist desire for his Mediterranean countryside; and he is also the first recorded man to climb a mountain just because he wanted to. In Goethe, four centuries later, an overpowering passion for the mountains, trees and plains of Italy expressed itself in haunting visions which fused his ideas of life, science, nature, poetry and morals in a single burning whole. Goethe's Wanderer, personifying the union of classicism and romance, is deeply moved by a moss-grown architrave and broken temple and columns in the vicinity of Cumae. The same contrast between this sunny, quiet countryside and its long since shattered glorious past has excited many an Englishman too.

> A marble shaft that stands alone
> Above a wreck of sculptured stone
> With grey green aloes overgrown.[13]

Byron saw in these foliage-entwined ruins the solemn passage of all Mediterranean history (1818).

> Cypress and ivy, weed and wallflower grown
> Matted and massed together . . .
> Temples, Baths, or Halls?
> Pronounce who can: for all that learning reaped
> From her research hath been, that these are walls.
> Behold the Imperial Mount. 'Tis thus the Mighty falls.

And in the following year Shelley, in his different way, was no less strongly affected by the same theme. *Prometheus Unbound*, he said,

> was chiefly written upon the mountainous ruins of the Baths of Caracalla, among the flowering glades and thickets of odoriferous blossoming trees, which are extended in ever winding labyrinths upon its immense platforms and dizzy arches suspended in the air. The bright blue sky of Rome, and the effect of the vigorous awakening spring in that divinest climate, and the new life with which it drenches the spirit even to intoxication, were the inspiration of this drama.

The painters of late republican and early imperial Italy had been as alive to its natural splendours as the writers. The vogue began when Demetrius of Alexandria (p. 218) came to Rome in the second century BC; and then the demand quickened. A house at Reate (Rieti) in the Sabine country was covered with pictures of agricultural and pastoral pursuits,[14] the kind of subjects which Egyptian artists had loved and later Greeks had occasionally attempted. But then the movement took wings, in what the elder Pliny called a delightful style of decorating walls with representations of villas, harbours, landscape gardens, sacred groves, woods, hills, fishponds, straits, streams and shores, any scene, in short, that took the fancy.[15]

The introduction of this treatment of landscape as a picturesque setting for rustic ritual or myth is ascribed by the same author to an artist named Studius – or perhaps the correct manuscript reading is Ludius. Pliny calls him a painter of Augustus' reign (31 BC – AD 14), but one set of landscapes of this kind, which happens to have survived, is as early as 40 or even 50 BC. This series, found on Rome's Esquiline Hill, comprises eight pictures and part of a ninth illustrating the *Odyssey*. They are impressionist narrative scenes displaying the most effective and delicate command of atmosphere, colour and light. The illusion is created of an open loggia through which the viewer is gazing, a method of treatment which may have come from Alexandrian copy-books and stage-sets. Broad, staccato brush-strokes have conjured up towering crags and limpid pools, summer sea-scapes in palest green or deepest blue, glowing with 'magic illumination produced by yellow Turneresque light'.[16] Ruskin gave medieval Italy the credit for a new sense that mankind acquired when landscapes were first painted, but it is hard to deny the same qualities to these pictures of the first century BC. Although the landscapes, like those described centuries before in the *Odyssey* itself, are still decorative backcloths to human activity, they have become more than merely digressions. Even if naturalism is not yet pursued single-mindedly for its own sake, this is Homer in modern dress, and the human beings, though purposeful, are small. There are signs of a historic reversal of the relative roles of man and nature, with the emphasis no longer wholly tilted towards man. A novel and delicate equilibrium, like Virgil's in his *Georgics*, has been reached between humanism and its Mediterranean background.

Very soon other artists began to devote themselves more thoroughly and exclusively to unmitigated nature, in which man, even if he has modified the scene, no longer visibly plays a part. Such is the bird-filled grove of firs, pines, palms, cypresses, laden orchard trees and blooming shrubs painted in the Empress Livia's villa at Prima Porta, just north of Rome (*c*. 30 BC). This 'paradise of the imagination in which the flowers and fruits of all the seasons bloom and ripen at one and the same time'[17] continuously covers all four walls of a single room. 'How dewy,' said Bernard Berenson, 'how penetratingly fresh the grass and trees and flowers, how coruscating the fruit! Pomegranates as Renoir painted them. Bird song charms one's ears. The distance remains magically impenetrable.'

Mural landscapes, pastoral and maritime scenes, more urbanised but possessing a glamour all of their own, abounded in the villas and public buildings of Campania. Although the artists used several vanishing points instead of one and allowed the light to fall from several directions, they exploited diminishing vistas so successfully that the walls seemed to recede, and the rooms looked much larger than they really were. Pompeii was decorated with many of these ornamental designs, and a picture from the neighbouring town of Stabiae (Castellamare) shows a harbour, perhaps Puteoli, in which the confidently painted flickering of sunshine on sea and buildings foreshadows nineteenth-century artists such as Pissarro.

The cruder but more spectacular mosaic, which became one of Rome's most conspicuous and characteristic arts, followed all the same trends of fashion, and indeed, as certain surviving examples show, actually copied paintings, transferring them in this different medium from walls on to pavements. A large floor-mosaic at Praeneste showing a rich variety of scenes on the Nile echoed the *Odyssey* pictures in its skilfully graded colouring of water, vegetation and rocks. Later mosaics throughout the empire were built up round central panels which displayed every sort of landscape, ranging from farm life at Zliten by the Tripolitanian coast to scenes of rocky landscape on the floors of Hadrian's villa at Tibur.

The mountains painted in illuminated books more than a thousand years later still show strange twisted rocks which go back to Greco-Roman pictures like the Esquiline *Odyssey*; and the Byzantine and Gothic illuminators, in their turn, foreshadow the early Renaissance, when the incomparable, austere lines of this Italian countryside again began to inspire painters in Florence and Umbria and Siena (*c.* 1410), including friends of Petrarch who rediscovered such scenery for literature (p. 286). Next the Venetians explored its glowing textures, and many an artist of seventeenth-century Rome dotted groups of figures and statues round his landscapes in the heroic manner of ancient times. Calm sunny woodland, or the play of dark tree trunks and light leaves against a stormy sky, convey Poussin's enormous vision of bygone dignity and repose; but then it seems, from the great pictures of his later life, that the underlying wildness came to appeal to him more. Meanwhile Claude Lorrain was evolving a dream-like past of his own. The magic rays of its sunlight, serenely bathing trees and hills, opened people's eyes to the lyrical significance of this Mediterranean land.

'A man,' said Samuel Johnson, 'who has not been in Italy is always conscious of an inferiority, from his not having seen what it is expected a man should see.' But whether people had carried out this fashionable purpose or not, there was a host of artists, enchanted by Claude's idea of the 'picturesque', who were willing and able to bring Italy before the world on canvas. Panini, and Piranesi, and Hubert Robert ('Robert of the Ruins'), all explored in various ways these dramatic contrasts of ancient remains and luminous spaces. The surroundings of Rome moved Richard Wilson to his own tranquil vision, and John Robert Cozens charged the same verdant woods and lakes with a haunting and poetic melancholy. Turner learnt from Cozens, but it was his own sight of the Venetian Adriatic in 1819 which inspired his unprecedented revelation of immaterial, shimmering gradations of light; while the gracious mists of Corot's grey and silver tones were again dispelled by a first visit to the transfiguring airs and contours of Rome and Naples before he, too, finally saw the luminosities of the Adriatic.

Round the Roman Mediterranean

Early imperial Italy, which its artists and writers so brilliantly evoked, was very prosperous. The imports of Rome were immense; besides grain, they included slaves, metals, marble, papyrus, linen, furs, ivory, silk and jewels. The city's exports too, though less in bulk, were nevertheless considerable, as many a cargo of wine, glass and woollen and linen goods was able to show. To undertake all this activity a large new port beside the old colony of Ostia at the Tiber mouth (p. 251) gradually supplanted the more distant Puteoli. Since the original Ostian roadstead had become unusable because of silt, Claudius (AD

41–54) constructed a new harbour in a marshy plain north of the estuary. As at the mouths of other principal rivers, a lighthouse was built, and the basin was enclosed by two enormous moles 1900 feet long and 180 feet wide. Within the space between the seaward extremities of the moles a concrete island was constructed to keep the waters of the harbour calm in any weather. Since, however, it was found that a gale could still sink ships inside the port, Trajan built a more compact and sheltered anchorage (*c.* AD 112). Although the Tiber, like other inland waterways, retained its importance in the communications system, sea-going ships could not go right up to the capital. Instead they had to trans-ship their cargoes on to smaller boats, and Ostia, where this trans-shipment took place, henceforward handled the largest volume of goods of any Mediterranean port except Alexandria.

The sections of Ostia so far excavated cover over eighty acres, and yet this represents only one half of the town's total extent. Like most Roman remains today, the buildings are made of excellent fire-baked bricks. These had first come into use in north Italy, and then were adopted at Rome and Ostia (*c.* AD 50). For even if Augustus claimed to have made a city of marble, its growing population soon began to be accommodated in enormous tenements which for architectural and financial reasons alike could not be made of stone; while mere sun-dried brick was not strong enough for structures of such a height. Moreover the concrete which was increasingly employed (p. 280) needed a covering for its coarse surface; and the ideal covering and building material alike was brick of the improved fire-baked variety. By *c.* AD 70–80 huge yards in Rome and nearby began producing accurately shaped bricks on an industrial scale. At first walls made of this material were faced with stucco, plaster or marble. Since these facings have now disappeared, the masses of brick that remain visible at Rome and elsewhere present a misleading appearance. That is also true of Ostia, but to a more limited extent; for there a great many of the brick buildings that survive never possessed any such facings, since they belong to a later period when bricks, though occasionally picked out in vermilion paint, were for the most part left deliberately unconcealed.

The other leading Italian port was Aquileia at the head of the

Adriatic. This had enormously expanded its trade with the increasingly prosperous northern lands which were now under Roman rule; and it was the terminal of a new amber route to the Baltic via Carnuntum (Petronell) on the Danube. The manufacture of woollen goods also began to develop in north Italy. Another centre of the same activity became established at Pompeii, and a further Campanian industry was the glass of Capua, whose craftsmen had learnt the technique from Syria (p. 296) and now made their own product from pure white sand found at the mouth of the River Volturno. Red-glazed ceramic ware from the clay-beds of Arretium (Arezzo) came from relatively small workshops, of which the largest known possessed only fifty-eight slaves, but these pots circulated to most parts of the Mediterranean world – until overtaken by Gallic industries in the middle of the first century AD (p. 293).

Even if some people may have seen in this decentralisation an omen for the future, Italy still remained generally supreme. The senate and the army alike gave preference to its sons, and Vespasian (AD 69–79), who founded the second imperial dynasty, encouraged his portrait sculptors to devote their novel, refined techniques of light and shade to the faithful record and indeed exaggeration of his small-town Italian idiosyncracies.

A new synthesis of realism and monarchic grandeur was attempted by artists portraying Trajan (98–117), who of all emperors did the most to advance the frontiers far beyond the Mediterranean into eastern Europe and Mesopotamia. Dacia, with its Transylvanian gold and access to Black Sea ports, was retained for a century and half, but the precarious hold on the Persian gulf did not outlast the conqueror's lifetime. Trajan's horizons were wide because he was the first emperor who did not come from Italy. He had been born at Italica near Seville, and although his father was of Italian descent he had a Spanish mother. The birthplace of his adopted son and successor Hadrian (AD 117–38) was again Italica, his mother being a woman from Gades descended from people who had emigrated from Hadria (Atri in the Abruzzi) several centuries earlier. Similarly, Marcus Aurelius (161–80), the most philosophical of emperors, came from a family which had settled long ago at Uccubi near Corduba but subsequently returned to Rome.

These Spanish provinces, which after prolonged wars under Augustus now covered the entire peninsula, exported not only minerals (p. 265), but corn, oil, wine, pickled fish of which the Romans were very fond, and the finest brand of the fish sauce that they likewise greatly enjoyed. There were many new city foundations with Roman or half-Roman status, and Gades ranked second in the whole empire for the number of capitalists among its population. Latin had taken root in such spectacular fashion that Spain's record of distinguished authors, the two Senecas and the epic poet Lucan from Corduba, the epigrammatist Martial from Bilbilis (Calatayud), and the educationalist Quintilian from Calagurris (Calahorra), was equalled by no other province and indeed not by Italy itself.

Between the great Spanish emperors ruled one whose family came from Gaul, Antoninus Pius (138–61). Just as it had been the southern, Mediterranean, mostly highly Romanised part of Spain which produced his predecessors, so again the Romanised Midi of France was the home of Antoninus. His place of origin was the city of Nemausus (Nîmes), which had profited from Massalia's decline to absorb a large territory including a vine-growing plain in the valley of the Rhone; before long it was the provincial capital.

But prosperity was by no means limited to the Mediterranean part of Gaul. The whole country drew profit from the raw materials it provided to Rome, and its principal city lay a hundred and forty miles north of Nemausus, outside the original province. This was Lugdunum (Lyon), centrally situated at the meeting point of Rhône and Saone, and of latitudinal land-routes. Not far from the city, moreover, were two successive groups of factories which supplanted Italy as the main producers of terracotta ware; though by *c.* 200 decentralisation had gone to still further lengths, when the distant Rhineland was rivalling these factories and next became Europe's principal industrial zone.

The western Mediterranean, then, was gradually left behind, but meanwhile the eastern areas of the empire continued to operate their old trades and manufactures, and benefited from the Pax Romana to an enormous extent. Moreover, a great many of the best, in addition to the worst, things that were done in Rome itself as well as the rest of the empire were the work of people from these deeply influential countries.

The mainland of Greece, although its new capital Corinth revived as a Roman colony, did not itself become particularly prosperous, but continued to live on its wits, with which St Paul tried to compete in his famous speech at Athens. Marcus Aurelius flattered the Athenians by the creation of four Chairs of Philosophy, and Plutarch of Chaeronea wrote biographies which have exercised profound effects on the literature of the world. But, above all, these Greeks saw infinite possibilities of profit in migration to Rome. Their pervasiveness in every sphere of metropolitan life inspired scandalised, old-fashioned indignation in the impoverished Juvenal, who could not abide this Greek-struck Rome.[18]

But a far greater part was played by Asia Minor, which was so varied, populous and rich that it seemed a continent rather than a country. Trimalchio, the slave who in Petronius' novel the *Satyricon* became a millionaire, is symbolical of a huge influx of slaves from the Asian province. Some of them rose to greater wealth than anyone else in Rome – or became the intimate advisers of emperors. 'Asia is so rich and fertile', Cicero had remarked, 'that it easily surpasses all lands in the fruitfulness of its soil, the variety of its products, the dimensions of its pastures, and the number of things for export.'[19] The sufferings of the peninsula during the civil wars had been extremely costly, and yet recovery was rapid and complete, and prosperity soon soared. The extent to which the Augustan Peace brought all this immense wealth to maturity is illustrated by the hundreds of rich, autonomous towns in Asia Minor which were still allowed to issue their own bronze coins. Pergamum remained the formal capital of Asia, but Ephesus was its chief city and the governor's place of residence; though Smyrna (Izmir) in due course become more prosperous than either.

The principal exports of the province included the wine of its offshore islands, olive-oil, dried and preserved fruits, salted fish, timber, marble, pigments and precious stones. There was also extensive exportation of manufactured products such as the silk of Cos, the soft 'raven-black' wool with which Laodicea on the Lycus (near Denizli) began to outdo even Miletus, the proverbial cheap clay-ware of Samos, work in many metals, and the sculptures of independent long-lived schools of artists at Aphrodisias and elsewhere, producing portraits and the sarcophagus reliefs which became from *c.* AD 180 the most favoured medium for sculptors.

Asia Minor also imported from the east, and reexported to the west, a rich crop of semi-philosophical, semi-religious sages, confidence-tricksters, charlatans, and missionaries for the numerous emotional religions which had always been specialities of the region. The cult of the earth-mother Cybele, whose exciting mysteries and initiations had come from Phrygia and Lydia, competed with the Egyptian Isis in the huge scale of its infiltration throughout the empire; and the Persian sun-god Mithras, worshipped in at least sixty-eight shrines in Rome and Ostia alone, wore a Phrygian cap which showed the area from which he had first been brought to Italy, perhaps, it was said, by Cilician ex-pirates. It was Asia Minor, again, that became the scene of Christianity's first widespread triumphs, and ensured its subsequent expansion (p. 308).

The distinguished educational centres of Asia included medical schools at Smyrna, Ephesus, Laodicea on the Lycus and above all Pergamum, which superseded Cos and produced Galen (d. 199) who dominated later doctors for many generations. Among countless writers from these parts were the two Dios from Bithynia, Cocceianus 'the golden-mouthed' of Prusa (Brusa) and Dio Cassius the historian and senator whose birthplace was Nicaea (Iznik). The spicy short stories of Miletus had long been best-sellers, and the three most talented Greek romantic novelists of the second century AD, Charito, Xenophon and Longus (author of *Daphnis and Chloe*) came from Aphrodisias, Ephesus and Lesbos respectively.

But the complex origins of the novel are more particularly to be sought farther south, partly in Egypt where ancient stories were translated and imitated (p. 219), and partly in Syria where from the time of Alexander onwards Greek romances continued for half a millennium to tap the legends of Mesopotamia and other neighbouring lands. In Roman mythological collections such as Ovid's *Metamorphoses*, Syrian and Babylonian influences are strong; and the Greek novelist Heliodorus from Emesa (Homs), second to none in the third century

AD(?), told a story (the *Aethiopica*) redolent of many parts of the east.

Syria rivalled Asia Minor in prosperity. Although the Roman frontier on the Euphrates was a disturbed zone often involved in military operations with the Parthians, there was a good deal of coming and going through caravan-centres such as Beroea (Aleppo) and particularly Palmyra (Tadmor), where a flourishing composite civilisation, including fine portrait sculpture, helped to transmit many oriental features to the art of the later Roman empire.

Israel, which became the Roman province of Judaea or Syria Palaestina, experienced two formidable rebellions (AD 66–73, 132–35) – the former resulting in a destruction of Jerusalem which the latest excavations show to have been complete – but these did not prevent the imperial government from safeguarding the rights of Jewish communities in many provinces against hostile Greeks. Apart from such outbreaks, the Levant for the first time in its long history was now enjoying two and a half centuries of almost continuous peace. An imposing array of Syrian exports included the wines of Laodicea (Latakia), which also became one of the leading distribution-points for the regional production of textiles. Other centres of this industry were Byblos, Tyre and Berytus (Beirut), and the dyeing works of those and other Phoenician cities still retained their reputation. It was also probably the people of this coast who discovered the art of glass-blowing in *c.* 40–30 BC, an invention (imitated in Italy) which brought glass utensils within the economic range of many people who had not been able to afford them before (p. 292).

The sun-cults of Emesa and of the huge architectural precinct at Heliopolis (Baalbek) attracted pilgrims from far and wide. Not only did Christianity come from the Levant, but so also, on its way from Persia, did the belief in an evil creator of the world, a doctrine which was turned into a thoroughgoing Gnostic dualism of two divine powers and swept through the entire Mediterranean world. Syrian culture, too, kept pace with religion. The university of Antioch was outstanding; rhetoric was taught at a variety of centres, astronomy at Sidon, and medicine at Laodicea and Apamea, which also produced a philosopher, Numenius, who exercised a formative influence on the greatest thinker of the third century AD, the Egyptian neo-Platonist Plotinus. The outstanding Roman lawyers of the early third century AD, Papinian and Ulpian, were Syrians; and although the country was such a stronghold of Greek and Greco-oriental culture Berytus became the leading Latin-speaking school of law. Guilds of Syrian merchants maintained branches at every port, and developed a virtual monopoly of the Mediterranean carrying trade. Countless Levantine slaves had poured into Rome, and they and their descendants occupied increasingly important posts in national and commercial affairs. 'For years now', complained Juvenal, 'Orontes has poured its sewerage into our native Tiber.'[20]

The climax of this process came when the masterful, highly cultured Julia Domna, daughter of the high priest of Emesa, moved into the palace at Rome as the empress of Septimius Severus; and before long her Syrian relatives were on the imperial throne (218–35).

Severus himself, however, came from another part of the Mediterranean, namely Tripolitania, now in Libya and at that time an extension of the province of Africa. His birthplace, Lepcis Magna, was made into a city of great magnificence. This and the two other towns which were later merged into Tripoli possessed a fertile hinterland that swelled the supplies of grain sent from these coasts to Rome. Recent investigations of Thapsus (Ras Dimas) show that the surviving four hundred and thirty-seven foot mole extends 2,926 feet under water, which makes it the largest free-standing Roman mole in existence. Great oil-presses, too, have been found in the African province; and the coincidence of the Roman Sahara frontier with the southernmost limit of olive terraces shows how much this slowly maturing tree needed the Pax Romana to flourish.

Rebuilt a century after its demolition (p. 272), Carthage became one of the empire's leading cultural centres, especially notable for its flamboyant orators and clever jurists. Moreover, for a very long time – from the second century AD right up to the fourth – north Africa succeeded Spain as homeland of the most remarkable Latin writers in the empire. The greatest of all legal authorities, Salvius Julianus (*c.* 100–69), came from a village south of Carthage, the scintillating versatile Latin novelist and popular speaker Apuleius originated from Madaurus – a Numidian town of ex-legionaries, Berbers and Carthaginians – and the most formidable eloquent of Latin Christian writers, Tertullian, was born at Carthage itself. Septimius Severus himself was a lawyer who spoke Latin with a Carthaginian accent.

His portrait-busts make him look rather like Marcus Aurelius, but this deliberate resemblance is deceptive. Although both were exceptional Romans – in the wider, non-racial sense in which the name must henceforward be used – Severus was the first emperor who was not a native of Europe, and he did not see Italy as the centre of the earth. For when the interests of imperial defence required that the whole Roman world must be controlled by a tough dictatorial bureaucracy and subjected to far stiffer taxes, Italy did not enjoy exemption any more. There had long been a centrifugal movement of trade into more northern countries (p. 293), and now this process of Italian decline was extended by Severus in the fiscal and political and military spheres. His son Caracalla went further still, by extending Roman citizenship, which had formerly been the closed preserve of Italy and relatively sparse centres overseas, to free men throughout the entire imperial world. Only 204 out of 479 senators now came from Italy; the fact that it was garrisoned for the first time with legionary troops illustrated this gradual relegation to the status of a province. And indeed, since all eyes were turned towards the distant, threatened frontiers, the whole Mediterranean area was soon subordinated to their needs and consequently began to lose the supremacy which it had held for so many centuries.

Mare nostrum

During the first two hundred years of the régime established by Augustus the unprecedented unity of this entire Mediterranean world had enormously facilitated intercommunication. Ports were full of trade-guilds from all over the empire, each devoted to a special aspect of maritime commerce, and enjoying legal rights and tax concessions. The most privileged of all were the shipowners who conveyed corn and other public cargoes to Rome and the army's maritime bases. But at Ostia, for example, there were not only shipowners, but shipwrights, caulkers, riggers, sandmen, divers, stevedores, warehousemen and watchmen, as well as groups composed of dealers in grain, wine, oil, hides and a host of other commodities.

Merchant vessels, some of them designed for the use both of sails and oars, had raked-forward mainmasts and foremasts and strongly built hulls, rounded like modern sailing trawlers but lower in the bows because they still sailed mainly before the wind. Corn-ships attained sizes that had never been seen in the Mediterranean before, carrying up to six hundred passengers and three hundred and forty tons of cargo, or even, in the top priority grain fleet, as much as twelve hundred, a burden not exceeded for another seventeen centuries.

One such craft of the second century AD, with its red top-sail, figure of Isis at the prow, and gilded goose's head at the stern, was described with admiration by the popular Greco-Syrian essayist Lucian, who remarked that the grain it carried on a simple voyage was enough to have fed the whole population of Athens for a year.[21]

In spite of all the technical improvements since earlier times, shippers still did not accept cargoes between 10th October and 31 March. Even imperial couriers would not risk long Mediterranean journeys during the winter; it was typical of the desperate determination of Agrippina, eager to avenge her husband Germanicus (d. AD 19), that she did not let even winter storms deter her. During the summer, freighters from Ostia to Alexandria took ten to fourteen days with the wind at their heels, travelling by way of Athens and Rhodes. But the return journey might take a very great deal longer since it usually involved a roundabout route via Cyprus, and northerly winds sometimes cut Rome off from Egypt for weeks at a time.*

For although poets might speak in their rhetorical way of the sea now being more thickly peopled than the land, the Mediterranean was still a hard master at any season. The ship Lucian so admired had been seven days out of Alexandria, with the north-west seaboard of Cyprus already in sight, when a contrary gale drove it into Sidon; and even then Cyprus was only reached after a narrow escape from shipwreck off the Cilician coast. Finally, after tacking against the northerlies, the vessel

* Though a favourable wind could bring travellers from Alexandria to Sicily in less than a week.

had got as far as the Piraeus, on the seventieth day after embarkation. And even then the western Mediterranean, much less safe than its easterly counterpart, was still to come.

Latin and Greek literature of the time remained full of shipwrecks and narrow escapes. Virgil devoted his full eloquence to the devilish hazards which Aeneas, like Odysseus, had to face at sea.[22] St Paul's missionary journeys included three shipwrecks; 'a night and day I have been on the deep'.[23] And then the Asian ship on which he went as a prisoner from Judaean Caesarea to Rome, travelling at the very end of the season, was caught in a storm off Crete, had to jettison part of its cargo, drifted westwards for fourteen days, and broke up on the coast of Melita (Malta) after its passengers had swum ashore.[24]

And yet, for all these perils, the outstanding feature of Paul's travels remains their enormous international range. 'Whensoever I take my journey to Spain', he assures the Romans, 'I will come to you . . . but now I go unto Jerusalem.'[25] Here is a Hellenised Jew from Tarsus writing from Corinth to plan a visit to Spain via Jerusalem and Rome, of which he is a citizen. A few years later Petronius shows how despite every hazard there were millions to be made amid these vast Mediterranean horizons. For Trimalchio is made to tell how, after losing his five ships and their wine cargo in a storm, he got together money to build bigger and better replacements, and then invested in a further cargo of wine, bacon, beans, scents and slaves, laying the foundation of his enormous fortune.[26]

The emperors did all they could to make the Mediterranean safe. When Augustus became sole ruler less than forty years had passed since Pompey broke the large-scale menace of piracy off the Cilician coast; and now further and final measures exterminated these robbers of the sea. The Roman fleet, which Pompey had revived for his campaign, was placed on a permanent basis in order to guard the sea from end to end. Its two main headquarters were on the Italian coast. The principal base guarding the home end of the grain routes was close to Cumae at the western extremity of the bay of Naples, where beneath the lee of Cape Misenum a submerged crater was converted into a sheltered harbour. This was linked by a narrow, bridged channel to an outer anchorage facing south-east and improved by parallel arcaded moles protruding from the promontory,

The port of Misenum could hold fifty large warships in addition to many smaller craft.

Augustus' second naval station, designed to patrol the Adriatic, was located at Ravenna, which five centuries later was destined to become the capital of Italy. This place, an offshoot of Spina in the distant days of Greek and Etruscan commercial activity, was situated south of the Po delta, and its shore was visited by just enough tide to keep sedimentation down to tolerable levels for a long time to come. The port of Ravenna with its moles and lighthouse stood on a lagoon linked by canals to the river and town, which was described in terms foreshadowing Venice as 'the largest city in the marshes, built of wood and intersected by water; bridges and ferries provide the thoroughfares.'[27]

In the east the emperors maintained three naval stations for light, fast squadrons, at Alexandria, Antioch's port Seleucia, and the island of Carpathos midway between Rhodes and Crete. In east and west alike the imperial sailors, all free men, belonged to the traditional seafaring nations of Phoenicia, Syria, Egypt and Greece.

So Mediterranean interchanges were protected from the brigandage of the past. There were internal customs-duties, but they were for purposes of revenue, not protection or restriction. This conversion of the entire area into a single commercial unit was an event without previous precedent or subsequent parallel. The unification had, it is true, largely been achieved by force; and yet its results could be enjoyed by all. The conversion of conquest into prosperity was the work of Augustus, and as during the last days of his life he was sailing past Puteoli, the passengers and crew of an Alexandrian ship hailed him as the man who had given them freedom to keep their possessions safely and sail the sea.[28]

Moreover, freedom of the Mediterranean meant easier travel far inland from its coasts. A Persian, as Seneca observed, can now take a drink from the Rhine,[29] and Aelius Aristides, an Asian Greek, delivered a long and lyrical tribute to the universal communications throughout the whole of the Roman empire. 'Greek and barbarian, with his property or without it, can go with ease wherever he likes, just as though moving from one homeland to another'.[30]

And yet the scope of this trading must not be exaggerated; for there were decided limitations. Not only was sea-transport hazardous and land-transport prohibitively expensive, but credit and banking facilities, in spite of improvements (p. 278), remained cautious and immature. And most significant of all, every kind of commercial and industrial operation was completely subordinated to the needs of agriculture, which remained incomparably the most important industry of almost every part of the empire and by far the greatest source of its wealth.

The principal cereal crop of the empire was wheat, and next came barley, used mainly by this time as animal food and in some regions also for beer. Water mills were known by the time of Augustus, but only came into common use in the third or fourth century AD. With regard to wine-making, on the other hand, an important technical change under the early emperors was the adoption from the Celts of metal-hooped wooden casks which kept wine in much better condition than the old terracotta jars.

On the whole, however, there were few technical advances, since a slave economy made no demand for them. And yet there were fewer prisoners of war, so that slaves were diminishing in numbers. This meant that the characteristic agricultural figure in early Italy was no longer the large ranch-owner, but a small or medium tenant farmer (colonus) who paid part of his produce (or the equivalent in money) in return for the use of land and stock.

To northern Italy, where the original settlers had been given quite large allotments (p. 269), this system came naturally; during the first and second centuries AD it spread to the rest of the peninsula. Nor was this the only respect in which the northern Italians now took the lead. Their provision of soldiers to the imperial armies had already been substantial, and so was the development of their cities and flourishing woollen trade. The fertile productivity of the Po valley was outstanding, and its heavy soils were now able to benefit from a wheeled plough introduced from the upper Danube. As the Italian peninsula gradually faded from the forefront after AD 200, north Italy, closer to the critical frontier zones, became ever more important.

From Rome to Constantinople

The displacement of Italy's focal point from Rome to the Po valley was related to a general diminution of the Mediterranean's significance in favour of more northern lands (p. 293); and both phenomena resulted, in part, from the time when Caesar had advanced the frontier to the Rhine, and Augustus, following up various explorations during the previous century, moved forward from the Alps along the whole length of the Danube.

But the full consequences of these enlargements only became apparent under Marcus Aurelius, when population pressures from the European interior impelled unprecedented hordes of Germans against the river boundary (166). They came as far as the head of the Adriatic, where Opitergium (Oderzo) near Aquileia was burnt, and Aquileia itself besieged; others even broke through into the Balkans and penetrated as far as Eleusis on the Corinthian Gulf. Such were the terrible happenings and portents which led Severus to a stringent tightening of government and taxation everywhere (p. 298). The need for such measures seemed greater still when the empire's frontiers in the east became as gravely menaced as its northern borders. For the Persian (Sassanian) empire replaced Parthia (*c.* 224), and confronted the Romans with a far more formidable enemy than they had ever faced in that region before.

During the half century that followed, both frontiers were repeatedly penetrated and overrun by Germans and Persians, while central authority in the empire crumbled. The Mediterranean region, wholly subordinated to the border-zones, was repeatedly plundered by invaders whom the defenders on the river lines had proved unable to stop. And so, after ravaging the northern confines of the empire, the German tribe of the Franks broke through as far as Tarraco in Spain; and in Asia Minor, already laid waste by the Persians, the Goths who were the most formidable of all German groupings sacked Ephesus, Chalcedon, and Trapezus, as well as Panticapaeum (Kertch), the capital of the corn-producing Crimean Bosphorus (p. 182).

A huge muster of hostile tribesmen at the mouth of the Dniester (268) led to further devastations, but in the same year a victory on land at Naissus (Niş) on the Morava enabled the emperor Gallienus to begin the turning of the tide. His successors,

Claudius II Gothicus and Aurelian, performed a stupendous task of recovery by overwhelming German armies (Alamanni) in three battles fought on north Italian soil (268–271); and then Probus finally reestablished the Rhine and Danube frontiers (277–79).

Aurelian had also dealt with another equally grave danger, the chaotic proliferation of dissident pretenders within the empire itself. At an exceptionally disastrous moment when Valerian was captured by the Persians (259), the western provinces of Gaul, Britain and Spain detached themselves under Postumus and his successors. Next, all the eastern provinces as well, already virtually autonomous under the powerful caravan city of Palmyra in the Syrian desert, were made into an independent empire by Queen Zenobia (268). Through a Herculean double effort Aurelian suppressed both these separatist régimes.

The Roman world had been forced to adjust itself to these grim years. State control was constantly on the increase, particularly in relation to guilds of national importance such as shipowners, who were eventually subjected to such severe compulsion that sons were forced to follow the profession of their fathers. Meanwhile, in the devastated countrysides, great landowners formed huge embattled ranches, which attracted crowds of refugees and displaced and starving persons.

Another result of these convulsions was the demonstration of the need to give this menaced empire a new capital, or more than one. For Rome, which had long been a parasite, was far away from the places that now mattered and from the communications networks on which imperial defence and unity depended (p. 307). Furthermore, most of the emperors who successively struggled with this crumbling world were men who had not originated from the Mediterranean area at all, but came from Danubian (Illyrian) provinces whose soldiers now bore the brunt of successive wars. For such was the origin of Decius (249–51) who lost his life against the Germans (in the Dobrogea), and of Claudius Gothicus and Aurelian and Probus who led the almost incredible revival.

Rulers of this type revered Rome for its prestige and traditions, but felt obliged to live nearer the principal camps and military operations. Since, however, there were two menaced frontiers and not one, Valerian (253–60) began to draw an inevitable conclusion when he instituted two separate imperial headquarters, moving to Antioch himself and leaving his son Gallienus in charge of the west. And when Gallienus subsequently formed a new and powerful cavalry army (264–68) to give him more mobility in dealing with his external and internal enemies, this was based not on Rome but on Mediolanum (Milan), which a new defence system linked with Aquileia, Verona and Ticinum (Pavia). This plan was all the more urgently needed because the enemy were now so close: the large reentrant area between the upper Rhine and Danube had been occupied by Germans and evacuated by Rome for ever, and Dacia (Rumania) was also soon to go.

The idea of dividing the empire between the ruler and his son persisted, and Diocletian (284–305), another Illyrian of genius, instituted its formal partition into two main parts. Each of these great units was ruled by one of a pair of senior imperial colleagues, and each of these Augusti, in their turn, divided his share between himself and a junior emperor or Caesar. For his own capital city Diocletian chose the Asian bank of the Sea of Marmara, establishing himself at Nicomedia (Izmit), a city founded by a king of Bithynia (264 BC) at the head of a deep gulf backed by a large and fertile territory. Nicomedia was now adorned with imposing architecture, which has vanished but can be imagined from the palace to which Diocletian retired after abdication, at Salonae (Split) in Dalmatia. But the main importance of the new imperial capital was derived from its central location, facing two ways upon the routes which linked the Danube and Euphrates frontiers.

Diocletian's subordinate emperor, Galerius Caesar, resided at Thessalonica (Salonica) in Macedonia. This city, dating from the early third century BC, possessed a silt-free port at a strategic situation on the Via Egnatia which led from the Adriatic towards the Black Sea. But more important still were longitudinal communications leading up into the Balkans. For the adjacent River Axius (Vardar) forms a southern extension of the valley of the Morava, which joins the Danube near Singidunum (Belgrade) and the even more important military centre of Sirmium (Sremska Mitrovica). Consequently Thessalonica served as strategic rear headquarters to the Danubian front. Its elevation to imperial status was signalised by the construction of a magnificent, massive palace complex, including an Arch of Galerius covered with reliefs which show a new anti-humanistic sort of flat, stocky, inorganic figures, dominated by the divine eternal supremacy of the rulers.

Both these eastern capitals are maritime, whereas each of their western counterparts lay inland – Mediolanum and Augusta Trevirorum (Trier). North Italy was an obvious place for a capital (p. 302), but Augusta Trevirorum on the Moselle, with its imperial buildings as great as Thessalonica's (and much better preserved), is an even more significant portent of the times, since the Mediterranean, round which the classical civilisations had centred, is nearly four hundred miles away from this place now selected as an imperial residence.

And yet, even if the armies, major industries, and attentions of the emperors were now concentrated upon the frontier areas, the sites of Nicomedia and Thessalonica supplied reminders that the sea was still a thoroughfare which provided a unique and irreplaceable service to the whole empire – and the only means whereby the new joint rulers, until the system broke down with Diocletian's departure, were able to act as colleagues rather than independent rulers. This continued importance of the sea was underlined by the new administrative arrangements of Diocletian, since the thirteen 'dioceses' (replacing the old provincial system) into which the empire was now subdivided still included no less than ten which possessed Mediterranean coastlines.

Constantine the Great (306–37) was able for the last dozen years of his life to rule over a single unified empire again. He had resided at a number of centres – and, being yet another Illyrian, was not influenced by traditional preoccupations in his choice of a capital. Indeed, he was said to have thought of his own birthplace, Naissus (Niş), where several roads meet. Another place which was believed to have crossed his mind (though the same thing had been rumoured of earlier rulers) was Troy. Yet the centre which he finally chose, and renamed Constantinople, was the ancient Greek colony of Byzantium. In addition to the unique general advantages of its geographical position (p. 178), the place was located even more favourably than Nicomedia for direct operations on the Danube and Euphrates fronts alike. For in Europe, a major line of communications ran through Hadrianopolis (Edirne), Serdica (Sofia), and Naissus up to Sirmium; and the eastern border was accessible not only by road but by sea-routes leading both to Syria and through the Black Sea to Trapezus.

It seemed to Constantine that this capital could control the east without losing its grip on the west. This proved, in the end, impossible, since when barbarian invaders had torn off one western territory after another, their recapture by Justinian (527–65) proved impermanent. Yet it was Constantinople which had sealed off and protected Asia Minor and the east from these barbarian incursions, and which then twice held out against the Arabs and prevented them from conquering the whole of the Mediterranean and Greco-Roman world.

As the city had already shown by prolonged resistance to Severus, impregnable fortification was possible both by sea and land, and a superb base was available for the navies which Constantine's operations against his own former colleagues had given a role larger than the policing duties of previous centuries. The new capital was within reach of the grain of Egypt and gave access to the rich industries, cities, cultures, teeming populations and recruiting agencies of Asia Minor, which had survived Gothic raids to become the empire's principal reservoir of all these resources. And so Constantinople displayed an 'extraordinary concentration, within a small, confined area, of all the forces making for survival'.[31] Before long, too, the city was destined to be enlarged on a glorious scale, and endowed with artistic masterpieces developing styles that embodied a subtle new intermixture of the qualities of Greece, Rome and the east.

But an even more remarkable example of such cultural adoptions and fusions was apparent in the second main element of Constantine's lifework, his adoption of Christianity as the official religion of the Roman state. Its non-Mediterranean origins were indicated by a transcendent Hebrew monotheism which firmly rejected the Greek idea that god was only man writ large. Yet, like its parent Judaism, the Christian doctrine had spread round the shores of the Mediterranean by means of the well-kept roads and peaceful sea routes of the imperial Pax Romana. After Paul had supported the section of opinion, among the first Christians, which decided to spread the new gospel outside the Jewish sphere, particularly strong roots had been laid down in the coastlands of his native Asia Minor, which were so receptive to all manner of beliefs; and the divine Mother, Mary, was herself widely held to have come to Ephesus. Nevertheless Ignatius (d. *c.* 117) felt it necessary to warn the cities of the region not to allow their faith to become just another worship of a suffering god, like all the many other offshoots of the old pagan cults of annual rebirth: never, he said, abandon belief in the humanity of Jesus, which is the distinctive feature of the religion.

For the early Church suffered from a host of varied interpretations and scriptures, especially in Asia Minor, and one of its most decisive achievements was the reduction of this mass of divergent literature into a limited and recognised canon. Greeks of those parts, such as Irenaeus of Smyrna, defended Christianity in many countries against its enemies, and then the Christian school at Alexandria, led by Clement and Origen (d. 254 and 255), sought to create a whole intellectually satisfying philosophy of Christianity. The religion also now received its first defenders in Latin, notably the scathingly eloquent north African Tertullian.

Nevertheless, the inevitable separateness of most believers from contemporary Greco-Roman society bred unpopularity which led to persecutions, especially under Decius and Valerian and Diocletian. Persecution caused a split among Christians, for in Asia Minor and then Syria and north Africa puritans accused the official churches of treating temporary renegades with too great leniency, which they attributed to an excessively Greco-Roman attitude. For what, asked Tertullian, 'has Athens to do with Jerusalem?'[32] The difficulty of reconciling his faith to the ancient Mediterranean culture could not have been more explicitly expressed; and Christianity, though gradually expanding, remained for the time being the religion of a comparatively unimportant minority.

And yet when the persecution of Diocletian was generally felt to have overreached itself, Constantine took the remarkable decision, inspired by sincere if theologically muddled personal belief, to make this his official religion. Many cults from the east had swept over the empire without such a sensational result. Here is the last, most spectacular and most influential example of the phenomenon, so frequent throughout antiquity, of an eastern institution moving westwards and taking roots in the Mediterranean area, but becoming transformed in the process.

The Council of Nicaea (Iznik) in Bithynia (325), summoned to deal with deviations, proclaimed three Mediterranean cities to be patriarchal sees: Rome, Alexandria in Egypt where a great wave of asceticism had led to the monastic movement, and Antioch – in Syria which had first given Christianity a strong regional native cast. But before long Constantinople, though respectful of Rome's traditions, claimed to be its equal, and the long history of the split between Catholicism and Orthodoxy was reaching a critical stage. The rift became accentuated when the empire was permanently cut in two parts, and divided between two emperors, by a longitudinal line running from Sirmium to the borders of Tripolitania and Cyrenaica (395). During the next century the west crumbled away out of Roman hands, creating a political as well as a religious division between Mediterranean lands. The unity of the area, which had lasted for only five centuries out of all these millennia of history, was at an end.

Appendix: Mediterranean Places and People

The people of the ancient world often believed that modes of life are directly created and differentiated by physical surroundings. 'Soft countries breed soft men', King Cyrus of Persia is reported to have said. 'It is not the property of any one soil to produce fine fruits and good soldiers too.'[1] And that, according to Herodotus, is why the Persians chose to live in a rugged land and rule, rather than cultivate rich plains and become slaves (p. 196). Another Greek author, whose name we do not know, pursued the same determinist approach in an essay *About Winds, Waters and Places* which explained national characteristics according to climates and soils.[2]

Such generalisations, though no doubt over-simplified, were at least right in attempting an analysis of environment, which the historian must consider in relation to communities just as a psychologist has to study the environment of individuals. Without a geographical basis, said Michelet (1833), the people who make history are walking on air; and H.T.Buckle pronounced that the four most influential physical agencies are climate, food, soil and the general aspect of nature, which he thought of as interacting with man by a process of reciprocal modification (1857).

Like many others after him, Buckle had less to say about man's action upon nature than about nature's upon man. In the hands of nationalistically minded geographers, this bias was intensified by the further idea that civilisations remain linked by a plant-like attachment to the territories in which they have come into flower. Historians too, adopting similar ideas, conceived of an almost mystical bond between state and soil which soon took on a racial character.

On a popular plane, this racialism is expressed today by

assertions – with more or less conscious biological implications – that all Frenchmen are like this, and all Germans like that. Such generalisations, however, tend to be wide of the mark, since there can as yet be little scientific basis for them, the genetical distinctions between racial groups being still unknown. Least of all can any racial conclusions be applied to the ancient world, because the science which attempts to deduce genes from the measurements of surviving skulls and skeletons has not yet produced any conclusive results. Furthermore, as the present study has suggested, races have always been deeply and inextricably mixed since the very beginnings of civilisation, and indeed of human life. In dealing, therefore, with the ancient Mediterranean peoples, racial factors cannot be made to yield any useful deductions.

Leaving race out of the question, then, we are back with environment; and many who refused to be racialists have preferred to join the ancients in the deterministic belief that it is environment, not heredity, which has dictated to us what we have to be. However, very few geographers would now venture to identify definite characteristics *inherent* in a particular region, or imply that cultures have permanent attachments to particular spots. A step towards a more subtle and flexible approach was reached with the declaration that 'earth has given man his problems – and at the same time *whispered hints* for their solution' (1911).[3] But why, in that case, since we must judge by results, has nature whispered one hint to one community, and quite another to the next, though apparently its circumstances may not be so very different?

This difficulty is met by the 'possibilist' interpretation, suggested to geographers originally by the variety-within-unity to be seen in France. The solution now was that any given area offers certain more or less limited possibilities, and that the occupants choose from these according to their needs, powers and whims. 'Geography can only recommend a site; if there are not men capable of using it, or if motives good or bad deter those who might have done so, she speaks in vain.'[4] An intermediate standpoint, agreeing that a region is a medal struck in its people's effigy,[5] yet still leaning towards the old idea of natural causes producing human effects, prefers a 'stop and go' position: nature changes the traffic lights and man acts accordingly. But the lights go on and off very irregularly, and they do not go on and off by themselves but because of the agency of man, who still remains, therefore, at least partly master of the situation.

Every land, then, presents different possibilities to every set of people that inhabit it. These possibilities are not infinite; there will not be a bronze industry where copper and tin are unprocurable. Yet at each successive stage man's geographical environment gives him certain opportunities for alternative decisions. He may select from among these alternatives, consciously or unconsciously, a course which leads to remarkable things. Ten million times more often, the courses chosen have led to nothing an historian can mention or regard as significant. But from time to time opportunities have arrived and been seized with both hands. The English industrial revolution was just such an opportunity, in which uniquely suitable time, place and circumstances coincided. The opportunity could be taken or left; and it was taken. The Portugal of the explorers, on the margin of the old Mediterranean world and facing the unknown ocean, could exploit its knowledge of the Mediterranean past to brave the unknown. When men rose to the occasion so remarkably, then and only then could nature's gifts produce their full effect in human achievement.

In about the tenth millennium BC people inhabiting the foothills between Taurus and Zagros had the astonishing good fortune to be living in a country where wheat, barley, sheep and goats all grew wild (p. 13). But this would have profited them nothing and been of no use to subsequent generations if they had not somehow decided and managed to begin domestication: which they did. Similarly, 'the Greeks were needed to develop Athenian civilisation, and neither the Greeks elsewhere norany other race in Greece would have been equal to the task'.[6]

As the ancient writer *About Winds, Waters and Places* already appreciated, climate has a good deal to do with this. 'Where the changes of the seasons are most frequent and most sharply contrasted, there you will find the greatest diversity in physique, in character and in constitution. It is changes of all things that raise the temper of man and prevent its stagnation.'[7] Abrupt climatic variations keep Mediterranean man in a perpetual state of readjustment which prevents sluggishness. And in particular, a climate which includes an unproductive season requires that a surplus be stored over against this season, and consequently stimulates invention, foresight and thrift: as well as providing months of unavoidable, invaluable leisure for the enterprises of higher civilisation.

This unproductive season is one form taken by the challenge which Arnold Toynbee saw as a dominant factor in social and cultural growth. Denying the necessity of a *favourable* climate on which others had tried to insist,[8] he concluded that the greater ease of the environment, the weaker the stimulus towards civilisation. Within limits, of course, since to be surmountable the challenge must not be too great; the north and south poles are ill-suited to become cradles of development. But provided that conditions are not so rigorous that they stunt man's mind or body, the greater his needs the more vigorous and effectively he will exert himself.

The Mediterranean area always provides a tantalising paradox of fruitfulness and frugality, rich both in suggestions and obstacles. Conditions are exceptionally discouraging and exceptionally favourable at the same time. People must never relax their efforts to direct nature and correct and check it, and keep it under control. Life is magnificent, but precarious;[9] marvellous growth and total extinction are both possible. The challenge is clearly seen in the great civilisations – in Egyptians taming their torrid water-logged jungles, Cretans exploiting their central position on stormy sea-routes, Syrians using their vulnerable situation to absorb and transmit alien cultures, Phoenicians and Greeks exploring beyond their mountain-bound narrowness, Romans overcoming the ring of enemies that history and geography had placed around them.

To make nature into an ally needed enormous efforts, and the changes imposed by human beings upon their environment from the most ancient times have been shown by much recent research to have been unexpectedly vast. This landscape, on which man has always exercised 'a profound effect much beyond what might be expected from his numbers',[10] has been compared to a print from a metallic plate of varied composition, texture and regularity, on which a corrosive fluid, namely human activity in all its manifestations and with all its experiences, has worked out a pattern and created a new surface.[11] Nowhere is this effect of man on nature as inextricably all-pervading as in the Mediterranean. To say that one of its inhabitants 'can see every day in his own harbours, and in his own fields, scenes which seem to be contemporaneous with Homer',[12] rightly and picturesquely calls attention to permanent, underlying conditions. Nevertheless, stated without qualification, it is also misleading. For it seems to suggest that these conditions are the predominating circumstance, whereas, in fact, there is no place on earth where so much has been changed by human agency. The French landscape first revealed that many of its characteristic and apparently native features in fact owe less to physical configuration than to systems of tenure and inheritance.[13] When Herodotus called Egypt the gift of the Nile, he was only telling half the story. The Egyptian landscape, like others, has been powerfully humanised. No wonder that Protagoras, who de-declared that man is the measure of all things, himself came from Mediterranean shores.

These considerations do not, of course, take away the importance of environment, since man can only redirect in accordance with whatever physical facts are offered, and these are as powerfully directive in the Mediterranean as anywhere else in the world. But what they have directed man to do is to change them: to transform them out of all recognition. Even such an apparently permanent feature as the coastline itself, which has so greatly influenced history, turns out to owe an enormous amount to human agencies. When a modern tourist visits Ephesus or a dozen other cities, and finds that the harbour is no longer even in sight, this is because it has been silted up owing to erosion which is largely due to man-made causes. Byron was mistaken in believing that Time wrote no wrinkle on the Mediterranean's azure brow.

Modern geographers have duly stressed these human alterations to nature. But they have usually left it to others to speak about the principal means by which the Mediterranean communities were able to create their stamp that was to be imprinted on the medal of nature. It is, instead, the archaeologists and art historians who have shown how this was done by borrowing from the east. If, as has lately been remarked, the essence of geography is movement, this applies with special force to the human movements which have brought cultures westwards to the Mediterranean area. Economic borrowings rapidly led to cultural, along the same great routes. Sometimes it was forms that travelled, and sometimes ideas, including Christianity.

And then, as has been seen, the elements imported from these varied eastern sources, or conveyed from one part of the Mediterranean to another, were fused and transformed almost out of recognition. Georges Braque described the obsession and hallucination of artists as preceded by impregnation. The impregnation of his ancient predecessors, the material which dictated the conditions they could exploit, came not only from their natural and partially man-made environment, but also from far away in the east. Mediterranean man on the whole disposed of no great gift of total originality, and yet he possessed this astonishing, peculiar talent for transfiguring these acculturations into something wonderfully new.

Borrowings from elsewhere, then, as well as natural environments and the changes men have wrought upon them, all contribute towards the total culture of the Mediterranean peoples. And yet, the picture still remains curiously incomplete. *Just why*, for example, Athens produced its plethora of brilliant practitioners in a host of different fields all at the very same time still remains imperfectly explained. The range of opportunities from which the Athenian was able to choose can be described. But there is a gap in our knowledge, because we still cannot give the actual reasons for their making the astonishing choices that they did.

The Greek historian Polybius recognised the problem and decided that it is best merely to identify this further, unknown, apparently indefinable factor with Chance or Fortune (Tyche). In his Greco-Roman world, disillusioned with the old religions, Chance was often spoken of and deeply respected, and Polybius' account of the foundation of Roman power, while trying in each individual case to provide other and specific explanations, felt obliged to add Chance as a further causative element built into the order of the universe. Fatalists preferred to call this factor destiny – often described in astrological terms.

> Time and the ocean and some fostering star
> In high cabal have made us what we are.

Religious people, on the other hand, seeing the hand of God or the Gods, instead described the additional, unaccountable element as Providence.

> All nature is but art, unknown to thee:
> All chance, direction, which thou canst not see.[14]

When the last of antiquity's great eastern influences, the Christian faith, invaded the Mediterranean world and finally abolished its already failing humanism, this providential view of history so strongly prevailed that the other accountable elements in history, such as environment and borrowing, tended to be lost sight of. But Renaissance writers, with various degrees of explicitness, suggested instead that the unaccountable factors, with a bit of research, might instead become accountable after all. If someone, said Francis Bacon, 'look sharply and attentively he shall see Fortune – for though she is blind, she is not invisible'. Such an attitude, however, now seems over-confident; though environments and borrowings explain many features in Mediterranean men and women, there still remain questions for which neither history or geography yet have any answer.

The Victorian, Carlylean view of history as a gallery of Great Men in their Hall of Fame became uncomfortably associated with fascist superman associations. Now, on the other hand, the contrary fashion of seeing great men as mere manifestations of tendencies or 'labels giving names to events',[15] has in its turn gone too far. During the ancient world in particular, leading men were far from being mere labels or cogs, since decisive happenings and developments were engineered by the minutest proportion of the population, the apex of a pyramid which is huge but totally invisible. All we can do is to 'see society as that part of the population which, at a certain time, can be regarded as the necessary background for the creative individual'.[16] But the principal theme has to be that creative individual himself – not owing to any lack of democratic feeling in the modern historian but because the history of antiquity depended to so vast an extent on these very few people. They were only labels for events in the sense that whatever influences of environment and borrowing their communities underwent affected them also, as members of those communities. But the creative individuals worked on these influences to understand and control and change them, while the influences at the same time stimulated, challenged and channelled their creative responses.

'I'll tell you what,' replied Themistocles to an islander's sneer that he owed all his success to his Athenian background. 'I should not have been honoured as I was if I had been born a Seriphian like you – nor would you, if you had been born at Athens.' Again Chance or Providence has intervened, because the influences have to come at just the right place and time. Themistocles' answer does justice to the significance of place; but the emergence of great men is equally susceptible to factors of timing. 'Not every man fits every hour. A given genius may come too early or too late. Peter the Hermit would now be sent to an insane asylum. John Stuart Mill in the tenth century would have lived and died unknown.'[17]

> Some village Hampden, that with dauntless breast
> The little tyrant of his field withstood,
> Some mute inglorious Milton here may rest,
> Some Cromwell guiltless of his country's blood.[18]

History being a success story (p. xvi), there is nothing we can do to make these *manqués* great men any less mute and inglorious. But a far more serious problem is raised by men who truly achieved great and famous things in their day, but are now not even names to us.

> Ere Agamemnon men were bold,
> But all in night are swept away.
> Because, of them, no bard has told,
> Unheard of and unwept are they.[19]

These words of Horace do pinpoint an embarrassing difference between history and prehistory. Even literate epochs of ancient history, it is true, are not quite the same thing as a more modern age, for we do not really know much, for certain and without bias, about most of their leading figures, and often we know very little indeed. The people of prehistory, on the other hand, are not imperfectly known, but totally unknown and lost. Occasionally an evident personality emerges for a moment from the mist – perhaps in a human-looking gold mask of Mycenae – but, except that he was not the Agamemnon he was prematurely proclaimed to be, we have no knowledge whatever about him or about anything he did or thought.

From some highly important regions, such as the Egyptian delta, scarcely anything of a fabulous past survives. Besides, even material remains are not always much use; as Thucydides pointed out while the classical cities were still standing, a visitor would make precious little of the extraordinary institutions of Sparta just by looking at the town. However, we do happen to know something at least about Sparta from literature, whereas most of the great cities of prehistory have left no such record but only material remains, and highly fragmentary remains at that.

And yet it is perfectly obvious that, however many processes were gradual, there were also huge pushes which must have come from individuals of immense calibre. In prehistory, as in history, it was certainly not through a lot of burrowing moles that all the great apocalyptic discontinuities occurred. The fact that we do not know who was responsible for them is subjective to ourselves, and means we have to use all available disciplines to find out, by peripheral means, such few things as we can. But it does not mean that we ought to regard prehistory and history as different orders of happenings, for they were not, and this applies to the Mediterranean area as much as to anywhere else, or even more (p. xiv). That is why an attempt has been made to bring them together in this book.

References

Preface

1 Samuel Johnson
2 O.Halecki
3 C.McEvedy (1967)
4 E.H.Carr

1 The Mediterranean and its Beginnings

1 Paul Morand
2 Lord Byron
3 Guy de Maupassant
4 T.S.Eliot
5 Freya Stark
6 E.M.Forster
7 Cf. Str. xvi, 2, 28, 759
8 Stuart Piggott
9 P.J.Ucko and A.Rosenfeld, *Palaeolithic Cave Art* (1967), p. 239
10 A.Leroi-Gourhan, cf. Grahame Clark (1967)
11 Virg. *Georg.* III, 314ff. (tr. C. Day-Lewis)
12 S.Runciman
13 Aesch. *PV.* 454–8 (tr. G. Thomson)
14 E.C.Semple
15 R.E.M. Wheeler
16 O.Spengler
17 Ar. *Pol.* I, 3, 4, 1256a
18 J.L.Myres
19 R.E.M.Wheeler
20 Livy, XXXVIII, 38, 3
21 N.Gatsos (tr. E.Keeley and P.Sherrard)

2 *Egypt*

1 *The Book of the Dead*
2 E.Meyer
3 Chester Beatty, IV, 3
4 C.Aldred
5 Numbers XI, 5
6 Cassiod. *Variarum* XII, 24, 29f.
7 Hom. *Od.* XI, 123
8 C.Aldred
9 Amelia Edwards
10 A.F.Weigall, *Short History of Egypt*, p. 166
11 F.Petrie, *Six Temples at Thebes*, p. 26

3 *The Easternmost Mediterranean*

1 Göran Schildt
2 J.E.Flecker
3 Karnak inscription
4 Gen. viii, 1
5 J.Ruskin, *Stones of Venice*, III, 195,
6 Judges, ix, 8
7 Psalms, iii, 8
8 Lawrence Durrell
9 Paul Morand

4 *The Straits and the Aegean*

1 Hom. *Il.* II, 461
2 Hom. *Od.* XIX, 172ff. (tr. R.Fitzgerald)
3 Thuc. I, 4
4 Exodus x, 21–2
5 C.M.Bowra
6 Hom. *Od.* IV, 605, 607–8 (tr. R.Fitzgerald)
7 A.E.Zimmern
8 Herod. VII, 102
9 Soph. *Ajax*, 1217
10 Pl. *Crit.* 110 e, 111 b–c (tr. R.G.Bury)
11 A.M.Snodgrass
12 Ar. *Mirabil.* 82

5 *The Expansion of Israel, Phoenicia and Carthage*

1 Amos ix, 7

2 Exodus iii, 8, Levit. xx, 24, cf. Deuteron. x, 11
3 I Kings v, 6–18
4 I Sam. vii, 1, I Kings xi, 23ff.
5 A.H.Gardiner, *Late Egyptian Stories*, 61–76
6 Isaiah xxiii, 8
7 E.g. Ezek. xxvii, 5–6, I Kings v, 6–18
8 D.Harden
9 Cf. App. VIII, 128
10 Ar. *Pol.* II, 8, 1, 1272b
11 Herod. IV, 42
12 Herod. IV, 43, cf. Plin., *NH.* II, 169, Justin, *Hist. Phil.* XIX, 2

6 The Homeric Age

1 Pl. *Laws*, 728 c
2 Thuc. I, 2, 6; cf. I, 12, 4
3 Ar. *Pol.* I, 1, 8, 1252b
4 Thuc. I, 7
5 Phocyl. 4 Diehl
6 Pl. *Rep.* IV, 423b
7 Theogn. 1197 (tr. A.R.Burn)
8 Hes. *WD.* 24
9 Pl. *Laws*, 626a
10 J.Beazley
11 Archil. 18 Diehl
12 Herod. I, 142
13 Paus. VII, 2, 5
14 Herod. I, 146, 2
15 Hom. Hymns, III, 143–8, 154–5
16 O.R.Gurney, *The Hittites*, p. 168
17 Plato, *Anth. Lyr. Graec.* (Diehl), I, p. 90, no. 10
18 Xen. *Anab.* IV, 7
19 Aesch. *PV.* 89f.
20 Hom. *Od.* V, 291–6 (tr. R.Fitzgerald)
21 Hom. *Od.* II, 420–9; cf. V, 244–6
22 Hom. *Od.* IX, 80–81
23 Thuc. II, 84, 3
24 Hom. *Od.* XIV, 245–359; cf. X, 87–132
25 Thuc. I, 2
26 Hom. *Od.* XII, 278–83
27 Archil. 79 Diehl
28 Soph. *Ant.* 332ff.
29 Alc. 148 Page LGS (18b, 46)

30 Paul Morand
31 Audiberti
32 Hes. *WD*. 663ff.
33 Hes. *WD*. 621–2 (tr. R.Lattimore)
34 Eratosth. *ap*. Str. I, 2, 14f., 23
35 Hom. *Od*. II, 420–9; cf. v, 244–6
36 Hom. *Od*. IV, 563ff., VI, 43ff.; cf. Gen. ii, 8–10

7 The Greek Civilisation Enriched and Diffused

1 Hes. *WD*. 651–9
2 Herod. v, 57–8
3 Hes. *WD*. 589
4 E.g. *Instruction of Amen-em-Opet*
5 E.g. Ninurtu of Enlil
6 Hes. *Theog*. 53–5
7 Herod. III, 73
8 Cf. Hom. *Il*. VI, 236
9 Plut. *Quaest. Graec*. 11
10 Theogn. 190; cf. Thuc. I, 13, 1
11 C.M.Bowra
12 Herod. VII, 125
13 Pseudo-Pl. *Epinomis*, 987d
14 Cf. Herod. II, 151–3
15 J.L.Myres
16 E.A.Freeman
17 Justin, *Hist. Phil*. XLIV, 4, 2
18 Asius *ap*. Ath. XII, 30
19 Eur. *fr*. 910 N
20 Matthew Arnold
21 Hom. *Od*. XII, 331
22 Ar. *Vesp*. 1087; cf. Aesch. *Pers*. 427
23 Polyb. IV, 38 (tr. M.Chambers)

8 Athens and Alexandria

1 Soph. *OC*. 861ff. (tr. W.B.Yeats)
2 Hes. *WD*. 428–35
3 Hom. *Od*. v, 69, VII, 112ff.
4 Eur. *Tro*. 801ff. (tr. R.Lattimore)
5 Soph. *OC*. 700ff. (tr. E.F.Watling)
6 Sappho *frs*. 150, 151 (tr. D.G.Rossetti)
7 Pind. *fr*. 114a

8 Ar. *Pax* 575f. (tr. B.B.Rogers)
9 Soph. *Oed. Col.* 154ff. (tr. R.Fitzgerald)
10 Ath. v. 206f., cf. XII, 542a
11 Alcm. *fr.* 65 (tr. A.E.Zimmern)
12 Ar. *Nub.* 276ff. (tr. B.B.Rogers)
13 Pseudo-Aristot. *De Coloribus*; cf. Plotinus and the Byzantines
14 Soph. *Phil.* 936ff. (tr. D.Grene)
15 Eur. *Hel.* 179ff. (tr. R.Warner); cf. *Iph. T.* 340–3, 1123–36
16 Eur. *Hippol.* 73ff. (tr. D.Grene)
17 R.W.Livingstone
18 Pl. *Phaedr.* 230 D
19 Hes. *Theog.* 902f.
20 Pind. *Ol.* II, 55–6, *Pyth.* v, 1–4, etc.
21 Solon *fr.* 11
22 Ezek. xxiii, 14f.
23 Herod. IX, 122, cf. I, 135
24 Aesch. *Pers.* 412ff. (tr. Lewis Campbell)
25 Thuc. I, 142–7, II, 60–4
26 C.M.Bowra
27 Hom. *Od.* IX, 12, 115 (tr. R.Fitzgerald)
28 Thuc. II, 40, 2 (tr. R.Warner)
29 Thuc. I, 70, 9 (tr. R.Warner)
30 M.R.Ridley
31 M.Cary
32 Pseudo-Zech. ix, 3–4
33 Hom. *Od.* IV, 358
34 P.Berl. 13045 line 28
35 Hirt. *B. Alex.* I
36 Jos. *C.Ap.* I, 60
37 W.W. Tarn
38 Anon. *ap.* Suid. s.v. *Basileia*
39 E.g. *Dream of Nectanebus* (cf. p. 151); and Egyptian romances of travel (p. 55)
40 J.J.Auchmuty (but there was also China)
41 Theocr. III, 12–14 (tr. G.S.Fraser)
42 Theocr. VII, 39–41
43 Anth. Pal. v, 16, VII, 717
44 Polyb. XVI, 14
45 Diogenianus, *Paroimiai*, v, 19
46 Cf. Str. XIV, 2, 5, 52

9 *The Etruscans and the Beginnings of Rome*

1 Dion. Hal. I, 37

2 H. Hencken
3 Herod. I, 94
4 Lord Macaulay
5 Sil. Ital. VIII, 485
6 D.H. Lawrence
7 Dion. Hal. I, 72–74
8 Cic. *Rep.* II, 19, 3
9 D.H. Tromp
10 Livy I, 33, 2
11 Livy I, 33, 4

10 The Republic Unites the Mediterranean

1 Prop. IV, 10, 27ff. (tr. A.E. Watts)
2 Rennell Rodd
3 Tib. II, 43f. (tr. G.H. Highet)
4 Virg. *Georg.* II, 531–4 (tr. G.H. Highet)
5 Virg. *Georg.* I, 121–4 (tr. C. Day-Lewis)
6 Virg. *Georg.* I, 316–17, 322–6 (tr. J. Dryden)
7 Hor. *Od.* III, 29, 36–41 (tr. J. Dryden)
8 Virg. *Georg.* I, 169–75
9 Virg. *Georg.* I, 82–3
10 Pl. *NH.* XIV, 11, 8
11 Pl. *NH.* XV, 3, 8
12 Virg. *Georg.* II, 179ff. (tr. C. Day-Lewis)
13 Pl. *NH.* XV, 3, 8
14 Varro, *RR.* I, 2, 6
15 Cato, *De Agr.* 10–14, 135
16 H.H. Scullard
17 Rose Macaulay
18 Polyb. I. 3f.
19 Livy XXXIV, 21, 7, Gell. *NA.* II, 22, 29
20 Polyb. XVIII, 12
21 M. Holleaux
22 Polyb. II, 15
23 Str. IV, 207f, V, 214
24 *OGI.* 338
25 Diod. Sic. XXXIV, 25ff.
26 Cic. *Rep.* III, 36, *Off.* II, 26
27 Vell. Pat. II, 21
28 Hor. *Ep.* II, 1, 156
29 Fest. p. 109 L
30 Pl. *NH.* XXXV, 47, 166 (tr. H. Rackham)

11 *The Imperial Sea*

1 Virg. *Ecl.* I, 51f. (tr. G.Highet)
2 Cf. Naev. *fr. com.* 122 Ribbeck
3 Virg. *Georg.* IV, 130–2, 134 (tr. C.Day-Lewis)
4 Cic. *De Or.* III, 5, cf. I, 8
5 Hor. *Od.* II, 9 (tr. Samuel Johnson)
6 Hor. *Ep.* I, 16, 7ff. (tr. G.Highet)
7 Hor. *Od.* III, 13
8 Petr. *Sat.* 131 (tr. W.Arrowsmith)
9 E.g. Ov. *Met.* III, 28–31, 155–64, 407–12, XI, 605–6, etc.
10 Pl. *Ep.* VIII, 8
11 Pl. *Ep.* V, 6 (tr. B.Radice)
12 *Perv. Vig.* V (tr. A.Tate)
13 Rennell Rodd
14 Varro *RR.* III, 5
15 Pl. *NH.* XXXV, 37, 116 (tr. K.Jex-Blake)
16 Eugènie Strong
17 J.M.C.Toynbee
18 Juv. *Sat.* III. 60–61
19 Cic. *Leg. Man.* 14
20 Juv. *Sat.* III, 62
21 Luc. *Navig.* 5
22 Virg. *Aen.* III, 192–204, etc.
23 II Cor. xi, 25
24 Acts xxvii, 1, 11
25 Rom. xv, 24, 1
26 Petr. *Sat.* 76
27 Str. V, 1, 7, 214
28 Suet. *Aug.* 98
29 Sen. *Med.* 370
30 Ael. Aristid. *Or. Rom.* 95
31 H.St.B.Moss

Appendix

1 Herod. IX, 122
2 Pseudo-Hippocr. *De Aeribus*, iiiff.
3 E.C.Semple
4 H.B.George
5 Vidal de la Blache; cf. L.Febvre
6 G.R.Crone
7 Pseudo-Hippocr. op. cit. XXIV

8 E. Huntington, C. E. P. Brooks
9 J.M. Houston, André Siegfried
10 G. Dimbleby (1967)
11 G.R. Crone
12 Jules Sion
13 Roger Dion
14 Alexander Pope
15 Leo Tolstoy
16 V. Ehrenberg
17 William James
18 Thomas Gray
19 Hor. *Od.* IV, 9, 25ff. (tr. Lord Dunsany)

Notes*

1 The Mediterranean and its Beginnings

Section 1. Creation of Mediterranean: in the Tertiary Age. Red soil: Terra rossa (sesquioxide of iron, of disputed origin. 'Trade winds': Etesians.

Section 2. Earliest known tools: Olduvai Gorge, Tanzania, *c.* 1,750,000 BC. N.India: Siwalik range. Chinese man *c.* 400,000 BC: Pithecanthropus Pekinensis (*homo erectus*), Choukoutien. Flint: hydrated silica. Carmel skeletons: Mugharet-es-Skhul (Levalloisio-Mousterian). Neanderthal man near Rome: Saccopastore, cf. M.Circeo. Dating: for limitations of radio-carbon method cf. L.de Paor, *Archaeology* (1967), p. 66. Blades instead of flakes: Upper Advanced Palaeolithic. Cyrenaica: Ed Dabba, Haua Fteah (trench now dug through 90,000 years, earliest period roughly datable by analogies with protoactinium-therium dates for Atlantic deep-sea cores). Greece: 1967 excavations at Kastritsa, cf. Asprochaliko. Centred upon W.Asia: Aurignacian. Female figures: Gravettian. Magdalenian: from La Madeleine (cf. Lascaux, Altamira). S.Ural site: Kapova cave (1962). S.Turkish caves: Kara' In, Öküzlü' In. Post-glacial west: Azilian (Mesolithic).

Section 3. N.Iraq *c.* 10,000: Shanidar (Zarzian), then Zawi Chemi-Shanidar. Domesticated goats from bezoar (capra hircus aegagrus). Wadi Natuf cave: Shukba (Proto-Neolithic). Early domestication in France: Chateauneuf-les-Martigues, Belloy-sur-Somme. Mid-way position: cf. Qalat Jarmo (E.Iraq), 8–7M. Carmel: Wadi Fallah (Nahal Oren: Tahunian). Turkish Mesolithic: Beldibi, Belbaşi. Obsidian finds: Aşiklihüyük. Obsidian source: Acigöl. The date of S.E.Spanish Mesolithic(?) paintings (Alpera, Cueva Remigiana) is uncertain.

Section 4. Hüyük (cf. Tepe, Tell) = hill-top (near spring) with low truncated cone, flat top and sloping sides. Emmer wheat (triticum

* M = Millennium, (BC), C = century, *c* = approximately, D = dynasty, r.c. = radio-carbon date.

dicoccum) developed from tetraploid wild T. dicoccoides. Less valuable einkorn (T. monococcum) from diploid T. boeoticum, probably by a gene mutation. Hexaploid bread wheat is T. aestivum. Two-rowed barley (hordeum distichum, tougher than wild H. spontaneum) replaced by six-rowed H. hexastichum. Çatalhüyük: baskets *c.* 6,500 from wheat straw; domestic loom early 6M; oil from crucifers, almonds, acorns, pistachios. Far eastern pottery: Japan 8M (r.c.). Neolithic (Holocene): distinction from Palaeolithic (Pleistocene) because axe-blades were now ground and polished. Asia Minor: Turkish Anadolu (Anatolia) covers wider area, i.e. all Asiatic Turkey. Amik excavations: Judaidah, Çatalhüyük (not to be confused with Asia Minor site), Ta'yinat; also Dhahab, Kurdu.
Section 5. Hacilar: agricultural settlement early 8M(?), mid-6M widespread copper. Cnossos: spinners and weavers by *c.* 55C. Argissa: cf. Soufli Maghoula, 59 or 58C. Transhumance: cf. Vlach (Sarakatsani, Mt Pindus) nomads today. Domesticated dog: Starr Carr (Yorkshire) *c.* 7538 r.c. (Natufian 'dog' may be wolf). E.Hungary etc. Körös (Kris)-Starcevo. Thessalian pottery: cf. walled Sesklo, end 6M(?). Rectangular porched house: megaron, cf. Dhimini (opposite Volo), then Karanova near Stara Zagora, *c.* 5000(?). Propped two-roomed house: Tsangli. Lepenski Vir: E. of Belgrade on Danube, *c.* 6000. Fine Neolithic figurines in Hamangia culture E.Rumania, *c.* 3600 r.c.
Section 6. Early and mid-6M Mesopotamia: Hassuna. 6M figurines with inlaid eyes: Tell-es-Sawwan (near Samarra). Later 6 and early 5M: Halafian (Tell Halaf, Arpachiyah). Later 5 and early 4M (S.Mesopotamia): Al Ubaid. Bitumen: from It springs. Mid 4M: Uruk (Erech, Warka; Protoliterate), Rumanian writing: Tartaria tablets (Mures valley). Model ship: Eridu. Late 4M and early 3M: Jemdet Nasr. Temple in N.E.Syria: Tell Brak. Seals in Persia: Siyalk. Sumerian language: ? cf. modern Transcaucasian group. Umma (24C): King Lugalzaggisi. Unidentified capital near Babylon: Agade (Sargon I from Kish). His grandson: Naram-Sin. Guardian of Forest: Huwawa, killed by Gilgamesh and Enkidu. Legal system at Ur: Ur-Nammu, 22–21C. Horse in Israel: Horvat Beter, 4M, chalcolithic; cf. Rana Ghundai, N.Baluchistan; Tarpan now extinct, a few Przewalski's Horse survive. Black Sea cultures (Sinop-Bafra): Ikiztepe, Demircihüyük, Maltepe (all different). Emery: near Alaşehir, and E. of Ephesus, and S. of Izmir.

2 Egypt

Section 1. Water-lift: *shaduf.* Palaeolithic finds at Abbasiyah, Hawara

(Fayum). Spanish analogies for leathery vessels: Neolithic Almeria culture. Early 4M: Badarian, Amratian, then Gerzian (*c.* 3600).
Section 2. Buto: house of the goddess Edjo. S.Mesopotamian tomb-prototypes: Jemdet Nasr. Tigris type ships: Gebel el Arak knife handle. Menes: = ? Narmer, Hor-aha or Scorpion king.
Section 3. First sea-journey to Syria: Peribsen, 2D. Sneferu: 4D. Cheops (Khufu): boat found 1954. Fleets of sailing ships: Sahure, 5D. 'Asiatics in sands': Pepi I (6D). 'Old Kingdom' is 3–6D. Oil from balanos, moringa, castor-oil. Vine: Astian fossils near Montpellier show that this was also indigenous to S.France. First large blocks: Sekhemkhet (3D). Calendar: Sothic, from observations of morning-star Sothis (Sirius). 23 statues: pyramid of Chephren (4D). Gratings: Hypostyle Hall, Karnak. 'Long level beam': Nefertari Temple, Abu Simbel. 27C paintings: tomb of Hesyre (3D). Gardens: of Methen (3D). Roof copying earlier materials: pyramid of Djoser (3D). Fluting, ribbing: cf. *heracleum gigantium* plant (but not known in Nile valley?). Lotus capitals: Uadji funerary stele (1D), cf. Jemdet Nasr. (This is *nymphaea caerulea*; food of 'lotus-eaters' was *cordia myxa* or *rhamnus zizyphus* or *celtus australis*).
Section 4. 'Men do not sail to Byblos': prophet Ipuwer (First Intermediate Period). El Lisht: Ithtowe (Amenemhet I, 12D, moved there). 'Middle Kingdom' is 11-13D. Fayum works: Amenemhet III (12D). Hyksos: 15–17D (Second Intermediate Period): capital has now been tentatively identified at Tell el Dabah (Zagazig). Horse *c.* 1900: Buhen (Wadi Halfa). Fortress with embankment: Tell-el-Yahudiyeh. Revival: Aahmes I (18D). 'New Kingdom' is 17–20D. Kings shown in chariots from Amenhotep I (18D). Importations of flowers and trees: Hatshepsut (18D), Rameses II (19D). Tanis: probably Zoan; residence of 21D. Frontier fortress: Tjel. Merenptah: 19D. Rameses III: 20D.

3 Easternmost Mediterranean

Section 1. Egyptian temple at Byblos: 4D. In mid-3M, Levant had been overrun from Asia Minor (Khirbet Kerak culture). Erosion: was there also a failure in rain-supply? Early ships: could only sail 80° (not 60°) off wind. Canaan: also Hamitic link (*Genesis* makes Canaan the son of Ham). Wild olive: also Spain, Po valley (Pliocene). Olive as criterion: but brought into California from Mexico in 1769. Its attraction of moisture: ? by osmotic pressure (flow of liquid through porous membrane).
Section 2. Amorites ('the west'): their homeland particularly in E. & N.Syria. Aleppo: kingdom of Yamhad. Carchemish (Karkamiş): Cerablus, Barak. Mari palace: king Zimri-Lim. Amorites in

Mesopotamia: Isin (king Ishbi-Erra). Assyrian capitals: Tell al Rimah, Chagar Bazar, Ashur, Nimrud, Khorsabad, Nineveh. Indo-European gods of Hurrians: Indra, Mithra, Nasaha. Capital of Mitanni: Washshukkani; perhaps at Tell Fecheriyah.

Section 3. Wave of assaults: e.g. Usatova movement from Russian steppes into Balkans. Hattusas: religious precinct of Yazilikaya is two miles E. Hurrian dynasty of Hittites: from Tudhaliyas II (15C). Iron: by unknown means had reached Shang rulers of Anyang by 12C. Beaten earth walls: Dan, Hazor, 17C inscriptions. Hittite unifier: Labarnas I. Black Sea enemies: Kaska. Cilicia: bronze (crescentic) axes of Mesopotamian type arriving by end 3M. Aleppo reduced 17C: by Hattusilis I. Cilicia's alliance with Hittites: Telepinus (16C). Tarsus: formerly identified with the Biblical Tarshish (which was not the Spanish Tartessus), but that appears to have been approached from Israel via the Gulf of Eilat. Adana: =? Egyptian Dnn, Danauna (? same as Greek Danaos). Ugarit's god of crafts: Kothar. Surviving syllabaries: Byblos (*c.* 1600), Tell Deir Alla (discovered 1963). Sinai alphabet: Serabit el Khadem. Byblos inscription 11 or 10C: Ahiram sarcophagus. Hittites allied with Cypriots: recently discovered Suppiluliumas II. Important Judaean towns: Hazor (S. of L. Huleh), Tell Beit Mirsim, Tell Abu Hawam, Lachish, Bethel. Peoples from across the sea: Lugga (? Lycians), Denen (? Danauna, Adana), Shrdn (? future Sardinians), Shkl (? future Sicilians), Trshw (? future Tyrrhenians, Etruscans).

4 *The Straits and the Aegean*

Section 1. Alacahüyük: ? capital of pre-Hittite Hatti. Cf. Horoztepe and Sardis where 3M settlement has now been found. Black earth of N. Caucasus: *chernozem.* Earlier S. Russian cultures: Mariupol, Nalchik (Ochre-Grave). Maikop: cf. stone chambers at Novosvobodnaya, more varied Kuban-Terek tombs (early 2M), then dolmens of Gelendshik, Beregovaya. Troy *c.* 3000: Troy I, cf. Thermi (Lesbos), Poliochni (Lemnos). Late 3M: Troy II (8 phases), cf. Poliochni. Spanish loom weights: Almizaraque (R. Almanzora). The view that there was actual colonisation of S. Spain from E. Med. (Los Millares) has been questioned. Dorak: L. Apolyont (Artyma). Beycesultan: destroyed *c.* 1750, *c.* 1400, and again later. After destruction: Troy III. *C.* 1800(?): Troy VI, Grey Minyan pottery. Supposedly captured by Greeks: Troy VIIa. Knobbed pottery: Troy VIIb. Was the Luvian language closely related to Hittite? Assuwa: a third (unidentifiable) Hittite dependency was the 'Seha river territory'. 13C Hittite victor over Assuwa: Tudhaliyas IV.

Section 2. Isthmus of E. Crete: Ierapetra (Hierapytna). Late 3M: Early Minoan II. Melos obsidian: already in Mesolithic cave at Scyros. Cnossos harbours: Amnisos, Nirou Khani and mouth of R. Kairatos. Phaestos: two (? or four) successive palaces; its later harbour was Komo. Santorin earth: *calcestruzzo*. Slated-paved town on islet: Pseira. Cretan script: Linear A. The Phaestos disc, in another script, may have been imported. Rhodes: a possible site of the sea-faring state of Ahhijawa (Achaea). Miletus: ? Millawanda, Milawatas. Trading colonies in Syria: also Minet el Beida. Presses 10m. S. of Cnossos: Vathypetro, 16C. Centres restored after eruption: Ceos, Cythera. Cretan pottery: Kamares (egg-shell) 18C, plant style joins marine style 16C. 'Impressionism': or eidetic memory images, cf. palaeolithic, and mental patients?

Section 3. Lerna House of Tiles: after destruction, Grey Minyan pottery (Early Helladic III) – named after Orchomenos in Boeotia (earlier pottery at Eutresis, 27C r.c.). Settlers before *c.* 1900: Late Bronze Age. Whetstone of N. European type: 'Arrow-shaft-polisher.' Largest Mycenae bee-hive tomb: 'Treasury of Atreus'. Attic figs: of Aegilla. L. Copais: fortress of Gla on island. Clay sarcophagi: e.g. Tanagra (found 1964). Agriculture: metal sickles, double-adzes. Armour: Dendra find (1960). Mycenaean script: Linear B. Oil jars at Mycenae: House of the Oil Merchant. Rhodes: distinctive pottery and cemetery, but settlement still undiscovered. Shipwreck *c.* 1200: off Cape Kilidonya (Gelidonya). Israel settlements: Tell Abu Hawam, Sarepta. Finds W. of Tbilisi: Trialeti (42 barrows). Rivers: Ister (Danube) often confused with Istria (Trieste). Coastal station N.W. Greece: S. of Parga. Sicily: Milazzo and near Syracuse (perhaps obsidian of Lipari Is. was incentive). S. Italy: Torre Castelluccia. Spain: El Argar etc.; gold treasure of Villena (found 1963) is perhaps *c.* 1000–850. Fall of Pylos: *c.* 1190–80 r.c. Cremation introduced to deal with bubonic plague?

5 Expansion of Israel, Phoenicia and Carthage

Section 1. Ashdod: Azotus, under sand-dunes. 'Philistine': from German students' slang for those who had not attended a university. Mid-11C. Philistine victory over Hebrews: battle of Ebenezer. Palestine: Judaea called Syria Palaestina by Romans, Falastin by Arabs *c.* AD 636). Philistine ships: oak from Edom. Canaanites' predecessors of Hebrews at Jerusalem: Jebusites. Valleys round city: Kedron, Hinnom. Jerusalem: recent excavations have revealed walls and part of a tower of 8C. Megiddo: horse-boxes 9C. Copper and iron: also from Wadi Arabah. Volute-capitals: Samaria, Megiddo, Hazor,

Ophel (Proto-Aeolic). Post-partition Israel: Jeroboam I (*c.* 931–910, house of Ephraim), capitals first at Shechem, then Tirzah; expansion under Jeroboam II (*c.* 783–743). Judah: Debir excavations; kingdom at height under Uzziah (*c.* 783–742). Jewish return later 6C: under Zerubbabel and Jeshua.

Section 2. Neo-Hittite states: Carchemish, Kummanu (Malatya), Gurgum (Maraş). Amik state: Ungi (Hattina, modern Hatay). Zincirli: state of Ya'diya (Samal). Cilicia: Que, Khilakku, Kizzuwatna. Karatepe: also Domuztepe. Aramaeans in Babylonia: if the same as 'Ahlamu'. Aramaean states: Bit Bahiani (Tell Halaf, Guzana), Aram-Sobah (Bekaa), M. Hermon (two), Geshur (Hauran), Bit Agushi (Aleppo-Arpad), Bit Adini (Tell Barsip, Nisibin). Urartian language: Vannic, Khaldian. Urartian drainage: cf. Assyrian of Sennacherib. Urartian conquerors in 8C: Argistis I, Sardur III. Aramaic: W. (six dialects) and E. (five including Syriac): dialects still spoken in N. Iraq. Byblos: late Bronze and Early Iron Age towns now shown to have been submerged by unrecorded earthquake. Phoenician ship: Luli, 8C. Cyprus: Salamis tumulus burials (excavated 1957–62). Phoenician tombs: both cremation and inhumation at Athlit and Achzib. Assyrian relief of Tyre: Gates of Balawat. *Phoinikes*: ? or name from red skins or date-palms; called *Fenkhw* by Egyptians *c.* 2000. Alphabet: inscription of Mesha of Moab *c.* 850; Hebrews much later developed method of indicating vowels. Assyrian governors: planted by Tiglath-pileser III. Princes of Tyre and Egypt on leash: Zincirli stele. Assyrians were expelled from Egypt with aid of 'Men of Bronze' (mercenaries). Assyrian libraries: Assur, Calah, Nineveh. Babylon: Hanging Gardens (*pensiles*, i.e. in form of terraces). Sidon; temporarily occupied by Hophra (Apries) of Egypt (589–570).

Section 3. Carthaginian houses: Dar Essafi, Djebel Mlezza painting. Settlements in Sicily: Drepanum (Trapani), Solus (identified in 1964 with 'Cannita'), Lilybaeum. Sardinia: Caralis, Tharros, Sulcis. S. France: Pyrene, Caccabarias, Pomègues, Ratonneau. Mixed race in N. Africa: Libyphoenicians; cf. later Bastulophoenicians in Spain. Mercenaries: especially from 5C. Population of Carthage *c.* 400,000 in 3C.

6 The Homeric Age

Section 1. Greek tin: Laconia, Euboea, Cyclades. Iron: two horse-bits in Athenian Agora *c.* 900, many objects in 9C grave. Chalcis-Eretria: Lelantine War. 11C pottery: first Protogeometric. Eastern contacts: Syrian cup in 9C grave, Greek vases in east. Earliest temples: Dreros (Crete), Sparta, Perachora (*c.* 850–750).

Section 2. Ionia (Yavan): no connection with Ionian Sea. Earliest Ionian Miletus: destroyed by fire 8C. Latmian gulf: L.Bafa. Samos: mainly settled from Epidaurus. Heraeum: Otomatik Tepe (identified 1964). First Cymaean tin importer: Midacritus. Early objects in Homer: e.g. boar's tusk helmet and shield of Ajax. Gilgamesh: Heracles also analogous.
Section 3. Greek navigation: normally began and ended with heliacal rising and setting of Pleiades. Odysseus' journeys: Drepanum and Aegates Is. have been invoked; 'stream of Ocean' is probably Strait of Gibraltar, not circumambient river. Odysseus' ship: merchantman, not warship as on vases. Odyssean wanderers: by D'Annunzio, Giono, Eyvind Johnson, Tennyson. Ithaca: identification with Leucas improbable.

7 Greek Civilisation Enriched and Diffused

Section 1. Alphabet: Attic jug *c.* 725. Alternative theory that Greeks received this in form of vowel-less syllabary is less probable. Sky-god consuming young: cf. Seti I cenotaph (*c.* 1300). Pandora: cf. Khnum myth, Deir el Bahri birth-oracle. Enuma Elish: Nebuchadnezzar I; finds at Sultantepe. Typhoeus in Cilicia: Apollodorus. Kumarbi myth and song of Ullikummi: fragments of Hurrian version found at Boğazköy. Emasculated sky-god: Anu.
Section 2. Gordion: 12m. N.W. of Polatli, near R. Sangarius (Sakarya); 'Tomb of Midas' found 1957. Earth-mother: statue found at second city near Afyonkarahisar. Music: Phrygian pipe (elegiac), cymbals, triangle. Greek alphabets resembling Phrygian: Crete and late Geometric Attica. Cimmerians: rulers probably Iranian (? from N.Caucasia). Lydia: E.boundary was R.Halys (Kizilirmak); language cf. Hittite, Luvian(?). Iron spit currency: found in Argive Heraeum. Lydian king's name on coins: Walwesh (Alyattes). Mycenaean Corinth: Korakou. Corinthian ports: excavations (1963) show subsidence of 6–10 feet since antiquity. Two-level ships: probably made by Corinthian Ameinocles for Samos; cf. Sennacherib reliefs. Chalcis: one of the few Greek place-names to have a Greek meaning. Argive king, 7C: Pheidon.
Section 3. Pottery: colour contrasts by reduction followed by partial reoxidation. *C.* 720–640 Protocorinthian, 640–20 transitional, 620–*c.* 550 Corinthian. Textile models: traces of Elamite influences; rosettes cf. Assyria. Boeotian statuette: Mantiklos bronze. 'Daedalic' statuette: Auxerre goddess, *c.* 630. Large sculpture like clay idol: Samos 'Hera' by Cheramyes, 575–550. Psammetichos I: 26D. Naucratis: granted monopoly by Apries; Amasis allowed Samians to trade in Fayum; Necho (609–594) made new attempt at Suez

canal. Echoes of wood construction in temples: abacus, tapering columns, triglyph pegs (but much disputed). Flutes: separated by fillets (Ionic) or arrises (Doric). Ionic prototypes: Samos 8C, Didyma 7C(?).

Section 4. Abdera: settled first from Clazomenae (twice), then Teos. Festivals: Pythian (Delphi), Olympian, Nemean, Isthmian (Corinth). Pithecusae: 1965–6 excavations brought total of tombs up to 914. Zancle (Messana): co-founders were Messenians. Sybaris: R. Crathis; Sila mountains. Villages at Rhône mouth: S.Blaise, La Couronne. Mistral: low pressure over sea attracts cold air (69 per cent of all Mediterranean depressions originate in, or near, Gulf of Genoa). Celts: La Tène culture replaced Hallstatt *c.* 450. Settlements also at Ensérune, M.Garou (recent excavations). Rhône: port of Theline (Arelate); leads up to Saône-Doubs groove and Belfort pass. Seine find: Vix (M.Lassois). Spain: date of Rhode (best natural harbour) unknown. Westernmost Greek settlement: Maenace.

Section 5. Wine: also Thasos, Lemnos, Lesbos, Cos. Tyrant of Naxos: Lygdamis. 6C Miletus: Theatre Hill (1961 excavations), Lion Bay. Guild: Aeinautai. Milesian pottery: formerly called 'Fikellura' after a Rhodian cemetery; Clazomenae produced grey pots, Lesbos black. Heraclitus: opposed by Parmenides of Elea who declared senses illusory (he may in old age have taught the atomist Leucippus of Miletus). Lydia: Cyme had preceded Ionian cities as main link. Cyzicus: pottery from inland Dascylium is of early 7C. Fish: Mediterranean (blue because of lack of plankton) far inferior to Atlantic. Tunny: Poseidon's trident was originally a harpoon. Breeding tunnies like hot salt water but not hotter than 38.5°. Chronicler on Constantinople: Odo of Deols, 12C AD. Current: reverse undercurrent as at Strait of Gibraltar. Black Sea: Aristeas said to have reached it *c.* 650(?). Geographers cannot agree why it has no summer droughts. Sinope: Greek ships painted red with its *miltos.* Trapezus: site still undiscovered. Tyras: Belgorod (Cetatea Alba, Akkerman). Polyglot bazaar: Dioscurias. 7C Caucasus tombs showing trade-route: Kelermes (other tombs at Kostromskaya, Chertomlyk). Silphium: probably a species of *ferula.*

8 From Athens to Alexandria

Section 1. Winter rest of plants: less complete for evergreen than for deciduous since the chlorophyll assimilation continues. City-emblems: bee at Ephesus, fig-leaf at Camirus, goat at Paros, cow at Carystus and Eretria.

Section 2. Sumerian code: Urukagina of Lagash. Babylonians: Hammurabi. Codes give stability: Thebes, W.Locri, Catana, Chalcidice. Codes promote change: Massalia, Heraclea Pontica, Rhegium. Pisistratus on Dardanelles: Sigeum (first foothold 690). Proto-Attic: Polyphemus *c.* 675–650, François vase *c.* 570. Gloss: produced by particles (plate-like illite) or sintering at kiln temperature. E.sculptors of *korai*: e.g. Archermus of Chios. Vermilion paint: kings of Rome painted their faces with this on public appearances. Golden hair: Acropolis boy, early 5C. Cleisthenes' regions: *astu*, *paralia*, *mesogeion*. Persian (Achaemenid) conquerors: Cyrus I (559–529) and Cambyses. Piraeus: war-fleet W., merchant-fleet E., and ferry-wharfs. Athenian League: by 448 only Chios, Lesbos and Samos had navies. New-style colonies of 440s: cleruchies. Peloponnesian War: Amphipolis fell to Spartans in 424, Byzantium, Chalcedon and Cyzicus revolted 412, final battle was at Aegospotami.
Section 3. Slaves: Hyperides' figure of 150,000 *adult male* slaves in 338 is probably too high. Festivals for dramatic performances: Great Dionysia, Lenaea. *Acanthus*: *spinosus*; Romans preferred *mollis* (Bear's Breech). Pentelic marble: gold patina due to oxidising iron ingredient; bluish-grey Hymettus marble had been used earlier. Apollodorus: influenced Zeuxis of Heraclea in Lucania, who added highlights.
Section 4. Dionysius' large ships: quadriremes, quinqueremes. Trade of Athens: its banker Pasion based his activity on Byzantium. Athens-Sparta agreement (371): Peace of Callias. 5C Macedonia: Archelaus (413–399). Philip's fast ships: *lembi*. Alexandria: on site of Rakotis; inner basins were royal port (E.), war-harbour (W.); architect was Democrates. Pharos' reflector: according to others a telescope. Succession states of Alexander: 'Hellenistic' age (term originally applied to non-Greek imitators of Greek customs). Egyptian oils: sesame, croton, linseed, safflower and colocynth, and a little from olives.
Section 5. Predecessor of Antioch: Antigoneia. Additions to Antioch: by Seleucus I and Antiochus IV. Seleucid vassal at Pergamum: Philetaerus. Achaean League; from 245 Aratus of Sicyon directs for 30 years. Three-fold rotation: cf. 4C rent contract from Euboea. Rhodes: union of Ialysos, Lindos, Camiros. *On Harbours*: by Timosthenes. Social services: Samos in *c.* 245 finally formed a permanent corn-fund.

9 The Etruscans and the Beginnings of Rome

Section 1. Arrivals from Balkans: Italian Neolithic (Mesolithic is obscure). Finest pottery: Serra d'Alto. Pile settlements: Lagozza di

Besnate *c.* 2845 r.c. Brenner immigrants: Remedello culture (contact with Aunjetitz culture of Bohemia). Early 2M: remarkable bronze figures of men, women and animals from Sardinia. 'Terramaricoli': *terramare*, rich soil, ancient refuse. Iron Age (*c.* 1200 ?): 'Villanovans' (after cemetery outside Bologna); outliers at Fermo, Pontecagnano. Biconical urns: cf. 'Urnfield' culture of mid-Europe. Alphabet: 8C 'Nestor Cup' recently found at Ischia. Etruscan shore, later abandoned: Maremma. Erosion: recent study at L. Monterosi. Evergreen: holm-oak has been suggested as the wild indicator plant of the Mediterranean, but its distribution is markedly western (it is also uncertain what permutation represents the 'climax'). Olive: unknown under Tarquins, Fenestella *fr.* 7P. Voltumna shrine: ? Orvieto, Montefiascone, Bolsena. Populonia: Massoncello promontory was once an island. Vetulonia: competitor at Rusellae, 10m. away (excavated since 1959). Caere harbour: Pyrgi, Punicum (S.Marinella), Alsium, Fregenae (?). City-gates: Perusia, Volterrae. Pottery: 'Caeretan' ware was made by Ionians at Caere (*c.* 540–530). E. contacts: perhaps also via Trapezus. Clusium 'portraits': Canopic urns. Metalwork: Populonia weapons also influenced from Talish region (S.W. of Caspian).

Section 4. Latium: there are more than 50 craters within 25m. of Rome. Sabines: Umbro-Sabellian. Convergence of paths 17m. N. of Rome: Eretum; Gabii road has also been discovered. Other half-Etruscan towns: Falerii Veteres, Nepet, Sutrium. Cattle market: Forum Boarium. Salt post: Ficana (Dragoncello). Bridge: Pons Sublicius.

10 The Republic Unites the Mediterranean

Section 1. Treaty of 493: Foedus Cassianum. Earliest Ostia: attributed to Ancus Marcius. Samnium: between R.Sangro and R. Ofanto, and Apulian and Campanian plains.

Section 2. Spelt: hexaploid triticum spelta, perhaps first grown in Bronze Age. Wine: also Caecuban, Falernian, Alban. Mago: also translated into Greek and abridged. Money: *pecunia.* Poultry in Italy from 3 or 2C BC. Tavoliere: from Sipontum to Lucera.

Section 3. First Punic War: Mylae (260), Ecnomus (256), Drepana (249). Land S. of Ariminum: Ager Gallicus et Picenus, taken from Senones. Flaminius' expedition: against Insubres and Cenomani. Roads: Via Aurelia, up W. coast, open on at least S. reaches by *c.* 240. Albanian coast annexed by Rome: from Lissus (Lesh) to Epirus border. Fertile land near Alicante: Elche oasis, Denia-Villajoyosa area. Second Punic War: Trebia, Trasimene, Cannae (218–16), R.Metaurus (207). Zama: Draa el Metnan plain(?).

Sierra Morena pass: Peñarroya. Mines: natural mercuric sulphide from Sisapo (Almaden). Roman refuse dump: M. Testaccio.

Section 4. 'Cloud rising': Agelaus of Aetolia. Illyrian exile: Demetrius of Pharos, betrayer of Corcyra to Rome (229). Victory over Philip V: Cynoscephalae (197). Victories over Antiochus III: Thermopylae, Myonnesus, Magnesia. Italian border-zone: Cisalpine (Cispadane and Transpadane) Gaul. Gridded plots: centuriation. Aquileia routes: through Julian and Carnic Alps. Victory over Perseus: Pydna. Scodra ruler: Genthius. Macedonian revolt: Andriscus. Thrace: invaded (e.g. 72–71, 29–28, *c.* 12 BC) but not made province until AD 46. Utopias: Euhemerus of Messene, Iambulus. Stoicism: founded by Zeno of Citium (Cyprus). Massalia routes: M.Genèvre and Little St. Bernard. Marius' victory over Germans in Italy: Vercellae. Murdered spokesman: M.Livius Drusus. Marsian War: or Social (*socius*, ally). Provinces: Cilician plain and interior (67) added to Rough Cilicia (102), Cyrene bequeathed (96), Crete added to it (67). Defeat by Parthia: Crassus at Carrhae (53). Triumvirates: Pompey, Caesar, Crassus; Antony, Octavian, Lepidus. Balance in Gaul: between Arverni and Aedui. Massalia penalised for siding with Pompey against Caesar (49). N.Africa: Numidia reverted briefly from province (46) to protectorate (30–25); Mauretania retained 'client' status until AD 44.

Section 5. Wall of 378: 'Servian' Wall (Grotta Oscura tufa). Puteoli: formerly Samian colony of Dicaearchia (*c.* 521). Building stones: tufa (including cappellaccio, peperino); travertine discovered *c.* 146; streets repaved 2C with hard lava from M.Albano. Basilica: Porcia (R.Forum). Bridge: Pons Aemilius (179, rebuilt 142). Early *pozzolana*: T.Concord, Castor and Pollux.

11 The Imperial Sea

Section 1. Pompeii paintings of scenery: House of Amandus; Villa of Agrippa Postumus nearby. Italian landscapes: unknown Florentine *c.* 1410 ('Thebaid'), Paolo Uccello; Gentile da Fabriano; Lorenzetti; Bellini, Giorgione, Titian; Caraccis, Domenichino; Roman landscapes began with Elsheimer and Brill.

Section 2. Brick in N.Italy: Augustan city-wall, Turin; first in Rome as roof-tiles. Pottery centres in Gaul: La Graufesenque (Tarn), then Lezoux (Allier). Sarcophagi: one of earliest from Lydia (*c.* 170); Sidamara 3C AD. Jewish revolts: AD 66–73, 132–5 (province since AD 6, except for 41–4).

Section 3. Navigation: except between Egypt and Rhodes, suspended 10 Nov.–10 March. Misenum: main harbour now shallow land-locked Mare Morto; Augustus gave up the silting Lucrine

Lake. Beer: e.g. Egypt, Illyricum, N. Gaul. Water-mill: e.g. Barbegal (Arles).

Section 4. Danube: Tomis, which superseded Istros as lower Danube port, was brought under Roman control in 72 BC, and later a frontier was drawn across the Dobrogea neck near this point. In 2C BC the Sarmatians had driven remnants of the Scythians into the Danube delta and Crimea. Persian devastations: Shapur I. Victories over Alamanni 268–71: L. Benacus, Fanum Fortunae (near Ticinum). Thessalonica: E. of delta, currents carry its silt westwards. Byzantium: had been the capital and naval base of Licinius (d. 324). Mission to Gentiles: Philip had made conversions among mixed Samaritans, and Peter baptised Cornelius at Caesarea. Greek Apologists: Irenaeus wrote in Greek in S. Gaul. Clement, Origen: Alexandrian Apologists. Puritan reaction: started with Montanism, the New Prophecy of Phrygian villages (*c.* 170). Monastic movement: St. Antony, Pachomius. Syrian churches: Antioch, Caesarea, Tyre.

Appendix

Kant had already seen physical geography as the primary basis of history. Genetical distinctions between racial groups: 'the question simply remains open' (E. Goldschmidt, 1967). Deduction of genes from bone measurements: palaeoserology. Geography and ancient history: O.G.S. Crawford, Sir Cyril Fox ('the farther a continental people was from the Mediterranean, the more barbarous it must be'). Challenges: Japan, with neither coal nor iron of its own, is the third steel producing and first steel exporting country in the world.

Further Reading

1 *The Mediterranean and its Beginnings*

E. C. Semple, *The Geography of the Mediterranean Region in its Relation to Ancient History*, English ed. (1931); A. Philippson, *Das Mittelmeergebiet*, 4th ed. (1931); J. H. Rose, *The Mediterranean in the Ancient World* (1933); E. Ludwig, *The Mediterranean* (1942); J. L. Myres, *Mediterranean Culture* (Frazer Lecture) (1944); A. Siegfried, *The Mediterranean* (1948); J. More, *The Mediterranean* (1956); J. Bradford, *Ancient Landscapes* (1957); H. d'Hérouville, *L'Economie Méditerranéenne* (1958); E. Naraghi (etc), *Bassin Méditerranéen et Proche Orient* (1961); J. M. Houston, *The Western Mediterranean World* (1961); G. R. Crone, *Background to Geography* (1964); P. Birot, *La Méditerranée et le Moyen Orient*, I (Birot-Gabert), II (Birot-Dresch), rev. ed. (1964); D. S. Walker, *The Mediterranean Lands*, 3rd ed. (1965); W. G. East, *An Historical Geography of Europe*, rev. ed. (1966).

C. B. M. McBurney, *The Stone Age of North Africa* (1960); P. Graziosi, *Palaeolithic Art* (1960); A. Leroi-Gourhan, *Préhistoire de l'Art Occidental* (1965); S. Piggott, *Ancient Europe* (1965); *Archaeology: Horizons new and old* (Amer. Philos. Soc. 110, 1966); G. Clark, *The Stone Age Hunters* (1967); P. J. Ucko and A. Rosenfeld, *Palaeolithic Cave Art* (1967); H. Frankfort, *The Birth of Civilisation in the Near East* (1951); V. G. Childe, *New Light on the Most Ancient East* (1952); J. Garstang, *Prehistoric Mersin* (1953); W. F. Albright, *The Archaeology of Palestine*, 2nd. ed. (1957); R. J. and L. J. Braidwood, *Excavations in the Plain of Antioch*, I (1960); C. Zervos, *Naissance de la Civilisation en Greece* (1962); E. Anati, *Palestine before the Hebrews* (1963); J. Mellaart, *Earliest Civilisation of the Near East* (1965) and *Catal Hüyük* (1967); S. Cole, *The Neolithic Revolution*, 4th ed. (1967); relevant fascicules of *Cambridge Ancient History*, 2nd ed.; N. K. Sandars, *Prehistoric Art in Europe* (1968).

2 *Egypt*

W. S. Smith, *The Art and Architecture of Ancient Egypt* (1958); W. B.

Emery, *Archaic Egypt* (1961); I.E.S.Edwards, *The Pyramids of Egypt* (1961); W.A.Fairservis, *The Ancient Kingdoms of the Nile* (1962); P. Montet, *Eternal Egypt* (1964); W.C.Hayes, *Most Ancient Egypt* (1965); C.Aldred, *Egypt to the end of the Old Kingdom* (1965); A. Badawy, *A History of Egyptian Architecture*, I (1954), II (1966).

3 Easternmost Mediterranean

C.F.A.Schaeffer, *Ugaritica* (from 1939); P.Jouguet (etc), *Les Premières Civilisations* (from 1950); H.Bossert, *Altsyrien* (1951); O.R.Gurney, *The Hittites* (1952); G.R.Driver, *Semitic Writings*, rev. ed. (1954); P.Thieme, *Die Heimat der Indogermanischen Gemeinsprache* (1954); H. Frankfort, *Art and Architecture of the Ancient Orient* (1954); C.L. Woolley, *A Forgotten Kingdom* (1953) and *Alalakh* (1955); S.Lloyd, *Early Highland Peoples of Anatolia* (1967); A.Gotze, *Kleinasien*, 2nd ed. (1957); F. E. Zeuner, *Dating the Past* (1958); T. B. Brown, *Early Mediterranean Migrations* (1959); L. Casson, *The Ancient Mariners* (1959); J. Gray, *The Canaanites* (1964); W. Culican, *The First Merchant Venturers* (1966); V. I. Georgiev, *Introduzione alla storia delle Lingue Indoeuropee* (1966); Z.Herman, *Peoples, Seas and Ships* (1967); J.Bottéro-E.Cassin-J.Vercoutter, *The Near East* (1967); W.S.Smith, *Interconnections in the Ancient Near East* (1967). See also chapter I.

4 The Straits and the Aegean

S.Marinatos and M.Hirmer, *Crete and Mycenae* (1960); G.L.Huxley, *Achaeans and Hittites* (1960); F.Matz, *Crete and early Greece* (1962); R.W.Hutchinson, *Prehistoric Crete* (1962); C.Blegen, *Troy and the Trojans* (1963); E.Vermeule, *Greece in the Bronze Age* (1964); W. Taylour, *The Mycenaeans* (1964); P.Demargne, *Aegean Art* (1964); R. Carpenter, *Discontinuity In Greek Civilisation* (1966); M.S.F.Hood, *The Home of the Heroes* (1967); F.Schachermeyer, *Agäis und Orient*, (1967); R.A.Higgins, *Minoan and Mycenaean Art* (1967).

5 Expanson of Israel, Phoenicia and Carthage

S.Grayzel, *History of the Jews* (1952); C.Roth, *A Short History of the Jewish People* (1953); H.M.Orlinsky, *Ancient Israel* (1954); S.W. Barron, *A Social and Religious History of the Jews*, I–V, rev. ed. (1952–1957); T.J.Meek, *Hebrew Origins* (1960); T.Kollek and M.Pearlman, *Jerusalem*, 1968.

D.Harden, *The Phoenicians* (1962); M.Cary and E.H.Warmington, *The Ancient Explorers*, rev. ed. (1963); S.Moscati, *The World of the Phoenicians* (1968).

B.H.Warmington, *Carthage* (1964); G.Picard, *Carthage* (1964); C.-A. Julien, *Histoire de l'Afrique du Nord* (1966).
See also chapter 3.

6–8 The Homeric Age; Greek Civilisation Enriched and Diffused; From Athens to Alexandria

M.I.Finley, *The World of Odysseus* (1954); M.B.Sakellariou, *La Migration Grecque en Ionie* (1958); D.L.Page, *History and the Homeric Iliad* (1959); T.J.Dunbabin, *The Greeks and their Eastern Neighbours* (1959); C.G.Starr, *The Origins of Greek Civilisation* (1961); G.S.Kirk (ed.), *The Language and Background of Homer* (1964); G.L.Huxley, *The Early Ionians* (1966).

T.J.Dunbabin, *The Western Greeks* (1948); A.Mongait, *Archaeology in the USSR.* (1955); A.R.Burn, *The Lyric Age of Greece* (1960); J.M. Cook, *The Greeks in Ionia and the East* (1962); A.G.Woodhead, *The Greeks in the West* (1962); J.Boardman, *The Greeks Overseas* (1964); A.J.Graham, *Colony and Mother City in Ancient Greece* (1964); P. Walcot, *Hesiod and the Near East* (1966); M.I.Finley, *Ancient Sicily*, 1968.

H.J.Rose, *A Handbook of Greek Mythology*, 6th ed. (1958); S.N. Kramer (ed.), *Mythologies of the Ancient World* (1961); M.Grant, *Myths of the Greeks and Romans* (1962).

R.E.Wycherley, *How the Greeks built Cities* (1949); A.Rumpf, *Malerei und Zeichnung* (1953); F.Villard, *Les Vases Grecs* (1956); A.W.Lawrence, *Greek Architecture* (1957); G.M.A.Richter, *Handbook of Greek Art* (1959); R.M.Cook, *The Greeks till Alexander* (1961); R. Carpenter, *Greek Art* (1962); J.Boardman, *Greek Art* (1964) and *Pre-Classical* (1967).

A.Philippson, *Das Griechische Klima* (1948); J.O.Thompson, *History of Ancient Geography* (1948); M.Cary, *The Geographical Background of Greek and Roman History* (1949); J.L.Myres, *Geographical History in Greek Lands* (1953); J.Du P.Taylor, *Marine Archaeology* (1965); M.Amit, *Athens and the Sea* (1965).

H.Bengtson, *Griechische Geschichte* (1950); J.B.Bury and R. Meiggs, *A History of Greece to the Death of Alexander the Great*, 3rd ed. (1952); C.M.Bowra, *The Greek Experience* (1957); N.G.L.Hammond, *A History of Greece to 322 BC* (1959); H.Lloyd-Jones (ed.), *The Greeks* (1962); M.I.Finley, *The Ancient Greeks* (1963); M.Grant (ed.), *The Birth of Western Civilisation* (1964); A.R.Burn, *The Pelican History of*

Greece (1965); G.Becatti, *L'età classica* (1965); F.Chamoux, *The Civilization of Greece* (1965); A.Andrews, *The Greeks* (1967).

W.W.Tarn and G.T.Griffith, *Hellenistic Civilization*, 3rd ed. (1952); M.Rostovtzeff, *Social and Economic History of the Hellenistic World* (1953).

9–11 The Etruscans and the Beginnings of Rome; The Republic Unites the Mediterranean; The Imperial Sea

P.J.Riis, *An Introduction to Etruscan Art* (1953); G.M.A.Richter, *Ancient Italy* (1955); M.Pallottino, *The Etruscans*, rev. ed. (1959); S.M.Puglisi, *La Civiltà Appenninica* (1959); R.Bloch, *The Origins of Rome* (1960); *Etruscan Culture, Land and People* (Columbia U.P. 1962); E.Richardson, *The Etruscans* (1964); H.Harrel-Courtès, *Etruscan Italy* (1964); G.A.Mansuelli, *Etruria and Early Rome* (1966); H.H. Scullard, *The Etruscan Cities and Rome* (1967); D.Strong, *The Early Etruscans* (1968); H.Hencken, *Tarquinia and Etruscan Origins* (1968).

A.J.Toynbee, *Hannibal's Legacy* (1965); A.H.McDonald, *Republican Rome* (1966); E.T.Salmon, *Samnium and the Samnites* (1967); E.Badian, *Roman Imperialism in the Late Republic* (1967).

Cambridge Ancient History to Vol. XII (1939); Methuen *Histories of the Roman World* (Scullard, Marsh, Salmon, Parker) ;M. Rostovtzeff, *Social and Economic History of the Roman Empire*, rev. ed. (P.M.Fraser) (1957); M.Grant, *The World of Rome* (1960); P.Grimal, *The Civilization of Rome* (1963); J.P.V.D.Balsdon (ed.), *The Romans* (1965); J.Rougé, *Recherches sur L'Organisation du Commerce Maritime en Méditerranéen sous l'Empire Romain* (1967); A.Maiuri, *Roman Paintings* (1953); H.Kahler, *Rome and her Empire* (1963); R.E.M.Wheeler, *Roman Art and Architecture* (1964); J.M.C.Toynbee, *The Art of the Romans* (1965); G.M.A.Hanfmann, *Roman Art* (1965).

A.H.M.Jones, *The Later Roman Empire* (1964) and *The Decline of the Ancient World* (1966); R.Remondon, *La Crise de l'Empire Romain* (1964); S.Mazzarino, *The End of the Ancient World* (1966); J.Vogt, *The Decline of Rome* (1967); M.Grant, *The Climax of Rome* (1968).

Maps

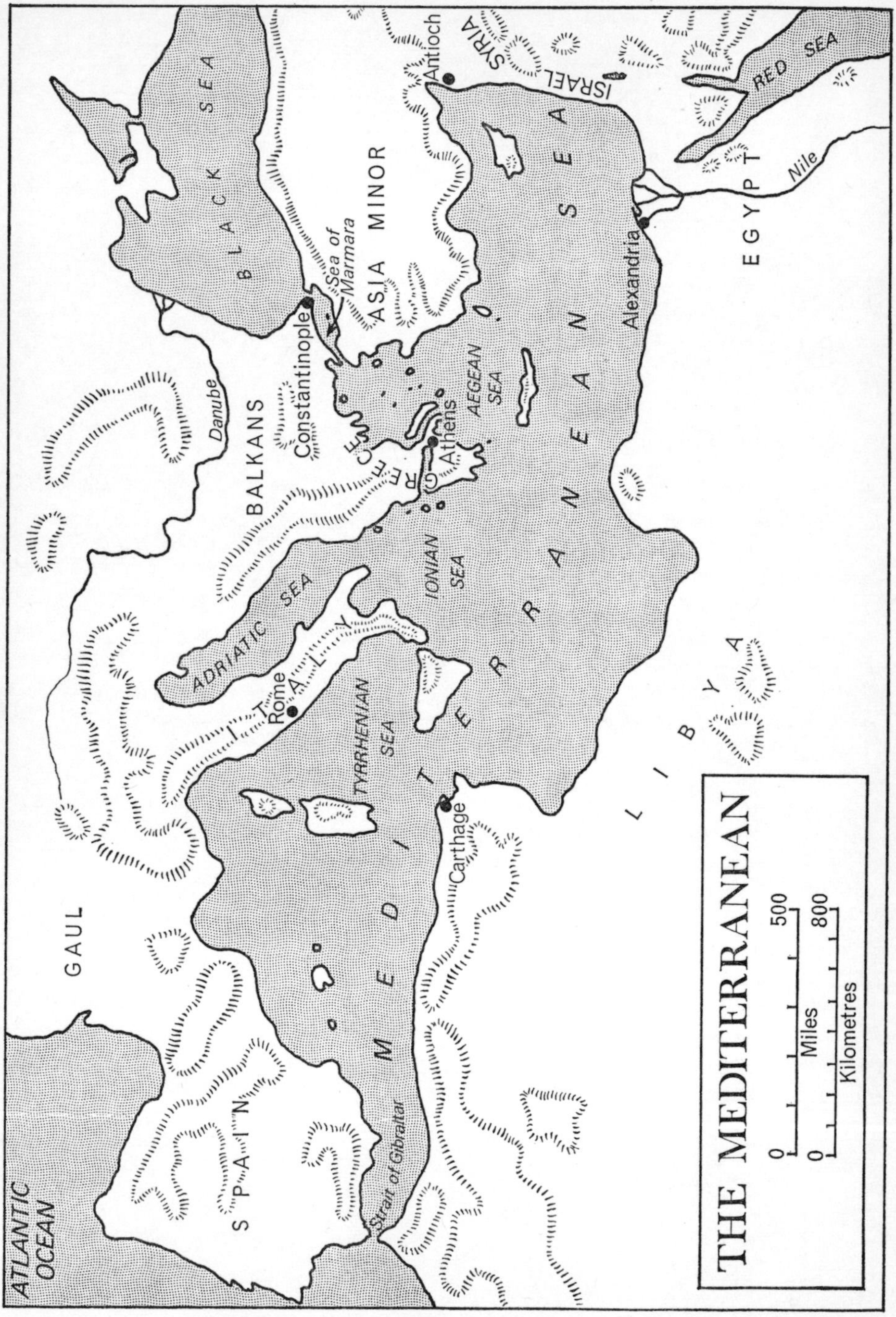
THE MEDITERRANEAN
ATLANTIC OCEAN
SPAIN
GAUL
Strait of Gibraltar
MEDITERRANEAN SEA
TYRRHENIAN SEA
Carthage
ITALY
Rome
ADRIATIC SEA
IONIAN SEA
LIBYA
BALKANS
Danube
GREECE
Athens
AEGEAN SEA
Constantinople
Sea of Marmara
BLACK SEA
ASIA MINOR
Antioch
SYRIA
ISRAEL
RED SEA
Alexandria
EGYPT
Nile
0
500
Miles
0
800
Kilometres

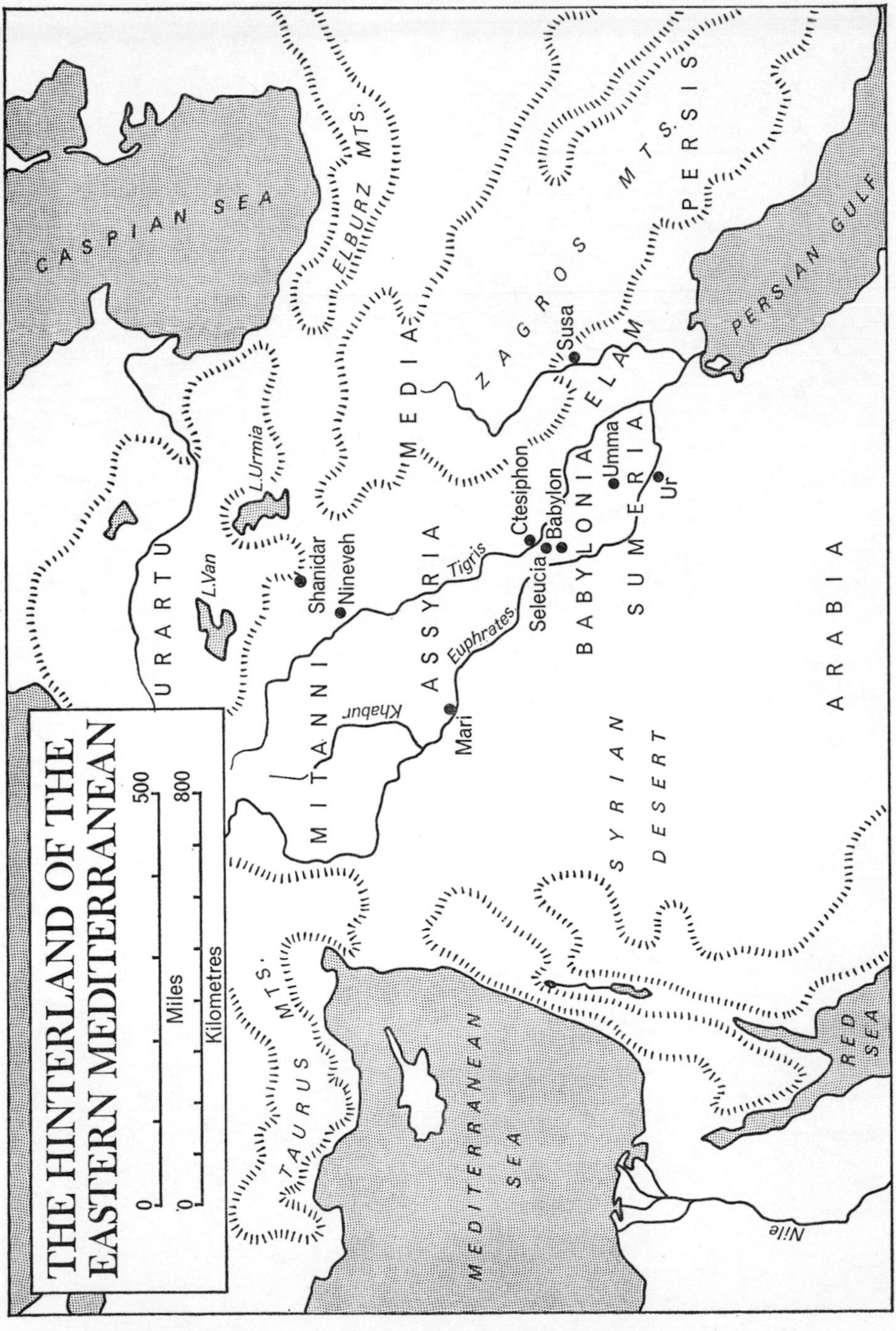
THE HINTERLAND OF THE
EASTERN MEDITERRANEAN
0
500
Miles
0
800
Kilometres
CASPIAN SEA
ELBURZ MTS.
ZAGROS MTS.
PERSIS
PERSIAN GULF
MEDIA
ELAM
Susa
URARTU
L.Van
L.Urmia
Shanidar
Nineveh
MITANNI
Khabur
ASSYRIA
Tigris
Euphrates
Mari
Ctesiphon
Seleucia
Babylon
BABYLONIA
Umma
Ur
SUMERIA
SYRIAN
DESERT
ARABIA
TAURUS MTS.
MEDITERRANEAN
SEA
RED
SEA
Nile

MAP 3

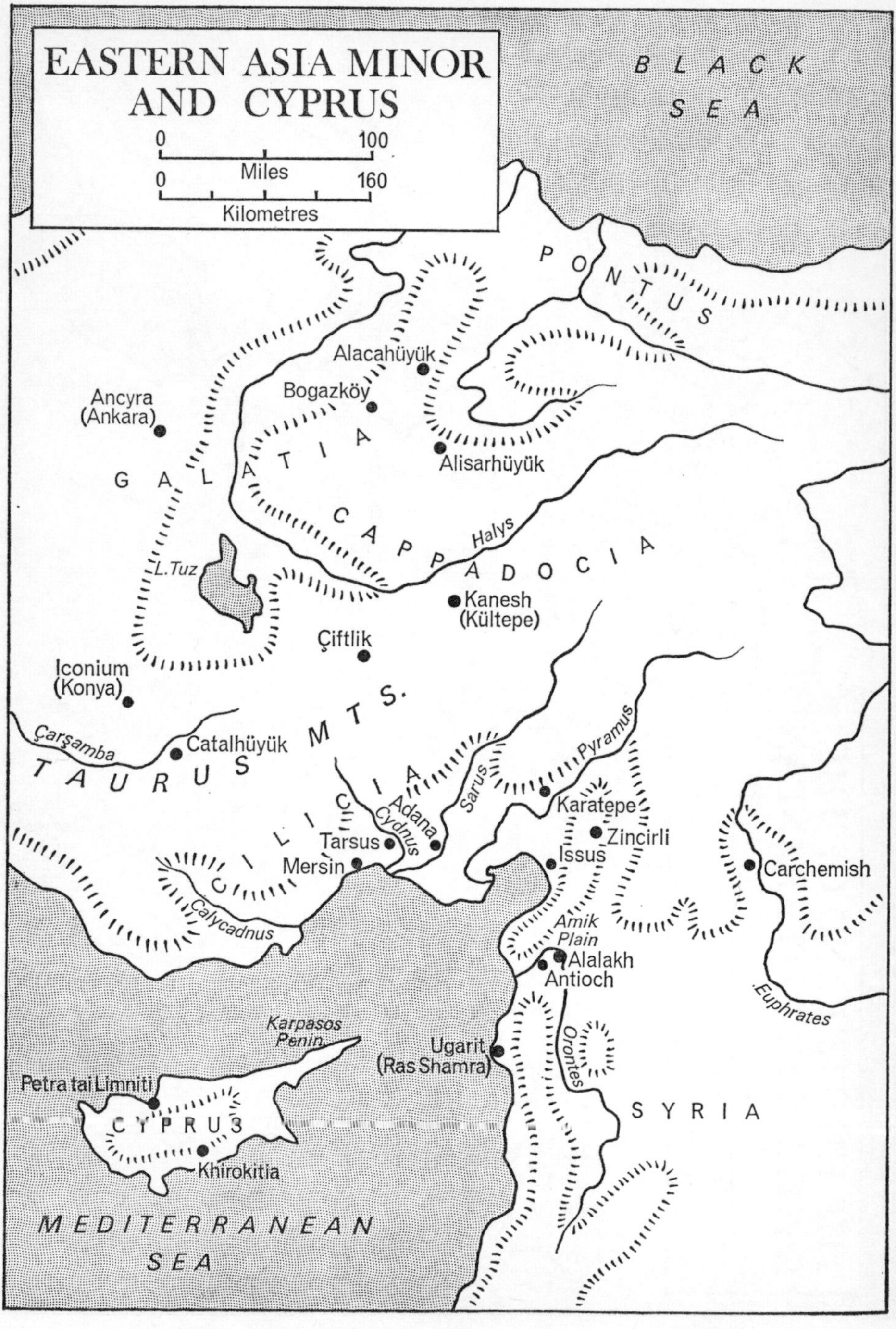
EASTERN ASIA MINOR AND CYPRUS
0
100
Miles
0
160
Kilometres
BLACK SEA
PONTUS
Alacahüyük
Bogazköy
Ancyra (Ankara)
GALATIA
Alisarhüyük
CAPPADOCIA
Halys
L.Tuz
Kanesh (Kültepe)
Çiftlik
Iconium (Konya)
TAURUS MTS.
Çarşamba
Catalhüyük
CILICIA
Pyramus
Sarus
Adana
Cydnus
Karatepe
Zincirli
Tarsus
Mersin
Issus
Carchemish
Calycadnus
Amik Plain
Alalakh
Antioch
Euphrates
Karpasos Penin.
Ugarit (Ras Shamra)
Orontes
Petra tai Limniti
CYPRUS
SYRIA
Khirokitia
MEDITERRANEAN SEA

BLACK SEA
Byzantium
Nicomedia
SEA OF MARMARA
BITHYNIA
Nicaea
Cyzicus
TROAD
Dardanelles
Troy
MYSIA
AEGEAN SEA
AEOLIS
Caicus
PHRYGIA
Phocaea
Cyme
Magnesia ad Sipylum
Hermus
Sardis
Smyrna
LYDIA
Colophon
Cayster
Ephesus
Maeander
IONIA
Priene
Mycale
Miletus
Aphrodisias
CARIA
Cnidus
DORIS
WESTERN ASIA MINOR
0
100
Miles
0
160
Kilometres

MAP 5

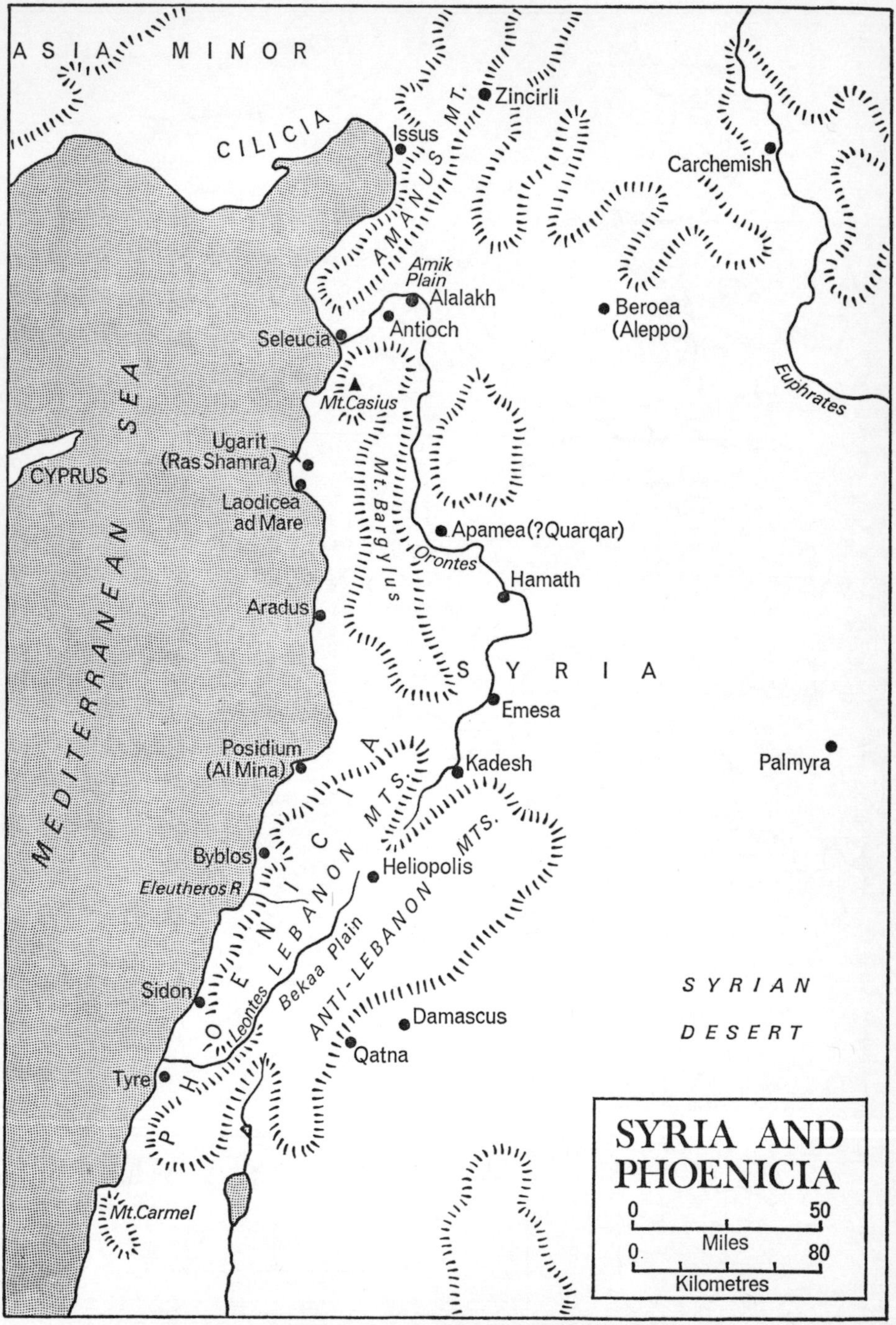
SYRIA AND PHOENICIA
0 50 Miles
0 80 Kilometres
ASIA MINOR
CILICIA
AMANUS MT.
Zincirli
Issus
Carchemish
Amik Plain
Alalakh
Antioch
Seleucia
Beroea (Aleppo)
Euphrates
MEDITERRANEAN SEA
Mt.Casius
Ugarit (Ras Shamra)
CYPRUS
Laodicea ad Mare
Mt. Bargylus
Apamea (?Quarqar)
Orontes
Hamath
Aradus
SYRIA
Emesa
Posidium (Al Mina)
Kadesh
Palmyra
PHOENICIA
LEBANON MTS.
ANTI-LEBANON MTS.
Byblos
Heliopolis
Eleutheros R.
Bekaa Plain
Sidon
Leontes
Damascus
Qatna
Tyre
SYRIAN DESERT
Mt.Carmel

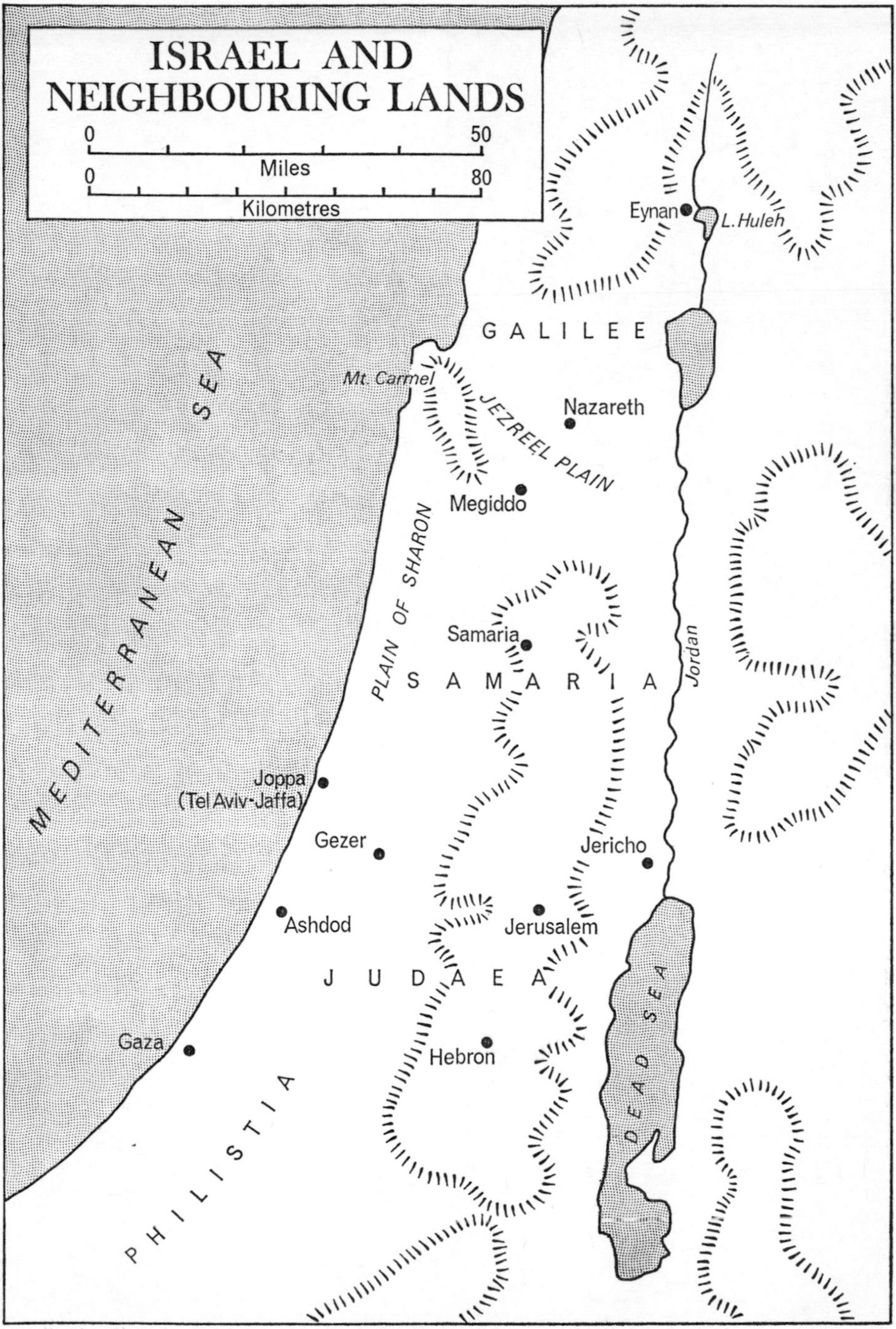
ISRAEL AND
NEIGHBOURING LANDS
0
50
Miles
0
80
Kilometres
MEDITERRANEAN SEA
Eynan
L. Huleh
GALILEE
Mt. Carmel
JEZREEL PLAIN
Nazareth
Megiddo
PLAIN OF SHARON
Samaria
SAMARIA
Jordan
Joppa
(Tel Aviv-Jaffa)
Gezer
Jericho
Ashdod
Jerusalem
JUDAEA
DEAD SEA
Gaza
Hebron
PHILISTIA

MAP 7

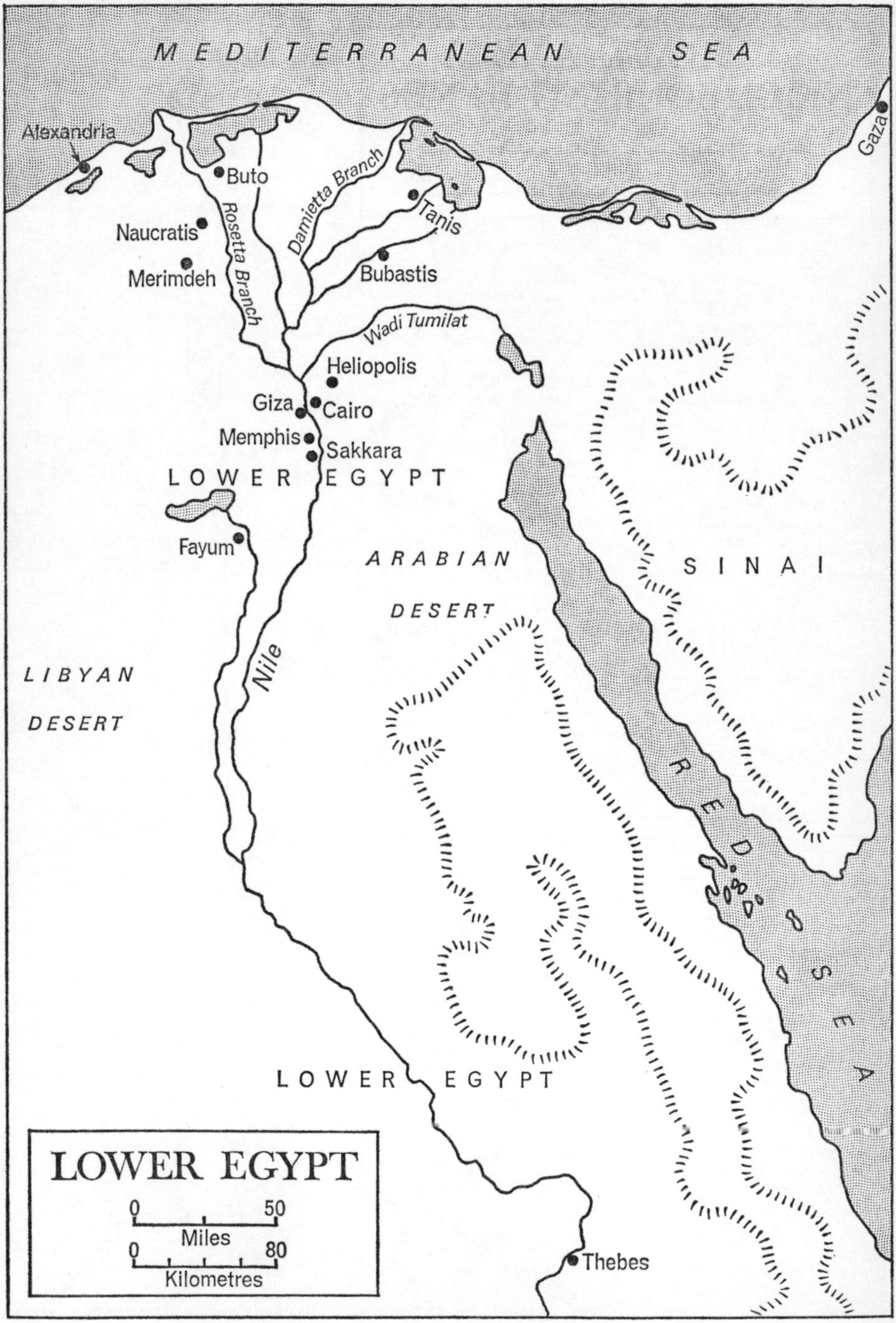
MEDITERRANEAN SEA
Alexandria
Buto
Damietta Branch
Gaza
Tanis
Naucratis
Rosetta Branch
Merimdeh
Bubastis
Wadi Tumilat
Heliopolis
Giza
Cairo
Memphis
Sakkara
LOWER EGYPT
Fayum
ARABIAN DESERT
SINAI
Nile
LIBYAN DESERT
RED SEA
LOWER EGYPT
LOWER EGYPT
0 50
Miles
0 80
Kilometres
Thebes

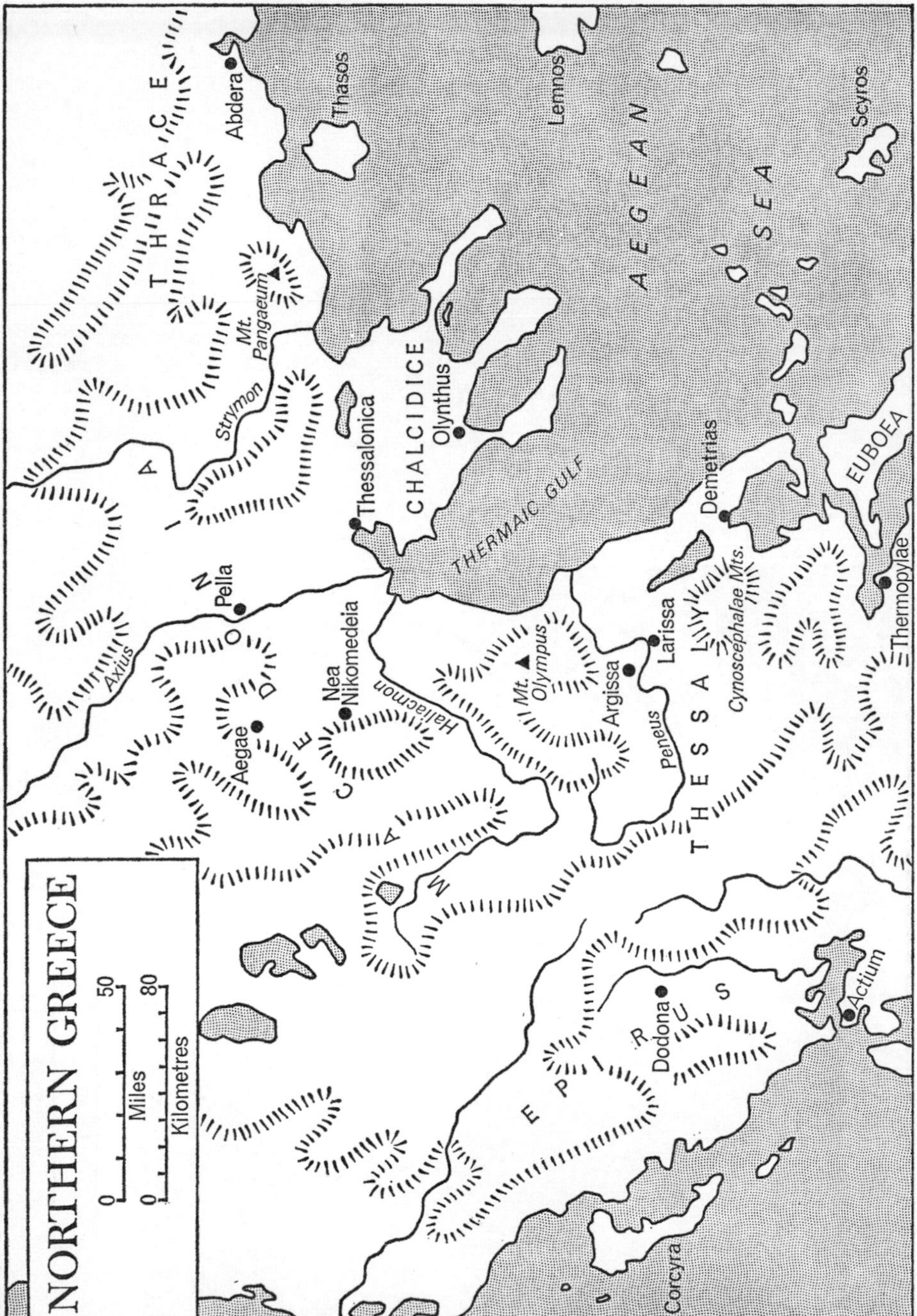
NORTHERN GREECE
0
50
Miles
0
80
Kilometres
THRACE
Abdera
Thasos
Lemnos
AEGEAN
SEA
Scyros
Mt. Pangaeum
Strymon
MACEDONIA
Axius
Pella
Thessalonica
CHALCIDICE
Olynthus
THERMAIC GULF
Aegae
Nea Nikomedeia
Haliacmon
Mt. Olympus
Argissa
Larissa
Peneus
THESSALY
Cynoscephalae Mts.
Demetrias
EUBOEA
Thermopylae
EPIRUS
Dodona
Actium
Corcyra

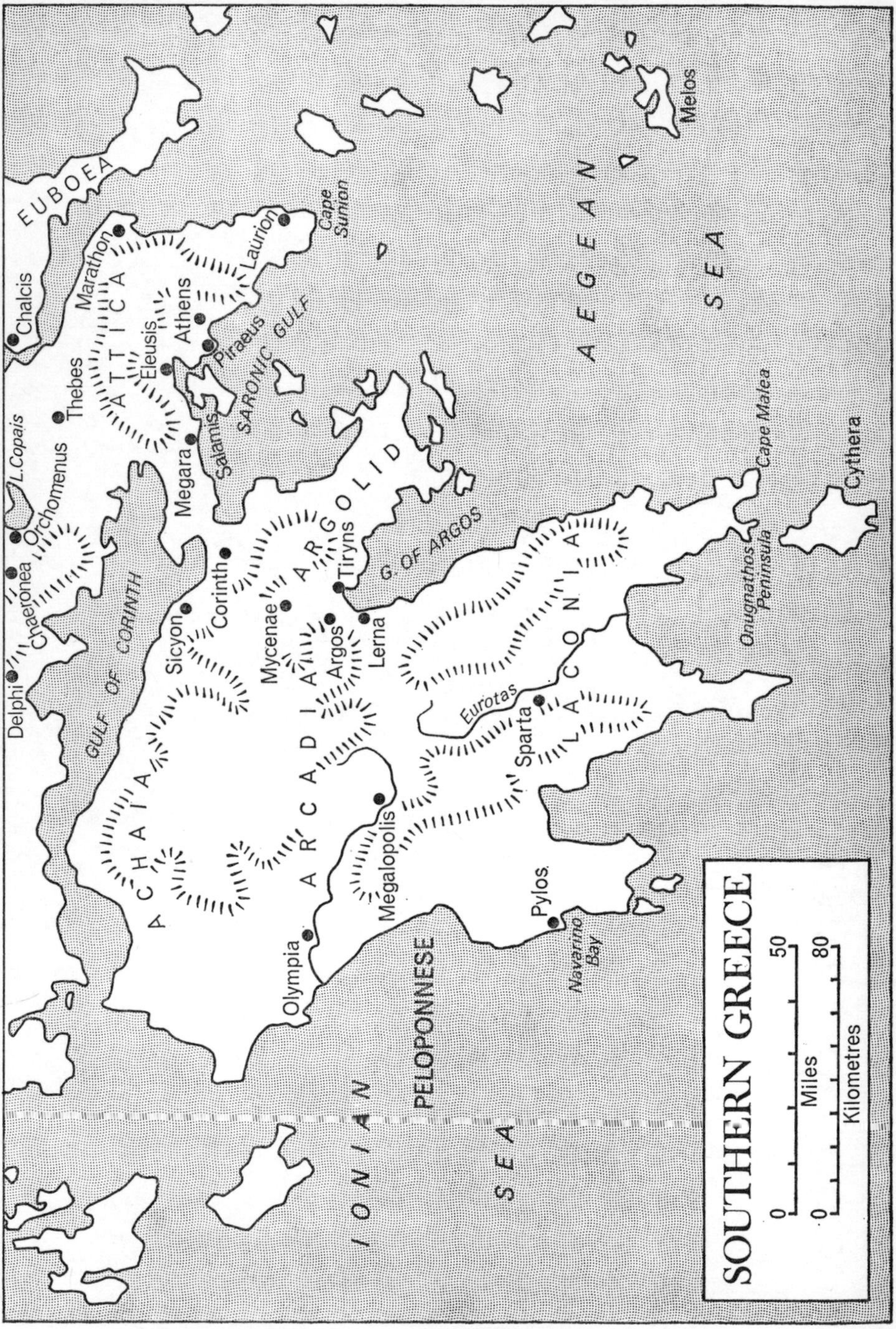
SOUTHERN GREECE
0 50
Miles
0 80
Kilometres
IONIAN SEA
PELOPONNESE
AEGEAN SEA
EUBOEA
Chalcis
Marathon
ATTICA
Athens
Eleusis
Piraeus
Laurion
Cape Sunion
SARONIC GULF
Salamis
Megara
Thebes
L.Copais
Orchomenus
Chaeronea
Delphi
GULF OF CORINTH
Corinth
Sicyon
ACHAIA
ARCADIA
ARGOLID
Mycenae
Argos
Tiryns
Lerna
G. OF ARGOS
LACONIA
Sparta
Eurotas
Megalopolis
Olympia
Pylos
Navarino Bay
Onugnathos Peninsula
Cape Malea
Cythera
Melos

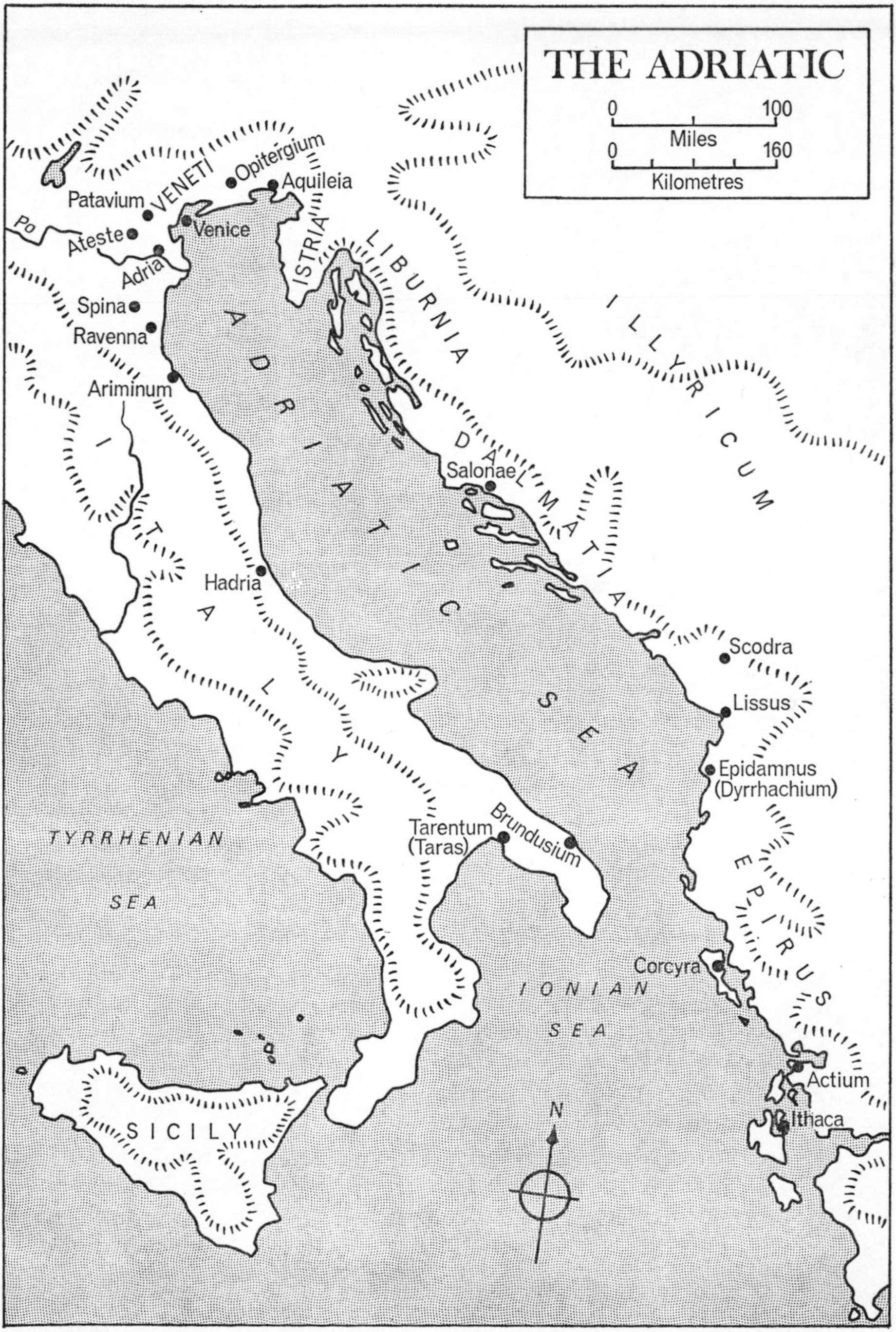
THE ADRIATIC
0
100
Miles
0
160
Kilometres
VENETI
Opitergium
Aquileia
Patavium
Venice
Po
Ateste
Adria
ISTRIA
LIBURNIA
ILLYRICUM
Spina
Ravenna
Ariminum
ADRIATIC SEA
DALMATIA
Salonae
ITALY
Hadria
Scodra
Lissus
Epidamnus
(Dyrrhachium)
Tarentum
(Taras)
Brundusium
TYRRHENIAN
SEA
EPIRUS
Corcyra
IONIAN
SEA
Actium
Ithaca
SICILY
N

MAP II

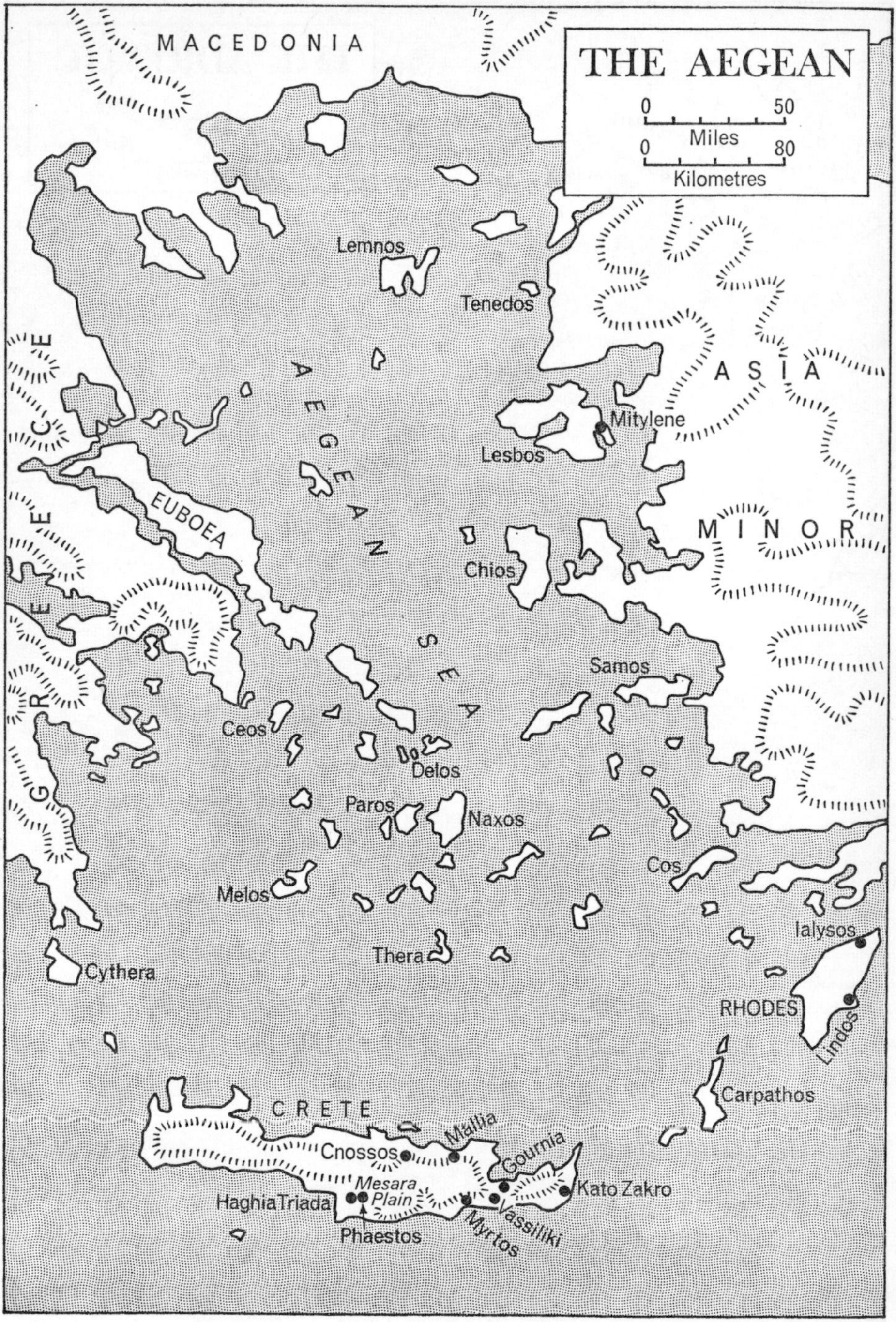
THE AEGEAN
0 50
Miles
0 80
Kilometres
MACEDONIA
GREECE
AEGEAN SEA
ASIA
MINOR
Lemnos
Tenedos
Mitylene
Lesbos
EUBOEA
Chios
Samos
Ceos
Delos
Paros
Naxos
Cos
Melos
Thera
Ialysos
Cythera
RHODES
Lindos
Carpathos
CRETE
Mallia
Cnossos
Gournia
Mesara
Plain
Kato Zakro
Haghia Triada
Phaestos
Myrtos
Vassiliki

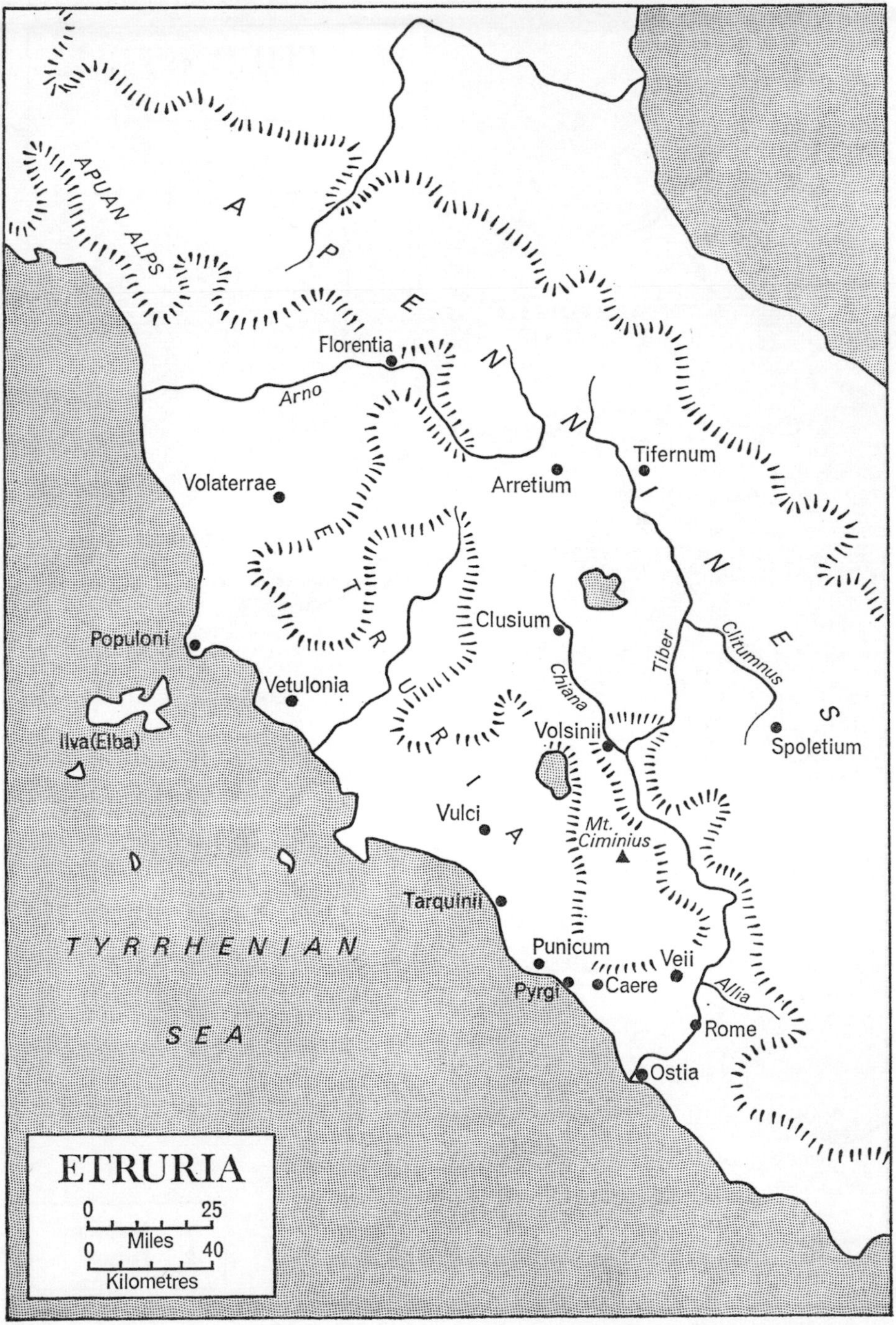
ETRURIA
0 25
Miles
0 40
Kilometres
APUAN ALPS
A P E N N I N E S
E T R U R I A
Florentia
Arno
Volaterrae
Arretium
Tifernum
Clusium
Populoni
Vetulonia
Ilva(Elba)
Tiber
Chiana
Clitumnus
Volsinii
Spoletium
Vulci
Mt. Ciminius
Tarquinii
Punicum
Veii
Pyrgi
Caere
Allia
Rome
Ostia
TYRRHENIAN
SEA

MAP 13

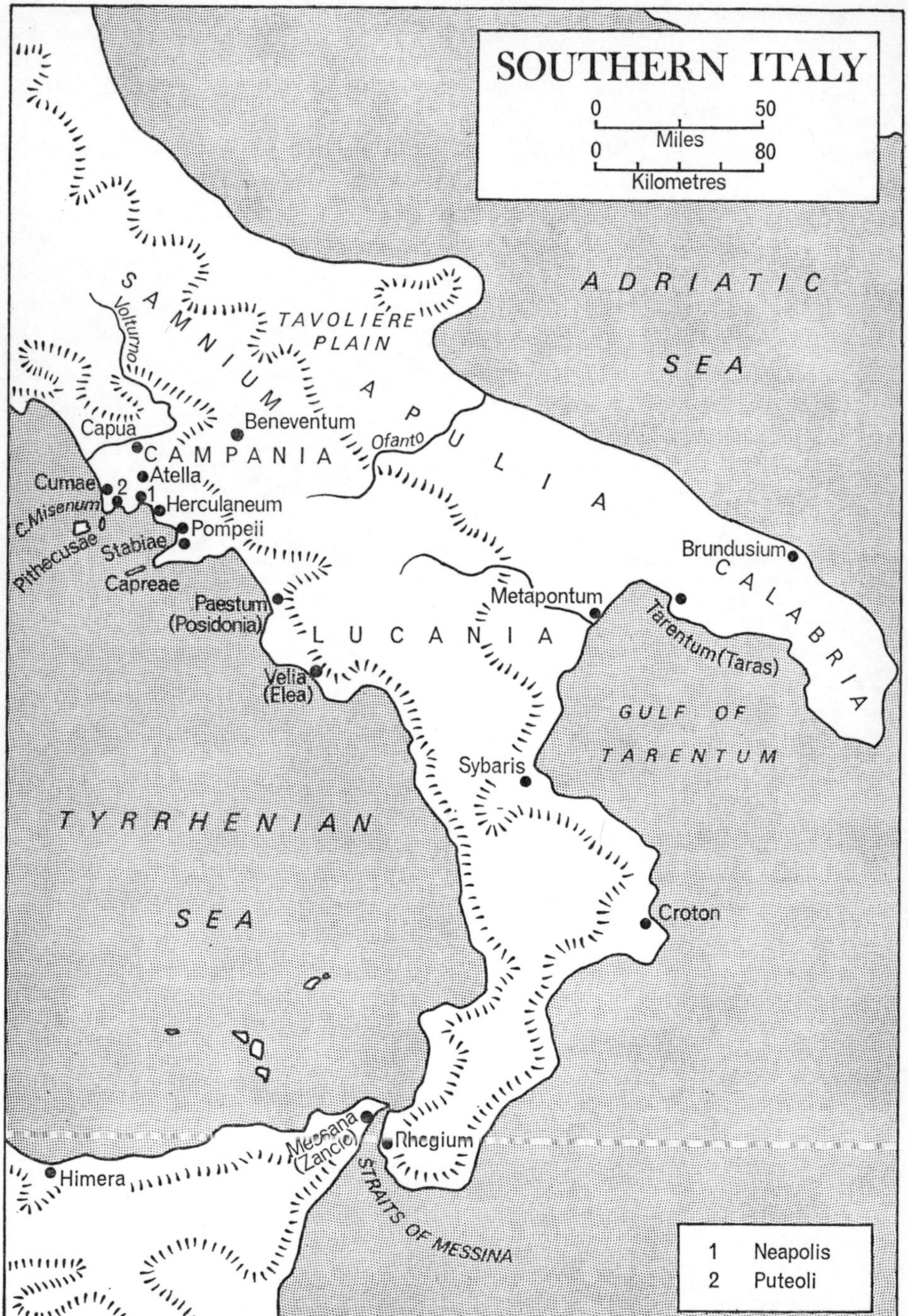
SOUTHERN ITALY
0
50
Miles
0
80
Kilometres
ADRIATIC
SEA
SAMNIUM
Volturno
TAVOLIERE
PLAIN
APULIA
Ofanto
Capua
Beneventum
CAMPANIA
Cumae
Atella
2
1
C. Misenum
Herculaneum
Pompeii
Pithecusae
Stabiae
Capreae
Paestum
(Posidonia)
LUCANIA
Velia
(Elea)
Metapontum
Brundusium
CALABRIA
Tarentum (Taras)
GULF OF
TARENTUM
Sybaris
TYRRHENIAN
SEA
Croton
Messana
(Zancle)
Rhegium
Himera
STRAITS OF MESSINA
1 Neapolis
2 Puteoli

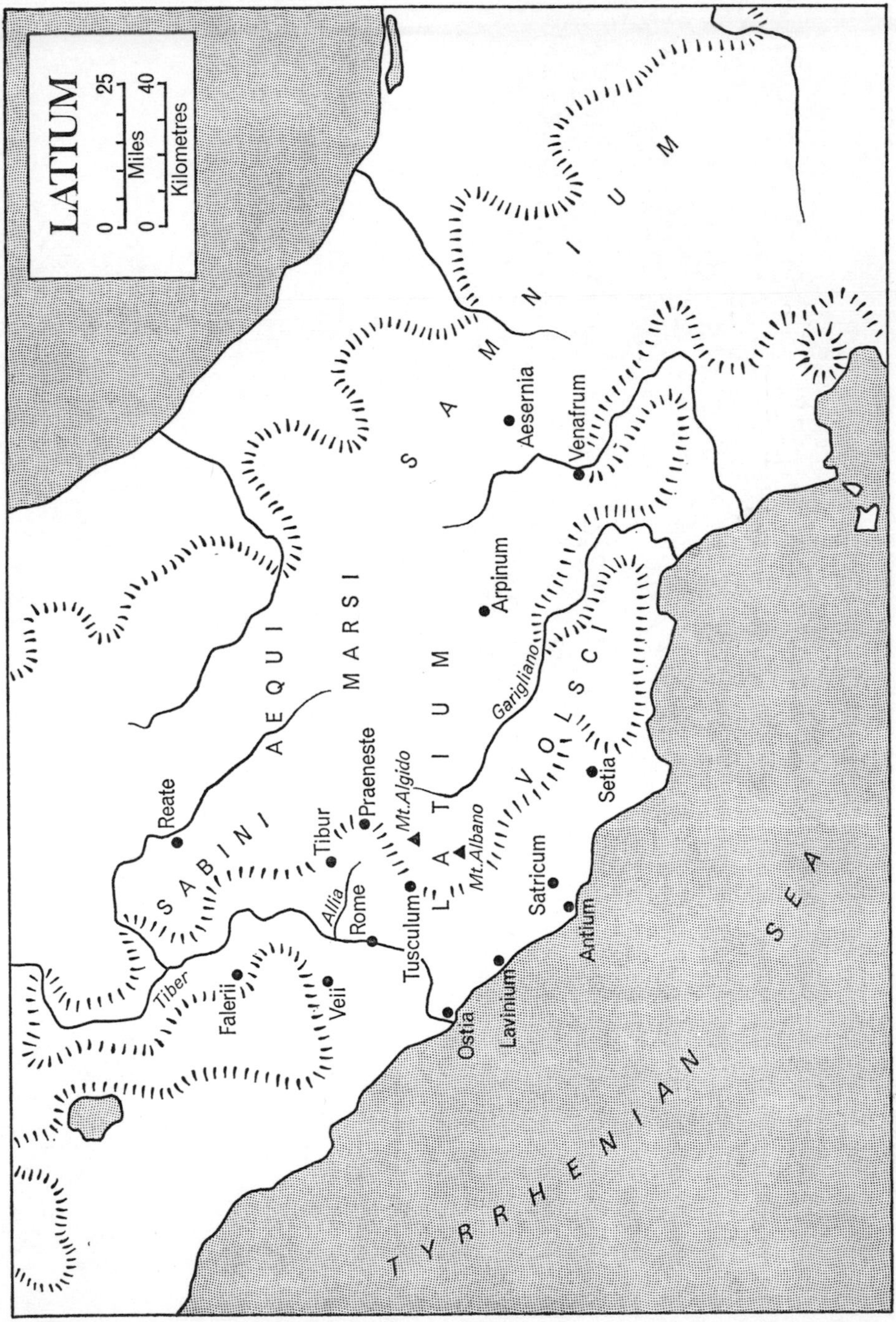
LATIUM
0 25
Miles
0 40
Kilometres
SABINI
AEQUI
MARSI
SAMNIUM
LATIUM
VOLSCI
TYRRHENIAN SEA
Reate
Tibur
Praeneste
Mt.Algido
Mt.Albano
Tusculum
Rome
Allia
Tiber
Falerii
Veii
Ostia
Lavinium
Antium
Satricum
Setia
Garigliano
Arpinum
Aesernia
Venafrum

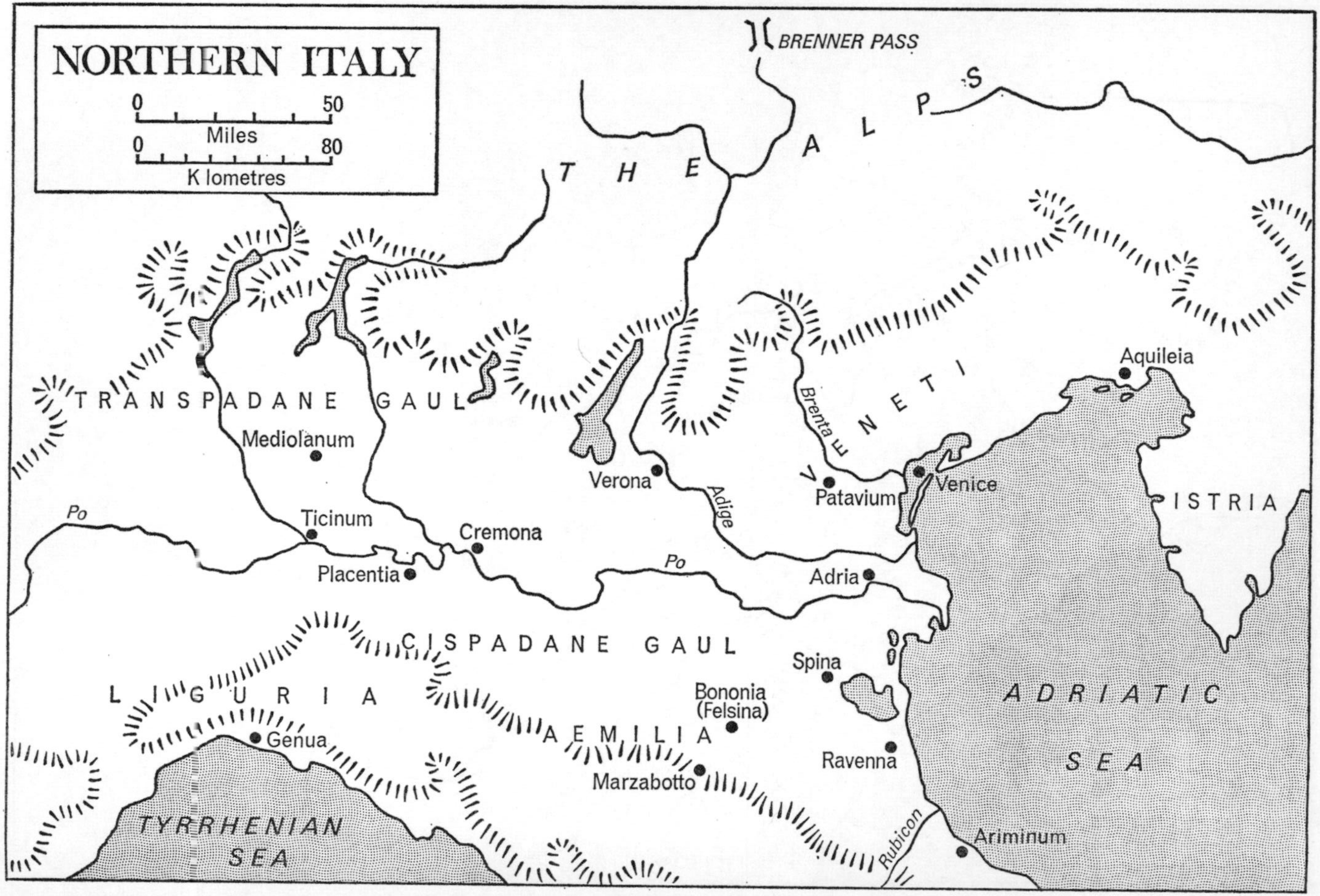

NORTHERN ITALY
0 50
Miles
0 80
K lometres
BRENNER PASS
THE ALPS
TRANSPADANE GAUL
VENETI
ISTRIA
Aquileia
Brenta
Venice
Patavium
Verona
Adige
Mediolanum
Po
Ticinum
Cremona
Placentia
Po
Adria
CISPADANE GAUL
LIGURIA
Spina
Bononia (Felsina)
AEMILIA
Genua
Marzabotto
Ravenna
ADRIATIC SEA
TYRRHENIAN SEA
Rubicon
Ariminum

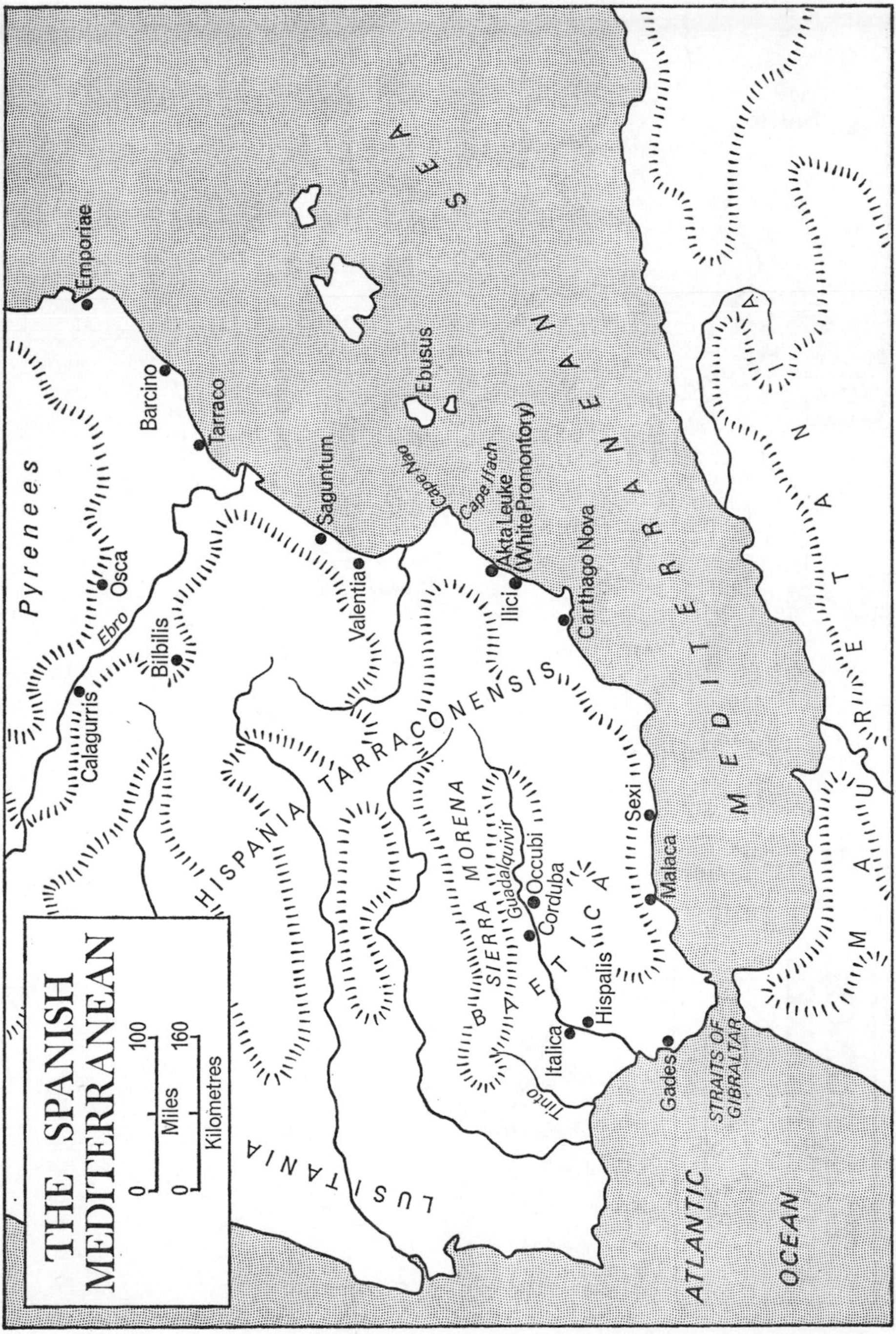
THE SPANISH MEDITERRANEAN
0 100 Miles
0 160 Kilometres
Pyrenees
Emporiae
Barcino
Tarraco
Osca
Ebro
Bilbilis
Calagurris
Saguntum
Valentia
Cape Nao
Ebusus
Cape Ifach
Akta Leuke (White Promontory)
Ilici
Carthago Nova
HISPANIA TARRACONENSIS
SIERRA MORENA
Guadalquivir
Occubi
Corduba
BETICA
Hispalis
Italica
Tinto
Sexi
Malaca
Gades
LUSITANIA
STRAITS OF GIBRALTAR
ATLANTIC OCEAN
MEDITERRANEAN SEA
MAURETANIA

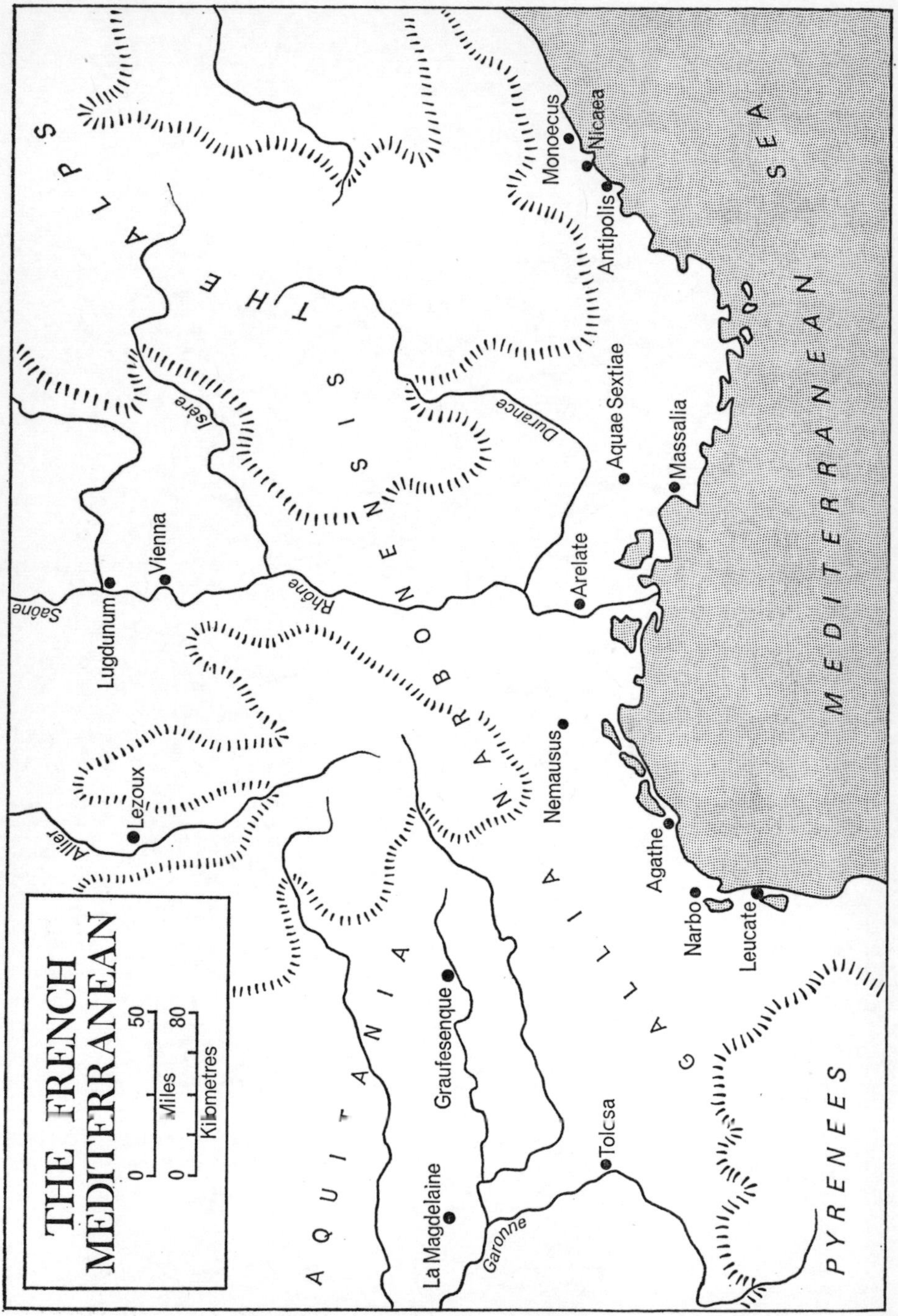
THE FRENCH MEDITERRANEAN
0 Miles 50
0 Kilometres 80
THE ALPS
NARBONENSIS
GALLIA
AQUITANIA
MEDITERRANEAN SEA
PYRENEES
Lugdunum
Vienna
Lezoux
Allier
Saône
Rhône
Isère
Durance
Garonne
Arelate
Aquae Sextiae
Massalia
Monoecus
Nicaea
Antipolis
Nemausus
Agathe
Narbo
Leucate
Tolosa
Graufesenque
La Magdelaine

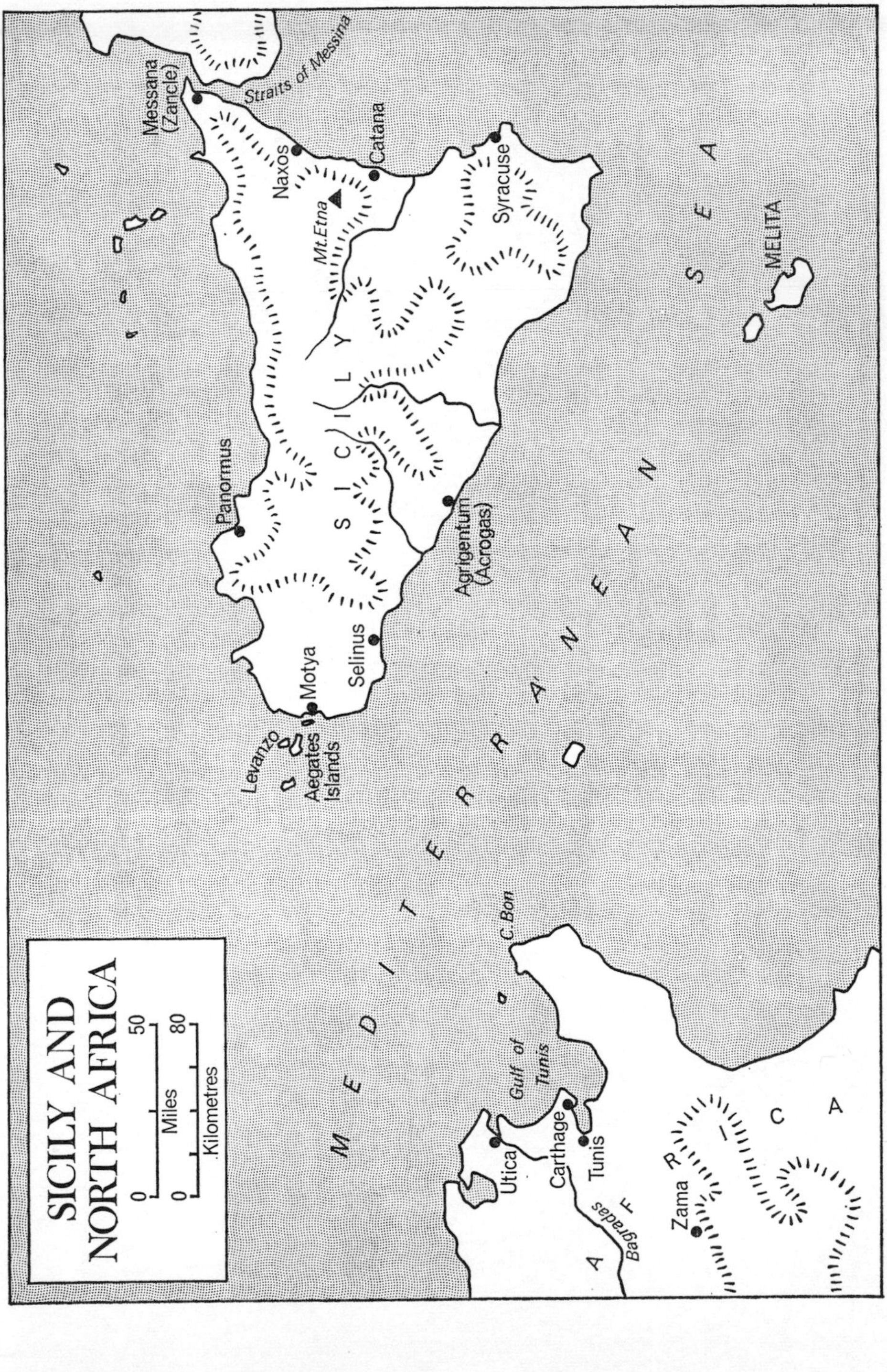
SICILY AND NORTH AFRICA
0
50
Miles
0
80
Kilometres
Messana (Zancle)
Straits of Messina
Naxos
Catana
Mt.Etna
Syracuse
Panormus
SICILY
Agrigentum (Acrogas)
Selinus
Motya
Levanzo
Aegates Islands
MELITA
MEDITERRANEAN SEA
C.Bon
Gulf of Tunis
Utica
Carthage
Tunis
Bagradas
Zama
AFRICA

MAP 19

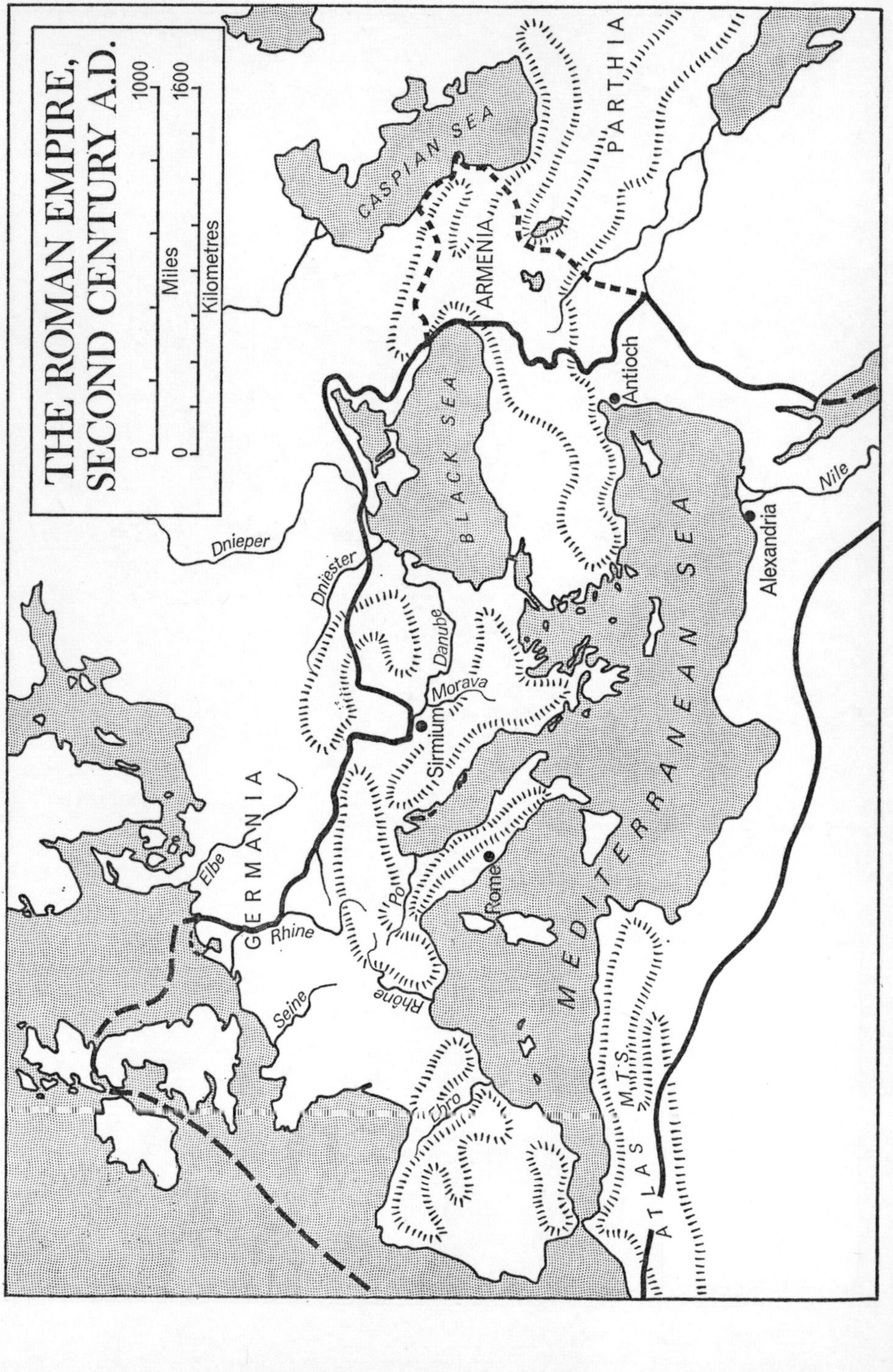
THE ROMAN EMPIRE,
SECOND CENTURY A.D.
0
1000
Miles
0
1600
Kilometres
CASPIAN SEA
PARTHIA
ARMENIA
BLACK SEA
Antioch
Nile
Alexandria
MEDITERRANEAN SEA
Dnieper
Dniester
Danube
Morava
Sirmium
GERMANIA
Elbe
Rhine
Po
Rome
Seine
Rhône
Ebro
ATLAS MTS.

Index

Grant, Michael

The ancient
Mediterranean

DATE			
MAY 8 '90			